MUHLENBERG LIBRARY

WITHDRAWN

REPRINTS OF ECONOMIC CLASSICS

THE NATURE OF CAPITAL AND INCOME

Also Published in

Reprints of Economic Classics

BY IRVING FISHER

MATHEMATICAL INVESTIGATIONS
IN THE THEORY OF VALUE AND PRICES [1892]
& APPRECIATION AND INTEREST [1896]
THE PURCHASING POWER OF MONEY [1922]
THE THEORY OF INTEREST [1930]

THE NATURE OF CAPITAL AND INCOME

BY

IRVING FISHER, Ph.D.

PROFESSOR OF POLITICAL ECONOMY, YALE UNIVERSITY

REPRINTS OF ECONOMIC CLASSICS

AUGUSTUS M. KELLEY · PUBLISHER
NEW YORK · 1965

ORIGINAL EDITION 1906

REPRINTED 1965
BY ARRANGEMENT WITH
IRVING N. FISHER

LIBRARY OF CONGRESS CATALOGUE CARD NUMBER
65-20921

Printed in the United States of America
by Sentry Press, New York, N. Y. 10019

TO

WILLIAM GRAHAM SUMNER

WHO FIRST INSPIRED ME

WITH

A LOVE FOR

ECONOMIC SCIENCE

PREFACE

THIS book is an attempt to put on a rational foundation the concepts and fundamental theorems of capital and income. It therefore forms a sort of philosophy of economic accounting, and, it is hoped, may supply a link long missing between the ideas and usages underlying practical business transactions and the theories of abstract economics. To some readers it may seem that certain elementary topics have been treated at undue length; but, as experience shows that economic structures built on hasty and inadequate generalizations inevitably collapse, it seems hardly possible to take too much pains in making the foundations secure. On the other hand, topics which are in their nature technical or which digress from the main theme — and in particular mathematical formulæ — have been relegated to appendices.

Many of the theses maintained will undoubtedly fail to command assent on a first reading, for in any orderly presentation of a subject it is impossible to forestall all objections as they occur. The aim has been to preserve a definite sequence by which each step prepares the way for those which follow; but this plan has necessitated the postponement of some topics beyond the point at which a consciousness of their difficulties might begin to trouble the reader. He is therefore asked to stay judgment until he has finished the work, and, if necessary, to reread those parts in which his difficulties were first encountered. This suggestion is especially urged in regard to the treatment of income, the concept of which forms the central theme of the book. Many of the friendly critics to whom the manuscript has been shown have at first dissented strongly from the conclusions of Chapter VII, but have invariably withdrawn their objections after finishing Chapter XIV.

The nature of income is a subject which has not hitherto received, in economic literature, the attention it deserves. Income plays an important rôle in all economic problems; it is income for which capital exists; it is income for which labor is exerted; and it is the distribution of income which constitutes the disparity between rich and poor.

Nor is the subject of interest solely to theoretical economists. It appeals to practical men of affairs and to those who are interested in problems of social reform, as well as to the special classes of accountants, actuaries, and mathematicians. The book is so arranged that the general reader may, if he so desires, omit the technical portions, such as the appendices and possibly Chapter XVII. It is suggested that all readers should give special attention to Chapters VI, VII, IX, and XIV.

The problem of nomenclature has proved not a little puzzling. In general, each term has been employed in one, and only one, sense; but to follow this plan exclusively has not been found practicable. Several words are sometimes used for the same concept,— for instance, "resources" and "assets," or "utility" and "desirability"; and sometimes the same word has been used in more than one sense, as in the case of "capital," which may mean capital-goods or capital-value. But special pains have been taken to avoid any confusion or uncertainty of meaning. The definitions have been carefully framed, and will be found collected in a glossary at the end.

A few fragments of the book have appeared in a somewhat different form in economic periodicals, and the whole book may be said to be only the elaboration of the ideas outlined some years ago in the *Economic Journal*. I would express my thanks to the publishers of the *Economic Journal* for permission to use unaltered some passages from "What is Capital?" 1897, "Senses of Capital," 1898, and "The Rôle of Capital in Economic Theory," 1898, and to the *Quarterly Journal of Economics* for similar permission with reference to "Precedents for Defining Capital," 1904.

I wish also to express my obligations to the many persons who have aided me in the preparation of this work, among them especially my wife; my brother, Mr. Herbert W. Fisher; my colleagues, Professor Henry C. Emery, Professor John P. Norton, and Dr. Lester W. Zartman; and my friends, Mr. Richard M. Hurd and Mr. Orland S. Isbell of New York City.

IRVING FISHER.

NEW HAVEN, CONN., June, 1906.

CONTENTS

FIRST SUMMARY

	CHAPTERS
INTRODUCTION. FUNDAMENTAL CONCEPTS	I–III
PART I. CAPITAL	IV–VI
PART II. INCOME	VII–X
PART III. CAPITAL AND INCOME	XI–XVI
PART IV. SUMMARIES	XVII–XVIII

SECOND SUMMARY

INTRODUCTION

CHAPTER		PAGE
I.	WEALTH	3
II.	PROPERTY	18
III.	UTILITY	41

PART I

IV.	CAPITAL	51
V.	CAPITAL ACCOUNTS	66
VI.	CAPITAL SUMMATION	90

PART II

VII.	INCOME	101
VIII.	INCOME ACCOUNTS	119
IX.	INCOME SUMMATION	141
X.	PSYCHIC INCOME	165

PART III

XI.	FOUR INCOME-CAPITAL RATIOS	183
XII.	CONCEPT OF RATE OF INTEREST	191
XIII.	VALUE OF CAPITAL	202
XIV.	EARNINGS AND INCOME	227
XV.	CAPITAL AND INCOME ACCOUNTS	256
XVI.	THE RISK ELEMENT	265

PART IV

XVII.	SUMMARY OF PART III	303
XVIII.	GENERAL SUMMARY	323
GLOSSARY.	SUMMARY OF DEFINITIONS	329

APPENDICES 341

INDEX 413

ANALYTICAL TABLE OF CONTENTS

CHAPTER I

WEALTH

		PAGE
§ 1.	Definition of wealth	3
§ 2.	Classification of wealth	5
§ 3.	Measurement of wealth	8
§ 4.	Price of wealth	9
§ 5.	Market-, asking-, appraised-price	11
§ 6.	Value of wealth	13
§ 7.	Quantity, price, and value contrasted	14
§ 8.	Accuracy in measurement of quantity, price, and value	15

CHAPTER II

PROPERTY

§ 1.	Definition of property	18
§ 2.	Definition of services	19
§ 3.	Definition of rights	20
§ 4.	Wealth and property correlative	22
§ 5.	Table illustrating this correlation	24
§ 6.	A guide for finding wealth underlying given property rights	24
§ 7.	A second guide: One property right overlaid by another	31
§ 8.	A third guide: Property rights are always to existing wealth	32
§ 9.	Total ownership is aggregate of partial rights	34
§ 10.	Classification of property rights	36
§ 11.	Importance of a clear understanding of wealth and property	38

CHAPTER III

UTILITY

§ 1.	Desirability vs. satisfaction	41
§ 2.	Synonyms for desirability (utility, etc.)	42
§ 3.	Desirability vs. services	43

ANALYTICAL TABLE OF CONTENTS

	PAGE
§ 4. Total and marginal desirability	44
§ 5. Law of decreasing marginal desirability	46

CHAPTER IV

CAPITAL

§ 1. Fund and flow distinguished. Capital and income	51
§ 2. Discordant definitions of capital	53
§ 3. Fundamental truths in these conflicting definitions	57
§ 4. Confusions resulting from neglect to introduce time element	58
§ 5. The weight of economic usage	60
§ 6. Popular and business usage	61
§ 7. Correct terminology less important than correct thinking	65

CHAPTER V

CAPITAL ACCOUNTS

§ 1. Senses of capital	66
§ 2. Book capitalization	68
§ 3. Book and market values	70
§ 4. Summary of senses of capital	72
§ 5. Case of decreasing capital-balance	73
§ 6. Effect of payments between stockholders and company	75
§ 7. "Rights to subscribe"	77
§ 8. Stock watering	79
§ 9. Insolvency	81
§ 10. Pseudo-insolvency	82
§ 11. Creditor nominally takes no risk	82
§ 12. But practically creditor is risk-taker	84
§ 13. Winding up a bankrupt company	86
§ 14. One bankruptcy leads to another	87
§ 15. Summary	89

CHAPTER VI

CAPITAL SUMMATION

§ 1. Methods of couples and balances	90
§ 2. Distinction between accounts of real and fictitious persons	92
§ 3. Summation by couples brings into relief concrete capital	93

ANALYTICAL TABLE OF CONTENTS

§ 4. Nature of credit 96
§ 5. Importance of distinguishing methods of couples and balances 97

CHAPTER VII

INCOME

§ 1. Difficulties of defining income 101
§ 2. The money-income concept 103
§ 3. The real-income concept 104
§ 4. Error of including as income both commodities and services . 106
§ 5. Vain attempts to escape the pitfalls thus laid 109
§ 6. Income not restricted to "enjoyable" elements . . . 112
§ 7. So-called social and individual income 113
§ 8. Conclusion 115

CHAPTER VIII

INCOME ACCOUNTS

§ 1. Introduction 119
§ 2. Specimen income and outgo accounts 121
§ 3. Cost of construction is to be included in outgo accounts . . 124
§ 4. Devices for making income regular 127
§ 5. Applications of income accounting 129
§ 6. Example of individual accounts 131
§ 7. Income and outgo account for *negative* capital (liabilities) . 134
§ 8. Limitations of practical bookkeeping 135
§ 9. Income accounts for fictitious persons 138
§ 10. Relation of income accounts to capital accounts . . . 139

CHAPTER IX

INCOME SUMMATION

§ 1. Summation by "method of balances" 141
§ 2. "Interactions" 143
§ 3. Interactions which change the form of wealth (production) . 145
§ 4. Interactions which change the place of wealth (transportation) 148
§ 5. Interactions which change the ownership of wealth (exchange) 149
§ 6. Accounts illustrative of the first class (production) . . 152
§ 7. Results of combining these accounts 156
§ 8. Methods of balances and couples contrasted 157
§ 9. Accounts illustrative of the third class, for fictitious persons . 158
§ 10. Accounts illustrative of the third class, for real persons . . 162
§ 11. Conclusion 164

xvi ANALYTICAL TABLE OF CONTENTS

CHAPTER X

Psychic Income

		PAGE
§ 1.	Objective income leads up to subjective	165
§ 2.	Illustrative cases	165
§ 3.	Concept of subjective income	167
§ 4.	Objective and subjective incomes differ in time	169
§ 5.	Objective and subjective incomes differ as to labor	170
§ 6.	Labor the only ultimate cost of production	173
§ 7.	Objective and subjective income differ as to pain	175
§ 8.	Summary	177
§ 9.	Classification of services	178

CHAPTER XI

Four Income-capital Ratios

§ 1.	Résumé of previous chapters	183
§ 2.	Physical- and value-productivity, physical- and value-return	184
§ 3.	Errors from confusing them	186
§ 4.	How costs, past and future, affect values	188

CHAPTER XII

Concept of Rate of Interest

§ 1.	The rate of interest as a case of "value-return"	191
§ 2.	Annual, semi-annual, quarterly, and continuous reckoning	192
§ 3.	Rate of capitalization or reciprocal of the rate of interest	194
§ 4.	The "premium" and "price" concepts of the rate of interest	194
§ 5.	The conditions under which they are interchangeable	196
§ 6.	Conditions under which they are not interchangeable	198
§ 7.	The rate of discount	199
§ 8.	Summary	199

CHAPTER XIII

Value of Capital

§ 1.	Capital-value of a single future item. The "discount curve"	202
§ 2.	Application to valuing capital, property, and wealth	204
§ 3.	Capital-value of a perpetual annuity	205
§ 4.	Application to valuing capital, property, and wealth	208
§ 5.	Capital-value of a terminable annuity	209
§ 6.	Application to valuing capital, property, and wealth	210
§ 7.	Capital-value of a bond	211
§ 8.	Capital-value of any income stream whatever	217

ANALYTICAL TABLE OF CONTENTS

		PAGE
§ 9.	Capital-value when alternative income streams are possible	221
§ 10.	Capital-value of a group of articles	223
§ 11.	General conclusion	223

CHAPTER XIV
EARNINGS AND INCOME

§ 1.	Capital-value less than total anticipated income	227
§ 2.	Effect of a change in the rate of interest	229
§ 3.	Value-return may be greater or less than rate of interest	229
§ 4.	Standard or earned income *vs.* realized income	231
§ 5.	Increase of capital equals excess of earnings over income	236
§ 6.	A depreciation fund as a means of standardizing income	238
§ 7.	Sinking funds	243
§ 8.	Other devices for making income regular	244
§ 9.	The device of keeping a large stock of instruments	246
§ 10.	Savings are not a part of realized income	247
§ 11.	Imaginary case of three brothers	249
§ 12.	An "income" tax on the three brothers	250
§ 13.	A misconceived income tax affects the use of capital	253
§ 14.	To consider "savings" income confuses capital and income	254

CHAPTER XV
CAPITAL AND INCOME ACCOUNTS

§ 1.	Capital and income accounts when items recur regularly	256
§ 2.	Case in which repairs occur at long intervals	257
§ 3.	The same, when there is a repair fund but no repairs as yet	259
§ 4.	The same, when repairs actually occur	261
§ 5.	Extraordinary increases or decreases	263
§ 6.	Conclusion	264

CHAPTER XVI
THE RISK ELEMENT

§ 1.	Subjective nature of chance	265
§ 2.	Definition of chance	269
§ 3.	Risk as applied to the rate of interest	271
§ 4.	Same, in case future income is dependent on rate of interest	273
§ 5.	Risk as applied to immediate income	275
§ 6.	"Riskless," "mathematical," and "commercial" values	276
§ 7.	Capital-value of a risky bond	277
§ 8.	Riskless, mathematical, and commercial rates of interest	279
§ 9.	Inverse case, where instead of risk of loss there is chance of gain	280

ANALYTICAL TABLE OF CONTENTS

	PAGE
§ 10. The general case, where both are present	281
§ 11. Difficulties in practice	283
§ 12. Enumeration of causes affecting capital-value	284
§ 13. Effect of chance on the form of the "discount curve"	286
§ 14. Effect of chance on bookkeeping	287
§ 15. Five methods of avoiding risk	288
§ 16. The method of guaranties	288
§ 17. The method of safeguards	289
§ 18. The method of increasing knowledge	291
§ 19. The method of insurance	291
§ 20. Forms of insurance	294
§ 21. Shifting risks to speculators. Dangers of imitative speculations	295
§ 22. Buying and selling futures	298

CHAPTER XVII

SUMMARY OF PART III BY MEANS OF DIAGRAMS

§ 1. Mode of representation adopted	303
§ 2. Capital-value as discounted income	304
§ 3. Capital-value as mean between past cost and future income	305
§ 4. How to combine capital curves	309
§ 5. Resultant in case of interactions	311
§ 6. Application to summation of capital of individuals	314
§ 7. Application to summation of capital of society	316
§ 8. An "interaction" as preparatory to enjoyable services	317
§ 9. The risk element	320

CHAPTER XVIII

GENERAL SUMMARY

§ 1. Picture of capital and income	323
§ 2. Summation of capital and income	324
§ 3. Subjective counterparts of objective capital and income	326
§ 4. Relative changes in values of capital and income	327
§ 5. Final summary	328

GLOSSARY

SUMMARY OF DEFINITIONS	329

APPENDICES

Appendix to Chapter I

	PAGE
§ 1 (to Ch. I, § 7). Dimensions of quantity, value, and price of wealth	341

Appendix to Chapter III

§ 1 (to Ch. III, § 4). Mathematical expression for marginal desirability. 344

Appendix to Chapter VII

§ 1 (to Ch. VII, § 1). Specimens of current definitions of income . 345

Appendix to Chapter XI

§ 1 (to Ch. XI, § 2). Mathematical dimensions of income-capital ratios 357

Appendix to Chapter XII

§ 1 (to Ch. XII, § 2). Mathematical relations between rates of interest reckoned annually, semi-annually, etc., when the rates are conceived in the "price" sense 357

§ 2 (to Ch. XII, § 4). The same, when the interest rates are conceived in the "premium" sense. Diagrammatic representation. Economic interpretation of e 358

§ 3 (to Ch. XII, § 6). A *premium* rate of 4 per cent in one year and 3 per cent thereafter, means a *price* rate of 3.03 per cent the first year and 3 per cent thereafter 362

§ 4 (to Ch. XII, § 6). A *price* rate of 4 per cent in one year and 3 per cent thereafter means a *premium* rate of $37\frac{1}{3}$ per cent the first year and 3 per cent thereafter 362

§ 5 (to Ch. XII, § 6). Mathematical relations between the rates of interest as a premium and as a price 363

§ 6 (to Ch. XII, § 7). Mathematical relations between the rates of interest and discount 364

§ 7 (to Ch. XII, § 7). Mathematical relations between rates of discount for different time reckonings 366

§ 8 (to Ch. XII, § 8). Dimensions of rates of interest, discount, and capitalization 367

Appendix to Chapter XIII

§ 1 (to Ch. XIII, § 1). Formula for capital-value of a sum due in one year 368

§ 2 (to Ch. XIII, § 1). Formula for capital-value of a sum V, due at end of any time t 368

§ 3 (to Ch. XIII, § 3). Formula for capital-value of a perpetual annuity 369

§ 4 (to Ch. XIII, § 3). Formulæ and diagrams for capital-value of annuities payable annually, semi-annually, quarterly, and continuously 369

§ 5 (to Ch. XIII, § 3). Diagrams for discontinuous and continuous income 371

§ 6 (to Ch. XIII, § 5). Formula for capital-value of a terminable annuity 374

§ 7 (to Ch. XIII, § 5). Discussion of formulæ for terminable annuities by diagrams. "Total discount." "Total interest" 374

§ 8 (to Ch. XIII, § 7). Formulæ for value of bond . . . 378

§ 9 (to Ch. XIII, § 7). Alternative method for computing value of a bond 380

§ 10 (to Ch. XIII, § 7). Formula for a bond when interest is reckoned oftener than yearly 382

§ 11 (to Ch. XIII, § 8). Formula for capital-value of any series of income installments 382

§ 12 (to Ch. XIII, § 8). Diagram and formula for deriving capital-value from a given continuous income stream 383

§ 13 (to Ch. XIII, § 8). Diagram showing the accumulated "amount" of a given income stream 387

§ 14 (to Ch. XIII, § 10). Effect of reckoning semi-annually, quarterly, and continuously, on the rate of interest realized from the income of a continuously replenished stock of articles . . 388

§ 15 (to Ch. XIII, § 11). Influence of variation in the rate of interest 390

§ 16 (to Ch. XIII, § 11). Representation of capital and income by polar coördinates 393

Appendix to Chapter XIV

§ 1 (to Ch. XIV, § 5). When the interest rate varies, there are two rival concepts of "standard income" 396

§ 2 (to Ch. XIV, § 12). Effect of foreknown tax on increase of capital 398

§ 3 (to Ch. XIV, § 13). Unrestricted application of a true income tax impracticable 400

Appendix to Chapter XVI

§ 1 (to Ch. XVI, § 6). Mathematical coefficients of probability, caution, and risk 403
§ 2 (to Ch. XVI, § 7). Formula for mathematical value of a risky bond 403
§ 3 (to Ch. XVI, § 10). Variability about a mean, as measured by the "standard deviation" 406
§ 4 (to Ch. XVI, § 20). Method of computing a pure level life insurance premium 410

INDEX 413

INTRODUCTION. FUNDAMENTAL CONCEPTS

    CHAPTER   I. WEALTH
    CHAPTER II. PROPERTY
    CHAPTER III. UTILITY

THE NATURE OF CAPITAL AND INCOME

CHAPTER I

WEALTH

§ 1

THE term "wealth" is used in this book to signify *material objects owned by human beings*. According to this definition, an object, to be wealth, must conform to only two conditions: it must be *material*, and it must be *owned*. To these, some writers add a third condition, namely, that it must be *useful*. But while utility is undoubtedly an essential attribute of wealth, it is not a distinctive one, being implied in the attribute of appropriation; hence it is redundant in a definition. Other writers, like Cannan, while specifying that an object, to be wealth, must be useful, do not specify that it must be owned. They therefore define wealth as "useful material objects." This definition, however, includes too much. Rain, wind, clouds, the Gulf Stream, the heavenly bodies — especially the sun, from which we derive most of our light, heat, and energy — are all useful, but are not appropriated, and so are not wealth as commonly understood. Still other writers insist that an article, to be wealth, must be "exchangeable." But this restriction would exclude parks, Houses of Parliament, the Hague Temple of Peace, and much other trusteed wealth; all wealth, in fact, which happens to fall into permanent hands. Although it is essential that wealth should be owned, it is not essential that it should continually change owners. Again, many writers, like McLeod, omit the qualifier "material" altogether, in order to make room for the inclusion of such "immaterial wealth" as stocks, bonds, and other property rights, and for human and other services. Property and services are, it is true, inseparable from wealth, and wealth from them, but they are not wealth. To embrace all these under one term involves a species of triple counting. A railway, a railway share, and a railway trip are not three separate items of wealth; they are respectively wealth, a title to that wealth, and a service of that wealth. Finally, a few economists, like Tuttle, have endeavored to break away from concrete objects entirely. The term "wealth," they maintain, applies, not to the concrete objects, but to the *value* of these objects. Much may be said in support of this contention. But as the question is chiefly verbal, that is, not a question of finding a suitable concept, but of finding a suitable word for a concept, it does not seem advisable to depart from the prevailing usage among economists.

Wealth, then, includes all those parts of the material universe which have been appropriated to the uses of mankind. It does not include the sun, moon, or stars, because no man owns them. It is confined to this little planet, and only to parts of that; namely, the appropriated portions of the earth's surface and the appropriated objects upon it. The appropriation need not be complete; it is often only partial and for a particular purpose, as in the case of the Newfoundland Banks, which are appropriated only in the sense that the fishermen of certain nations have the right to take fish in their vicinity, while their waters are open to all men for all other purposes. In fact, it is doubtful if there are any objects owned so unrestrictedly that the owner of them may use them in absolute defiance of the wishes of others. By appropriation of any object is therefore meant that degree of appropriation to which the object is subjected.

Any single object of wealth is called an *article* of wealth, an *item* of wealth, or an *instrument*. The term "instrument" is perhaps the most convenient. It appears to have been first employed by John Rae in 1834.[1]

§ 2

Various classes of wealth may be distinguished. Wealth which consists of the earth's surface is called *land;* any fixed structures upon it, *land improvements;* and the two together, constituting immovable wealth, *real estate.* All wealth which is movable (except man himself) we shall call *commodities.* A third group includes *human beings* — not only slaves who are owned by other human beings, but also freemen who are their own masters.

It is true that freemen are not ordinarily counted as wealth; and, indeed, they are a very peculiar form of wealth, for various reasons: first, because they are not, like ordinary wealth, bought and sold; secondly, because the owner usually estimates his own importance so much more highly than any one else; and finally, because the owner and the thing owned in this case coincide. Yet they are, like other wealth, "material" and "owned." These attributes, and others which depend on them, justify[2] the inclusion of man as wealth. But in order to concede as much as possible to popular usage, the following supplementary definition is framed: By wealth (in its more *restricted* sense) we mean *material objects owned by man and external to the owner.* This definition obviously includes slaves, but not freemen. But it is more difficult of application than the wider definition first given, as it requires

---

[1] *New Principles of Political Economy*, recently reprinted under the title *Sociological Theory of Capital*, Macmillan, 1905.

[2] Among those writers who have included man in the category of wealth are Davenant, Petty, Canard, Say, McCulloch, Roscher, Wittstein, Walras, Engel, Weiss, Dargun, Ofner, Nicholson, and Pareto.

us to separate into arbitrary classes those persons who are intermediate between freemen and slaves, such as vassals, indentured servants, long-time apprentices, and negroes held in peonage. A man bound out to service for thirty years is almost indistinguishable from a slave, and if the term of service be long enough and the control absolute enough, the distinction becomes a distinction without a difference. On the other hand, the shorter the term of service, the nearer does his condition approach freedom. As a matter of fact, most workers in modern society are "hired," $i.e.$ bound by contract to some extent and for some period of time, even though it be for no more than an hour, and to that extent are not free. In short, there are many degrees of freedom and many degrees of slavery, with no fixed line of demarcation.

Two concepts have been defined which may be designated as "wealth in its more general sense" and "wealth in its more restricted sense." There need be no confusion between them. Ordinarily, when the simple term "wealth" is used, the former concept will be understood, and any propositions which hold true of this broader concept will necessarily apply also to the narrower one. If we have occasion at any time to refer to the latter exclusively, we may always make use of the full phrase, "wealth in its more restricted sense."

There are many admissible ways of classifying wealth, one being more or less desirable than another according to the purpose for which it is intended. The scheme on page 7 is not based on any one logical criterion, but is intended merely to give the principal groups into which wealth, as it actually exists, naturally falls. It scarcely needs to be stated that the various classes are not always absolutely distinct. Like all classes of concrete things, they merge imperceptibly from one into another. For this reason the classification is of little importance except to give a bird's-eye view of economic science. In fact, the classification of concrete things is seldom of paramount importance in scientific study. Not classification, but analysis, solves scientific problems.[1]

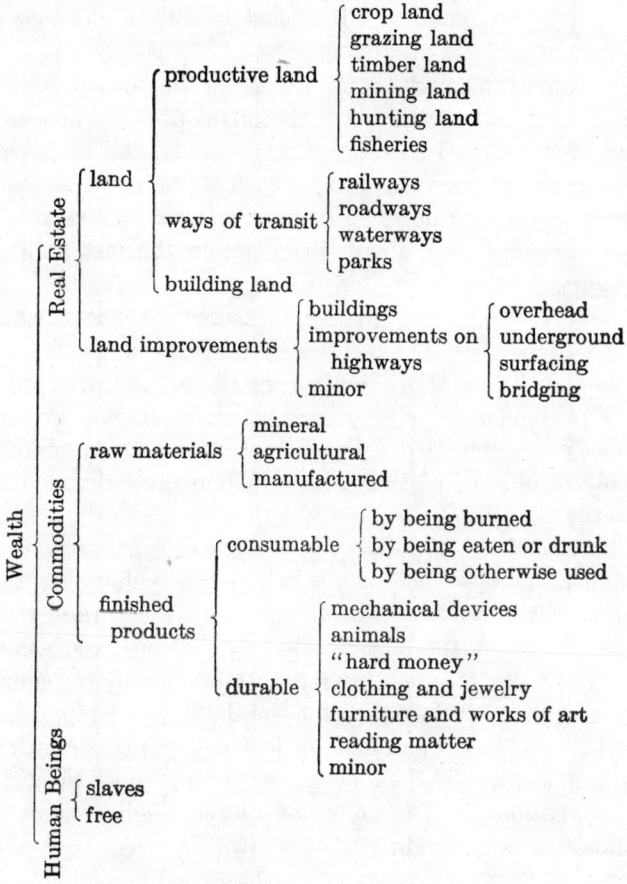

[1] See the writer's "What is Capital?" *Economic Journal*, December, 1896, p. 516; and "Precedents for Defining Capital," *Quarterly Journal of Economics*, March, 1904.

§ 3

In the definition of wealth were included two attributes: wealth is *material;* and, it is *owned*. These attributes, materiality and appropriation, need to be considered separately. The remainder of this chapter will be devoted to the former.

An important and useful result of the materiality of wealth is that it provides a basis for the physical measurement of wealth. Wealth is of many kinds, and each kind is measured in its own proper physical unit. These units have been handed down to us from various sources and in great diversity, but all of them are in the last analysis arbitrary.

Many kinds of wealth are measured by *weight-units*. This is true of coal, iron, beef, and in fact, of most "commodities." Each unit consists of the weight of some particular piece of matter which is adopted for convenience as a standard. For instance, the English pound is simply a lump of platinum kept in London and called arbitrarily the pound.

Many articles are not so conveniently measured by weight-units as by *space-units*, whether of volume, area, or length. Thus we have, for volume, milk measured by the quart, wheat by the bushel, wood by the cord, and gas by the cubic foot; for areas, we have lumber sold by the square foot and land by the acre; for length, we have rope, wire, ribbons, and cloth measured in feet and yards. All these units of length, area, and volume are also quite arbitrary or conventional. The definition of the English yard, for instance, is an imaginary line drawn between two small dots on gold plugs in a particular brass rod in London.

Many articles exist in more or less definite units which need only to be counted, as for instance, eggs or oranges, which are measured by the dozen. Similarly, writing paper is reckoned by the quire; pencils and screws by the gross.

In such cases we say that the article is measured *by number*. But "number" is by no means peculiar to the last-named case. All measurement implies both an abstract number, and a concrete unit, as "ten screws," "six eggs," or "four pounds-of-granulated-sugar."

The last example suggests that in order to specify fully the unit of any kind of wealth, it is necessary to enumerate its particular attributes, or enough of them to distinguish it from other sorts of wealth with which it may become confused. Thus, it is often necessary to specify what "grade" or "brand" is meant, as "Grade A," "Eagle Brand," "Lackawanna" coal. Sometimes the special sort is denoted by a trade mark or hallmark. It is in this way that the attributes of particular kinds of wealth enter into the consideration of economic science, and not, as some have erroneously supposed, separately as an "immaterial" sort of wealth. The "fertility" of land is not to be counted as wealth apart from the land itself; it is the "fertile land" which is wealth. The "skill" of a mechanic is not wealth in addition to the man himself; it is the "skilled mechanic" who should be put in the category of wealth.

Of course, the number expressing the measure of wealth may be unity, as for instance, "one dwelling." Sometimes there is only one article of the particular kind in existence. There is but one Battery Park, one Buckingham Palace, one Koh-i-noor diamond, one Rhynd papyrus. Dealers call such articles "uniques." Strictly speaking, every article might be called a unique, even as no two grains of wheat are precisely alike; but for practical purposes we overlook minor differences and regard articles sufficiently similar as homogeneous.

§ 4

Thus each individual kind of wealth may be measured in its own special unit, — pounds, gallons, yards; but for most purposes it is more important to measure the *value* of wealth, and this may be done in dollars and cents, pounds and shillings, francs and centimes, and so forth. This is also a species of physical measurement, but involves the principle of *exchange*. So much mystery has surrounded the term "value" that we cannot be too careful to obtain correct and simple ideas on the subject. In the explanation which follows, the concept of value is made to depend on that of price; that of price in turn on exchange; and finally, that of exchange on transfer.

An article of wealth is said to be *transferred* when it changes owners. It is to be observed that such a change does not necessarily imply any change of place. Ordinarily, the transfer of an article involves change in its position. The purchase of tea or sugar is accompanied by the delivery of these articles across the counter from dealer to customer. But in many cases such a change of position does not occur, and in the case of real estate it is even impossible. This distinction between change of ownership and change of position is not always borne in mind. It is sometimes said, for instance, that exports and imports must balance in a certain manner. But if by "exports" we mean articles that are sent out of the country, and by "imports" those which come into it, the proposition will not hold true. When, some years ago, Englishmen were buying American breweries, these articles, of course, were not exported, though they were transferred to foreign ownership.

Transfers may be voluntary or involuntary. Examples of involuntary transfers of wealth are transfers effected either (1) through force and fraud of individuals, as in robbery, burglary, embezzlement, etc.; or (2) through force of government, as in taxes, court fines, etc. But at present we have to do with voluntary transfers.

Voluntary transfers are of two kinds: (1) one-sided transfers, *i.e.* gifts and bequests; and (2) reciprocal transfers or *exchanges*, which are the most important for economic science.

Exchange of wealth, then, means the *mutual and voluntary transfer of wealth between two owners, each transfer being in consideration of the other.* If either of the two quantities of wealth exchanged is divided by the other, the quotient is called the *price* of the latter. Thus, when three bushels of wheat are traded for two dollars of gold, the price of the wheat is ⅔ of a dollar per bushel, and the price of the gold is 1½ bushels of wheat per dollar. In modern times, one of the two articles is usually money, but this condition is not essential, and in primitive times was not even common. When the exchange is one of money for other wealth, it is called a *purchase* (with reference to the one who parts with the money) and a *sale* (with reference to the person who receives the money).

§ 5

In order that there may be a price, it is not necessary that the exchange in question should actually take place. It may be only a contemplated exchange. A real estate agent often has an "asking price," that is, a price at which he tries to sell, usually above the price of an actual sale. In the same way there is often a "bidding price," which is usually below the price of actual sale. The price of sale thus generally lies between the prices first bid and asked. But it sometimes happens that the bidder refuses to raise his bid and the seller refuses to lower his asking price. In such a case no sale takes place and the only prices are those bid and asked. Trade journals report, for many commodities, the price of sale if there is a sale, otherwise the two prices bid and asked, or if both do not exist, the one which does.

When there is no sale, and especially when there is no price bid or asked, it is not so easy to answer the question, What is the price? Recourse is then had to an "appraisement" or appraisal, which is simply a more or less skilful guess as to what price the article would or should fetch. Appraising or guessing at prices is often very difficult in practice. It is necessarily employed, however, by the government in assessing taxes and customs and condemning land; by insurance companies in settling claims and adjusting losses; by merchants in making up inventories and other statements; and by statisticians and others. In fact, some people make a living by simply appraising wealth on which, for one purpose or another, a price of some sort must be set. Evidently, the purpose makes a great difference in the appraisal. Sometimes we need to know the price for which an article could be sold at an immediate forced sale; sometimes, what it might be expected to bring if a reasonable time were allowed; sometimes, what the owner would probably take; sometimes, what a possible purchaser would probably give. These appraised prices may all be different. A family portrait may be worth an untold amount to the owner, but might bring next to nothing if actually sold. The owner would endeavor to appraise it at a high figure if he wished to insure it against fire; but if he wished to borrow money on it, the appraisement would doubtless be small, for the pawnbroker would consider it almost worthless.

Thus, in practically making an appraisement we encounter many difficulties, owing partly to the unknown character and condition of the parties involved, and partly to the variety of interests to be served by the appraisal. But whatever the difficulties and ambiguities in ascertaining a price or prices for any article, the price or prices do actually exist without ambiguity. The vagueness comes wholly from failure to specify sufficiently the conditions under which the exchange is to take place. If we specify in sufficient detail the conditions of the contemplated exchange, its terms will be quite definite; but whether or not we can guess at those terms correctly is quite another matter.

§ 6

Having obtained the *price* of any kind of wealth, we may compute the *value* of any given quantity of that wealth, without necessarily supposing that particular quantity to be exchanged. The value of a given quantity of wealth is found by multiplying the quantity by the price. Thus, if the price of wheat is $\frac{2}{3}$ of a dollar per bushel, then a lot consisting of 3000 bushels would have a value of 3000 × $\$\frac{2}{3}$ per bushel or $2000. In other words, the value of a certain amount of one kind of wealth is the quantity of some other kind for which it would be exchanged, if the whole amount were exchanged at the price set upon it. The exchange which sets the price need not be the exchange of the particular 3000 bushels which we are valuing; some other exchange of, say, 300 bushels for $200 may set the price. This is one reason why it is preferable to explain price first and value afterward.

The definition of value which has been given, applying, as it does, to an aggregate of wealth instead of the unit, departs somewhat from economic usage; but it follows closely the usage of business men and practical statisticians. Economists have not usually thought it necessary to distinguish between the purchasing power of the unit and the aggregate, but have employed the term "value" indiscriminately to both. In other respects also their usage has been somewhat different from that here employed. Some of them have confined "price" to a money expression, *i.e.* to what is here called *money* price, and applied the term "value" to purchasing power in "goods." Others have used the term "price" in the sense of what an article actually sells for (market price) and "value" in the sense of what it *ought* to sell for (appraised price or reasonable price). Others, in turn, have used the term "price" in the sense employed in this book, but "value" in the sense of the degree of esteem in which an article is held ("marginal utility" or "subjective value"). It seems preferable to conform our definitions of value and price as closely as possible to business usage, which instinctively and consistently applies the term "price" to the unit and "value" to the aggregate.

§ 7

The distinction between quantity, price, and value of wealth may be seen clearly in any "inventory," such as the following: —

	Quantity	Price in Wheat	Value in Wheat
Shoes	1000 pair	4¼ bu. per pair	4,250 bu.
Beef	300 lbs.	⅕ bu. per lb.	60 bu.
Dwelling House	1 house	10,000 bu. per house	10,000 bu.
Wheat	100 bu.	1 bu. per bu.	100 bu.
			14,410 bu.

In the first column are recorded various quantities of wealth, measured each in its own special unit; in the second column are the prices of these in wheat; while in the last column are their values, also in terms of wheat. The first and last columns represent two different modes of measuring wealth. Statistics of wealth, such as those published monthly by the Department of Commerce, usually give both "quantities" and "values." To translate from one to the other we need always a *price* as go-between.

It is important not to confuse the three columns with each other. The *quantity* of beef is a totally different thing from its *value*, and each of these is different from its *price*. The quantity is measured in *pounds* of beef, its value in *bushels* of wheat, and its price in *bushels per pound*. These three magnitudes are all of different "dimensions." Both quantity and value are simply physical magnitudes. "Value" as here explained is not a subjective magnitude in the mind of man, but purely objective, as *money value,* or *wheat value.* It has, of course, subjective causes, but these do not concern us yet.[1]

The measurement of wealth in "value" has this great advantage over its measurement in "quantity," that it translates the many kinds of wealth into a single kind. All the items in the third column of the inventory are thus expressed in a common unit, the bushel. We may consequently add together this column and obtain a single sum, namely, 14,410 bushels; but summation of the first column is impossible, because shoes, pounds of beef, houses, and bushels of wheat are incommensurable. We see here one of the important functions of money; it brings uniformity of measurement out of diversity.

But, although this reduction to a common measure is practically convenient, it would, of course, be a great mistake to suppose that it gives what may be called "the true measure of wealth." "The value of wealth" is an incomplete phrase; to be definite we should say, "the value of wealth in terms of gold," or in terms of some other particular article. We cannot, therefore, use such values for comparing different groups of wealth except under certain conditions and to a limited degree. To compare the wealth-values of America and England, of Ancient Rome and Modern Italy, of Carnegie and Crœsus, will give different results according to the standard of value employed.

§ 8

We have seen how to measure the three magnitudes,— quantity, price, and value of wealth. This measurement is, practically, a very inaccurate affair. The degree of accuracy attained is exaggerated in the minds of most persons, even including business men. In measurements of quantities of wealth there are two sources of error, for every

[1] Further explanation as to the dimensions of the quantity, price, and value of wealth are given in the Appendix to Chap. I, § 1.

measurement includes, as we have seen, two elements: a *unit of measure*, which may be inaccurate; and a *number* or ratio between the quantity to be measured and the unit, which number may also be inaccurate. In modern times the first source of error is practically eliminated. Our units of weight and measure are standardized by law, and a pound weight in California is equal to one in Connecticut, within one part in many thousand. The chief source of error, therefore, lies not in the unit, but in the ratio of the wealth to that unit. In retail trade the inaccuracy is as great as five per cent, or greater. Wholesale transactions are more accurate. A large manufacturing concern of Syracuse had its measurement of the weight of caustic soda sold in carload lots compared with the measurement made by its customers, and the results agreed within one fifth of one per cent on two fifty-carload lots. Probably the greatest degree of accuracy ever obtained in commercial measurements is on the Mint scales used by the United States in Philadelphia and San Francisco. These scales weigh accurately to within about one part in ten million.

When we proceed from quantities of wealth to values, we introduce still a third source of inaccuracy, namely, in the price factor by which we multiply. This is especially true if the price be merely an "appraised" price. The price of any actual sale is an absolute fact and cannot be said to have any inaccuracy; but the price at which we estimate that a thing *would* sell under certain conditions is always uncertain. In the case of staple articles, *i.e.* articles regularly on the market, a dealer can often appraise correctly within one per cent. Real estate in certain parts of a city where sales are active can sometimes be appraised correctly within five or ten per cent; but in the "dead" or out-of-the-way parts of some towns, where sales are infrequent, the appraisement becomes merely a rough guess. Again, in the country districts, while farms in the settled parts of

Iowa and Texas can be appraised within ten or fifteen per cent, in the backward parts even an expert's valuation is often proved wrong by more than fifty per cent. In some cases, in fact, where a sale of the article is scarcely conceivable, an appraisement is almost out of the question. To estimate the value of the Yellowstone Park is impossible, unless we allow ourselves a range of several hundred per cent. Similar wide limits must be allowed when we try to value free human beings. We can often give a lower limit, but seldom an upper one. The estimates may vary enormously with the point of view. It is sometimes said, "If I could buy Mr. So-and-So at my valuation and sell him at his, I'd get rich." It would be wrong, however, to conclude, as some writers have, that because we cannot value them accurately, public parks or freemen cannot be called wealth. When the slaves in the South became freemen they ceased to be appraised as wealth. The result has been somewhat confusing to our census statistics. The *Manufacturers' Record* of Baltimore recently issued figures showing a sharp drop in the assessed valuations of wealth in the South after the war, and the inference was drawn that wealth had immensely decreased. But a large part of this so called decrease consisted merely in the change of ownership of slaves from their old masters to themselves, and the consequent omission of them from the statistics.

Various writers, from Petty down to Engel and Nicholson, have tried to assess the value of human beings. Professor Nicholson estimates roughly that the English nation is worth at least five times the value of other existing wealth in England.[1] Such calculations are of course of more theoretical than practical moment. They are also necessarily inaccurate, and involve in each case some particular supposition as to the purpose of the appraisement; for instance, whether it is to indicate the earning power of the population, their value to themselves, or to others.

[1] *Economic Journal*, March, 1891, p. 95.

CHAPTER II

PROPERTY

§ 1

THE definition of Wealth in the previous chapter restricts its meaning to concrete material objects. But economics has also to deal with abstract services, utilities, and property rights. These, like material wealth, are bought and sold, and are, in fact, often regarded as a sort of "immaterial" or "incorporeal" wealth. It is, however, needless as well as confusing to include these elements under the general category of wealth. They are not wealth, though they are intimately related to wealth. The definition given shows that wealth has two attributes: it must be material, and it must be owned. Its materiality was the subject of the previous chapter; its ownership will be the subject of the present chapter.

But what is meant by owning wealth? We answer: to have the right to use it. Such a right is called *property*, or, more explicitly, a *property right*. To own a loaf of bread, or to have property or proprietorship in it, means nothing more nor less than to have the right to eat it, or sell it, or otherwise employ it to satisfy one's desires. To own a suit of clothes is to have the exclusive right to wear it. To own a carriage is to have the right to drive in it or otherwise utilize it as long as it lasts. To own a plot of land means to have the right to its use forever. The concept of property — the "right to use wealth" — is more fully expressed by the phrase, the "right to the uses of wealth." In this phrase we have to deal with two new ideas — rights and uses — each of which needs to be treated separately.

§ 2

We need first to understand what is the nature of the uses or services of wealth. The services of an instrument of wealth are the desirable changes effected (or the undesirable changes prevented) by means of that instrument. For instance, the services of a loom consist in changing yarn into cloth, or what is called weaving. Similarly, a plow performs the service of changing the soil in a particular manner; a bricklayer, of changing the position of bricks. A dam or dike performs the service of preventing the water from overflowing the land; a fence, of preventing cattle from roaming; a necklace, of sparkling or reflecting light, and thereby satisfying the love of beauty or the vanity of the owner.

When services are described as *desirable* events, it is meant that they are desired or esteemed by the owner or owners, not necessarily by every one, or even any one, else. It may even happen that the events are distinctly distasteful to others. A factory whistle may be a nuisance to every one except the factory owner.

In this connection it is important to distinguish between the uses or desirable events, and the utility or desirability of those events. The desirable service is a thing; it is usually objective. The desirability of the service, on the other hand, is a quality, and is purely subjective. It is a feeling toward the events, not the events themselves. In the present chapter we do not have to deal with the desirability, and it will form the subject of the next chapter.

Each sort of service is measured in its own appropriate unit. Sometimes the measurement is by *number*, i.e. obtained by simply counting the acts in which the specified service consists, as, for instance, in the case of the strokes of a printing press; sometimes the measurement is by *time*, as in the case of the day laborer; while sometimes the measurement of the services is expressed in terms of the *units of wealth* affected by those services, as in the case of so-called piecework. The services of a miner are measured by reference to the quantity of coal mined; the services of a planter, by the number of acres planted; and of a spinning machine, by the number of yards spun. Services, like wealth, are subject to exchange and, in consequence, have *prices*. The quantity of any service multiplied by its price gives its *value*. When reduced to value in a common standard, all varieties of services become commensurable with each other and with wealth.

The opposite of a service is a disservice, which is an undesirable change effected (or a desirable change prevented) by means of wealth. For instance, a locomotive renders disservices by consuming coal; a farm, by requiring fertilizers and labor; a factory, by requiring costs of working. Disservices, like services, are measured in quantity by special units and made commensurable in value by reduction to a common standard.

§ 3

Having seen what is meant by services of wealth, we next ask what is meant by the *right* to those services. "Right" is a term of jurisprudence, and brings economics into contact with the whole subject of legal and custom-sanctioned relations; but, for our present purpose, it is not necessary to go far in this direction. The right of a person to the uses of an article of wealth may be defined as his liberty, under the sanction of law and society, to enjoy the services of that article.

Lawyers distinguish between property rights and personal rights; but, to the economist, all rights are proprietary. The distinction between property and personal rights exists only so long as we restrict the meaning of wealth to the narrower of its two definitions, that is, only so long as we exclude free human beings. Here we have an instance in which logical convenience is served by adopting the broader definition of wealth, which includes human beings even when free, and by adopting also a coextensively broad definition of property so as to include all rights known to jurisprudence. This being premised, it follows that every right is a property right. No rights have ever been suggested which are not rights to obtain and enjoy the uses of wealth, either persons or things. Even the "right to life, liberty, and the pursuit of happiness" is simply one's right to certain uses of his own person. The rights of a husband over his wife and of a wife over her husband, and the reciprocal rights between parents and children, as well as all other rights *in personam*, are claims against particular persons; while the right to reputation, to the free exercise of one's calling, to immunity from boycott, persecution, etc., are claims upon the community generally.[1] These rights are not ordinarily called property rights, just as persons are not ordinarily called wealth, and for a similar reason, — they do not enter into trade. When wives were bought and sold they were regarded as wealth, and marital rights as property. To-day, both are taken out of commerce and therefore removed from commercial ideas and terms. The economist need not, perhaps, absolutely insist on restoring them; like the business man, he is chiefly interested in what is salable. But in framing his definitions he finds it difficult, if not impossible, to confine the terms "wealth" and "property" to objects which are exchangeable, without thereby sacrificing simplicity and logical convenience, and excluding certain objects, such as public parks and former English entails, which, though never sold, even business men would call wealth and property respectively. We therefore choose in this book to frame our definitions so as to include such elements, even though they be not further referred to. In definitions, it is usually better to include too much rather than too little, and in this case,

[1] Cf. T. E. Holland, *Jurisprudence*, Macmillan, 1898, pp. 50, 80, 87, 90, 128.

at least, the superfluous which is included will seldom concern and never embarrass us.

Property rights, then, consist of rights to the uses or services of wealth. But the services which we own are always and necessarily future services; the past have perished. Moreover, since all future events are uncertain, we are always constrained to reckon with the element of *chance*. A strictly complete definition of a property right, therefore, would read as follows: *A property right is the right to the chance of obtaining some or all of the future services of one or more articles of wealth.*

Property is measurable, just as are wealth and services, each in its own particular unit. Usually the measurement is "by number," that is, by counting the number of rights of the same kind. Thus, one hundred shares of preferred stock in a particular company is a statement of the amount of that particular property. The concepts transfer, exchange, price, and value apply to property as to wealth and to services. Indeed, as an exchange of wealth is but a concealed exchange of services, so an exchange of services is but a concealed exchange of the right thereto, namely, property. Hence the exchange of property is the final form of exchange, and includes in itself all other forms whatsoever.

§ 4

Wealth and property, then, are correlative terms. Wealth is the concrete thing owned; property is the abstract right of ownership. The two concepts mutually imply each other. There can be no wealth without property rights applying to it, nor property rights without wealth to which they apply. In fact, the proposition that property and wealth are coextensive follows necessarily from the definitions of wealth and property which we have adopted. But it may readily be objected that in the actual concrete world, for which these definitions were designed, the correspondence between what are known as wealth and property does not hold true. A thorough examination of the case, however, will remove this objection.

Sometimes wealth and property rights are so closely associated as to be confused with each other, so that, unless one stops to consider the matter, the existence of the two separate concepts would not be suspected. This is true in the case of "fee simple," where a piece of land is spoken of as a "piece of property." For practical purposes, little objection can be raised to such popular usage, but even in such cases strict accuracy requires that the two ideas should be distinguished. The distinction is more easily remembered if we employ the full phrase "property right." A loaf of bread is concrete wealth, not a property right; the right to eat it is the property. On the other hand, in the more involved cases of property rights, we encounter the opposite difficulty. The danger here is in separating the concepts of wealth and property too far, so as to consider them as independent instead of interdependent. When railway shares are sold in Wall Street, the investor is prone to think of those shares as entirely detached from any concrete wealth. It is unlikely that he has ever seen or ever will see the steel rails, cars, and locomotives upon which those shares are based; and indeed, the only concrete object of which he is likely to be distinctly conscious is the paper certificate itself. But it is clear that this paper certificate is not itself the property, but merely the written evidence of it and that the railway shares, to be property, involve a real railway (wealth) underneath.

That all wealth involves a property right is not likely to be denied by any one; and that all property rights involve underlying wealth should be equally evident. But this is not the case. In fact, some of the most dangerous fallacies which beset the business world, including many of the sophisms of credit, are due to the difficulty of recognizing the wealth lying behind property in some of its sublimated forms.

§ 5

In order not to devote too much space to this subject the best procedure will be to give types of the chief forms of property, and to specify in each case what wealth underlies the right. This is done in the table on pages 26 and 27, which also specifies the services involved, and (where they exist) the certificate or written evidence of the property right.

§ 6

Probably ninety per cent of the actual property in the United States would be included under the cases entitled Fee Simple, Partnership Rights, Stocks, Bonds, Notes, and Lease Rights. In all of these cases, the existence of the real wealth behind them is well known and acknowledged. For practical purposes, therefore, the proposition that wealth and property are coextensive is already established.

Of the remaining cases some seem a little obscure at first, but they may be readily solved if we bear in mind a few general principles:

The first thought which should guide us is that, given any particular property right, we should first discover the benefits or "services" secured by that right, then the physical means by which those services are obtained. These means are not always identical with the "cause" of those services. For instance, real estate with a southern exposure is especially desired because of the sunlight which falls upon it. The sun may be called the *cause* of the sunlight, but the land is the practical *means* of obtaining it. To own or not to own the land is to obtain or not to obtain the sunlight which goes with it. It is the land which puts the sunlight at the disposal of its owner. On the other hand, when a lamp gives its light it is not only means, but also cause.

Following this idea, that wealth is simply the means and not necessarily the cause, we can better understand some of the items in the table. We see clearly what it is that lies behind a street railway franchise, or the franchise of the underground system of New York City. It must be the wealth by means of which the transportation can take place. The streets which the railway has the right to use form the necessary means for its transportation services. To own the streets involves the possession of the right to use them for transportation purposes, and, when this right is given or sold, as when a franchise is granted, this act constitutes a partial surrender of the ownership of the streets.

Again, let us consider the case of a promise. The physical means of fulfilling a promise are evidently the person who made the promise and the wealth which that person can or will use for that purpose. Thus, a debt or bond secured by a mortgage is primarily a claim upon the promisor which he may satisfy out of his earnings or his general wealth. But it offers this great advantage over other forms of indebtedness, that it is also a contingent claim upon a *specific* portion of the promisor's wealth, which may be taken in payment even against his will, if the promisor otherwise fails to make good his promise. Here the means of perfecting the right evidenced by the bond include the person of the promisor, his general wealth, and the specific part of that wealth covered by the mortgage. On the other hand, a "labor due" is principally a claim upon the person of the laborer, for he must be the means of performing the labor required. In country districts farmers are often under obligations to the county to furnish a certain amount of roadwork of men and horses. The right to such work is a species of property belonging to the county. A still better example is found in cases where the labor or services to be rendered are of a personal or artistic character, such as the singing of a Patti or the acting of a Bernhardt; for, while one under contract to lay bricks might reasonably

TYPICAL CASES ILLUSTRATING THE EXISTENCE OF WEALTH BEHIND PROPERTY RIGHTS

Name of Case	Wealth on which the Property Right is Based	Services of that Wealth	Description of Property Right	Certificate of Ownership, if Any
Fee Simple	farm	yielding crops	right to use it exclusively forever	deed
Partnership	dry goods	yielding profits from sales	one partner's "undivided one-third interest", other partners' "undivided two-thirds interest"	articles of agreement
Joint Stock	railway	yielding profits	the shares of stock	stock certificate
Different Usufructs	ranch	yielding products	right of farming, right of lumbering, right of fishing, right of mining	written contracts
Street Franchise	street	use of same for passage, etc.	right to run cars through it, right to run wires through it	charter
Lease or Hire	dwelling	use of same for shelter, etc.	right of tenant till fixed date, right of landlord thereafter	lease
Lease or Hire	horse and buggy	driving	right of customer to an afternoon drive, residual rights of liveryman	none
Lease or Hire	theater	use of same for amusement	right to opera box for season	receipt
Railway Ticket	railway	transportation	right to specified trip	ticket
Work Dues	workman	his work	right of employer to performance of same	per-written contract
Railroad Bond	railway	payment of "interest" and "principal"	right to same and contingent right to foreclose	bond certificate
Personal Note	all the possessions of the signer	payment	right to same and in default thereof right to collateral security	note

Bank Note	bank building, cash, and all wealth underlying bank property	payment on demand	right to same on demand	note
Bank Deposit	bank building, cash, and all wealth underlying bank property	payment on demand	right to same on demand	pass book
Promises of Refraining	person and his (other) wealth	leaving the field open	right to same	articles of agreement
Good Will of Newspaper	subscribers, advertisers, and their (other) wealth	resubscribing and readvertising	right of the "paper" to chance of their patronage	none
Irredeemable Paper money	general wealth of community	any uses thereof	right to portion of same	paper money
Copyright	general wealth of community (persons included)	leaving the field open	right to compel same	official record
Patent Right	general wealth of community (persons included)	leaving the field open	right to compel same	official record
Monopoly Franchise	general wealth of community (persons included)	refraining from doing similar business	right to compel same	charter
Taxing Power	general wealth of community	paying taxes	right of government to collect	none
Rights in Common	club building furniture and members	use of same	right to use of same	certificate
Government Property	streets, public parks, and buildings	use of same	right to walk over and otherwise use same	official recorded plats, old grants, individual dedications, deeds

fulfil his contract by furnishing another equally skilful bricklayer, no audience attracted by either of those artists would accept in return for its entrance money the performance of any understudy, no matter how capable. This right to the services of a particular person, as distinguished from the right .to services of a particular character, gives rise to many curious cases in law. Similarly, a personal note is to a large extent a claim upon the person of the drawer, though also a claim upon his other wealth; for both the man himself and his external wealth are the means of keeping good the promise and finally paying the debt. Another case is that of a "factor's agreement" or some other promise by which a firm or person agrees to refrain from certain acts, such as selling in competition with the promisee. Some years ago a paper manufacturer near New Haven was offered a round sum if he would close his mills. This he did, to the benefit of both himself and his former rivals, though not of the public. In this case the contract which he made with his rivals constituted a kind of property for them; the wealth by *means* of which his promise was made good was evidently his own person, together with his plant; and the service performed was the inactivity of both.

Good will is a less certain though still a valuable form of property. A few years ago one of the largest newspapers in the United States was sold. The property included, besides presses, type, linotype machines, office building, etc., the items of overdue subscriptions and good will. An overdue subscription is a debt which constitutes a virtual promise of the subscriber, and thousands of these in the aggregate make up a considerable value. By good will is meant something very similar; namely, the quasi-promise of the subscribers to continue to pay as long as the newspaper is sent to them and they are satisfied. These quasi-promises are also property, being almost equivalent to a signed agreement of the subscribers to the effect: "We hereby promise to pay the annual sum of $8 to the —— Publishing Company, provided that and so long as its newspaper is received and is satisfactory." Thus good will is merely the right to a tacit, loose, and contingent promise of support and patronage, less cost. The firm possessing good will owns a precarious yet valuable claim upon its patrons, namely, the chance of their continued patronage. The persons of these subscribers, and their other wealth, are what underlie the property right, because they are the means to the desired services to which those rights apply. Of course the chance of obtaining these services is very much less than it would be if the services were specifically promised; but chance, either large or small, is involved in all property rights.

In the same way, the "custom" of a tailor or the "practice" of a physician is simply the right to the chance of future patronage.

A franchise in the sense of a monopoly privilege granted by a government is quite different from a street railway franchise. The object of the monopoly is to prevent certain acts of certain persons. The means to that end are, in the last analysis, the persons who are constrained to refrain, and the wealth withdrawn from competition.

We may similarly regard a copyright. Recalling the case of the paper trust, part of whose property was the promise of a paper manufacturer not to compete, we may regard a copyright as the right to a similar refraining from or restraining of competition. At one time, an English publisher would obtain the promise of an American publisher not to "pirate" his works. It would have been property of great value to the publishers of the Encyclopædia Britannica if they could have prevented the pirating of their work in this country. Prevention can now be accomplished through the instrumentality of international copyright. The wealth underlying this property right is the wealth which, if employed in the specified line, would enter into competition with the property owner. It mainly consists of the persons and plants of possible competing publishers; and it does not matter whether their inactivity — their non-competition — is purchased by a money payment or enforced by government intervention.

In like manner we may resolve the problem of irredeemable paper money. Where this exists in its purest form, with no promise or intention of ultimate redemption by the government which issues it, it amounts to a forced loan, or rather, a levy. It is like a check drawn by the government upon the public, which each individual is obliged to cash. It is an order to surrender on demand a certain amount of the community's goods. The government usually employs paper money to obtain ammunition or soldiers' supplies. The merchants who give these goods are forced to accept paper money in return, and allowed to recoup themselves by passing on these orders to others. In this way people are deluded into believing that no one really loses, but that the loss is perpetually passed on. The loss is shifted, but nevertheless it exists; for, since a definite quantity of supplies has been abstracted from the public by the government, it is clear that this much loss has been suffered, however it may be distributed by rotation. Thus, irredeemable paper money is a claim on the general wealth of a community. Of course it seldom occurs that it continues irredeemable, and when it becomes redeemable it changes its character; for when the government assumes the obligation involved, it becomes a special claim upon the government gold and other wealth.

A somewhat similar vague property right is the government's taxing power, which is the right to take from the individual so much of the services or product of his wealth as may be necessary for the public good. The heavier the tax, the greater the reduction in the value of the individual wealth of the community. It is well known that to nationalize land, as Henry George proposed, means merely to increase the tax upon it until all its value has been taxed out of it; that is, to take from the individual all of the services or profit of his landed wealth for the benefit of the public, leaving him merely the empty shell of nominal ownership. The case is analogous to that of a person or a community which has mortgaged its wealth so heavily that the value of its services is entirely consumed in the payment of interest, and nothing is left with which to redeem the pledge. The same principle applies to all taxes, even when not carried to such an extreme.

§ 7

A second helpful guide in resolving the various obscure forms of property is found in the fact that one property right is often overlaid by another. For instance, a mill is owned in shares; a railway company owns some of those shares; a bank owns some of the railway shares; and John Smith owns some of the bank shares. It is evident that John Smith has a claim upon the wealth constituted by the mill, although his property is only distantly connected with it, and through several intermediate layers of property rights.

A common example of such secondary relation between wealth and property occurs when the property is held in trust. At common law, the trustee is the legal owner; but the law of equity recognizes the fact that the beneficiary is the true owner. He has a claim against the trustee, and the trustee holds the right to the wealth as against the rest of the world. The beneficiary must work out his rights through the rights of the trustee.

Another good example is that of a claim upon a government, as, for instance, a government bond. This is really a claim against the community, for the government is merely an intermediary between the bondholder and the public wealth which is taxed to satisfy the bondholder's claims. The government owns property only as a sort of trustee for the public. The Boston Common is held by the city of Boston, but is really owned by the citizens, who are the true beneficiaries. Each individual who has the right to enjoy it is to that extent a part owner.

It is not uncommon thus to have, between a property right and the wealth underlying it, several layers of property. A man who owns an ordinary foreign bank note has a claim upon the property of the bank. But the bank's property consists, for the most part, not of tangible wealth, but of promissory notes and other claims on merchants. These notes represent a part right in the wealth (including persons) of the community; consequently the holder of a bank note quite unconsciously owns a claim upon the dry goods, groceries, and other wealth of merchants, which make good the debts of these merchants to the bank.

In the case of United States bank notes he also owns an alternative claim on government bonds, and therefore on the taxable wealth which makes these bonds good. It is erroneous to think of a bank note as representing simply money. This is true of gold certificates; for there are in the United States Treasury as many actual gold dollars as there are certificates in circulation. A bank note, on the other hand, is made good, not solely by the metallic reserve of the bank, but also by the other property or "assets," which the bank is constantly changing or transforming into cash. The Bank of England, for instance, had £60,000,000 of notes out at a given date, and only £43,000,000 of gold in its vaults. But the £17,000,000 deficiency which thus seemed to exist was represented by securities, that is, other property held by the bank.

§ 8

A third guide is that the correspondence between property and wealth is a contemporaneous correspondence. That is to say, the existing property rights are rights to the use of existing wealth, so that *existing* wealth underlies all *existing* property rights. It would seem at first sight that "credit" forms an exception, for credit is a present right to a future payment. But it is impossible to have a right to any future wealth which is not also a right to some present wealth as a means of securing that future wealth. The right to next year's fruit is a right to or in present fruit trees. The right to next year's wheat is a right to or in the present farm, farmer, and farm implements. The right to receive a future chair or table yet unmade is the right to or in the present person, tools, and other wealth of the carpenter, which are the means by which that chair or table is to be secured. To own a note falling due next year is a part right in the person and other "assets" of the promisor, and ceases to have value as soon as he ceases to be "good for it." The courts do not restrict a debtor in the disposition of his possessions prior to the maturity of a note. He may elect to squander these, and even to commit suicide. But such destruction of the present means of providing for future payment carries with it the impairment or destruction of the value of the note. No future commodities or benefits whatever can be owned in the present except as claims on certain requisites of their production now in existence. We cannot own next year's goods suspended in mid air, as it were, any more than we can fly a kite without a cord. There must always be some present means of controlling the future. Thus, credit, like every other property right, is a part right upon existing wealth.

And not only is every right to a future benefit a claim on present wealth, but conversely, every claim on present wealth is a right to a future benefit. Owning rights to "futures" is therefore not an exceptional case, but the general one. As we have seen, all wealth is merely existing means toward *future* services, and all property, merely present rights to some of those future services. It is only through the future services that wealth and property are bound together at all. The sequence of ideas is, first, present wealth; second, future services; third, present rights to these future services and therefore to the present wealth which yields them. Property is thus always a right to the chance of a future benefit. It always contemplates both present and future time. We are here emphasizing the fact that property always constitutes an interest in the *present* means for acquiring it. Property in nothing is nothing. This principle applies even to the extreme case of good will. We saw that good will is the ownership of a chance of continued patronage. The future patronage may in some cases include that of persons yet unborn; but the road to their patronage must lie through the present generation. Existing persons and things must always constitute the means for the attainment of any benefits expected in the future.

§ 9

A fourth guide is that, in the case of partial ownership of wealth, the aggregate of all the partial rights constitutes the total ownership. We may picture to ourselves all articles of wealth as having attached to them streams of services stretching out into the future. These services are cut up among separate owners in different ways, sometimes transversely, sometimes longitudinally, and sometimes definite parts of them are separated out. The total ownership of the wealth is simply the aggregate of the rights to the entire stream of future services. It may, of course, be true that the character and size of this stream of services will differ according to the different methods by which its ownership is parceled out. This fact, however, does not invalidate the principle that the total ownership is the combination of all the partial rights.

In common speech the minor rights to wealth are not ordinarily dignified as rights of ownership. Thus, a tenant's right in the dwelling he occupies is sharply distinguished from the right of the owner. Yet the law recognizes a leasehold as an estate in the land, and when the owner of land wishes to sell and convey an unencumbered fee simple title, he finds it necessary to extinguish all outstanding leases, or claims for future services, often at considerable cost. Recently the New York Reform Club sold its leasehold in a building for $25,000, because the purchaser could not afford to wait for the expiration of the lease. The total ownership always includes the ownership of the tenant.

In like manner, the total value of any concrete wealth is the total value of the property rights in it. The close correspondence between wealth and property gives us a new method of appraising wealth, namely, by appraising the property rights to it. In fact, we are here provided with another sense of appraisement of wealth, in addition to the several already given in Chapter I. Such appraisement may mean, not what the whole article of wealth would sell for *en bloc*, but the sum of the values of the partial rights to it when these latter are appraised on the basis of small individual sales. Thus, the value of a railroad, operating under normal conditions, is found by taking the sum of the values of its stocks and bonds. Railways are seldom sold as a whole, but their stocks and bonds are constantly on the market, and are often the only means of affording a valuation.

It is true that under these circumstances the market price of the stock would form no basis for judging what would be the value of the road if sold as a whole. There would need to be added the value of "control." But this will be accounted for by an addition to the value of such of the shares as will secure this control. "Control" is the power, coming from a majority of votes, to obtain from the road some services which would not be possible without such majority ownership. The additional benefit thus obtained may be illegitimate, as when the parties in control vote themselves large salaries. But whether legitimate or illegitimate, the power to make the road better serve one's interest often affects profoundly the value of the shares. The stock of the Chicago, Burlington, and Quincy Railroad was quoted at $132 when a certain capitalist determined to buy it. Knowing that it would be almost impossible to acquire all the stock by ordinary means, he offered instead to take over as much as should be offered to him, provided it was more than half, and to give $200 in four per-cent bonds for each $100 share,—an offer which was accepted by most of the stockholders. The acceptance added at once fifty per cent to the market value of the stock, and improved even the value of the bonds; so that the value of the system, sold virtually as a whole, was much more than of the stock and bonds before the negotiation was opened. The valuation of the road will thus be different according to whether it is under the control of a particular interest or whether its ownership is widely distributed, as well as according to the purpose for which the valuation is made.[1] But in every instance the value of the railroad is the sum of the values of the complete aggregate of rights in it.

If one bears in mind the explanations which have been given, there can scarcely be any difficulty in tracing out for each property right some underlying wealth, so that we may give adherence to the general principle that wealth and property are coextensive. That this is true as a "general fact" cannot fail to be admitted even were it necessary to reject it as a "necessary truth." But if our definitions of wealth and property are adopted, it becomes also a necessary truth.

§ 10

Having seen what property is, we may now classify property rights. There are two chief classes, complete rights and partial rights. A complete, or practically complete, right, or "fee simple" to an article of wealth, is a right to all those uses of that article which are owned; a

---

[1] The completest account of railway valuation is that contained in Bulletin 21, "The Commercial Valuation of Railway Operating Property," United States Census, 1905.

partial right is a right to a part of its uses. The partial rights are the only ones which make difficulty.

The services of an article of wealth may be apportioned among different part owners in many ways. If they are divided longitudinally in time, the rights of the various coöwners are similar to each other. The chief examples are the rights of partners and stockholders, and the less well-defined rights of the individual members of a club, family, or commune to the common property and all rights in common, and, finally, the rights to the different kinds of uses, as, for instance, where one person owns the right of farming a piece of land, another the right of mining its minerals, and a third the right of fishing in the streams which run through it.

If the services are divided transversely in time, one person has the rights of all services up to a particular date, and another all the rights beyond that. The former person is called the tenant and the latter the landlord.

If the services are limited both in time and also in quantity or value, we have still another group of property rights. These and other classes are seen in the following scheme of classification.

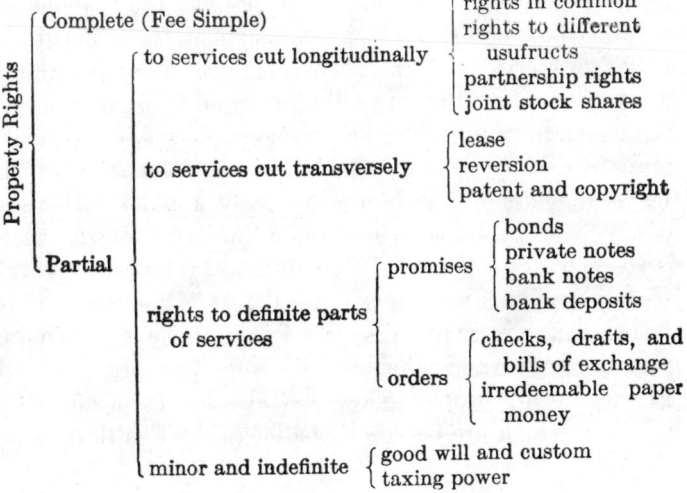

§ 11

Since wealth and property are each the opposite aspect of the other, economics might be described as the "science of property" quite as truly as the "science of wealth." If we are studying the economic condition of a whole country, we prefer to fix our attention upon wealth, caring less about how its ownership is divided. We are then interested in the acreage of wheat fields, the extent of coal mines, railways, factories, and homesteads, and not in their owners. On the other hand, if we are studying the "distribution of wealth" — the condition of individuals or of classes — it is property on which we need to fix attention. The idea of wealth, therefore, is associated with the welfare of the community in general, while that of property is associated with the welfare of the different individuals in the community.

But, it may be asked, why is so much stress laid on the principle that wealth and property are coextensive? It may be conceded that most of the principles of political economy will be unaffected whether or not this one is accepted as rigorously true. Its usefulness consists in helping us to arrange our ideas. At present there seems to exist in the popular mind a confusion of the concepts of wealth, property, certificates of property, services, and utility, all of which should be carefully separated from each other. No one can fully understand monetary problems, for instance, unless he distinguishes carefully the three elements to which the term "money" is indiscriminately applied. There is money-*wealth*, such as a gold eagle; money-*property*, such as the right of a holder of "greenbacks"; and money-*certificates*, such as the paper "greenbacks" themselves. If the fact that wealth and property are coextensive were more generally known and acknowledged, some very practical and salutary results would follow. Wild schemes of currency inflation, which are based on the idea that wealth may be increased simply by multiplying the titles to it, would be checked, and the usual atrocities of double taxation, for instance, of farm and mortgage, or of railways and railway shares, would be avoided.[1]

If we bear in mind the distinctions in this and in the previous chapter, we shall see that there is no advantage, but much disadvantage, in including any "immaterial" elements in wealth. "Immaterial wealth" is, in fact, one of those bugaboos which have done a great deal to obscure the simplicity of economic relations. Legal advice or medical attendance are not "immaterial wealth"; they are, as we have seen, simply *services* of wealth (human wealth in this case). The "properties and powers of nature" are not wealth, but, as explained in the previous chapter, are *attributes* of land and enter economic science merely as giving characterization to that particular kind of wealth. They cannot be counted as wealth in addition to the land any more properly than can the elasticity of rubber be counted as wealth in addition to the rubber. Likewise, swift horses are wealth, but not their swiftness; honest, wise, successful, and healthy men are wealth, but not their honesty, wisdom, skill, or health. Most of the mystery of banking to the ordinary mind consists in the mistaken notion that credit is something "inflated," without a tangible basis. A mere inspection of a bank's balance sheet should serve to make clear the fact that behind every claim upon the bank is something to make it good. If the anterior something be itself a claim on some other bank or person, there lies behind it, in turn, some basis, and so on until a concrete instrument is finally found.

Another common error is the belief that "wealth consists of utility." If this were true, the law of diminishing

---

[1] See Report of Professor Edward W. Bemis and Carl H. Nau, on *Value of Ohio Railroads*, 1903; also, Report of the Interstate Commerce Commission on *Railways in the United States in 1902*, 1903, Part V.

utility, that equal increments of wealth have decreasing increments of utility, would be a contradiction in terms.

To plead in extenuation of such confusions the fact that popular usage is guilty of them, is like trying to justify in the science of physics a jumbling together of the concepts of mass and density, or of velocity and acceleration, or of force and energy, on the ground that the ordinary man does not distinguish between them. The proper method of avoiding large errors in any science is to avoid small ones at the outset. This can be accomplished only by scrupulous attention to elementary distinctions.

CHAPTER III

UTILITY

§ 1

WE have seen that all wealth and property imply prospective services or "desirable events." It is the desirability of these future expected services which gives meaning to all economic phenomena. It would therefore be impossible, in any full view of the subject, to confine ourselves strictly to the study of objective wealth, property, and services. In the present chapter we shall consider briefly the subjective or psychical element in economics.

Wealth is wealth only because of its services; and services are services only because of their desirability in the mind of man, and of the satisfactions which man expects them to render. Indeed, the desirability of services is implied in their very definition as "desirable events." The mind of man supplies the mainspring in the whole economic machinery. It is in his mind that desires originate, and in his mind that the train of events which he sets going in nature comes to an end in the experience of subjective satisfactions. It is only in the interim between the initial desire and the final satisfaction that wealth and its services have place as intermediaries.

We are thus led to consider two new concepts, — that of "desirability" and that of "satisfaction." Both of these enter into our consideration only as they are applied to the three economic elements, — wealth, property, services. To avoid unnecessary repetitions, we may treat these three elements under the one rubric of "goods."

§ 2

The *desirability*, then, of any particular goods, at any particular time, to any particular individual, under any particular conditions, is the strength or intensity of his desire for those goods at that time and under those conditions. What is here called desirability is identical with what has usually been called in economic writings "utility." But utility, though not to be utterly displaced, is not the happiest term for our purpose. To say nothing of the mere awkwardness of its only antithetical term — "disutility" — as compared with "undesirability," it has fallen heir to so many different meanings that its use here is apt to be confusing. The term "useful," for instance, in ordinary language is employed in opposition to "ornamental." In this sense diamonds are said to be ornamental and not useful, though in economic science they are adjudged useful. Again, "utility" usually implies intrinsic merit, whereas, when we employ it in economic science, we are obliged to apply it to any noxious thing considered by its owner *desirable*, for instance, opium, alcohol, or degrading literature. Finally, in the last few years, the word "utility" has come into a new and technical meaning as employed in the phrase "public utilities," which designates electric lighting plants, street railway systems, gas works, and many other things which are merely collections of wealth of a peculiar kind.

In order to obviate these objections, Professor Pareto has proposed an entirely new term, "ophelimity." This has both the advantages and the disadvantages of any newly invented technical term, and has thus far shared the fate which usually befalls the attempt to coin words. The word "utility" is still employed, and it is not likely that "desirability," "ophelimity," or any other term will soon displace it. In the present book we shall use both "utility" and "desirability," but preferably the latter.

In proposing that economists substitute so far as possible the term "desirability" for "utility," the author is simply following the example of Professor Gide [1] and Professor Marshall.

§ 3

If the term "utility" is to be used at all, we must distinguish the utility of goods from the *use* of the goods. As has been pointed out, the uses or services of goods are the desirable events which occur by their means. Utility, on the other hand, is not these desirable events, but their desirability.

Again, the desirability or utility of goods must not be confused with the pleasure which may be ultimately obtained from those goods. Here our second concept is involved, for pleasure is not the desire, but the *satisfaction* of the desire. It is an experience in time, and requires *duration* of time for its existence. Desirability, which means the intensity of desire of an individual under certain conditions, merely indicates a state of mind at a particular *point* of time, namely, the point of time at which he mentally weighs and measures the desirability of any contemplated service, property, or wealth. We may speak of the desirability of a fruit orchard to a particular person on January 1, 1905; but the pleasure derivable from that orchard is only to be experienced during future years, as it bears fruit and the fruit gives enjoyment to those who eat it. Thus we have two concepts: utility or desirability, — a state of mind at a point of time; and pleasure or satisfaction, — an experience of mind through a period of time. These two concepts are closely related; for the desirability of goods is simply the present esteem in which the future

---

[1] Gide's *Principles of Political Economy*, 2d American ed., 1904, p. 48. See also the present writer's "Mathematical Investigations in the Theory of Value and Prices," *Transactions of the Connecticut Academy*, 1892, p. 23.

satisfactions from those goods are held. But the two are none the less distinct. It is with utility or desirability that we are concerned in this chapter.

§ 4

The desirability of any particular goods may relate to the whole or to any part of the group of goods. The desirability of the entire group is called the total desirability; the desirability of one unit more or less of the group is called the marginal desirability. In economic science we have to do more with marginal than with total desirability, and it is important that the concept of marginal desirability should be thoroughly understood.

That *marginal desirability* is the desirability of one unit, more or less, may be illustrated as follows: If a person possesses ten chairs, their marginal desirability is the difference, in his mind, between the desirability of having ten chairs and the desirability of having nine chairs; that is, it is the desirability sacrificed by having one chair less. Or, what is almost the same thing, the marginal desirability of the group of ten chairs is the desirability of one chair more, — the difference in desirability between eleven chairs and ten. Whether the marginal desirability is taken as referring to one unit more or to one unit less is usually of so little importance as not to require separate designations to distinguish them, and in case the commodity is one which admits of indefinite subdivision, as flour, wheat, coal, etc., the two coalesce as the size of the increment is reduced indefinitely.[1] This fact is usually expressed by saying that the marginal desirability of the chairs is the desirability of "the tenth" chair. But though this mode of statement is correct, it is not intended to convey the idea that any particular chair is the "tenth" chair.

The group of goods the marginal desirability of which is under consideration may be any specified group of goods

[1] For a mathematical treatment see Appendix to Chap. III, § 1.

whatever. Reference may be had to a specified group of goods now existing, or to a specified group of goods in the future, or to a specified flow of goods through a period of time. For instance, the marginal desirability of coal to an individual may be taken to refer to the particular stock of coal in his bin at the present moment. If this stock consists of fifteen tons, its marginal desirability is the desirability of the fifteenth ton, or the difference to him between the desirability of having fifteen and that of having fourteen tons. Or, reference may be had to an intended purchase of coal to be delivered in three months. If we consider a possible purchase of future coal to the extent of fifteen tons, its marginal desirability then represents the present desire for the fifteenth ton, in exactly the same way as though reference were had to an existing stock. Again, if a person is consuming in his household fifteen tons of coal a year, its marginal desirability at any instant is the desirability of the fifteenth ton, or the sacrifice which would be occasioned were he to reduce his yearly consumption from fifteen tons to fourteen.

Again, the group of goods considered may consist of articles all of which are of the same kind, or of a heterogeneous collection. In the preceding examples the goods were of exactly the same kind. As an example of the marginal desirability of a group consisting of diverse kinds, we may cite the desirability of an additional monthly magazine or newspaper. If a subscriber is already taking ten periodicals of different kinds, the desirability of a specified journal additional to the existing assortment may be regarded as the marginal desirability with reference to the entire group of journals.

In the same way we may speak of the marginal desirability of a series of characteristics or features connected with any article or articles of wealth. A person contemplating the building of a house may have to decide how many windows he will put in. If he contemplates fifty windows, the marginal desirability of the windows is the desirability of the fiftieth window, or the difference in the desirability of having fifty windows rather than forty-nine.

§ 5

The first principle in regard to marginal desirability is that an increase in the quantity of goods in the group the marginal desirability of which is under consideration, results in a decrease in the marginal desirability of the group. Each successive increment is less desirable than the preceding increment. The marginal desirability of sugar to the householder consuming five pounds weekly is greater than the marginal desirability if six pounds are consumed, and is successively diminished as each successive pound is added to his consumption.

It is well to remember that when the term "successively" is here employed, it is not used in a temporal sense. The succession to which it refers is not a succession in time, but a succession in thought. We consider the consumer of sugar under a series of different hypotheses which we *examine* successively. We begin with the hypothesis of a weekly consumption of five pounds, and take up successively the hypotheses of six pounds, seven pounds, eight pounds, etc. The desirability of the "last" pound in this series is the marginal desirability for the group ending at that point; but the "last" pound refers to the one *considered* last in our mental review, and not the one *acquired* last by the consumer. This fact needs to be emphasized, in view of frequent confusion on the subject occasioned by too loose an employment of the words "last" and "successive." It is presumably because of the time confusions involved in these words that, under the leadership of Wieser[1] and Marshall,[2] economists have substituted the phrase "marginal utility" for the older phrase of Jevons, "final utility."

With these provisos and explanations in view, it is clear

---

[1] *Ursprung des Werthes*, p. 128.
[2] *Principles of Economics*, 3d ed., 1895, p. 168.

that the total desirability of any group of goods is the sum of the desirabilities of the successive units. The total desirability of the ten chairs, for instance, is found by adding together (1) the desirability of having only one chair, (2) the desirability of having a second chair, (3) a third, (4) a fourth, etc., until ten chairs have been considered. These successive desirabilities will evidently continually diminish. Hence their sum, or the total desirability of the group, is not the same thing as ten times the marginal desirability. In this is found the explanation of the fact that the possessor of the chairs regards them as possessing much more total desirability to him than the total desirability of the money which they cost, although the loss of any one of the ten chairs may not represent more desirability than the desirability of the money which that one chair cost.[1]

As is well known to all students of the modern theory of value, marginal desirability lies at the root of the determination of value and price. We are here concerned, however, not in applying the concept of marginal desirability to the determination of economic magnitudes, but merely in explaining its nature.

Although the definitions which have been given of desirability serve to explain its nature, they do not enable us to employ it in a quantitative manner. The exact measurement of desirability is a subject of much importance, as well as of great difficulty. Inasmuch as in the present work only an incidental use will be made of these concepts, it does not seem proper here to enter into these discussions.[2]

[1] Cf. Fetter's *Principles of Economics*, New York, 1904, pp. 25-26.
[2] See the writer's "Mathematical Investigations in the Theory of Value and Prices," *Transactions of the Connecticut Academy of Arts and Sciences*, 1893, Vol. IX; Pigou, *Economic Journal*, March, 1903, Vol. XIII; Pareto, *Cours d'Economie Politique*, Vol. I; *Giornale d'Economisti*, August, 1892; J. B. Clark, "Ultimate Standard of Value," *Yale Review*, November, 1892; Seligman, *Principles of Economics*, Longmans, Green & Co., 1905, Chap. XIII; Chin tao Chen's *Societary Circulation*, a doctor's thesis, Yale Univ., 1906.

PART I. CAPITAL

CHAPTER IV. CAPITAL
CHAPTER V. CAPITAL ACCOUNTS
CHAPTER VI. CAPITAL SUMMATION

CHAPTER IV

CAPITAL

§ 1

IN the foregoing introduction we have set forth several fundamental concepts of economic science, — wealth, property, services, satisfactions, utility, price, and value. We have seen that wealth consists of material appropriated objects, and property, of rights in these objects; that wealth in its broadest sense includes human beings, and property in its broadest sense includes all rights whatsoever; that services are the benefits of wealth, satisfactions the enjoyment of services, and desirability or utility the desire for wealth, property, services, or satisfactions; that prices are the ratios of exchange between quantities of wealth, property, or services; and, finally, that value is the price of any of these multiplied by the quantity. These concepts are the chief tools needed in economic study.

Nothing has yet been said as to the relation of these various magnitudes to that great "independent variable" of human experience, *time*. When we speak of a certain quantity of wealth we may have reference either to a quantity existing at a particular instant of time, or to a quantity produced, consumed, exchanged, or transported during a period of time. The first quantity is a *stock* (or *fund*) of wealth; the second quantity is a *flow* (or *stream*) of wealth. The contents of a granary at noon, January 1, 1906, is a stock of wheat; the amount of wheat which has been hoisted into it during a week, or the amount of wheat which has been exported from the port of New York during

1905, is a flow of wheat. The term "wealth" by itself is insufficient to determine which of these two kinds of magnitudes is meant. Similarly, when we speak of property or of value, we may have in mind either a fund or a flow. A thousand shares in a certain company owned by a certain man at a certain time constitute a particular fund of property; the number of shares transferred in a week on the stock exchange constitute a flow of property. Again, the value of the checks held at noon of any day by one bank drawn on other banks constitutes a fund of value; the value of the checks which pass through a clearing-house in twenty-four hours constitutes a flow of value. Services and satisfactions, unlike wealth and property, can exist only as flows; a fund of either is impossible.

A fund is fully specified by one magnitude only; a flow requires two, — the *amount* of flow and the *duration* of flow. From these two a third follows, — the *rate* of flow or the quotient of the amount divided by the duration. The rate of flow is often of more importance than the amount of flow. Thus we care less to know the aggregate wages of a workman during a lifetime than the rate of his wages during various periods of his life.

The distinction between a fund and a flow has many applications in economic science.[1] The most important application is to differentiate between capital and income. Capital is a fund and income a flow. This difference between capital and income is, however, not the only one. There is another important difference, namely, that capital is *wealth*, and income is the *service* of wealth. We have therefore the following definitions: A *stock of wealth* existing at an *instant* of time is called *capital*. A *flow of services* through a *period* of time is called *income*. Thus, a dwelling house now existing is capital; the shelter it affords or the bringing in of a money-rent is its income.

---

[1] For some of these applications, *e.g.* to monetary circulation, see: "What is Capital?" *Economic Journal*, 1897.

The railways of the country are capital; their services of transportation or the dividends from the sale of that transportation are the income they yield.

The distinction between capital and income is somewhat analogous to the distinction between *desirability* and *satisfactions*, which was emphasized in Chapter III; for desirability was shown to relate to a point of time and satisfactions to a period of time.

§ 2

The foregoing definitions of capital and income are not, it is true, universally accepted. Many authors attempt to define capital, not as wealth in a particular aspect with reference to time, but as a particular kind or species of wealth, or as wealth restricted to a particular purpose; in short, as some specific part of wealth instead of any or all of it. We are obliged, therefore, to pause a moment to consider these opinions. In this chapter we are concerned with the concept of capital only.

From the time of Adam Smith it has been asserted by economists, though not usually by business men, that only particular kinds of wealth could be capital, and the burning question has been, *What* kinds? But the failure to agree on any dividing line between wealth which is and wealth which is not capital, after a century and a half of discussion, certainly suggests the suspicion that no such line exists.[1] What Senior wrote seven decades ago is true to-day: "Capital has been so variously defined, that it may be doubtful whether it have any generally received meaning."[2] In consequence, "almost every year there appears some new attempt to settle the disputed conception, but, unfortunately, no authoritative result has as yet followed these attempts. On the contrary,

[1] For a fuller statement than that which follows of the disagreements and confusions on this subject, see the writer's "What is Capital?" *Economic Journal*, December, 1896.
[2] "Political Economy," *Encyclopædia Metropolitana*, Vol. VI, p. 153.

many of them only served to put more combatants in the field and furnish more matter to the dispute."[1] Many authors express dissatisfaction with their own treatment of capital, and even recast it in successive editions.[2]

Adam Smith's[3] concept of capital is wealth which yields "revenue." He would therefore exclude a dwelling occupied by the owner. Hermann,[4] on the other hand, includes dwellings, on the ground that they are durable goods. But a fruiterer's stock in trade, which is capital according to Smith, because used for profit, according to Hermann does not seem to be capital, because it is perishable. Knies[5] calls capital any wealth, whether durable or not, so long as it is reserved for future use. Walras[6] attempts to settle the question of durability or futurity by counting the uses. Any wealth which serves more than one use is capital. A can of preserved fruit is therefore capital to Knies if stored away for the future, but is not capital to Walras because it will perish by a single use. To Kleinwächter,[7] capital consists only of "tools" of production, such as railways. He excludes food, for instance, as passive. Jevons,[8] on the contrary, makes food the most typical capital of all, and excludes railways, except as representing the food and sustenance of the laborers who built them.

While most authors make the distinction between capital and non-capital depend on the kind of wealth, objectively considered, Mill[9] makes it depend on the intention in the mind of the capitalist as to how he shall use his wealth,

[1] Böhm-Bawerk, *Positive Theory of Capital*, English translation, London and New York, 1891, p. 23.
[2] *E.g.* Roscher, Marshall, Schäffle.
[3] *Wealth of Nations*, Book II, Chap. I.
[4] *Staatswirtschaftliche Untersuchungen*, Munich, 1832, p. 59.
[5] *Das Geld*, 2d ed., Berlin, 1885, pp. 69–70.
[6] *Éléments d'Économie Politique Pure*, 4th ed., Lausanne, p. 177.
[7] *Grundlagen des Socialismus*, 1885, p. 184.
[8] *Theory of Political Economy*, 3d ed., 1888, Chap. VII, pp. 222, 242.
[9] *Principles of Political Economy*, Book I, Chap. IV, § 1.

Marx [1] makes it depend on the effect of the wealth on the laborer, and Tuttle,[2] upon the amount of wealth possessed. Again, while most authors confine the concept of capital to material goods, MacLeod [3] extends it to all immaterial goods which produce profit, including workmen's labor, credit, and what he styles "incorporeal estates," such as the Law, the Church, Literature, Art, Education, an author's Mind. Clark [4] takes what he styles "pure" capital out of the material realm entirely, making it consist, not of things, but of their utility. Most authors leave no place, in their concept of capital, for the value of goods as distinct from the concrete goods themselves, whereas Fetter,[5] in his definition, leaves place for nothing else. Some definitions are framed with especial reference to particular problems of capital; many, for instance, have reference to the problem of capital and labor, but they fail to agree as to the relation of capital to that problem. MacCulloch [6] regards it as a means of supporting laborers by a wage fund; Marx,[1] as a means of humiliating and exploiting them; Ricardo,[7] as a labor saver; MacLeod,[3] as including labor itself as a special form of capital.

Many definitions have reference to the problem of production, but in no less discordant ways. According to Senior,[8] Mill,[9] and many others, capital must be itself a product. Walras,[10] MacLeod,[3] and others admit

[1] *Capital*, English translation, London, 1887, Vol. II, p. 792.
[2] "The Real Capital Concept," *Quarterly Journal of Economics* November, 1903.
[3] *Dictionary of Political Economy*, article "Capital," p. 331.
[4] *Capital and its Earnings*, Publications of American Economic Association, 1888, pp. 11-13.
[5] "Recent Discussion of the Capital Concept," *Quarterly Journal of Economics*, November, 1900, and *Principles of Economics*, 1904.
[6] *Principles of Political Economy*, 4th ed., p. 100.
[7] *Principles of Political Economy*, § 37.
[8] "Political Economy," *Encyclopædia Metropolitana*, Vol. VI, p. 153.
[9] *Principles of Political Economy*, Book I, Chap. IV, § 1.
[10] *Éléments d'Économie Politique Pure*, Lausanne, 4th ed., p. 177.

land[1] and all natural agents under capital. Böhm-Bawerk,[2] while agreeing that it must be a product, insists that it must not apply to a finished product. Marx[3] denies that capital is productive. Böhm-Bawerk[4] admits that it is not "independently" productive, but denies the Marxian corollary that it should not receive interest. Other writers make it coördinate with land and labor as a productive element.

As to what it is that capital produces there is further disagreement. Adam Smith[5] affirms that capital produces "revenue," Senior,[6] that it produces "wealth." Others vaguely imply that it produces value, services, or utility.

Most of the definitions involve some reference to time, but in many different ways. Hermann[7] has in mind the time the wealth will last; Clark,[8] the permanency of the fund capital as contrasted with the transitoriness of its

---

[1] The fancied distinction between land and capital, viz., that the former yields rent and the latter interest, and that rent varies with different grades of land whereas interest is uniform for all sorts of capital, is based on a confusion between *quantity* and *value* of wealth. The return from land *per acre* will, it is true, vary according to the quality of the land. But so also the return from machinery of different grades will vary *per machine*. The return from different kinds of capital per $100 worth will, it is true, be uniform; but so will the return from land per $100 worth. For a full treatment of this confusion see Fetter's "The Relations between Rent and Interest," a paper presented before the American Economic Association, December, 1903. Cf. Clark, *Capital and its Earnings*, p. 27, and *Distribution of Wealth* (Macmillan, 1899), Chaps. IX and XIII. Cannan developed the same idea in "What is Capital?" *Economic Journal*, June, 1897. Cf. the writer's "Rôle of Capital," *Economic Journal*, December, 1897, pp. 524, 526.

[2] *Positive Theory of Capital*, English translation, London and New York, 1891, p. 38.

[3] *Capital*, English translation, London, 1887, Vol. II, p. 792.

[4] *Capital and Interest*, Book VI.

[5] *Wealth of Nations*, Book II, Chap. I.

[6] "Political Economy," *Encyclopædia Metropolitana*, Vol. VI, p. 153.

[7] *Staatswirtschaftliche Untersuchungen*, Munich, 1832, p. 59.

[8] *Capital and its Earnings*, Publications of American Economic Association, 1888, pp. 11–13.

elements, "capital goods"; Knies,[1] the futurity of satisfactions; Jevons,[2] and Landry,[3] specifically the time between the "investment" of the capital and its return.

§ 3

It is idle to attempt any reconciliation between concepts of capital so conflicting, and yet there are elements of truth in all. Though generally wrongly and narrowly interpreted, there are certain recurrent ideas which are entirely correct. The definitions concur in striving to express the important facts that capital is *productive*, that it is *antithetical to income*, that it is a *provision for the future*, or that it is a *reserve*. But they assume that only a part of all wealth can conform to these conditions. To the authors of the definitions quoted, it would seem absurd to include all wealth as capital, as there would be nothing left with which to contrast it and by which to define it. And yet, as Professor Marshall says, when one attempts to draw a hard-and-fast line between wealth which is capital and wealth which is not capital, he finds himself "on an inclined plane," constantly tending, by being more liberal in his interpretation of terms, to include more and more in the term capital, until there is little or nothing left outside of it. We are told, for instance, that capital is "wealth for future use." But "future" is an elastic term. As was shown in Chapter II, all wealth is, strictly speaking, for future use. It is impossible to push back its use into the past; neither is it possible to confine it to the present. The present is but an instant of time, and all use of wealth requires some duration of time. A plateful of food, however hurriedly it is being eaten, is still for future use, though the future is but the next few seconds; and if by "future" we mean to exclude the "immediate future," where is the

[1] *Das Geld*, 2d ed., 1885, pp. 69–70.
[2] *Theory of Political Economy*, 3d ed., 1888, Chap. VII, pp. 222–242
[3] *L'Intérêt du Capital*, Paris (Giard), 1904, p. 16.

line to be drawn? Are we to say, for instance, that capital is that wealth whose use extends beyond seventeen days? And as all wealth is for future use it is also, by the same token, all a "reserve." To call capital a reserve does not, therefore, in strictness, delimit it from other wealth. Even a beggar's crust in his pocket will tide him over a few hours.[1]

Equally futile is any attempt definitely to mark off capital as that wealth which is "productive." We have seen that all wealth is productive in the sense that it yields services. There was a time when the question was hotly debated what labor was productive and what unproductive. The distinction was barren and came to be so recognized. No one now objects to calling all labor productive. And if this productivity is common to all labor, it is equally common to all wealth. If we admit that a private coachman is a productive worker, how can we deny that the horse and carriage are also productive, especially as the three merely coöperate in rendering the very same service, — transportation?

Finally, we cannot distinguish capital as that wealth which bears income. All wealth bears income, for income consists simply of the services of wealth. But the idea that some wealth bears income and some not has been persistent from the time of Adam Smith, who, meaning by income only *money* income, conceived capital as the wealth which produces income in this sense, as distinguished from the wealth, such as dwellings, equipages, clothing, and food, which dissipates that income. A home, according to him, is not a source of income, but of expense, and therefore cannot be capital.

§ 4

In these and other ways have economists introduced, in place of the fundamental distinctions between fund and flow, and between wealth and services, the merely relative dis-

[1] See the writer's "Precedents for Defining Capital," *Quarterly Journal of Economics*, May, 1904, p. 404.

tinction between one kind of wealth and another. As a consequence, their studies of the problems of capital have been full of confusion Among the many confusions [1] which have come from overlooking the time distinction between a stock and a flow was the famous wage fund theory, that the rate of wages varies inversely with the amount of capital in the supposed "wage fund." MacCulloch wrote: [2] —

"To illustrate this principle, let us suppose that the capital of a country appropriated to the payment of wages would, if reduced to the standard of wheat, form a mass of 10,000,000 quarters; if the number of laborers in that country were *two* millions, it is evident that the wages of each, reducing them all to the same common standard, would be *five* quarters."

"The wages would be five quarters" — thus MacCulloch — but five quarters in what time? Five quarters per hour, per day, or per year? Divorced as it is from any time concept, this definition is meaningless.

Even so acute a writer as John Stuart Mill unhesitatingly states: [3] —

"Wages, then, depend mainly upon the demand and supply of labour; or, as it is often expressed, on the proportion between population and capital. By population is here meant the number only of the labouring class, or rather of those who work for hire; and by capital, only circulating capital, and not even the whole of that, but the part which is expended in the direct purchase of labour. To this, however, must be added all funds which, without forming a part of capital, are paid in exchange for labour, such as the wages of soldiers, domestic servants, and all other unproductive labourers. . . . With these limitations of the terms, wages not only depend upon the relative amount of capital and population, but cannot under the rule of competition be affected by anything else. Wages (meaning, of course, the general rate [sic]). . . ."

A little attention to business bookkeeping would have saved economists from such errors; for the keeping of records in business involves a practical if unconscious recog-

[1] See "What is Capital?" *loc. cit.*
[2] *Principles of Political Economy*, 1st ed., pp. 327–328, 2d ed., pp. 377–378. See Cannan, *History of Theories of Production and Distribution*, p. 264.
[3] *Political Economy*, Book II, Chap. XI, § 1.

nition of the time principle here propounded. The "capital account" of a railway, for instance, gives the condition of the railway *at a particular instant of time*, and the "income account" gives its operation *through a period of time*.

§ 5

It has been objected that the proposed definition does not conform to established usage. So far as economic precedent is concerned, we have already seen that there is no established usage.[1] Moreover, in the immense literature on the subject there is no lack of precedent for the definition here proposed. Turgot[2] employed the term capital in practically the sense of a stock of wealth. J. B. Say,[3] Courcelle-Seneuil,[4] and Guyot[5] followed. Edwin Cannan,[6] among present economists, reintroduced it, and in a very clear and explicit way. To-day it is used in five or six standard works,[7] as well as in some minor writings. Many economists have orally expressed their approval of the proposed definition.

Others virtually or approximately adopt it, as, for instance, Knies,[8] Clark,[8] Pareto,[8] Giffen,[9] De Foville,[10] Flux,[11]

[1] For a fuller statement of this fact see the writer's "Precedents for Defining Capital," *Quarterly Journal of Economics*, May, 1904.

[2] *Formation and Distribution of Riches*, § 58, Ashley's translation (Macmillan, New York), pp. 50–59.

[3] See Tuttle, "The Real Capital Concept," *Quarterly Journal of Economics*, November, 1903, p. 83; but cf. Böhm-Bawerk, *Positive Theory*, English translation, p. 59, n.

[4] *Traité théorique et pratique d' Économie Politique*, 1867, tome I, p. 47.

[5] *Principles of Social Economy*, English translation, p. 50.

[6] *Theories of Production and Distribution*, London, 1894, p. 14.

[7] Among them are Cannan's *History of Theories of Distribution*, Hadley's *Economics*, Smart's *Distribution of Income*, Daniels's *Finance*, Fetter's *Principles of Economics*, Seligman's *Principles of Economics*.

[8] See "What is Capital?" *loc. cit.*

[9] In his *Growth of Capital*.

[10] In his "Wealth of France and of Other Countries," English translation, *Journal of the Royal Statistical Society*, 1894.

[11] *Economic Principles*, London (Methuen), 1904, pp. 16–18.

Nicholson,[1] Hicks,[2] and the "Committee [of the British Association for the Advancement of Science] on a Common Measure of Value in Direct Taxation."[3] Professor Marshall says that in earlier years he "invariably thought of capital as the whole stock of goods, and of interest as the whole of the usance or benefits derived from the use of that stock";[4] that "when one approaches the problem of distribution from the mathematical point of view, there is practically no choice"[5] but to do so; and that "wealth in the form of houses or private carriages helped to give employment to labour as much as when in the form of hotels or cabs."[6] He expressly concedes what is really the chief contention of the present writer when he says: "I concur in his [my] conclusion that whatever we do with the *word* capital, we cannot solve problems of capital by classifying wealth."[7] Yet he concludes, "not without doubt, that it is best to"[8] base his definition of capital on such a classification, purely out of deference to what he conceives to be the dominant usage.

§ 6

As to popular and business usage, it may be said that a careful study of this usage as reflected by lexicographers, who have sought from time to time to record it,[9] reveals the fact that before the time of Adam Smith capital was not regarded as a part of the stock of wealth, but as synonymous with that stock.[10] Sometimes the inclusion of *all*

[1] In his *Elements*, pp. 42, 43.
[2] *Lectures on Economics*, Cincinnati, 1901, pp. 91, 244.
[3] Report of British Association for Advancement of Science, 1878, Dublin, p. 220.
[4] "Distribution and Exchange," *Economic Journal*, 1898, p. 56.
[5] *Ibid.* p. 55.   [6] *Ibid.* p. 57.   [7] *Ibid.* p. 50.   [8] *Ibid.* p. 56.
[9] See the writer's "Precedents for Defining Capital," *loc. cit.*, where are presented the results of an examination of seventy-two dictionaries.
[10] Originally.the term "capital" was not a noun, but an adjective. "*Capitalis pars debiti*" indicated the principal part of a debt, *i.e.* the "principal" as distinguished from the interest. This virtually repre-

stock as capital was explicit, as, for instance, in the year 1611, Cotgrave defined capital as, "wealth, worth; *a stocke.*" Again, we find: —

1678, Dufresne du Cange, *Glossarium.* — Capitale dicitur *bonum omne quod possidetur.* . . .

More often capital is explained as a term employed in business, as : —

1759, Rider, W. *A New Universal English Dictionary.* . . . London. — Capital. Among merchants, the sum of money brought in by each party to make up the common stock. Likewise the money which a merchant first brings into trade on his own account.

Here the phrase "among merchants" is perhaps intended to specify the sphere in which the term is generally found, rather than as a necessary limitation to that sphere, just as "hawser" is explained as a "nautical term" without implying that a hawser could not be employed on shore.[1]

With the advent of the economists the dictionary definitions were thrown into confusion, although the great majority of them continue still to adhere to the original usage; *e.g.* : —

1883, Simmonds, P. L. *The Commercial Dictionary.* . . . Capital . . . the net worth of a party.

1894. Palgrave's *Dictionary of Political Economy*, under "Assets." The assets remaining after the discharge of liabilities are a person's actual capital.

In many cases it is thought necessary to distinguish between the meaning of capital among economists and its meaning among business men; *e.g.* : —

1893, Murray, J. A. H. *A New English Dictionary.* . . . Vol. II, Oxford. — Capital, B. *sb.* 3. A capital stock or fund. *a. Commerce.* The stock of a company, corporation, or individual with which they enter into business and on which profits or dividends are calculated;

---

sented the distinction between a fund and a flow. The term soon became applied to a merchant's stock in contradistinction to the flow of profits springing from it, and hence to any fund or stock whatever. See "Precedents for Defining Capital," *Quarterly Journal of Economics*, May, 1904, p. 395.

[1] See "Precedents," pp. 8, 9.

in a joint stock company, it consists of the total sum of the contributions of the shareholders. *b. Pol. Econ.* The accumulated wealth of an individual, company, or community, used as a fund for carrying on fresh production; wealth in any form used to help in producing more wealth.

In business manuals and articles on practical accounting we find that capital is employed in the sense of the net value of a man's wealth. Thus L. W. Lafrentz, speaking of the difference between assets and liabilities,[1] states: "The residue will be the net worth of the proprietor — the capital of the proprietor."

Inquiry among business men also reveals the fact that in business usage all wealth is included in the term "capital." It would astonish a business man to have an economist strike out from his assets as non-capital his raw materials, as would Kleinwächter; his perishable goods, as would Hermann; his fuel, as would Walras; or, above all, his land, as would most of the classical economists. That land is capital, business men all emphatically declare. As the manufacturer would express it, land is the very first thing into which the "paid-in" capital of a new concern is converted. Again, business men maintain that the *function* of any given wealth has nothing to do with its classification as capital. It need not be "for production" nor "for sustaining laborers," nor for any particular object whatever. The only point on which some of them hesitate is whether or not all articles in *consumers'* hands are capital. The reason for this hesitation may possibly be found in the customs of bookkeeping. As one business man expressed it, "Capital is simply a bookkeeping term." Consequently the business man naturally associates the term with his shop and not his home, for he keeps a balance sheet in the former and not in the latter; but, once given a balance sheet,

[1] "Economic Aspects of Accounting and Auditing," *Journal of Accountancy*, April, 1906, p. 482. Cf. Victor Branford, *Economics and Accountancy*, London (Gee & Co.), 1901, and Charles E. Sprague, *The Accountancy of Investment*, New York (Business Publishing Co.), 1904, p. 12.

it does not matter what purpose is behind it. A social club, an art gallery, or a hospital may have a capital. In one year a joint stock company with capital stock was proposed for the purpose of building the yacht for defending the America Cup. If a private family should call itself a joint stock company and draw up a balance sheet, entering all its property, house, furniture, provisions, etc., on one side, with the debts on the other, no business man, we imagine, would hesitate to call the balance of assets over liabilities, which is the total wealth-value of the family, by the name "capital." As a business man said to the writer, "Capital isn't a part of wealth, but all a man has got, including his automobile." "Is that cigar in your mouth capital?" he was asked. "No," he said, hesitatingly; but this opinion he quickly reversed as inconsistent with his former statement, and admitted that a box of cigars and each cigar in it, or out of it, for that matter, were a part of his stock or reserve.

The phrases "to capitalize" and "to live on capital," as used by business men, imply that capital is simply a fund. When we "capitalize" an annuity of $5 a year at a given sum, as $100, we mean that $100 is the *fund* of ready-money equivalent of $5 *flowing* in annually. It does not matter what kind of goods the $5 of income or the $100 of capital represents. Again, when we say that a man is "living on capital," we mean that he is using up his stock faster than he is replacing it. The reference is not to any particular part or kind of the stock. A wealthy New Yorker who was recently forced to "live on capital" did so by selling his accumulations of art treasures; it would be the same if he had sold his stocks and bonds.

So far, then, as popular and business usage is concerned, we have ample warrant for the definition of capital here accepted, and no warrant whatever for the definitions ordinarily found in economic text-books.

§ 7

Should economists continue to reject the simple definition above explained, and insist on restricting the term capital to some narrower meaning, our only recourse will be to follow the example of John Rae,[1] and, after defining capital as a part of stock, quietly shelve the term and proceed to the analysis of "stock" instead.[2] We shall then be in the curious position of acknowledging that the "problems of capital" are not problems of " capital" only, but of stock, and shall have to regard such common phrases as "the interest on capital," "*l'intérêt du capital*," and "*capitalzins*" as misnomers. But this or any other settlement of the difficulty will be welcome to all who are tired of the present confusion of tongues. A business friend recently complained that he was chiefly deterred from reading the books of economists because they seemed to have no settled terminology. It does not so greatly matter what *name* we select by which to call a concept. The important matter is to select for consideration those *concepts* which are fruitful in scientific analysis. That the concept — by whatever name we call it — of a *stock of wealth at an instant of time* is thus fruitful will, we believe, appear more plainly as we proceed to apply it to what have been called, rightly or wrongly, the "problems of capital."

[1] *Sociological Theory of Capital*, edited by Professor Mixter, Macmillan, 1905.

[2] It is not, of course, denied that "stock" falls into several more or less distinct groups. One classification has already been given in the chapter on "Wealth," and there are many others. One of the most striking divisions of the stock of wealth as it exists in modern society is between that *at home* and that *in business*. This is the basis of many definitions of capital, especially that of Komorzynski (*Credit*, Innsbruck, 1903, p. 138). But the distinction applies only to modern and highly differentiated societies. Like all classifications of concrete things, it serves a descriptive purpose but does not help analysis. It is well known that in science the most general conceptions are the most fruitful. Professor J. Willard Gibbs, noted for the generality and simplicity of his methods in mathematical physics, used to say, "The whole is simpler than its parts."

CHAPTER V

CAPITAL ACCOUNTS

§ 1

WE have defined capital as a quantity of wealth existing at an instant of time. A full view of capital would be afforded by an instantaneous photograph of wealth. This would reveal, in addition to the durable wealth, a large amount of goods of rapid consumption. It would disclose, not the annual procession of such goods, but the members of that procession that had not yet been transmuted in form or passed off the stage of existence, however swiftly they might be moving across it. It would show train-loads of meat, eggs, and milk in transit, cargoes of fish, spices, and sugar, as well as the contents of private pantries, ice chests, and wine cellars. Even the supplies on the table of a man bolting his dinner would find a place. So the clothes in one's wardrobe or on one's back, the tobacco in a smoker's pouch or pipe, the oil in the can or lamp, would all be elements in this flash-light picture of capital.

Such a collection of wealth is, however, heterogeneous; it cannot be expressed in a single sum. We can inventory the separate items, but we cannot add them together. They may, however, be reduced to a homogeneous mass by considering, not their kinds and quantities, but their values. And this *value* of any stock of wealth is also called "capital." To distinguish these two senses of capital, we call a stock, store, or accumulation of existing instruments of wealth, each instrument being measured in its own unit, *capital-instruments*, or capital-wealth, and we call the value of this stock, when all articles are measured in a common unit, *capital-value*. Similarly, a quantum of property rights existing at any instant is called *capital-property*, and its value, *capital-value*. As a general term to include both capital-instruments and capital-property, we may employ *capital-goods*, a term first suggested by Professor Clark.

We have, then, a definite antithesis between capital-goods and capital-value, capital-goods being measured in various units appropriate to the various goods, as, for instance, in bushels of wheat, gallons of oil, acres of land, shares of stock, and capital-value being measured in a single uniform manner, as in dollars or other convenient units of value. The simple term "capital" is only employed as an abbreviation of either of the compound terms "capital-goods" and "capital-value." The business man ordinarily uses the term "capital" in the sense of capital-value, and hereafter, unless it is otherwise specified, the term "capital" will be understood in this sense. In adopting this nomenclature we find ourselves in harmony with Professors Clark, Fetter, Tuttle, and others referred to in the preceding chapter.

We are now ready to consider the "capital accounts" employed in business. It is strange that any treatment of these accounts is generally omitted from economic text-books. There seems to be no systematic study of capital accounts in any work on political economy.

A capital account is a statement of the amount and value of the property of a specific owner at any instant of time. It consists of two columns, — the assets and the liabilities. The liabilities of an owner are the debts and other obligations owing to others; that is, they are the property-rights of others for which such owner is responsible. The assets or resources of the owner are all his property-rights, irrespective of his liabilities. The assets include both the property which makes good the liabilities, and the property, if any, in excess of the liabilities. They also include, if exhaustively considered, the person of the owner himself.

The owner may be either an individual human being, or a collection of human beings, such as a family, an association, a joint stock company, a corporation, or a government. With respect to a debt or liability, the person who owes it is the debtor and the person owed is the creditor.

Every item in a capital account is an *element* of the owner's total capital, the assets being positive elements and the liabilities being negative. Consequently, the algebraic sum of the elements of capital, or the difference in value between the total assets and the total liabilities, is the *net capital*, or *capital-balance* indicated in the account.

§ 2

The items in a capital account are constantly changing, and their value also, so that when, after one statement of assets and liabilities is drawn up, another is constructed at a point of time six months later, the balancing item, or net capital, may have changed considerably. However, bookkeepers are accustomed to keep the item "capital" intact from the beginning of their account, and to denominate any increase of it as "surplus" or "undivided profits." There are several reasons for this. In the first place, the less often the bookkeeper's entries are altered, the simpler the bookkeeping. Again, by stating separately the original capital and its later increase, the books show at a glance what the history of the company has been as to the accumulations of capital. Finally, in the case of joint stock companies, the capital is represented by stock certificates, the engraved "face value" of which cannot conveniently be altered to keep pace with changes in real value. Consequently it is customary for bookkeepers to maintain the book value of the "capital" equal to the face value of the certificates.

The following two balance sheets will show the accumulation of "surplus."

JANUARY 1, 1900

Assets		Liabilities	
Plant	$200,000	Debts	$100,000
		Capital	100,000
	$200,000		$200,000

JANUARY 1, 1901

Plant, etc.	$246,324	Debts	$100,000
		Capital	100,000
		Surplus	46,324
	$246,324		$246,324

But not only is the book item, capital, maintained intact as long as possible, but often the surplus also is put in round numbers and kept at the same figure for several successive reports. All the smaller fluctuations have an effect simply on a third item called "undivided profits." The distinction between surplus and undivided profits is thus merely one of degree. The three items — capital, surplus, and undivided profits — together make up the present net capital. Of this, "capital" represents the original amount, "surplus" the earlier and larger accumulations, and "undivided profits" the later and minor. The undivided profits are more likely to appear in dividends, that is, to become *divided* profits, although this may also happen to the surplus, or even in certain cases to the capital itself.

We see, then, that the capital of a company, firm, or person is to be understood in two senses; first, as the item entered by the bookkeeper under that head, — the *original* capital; and, secondly, this sum plus surplus and undivided profits, — the true net capital at the instant under consideration.

Inasmuch as the stock certificates were issued at the formation of the company and cannot be perpetually changed, they ordinarily correspond to the original instead of to the present capital. Recapitalization may be effected, however, by recalling the stock certificates or issuing new ones. In these ways the nominal or book value may be either decreased or increased. It is sometimes scaled down because of shrinking assets, and often increased because of new subscriptions or expanding assets. If, for instance, the original capital was $100,000, and the present capital (that is, including surplus and undivided profits) is $200,000, it would be possible, in order that the total certificates outstanding might become $200,000, and the surplus and undivided profits be enrolled as capital, to issue free to each stockholder stock certificates of a face value equal to those already held. In practice, however, such a proceeding is very rare. Ordinarily the stock certificates remain as originally, and merely increase in value. Thus, if the present capital is as in the above example, $200,000, whereas the original capital and the outstanding certificates amount to only $100,000, the market value of the shares will be double the face value; for the stockholders own a total of $200,000, represented by certificates of the face value of $100,000.

§ 3

If, however, we attempt to verify such a relation by reference to the company's books, we shall find some discrepancies in the results. For instance, the Second National Bank of New York had, at a recent statement, a total capital, surplus, and undivided profits of $1,295,952.59, of which the original capital was only $300,000. We should expect, therefore, that the stock certificates, amounting to $300,000, would be worth $1,295,952.59, or, in other words, that each $100 of stock certificates would be worth $432. The actual selling price, however, is found to be $700. Again, the Fourth National Bank of New York City had a total capital, surplus, and undivided profits of $5,700,000, of which $3,000,000 was capital. From this we should expect the shares to sell at $\frac{5,700,000}{3,000,000}=190$. The actual selling price, however, is $240. Here are discrepancies which call for explanation. If a business man were called upon to explain them, he would say that book values and market values are entirely distinct, the latter depending on estimated "earning power." The stock is worth its "capitalized earning power," and its value fluctuates from day to day in response to a thousand causes. This is quite true, but it does not constitute a distinction between book values and market values, for book values also represent estimated earning power. The book valuations of the company's lands, buildings, machinery, etc., were originally determined by their earning power; their cost value was, at the time of purchase, a market estimate of earning power as truly as the market price of stock. This principle holds true of liabilities as well as of assets. The liabilities are simply capitalized charges, interest, rentals, and other expenses.

The meaning of the discrepancy is, therefore, not that one valuation depends on earning power and the other not, but that there are two estimates, one that of the bookkeeper, which is seldom revised and usually conservative, and the other that of the market, which is revised daily. Thus the stockholders of the Second National Bank are credited by their bookkeeper with owning $1,295,952.59, whereas in reality the total value of their property is more nearly $2,100,000. The bookkeeper has systematically undervalued the assets of the bank, and even omitted some valuable assets altogether, such as good will. The object of a conservative business man in keeping his books is not to give mathematical accuracy, but to make so conservative a valuation as to be well within the market, even in times of financial stress. He is more interested in safety than in precision, and in maintaining his solvency even in the face of heavy shrinkage of market values than in meeting the requirements of ideal statistics.

There are thus two valuations of the capital of a company, — the bookkeeper's and the market's. The latter is apt to be the truer of the two, although it must be remembered that each of them is merely an appraisement. We see, therefore, that the balance of a company's books which is so carefully worked out to the last cent, and which has so imposing an appearance of accuracy, may be in reality very wide of the mark.

§ 4

Not only is there a discrepancy between the market estimate of the present capital of a company and the bookkeeper's entries, but the original capital paid in to the company may itself have been quite different from the nominal capitalization, for the stock may have been sold below or above par. We see, then, that the "capital" of a person or firm has four separate meanings: — the nominal "capitalization"; the actual original "paid-in capital"; the present accumulated capital, or "capital, surplus, and undivided profits" as given by the bookkeeper; and the market estimate of the same, *i.e.* the "value of the shares." These and the other senses of capital are given in the following scheme, which displays the various uses of the term "capital."

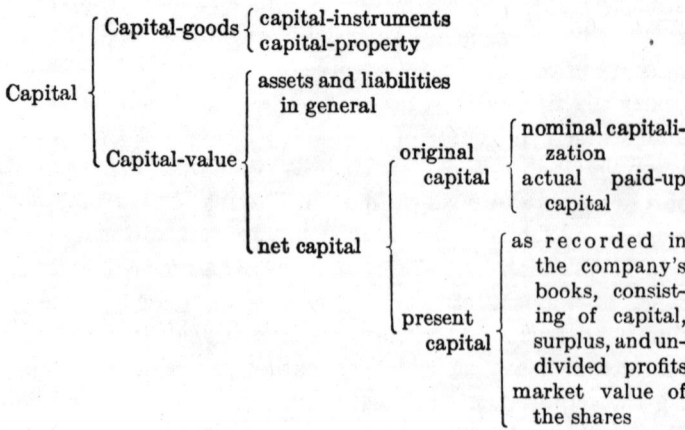

§ 5

We have seen that the effect upon the balance sheet of an increase in the value of the assets was to swell the surplus or the undivided profits. Reversely, a shrinkage of value tends to diminish those items. For instance, if the plant of a company having a capital of $100,000 and a surplus of $50,000 depreciates to the extent of $40,000, the effect on the books will be as follows: —

ORIGINAL BALANCE SHEET

Assets		Liabilities	
Plant	$200,000.00	Debts	$150,000.00
Miscellaneous	101,256.42	Capital	100,000.00
		Surplus	50,000.00
		Undivided profits	1,256.42
	$301,256.42		$301,256.42

PRESENT BALANCE SHEET

Assets		Liabilities	
Plant	$160,000.00	Debts	$150,000.00
Miscellaneous	101,256.42	Capital	100,000.00
		Surplus	10,000.00
		Undivided profits	1,256.42
	$261,256.42		$261,256.42

Here the shrinkage in the value of the plant, as recorded on the assets side, comes out of the surplus as recorded on the liabilities side.

In case the surplus and undivided profits have both been wiped out, the capital itself becomes impaired. In this case the bookkeeper may indicate the result by scaling down the capitalization. This sometimes occurs in banks and trust companies, but not often in ordinary business. It is often avoided by making up the deficiencies through assessment of stockholders or postponement of dividends. This is required by law in many cases, as in that of insurance companies. Dishonest concerns, however, often conceal the true state of the case by the reverse process of exaggerating the value of the assets. Sometimes this is done systematically, as in the case of stock-jobbing concerns. Unscrupulous promoters often invest the sums entrusted to them by confiding stockholders, in unwise or fraudulent ways. For instance, we may imagine an Oil Well Company in California, of the type called "stock-producing wells," which borrows $50,000 and collects $50,000 more from the sale of stock (at par), and with this $100,000 purchases land of friends at a fancy price, collusively providing that the proceeds be returned in large part to the promoter. In such a case the books of the bubble concern will show the following figures: —

Assets		Liabilities	
Land	$100,000	Debts	$50,000
		Capital	50,000
	$100,000		$100,000

But if the land is worth, say, only $60,000, these accounts *should* read: —

Assets		Liabilities	
Land	$60,000	Debts	$50,000
		Capital	10,000
	$60,000		$60,000

In other words, the investor has only $10,000 worth of property, instead of the $50,000 which he put in, or 20 cents for every dollar he invested. The rest has been diverted into the pockets of the promoter and those in collusion with him.

A favorite method of concealing the real condition of a company is to enter among the assets the bad debts due it, at their nominal value. Sometimes bad debts are bought up for that special purpose, the fraudulent company investing in the notes of some bankrupt concern, which can be obtained for very little, but may be entered on the books at face value. It is clear that any exaggeration on the assets side of the ledger produces an equal exaggeration of the capital, surplus, and undivided profits, on the opposite side. A great responsibility, therefore, rests on those who construct commercial accounts.

§ 6

Thus far we have considered the fluctuations of the items of a capital account independently of any payments between the company and the stockholders. When payments are made to the stockholders in the shape of dividends, the effect is to reduce both sides of the account, depleting the cash on the assets side, and the undivided profits on the liabilities side, each by the amount of the dividend. If a dividend is declared larger than the undivided profits, the effect will be to reduce the surplus, or even the capital. For most business concerns it is regarded as bad policy, or even fraudulent, to pay dividends out of capital. However, there is no inherent reason why such dividends should not be paid, and in some sorts of business it is not only proper but necessary. In these cases when dividends are paid out of capital there should be a corresponding reduction in the amount of outstanding capital stock, in order that those dealing with the concern may not be deceived. For instance, land companies in Colorado and California, such as the Redondo Land Company, are formed for the express purpose of investing in land and selling it again. As fast as it is sold, the proceeds are divided among the stockholders, and stock certificates cancelled, until the whole capital of the company is cleared away. Ordinarily, however, reduction in capital takes other forms than dividend payments. The payment of dividends out of capital is, generally speaking, unlawful, otherwise the creditors of a company might suddenly find themselves without any adequate security for their loans.

Payments are, of course, also made from the stockholders to the company. We will suppose that a company is formed with a capital stock of $100,000, but that when its first statement is made only $60,000 of this stock has been subscribed. It would be possible for the bookkeeper to enter the capital at that moment as $60,000; but, following his rule of keeping the capital item the same in all successive accounts, he will place the whole $100,000 on the *liabilities* side, and, to offset it, will insert on the other side assets of $40,000 in the form of treasury stock, the idea being that the company holds, in its treasury, stock certificates for $40,000, which are to be regarded as an asset. Of course this mode of entering treasury stock is a bookkeeping fiction, for this sum of $40,000 represents what is neither owned by nor owing to the company, except in the sense that the company owes itself; yet promoters will often impose upon the credulous investor the statement that to keep a certain amount of the stock of the company in its own treasury increases by that much the property of the stockholders.

After the capital stock has been fully paid in, it is often necessary to enlarge it. Let us suppose that before the increase in capital the account stands as follows: —

Assets		*Liabilities*	
Miscellaneous . . .	$300,000	Debts	$100,000
		Capital	100,000
		Surplus and undivided profits . . .	100,000
	$300,000		$300,000

Next let new capital to the extent of $100,000 be issued and sold to old stockholders at par, in lots proportionate to their original holdings. The new stock certificates of face value of $100,000 are thus sold for $100,000. The accounts will then stand as follows: —

Assets		*Liabilities*	
Miscellaneous . . .	$400,000	Debts	$100,000
		Capital	200,000
		Surplus and undivided profits . . .	100,000
	$400,000		$400,000

The additional capital will first take the form of cash, but afterward, by the purchase of plant, equipment, etc., will be changed into these or other forms of wealth or property. We shall suppose, however, for the present, that in whatever form invested, the value remains exactly equal to the cost, namely, $100,000, so that the assets are changed from $300,000 to $400,000.

§ 7

Let us assume that the books accurately represent actual values and correspond to market prices. After the new issue of stock, we find $200,000 of stock certificates representing $300,000 of actual value of capital, surplus and undivided profits, or $150 per share. But the new stock was, we assumed, issued to them at $100 a share. Hence the original stockholders will be able to make a profit on their new stock by buying at the issue price of $100 and then selling at $150; or they may shorten this operation by selling their "right to subscribe" for $50. At first sight it would seem as though this right to subscribe represented a mysterious bonus to the stockholders, due to the issue of the new stock. It must be remembered, however, that the $100,000 par value of original stock certificates represented, including the surplus, $200,000 worth of property belonging to the stockholders, consequently the original certificates were worth $200 per share. That is, the effect of issuing new stock below the original market price was to lower the value of the *old* stock from $200 per share to $150 per share. Consequently the loss of $50 to the stockholders on their old stock will exactly compensate for the $50 of excess value represented in the rights to subscribe. An individual stockholder owning 10 of the original shares will find them worth, instead of $2000, only $1500, that is, he will lose $500. This will equal the profit of $500 on his 10 new shares or the value of his rights to subscribe for them. The outside public would be willing to pay him $500 for the privilege of buying $1500 worth of stock for $1000.

We thus see that the price at which the new stock is issued does not of itself affect the balance due the shareholders. And yet the price of issue is not a matter of indifference. The lower the price of issue, the greater the inducement to the individual stockholder to subscribe, or to find some one else to subscribe instead, and buy his "right." Neglect to subscribe (or to sell the right to subscribe) would then cause a loss. The value of the old shares will be lowered in any event, and in such subscription or sale lies the only means of indemnification. For these reasons, it is usual for new stock to be offered to the original stockholders below the market price.

The exact compensation between the value of the new rights and the depreciation of the old stock is seldom realized in practice, because the company may be in a position to invest the new sums to advantage, in other words, to buy assets which are worth more than cost. In this case there may be little or no loss in the value of the old shares. But the point emphasized still remains true, that the price of issue does not of itself create additional capital value through the "right to subscribe." Any increase of value will be due to unusual opportunities for investment, — to economic causes and not to mere bookkeeping changes.

Of course, it may be true that the very fact of issuing new shares may of itself create a different opinion in the stock market and influence prices there for better or worse. A low price of issue may, for instance, make the stock more available for small investors, and the consequent increase in the volume of the stock on the market may make it, temporarily at least, a subject for the speculation of pools. Such facts, while they modify the results, do not affect the principle.

§ 8

We have considered two ways through which the book-value of capital, surplus, and divided profits may exaggerate the true condition of the stockholders' property, namely, through misfortune or the unforeseen shrinkage of the assets, and through misappropriation of stockholders' funds, even when stock had at the outset been issued at par. There remains to be considered a third way, namely, through the issue of stock below par, or for services, patents, etc., at unduly high prices.

To illustrate this way of overvaluing capital, or "stock-watering," suppose a company to be capitalized at $200,000, and that this company issues at the beginning 1000 certificates of the par value of $100,000, but sells them for only $60 per share actually paid into the treasury. Here is $60,000 paid-in capital, represented by $100,000 face value of stock certificates, leaving a margin of $40,000 "water." Suppose, further, that another block of $100,000 of the stock is given to an inventor for his patent, the real value of which is only $10,000. Finally, suppose that bonds are issued to the extent of $300,000, and are floated at par. Then the company has received in actual cash only $360,000. Of this sum only $60,000 has been received from the stockholders. The patent, which has also been contributed in return for $100,000 of stock, and which is worth only one tenth of that sum, makes the total balance due the stockholders $70,000. But, the company is capitalized at $200,000. Consequently it will be necessary for the bookkeeper to exaggerate the assets to the extent of $130,000.

He may do this as follows: —

Assets		Liabilities	
Plant [cost $360,000]	$400,000	Bonds	$300,000
Patent [worth 10,000]	100,000	Capital	200,000
	$500,000		$500,000

Here $90,000 of the exaggeration is put under patent and the remainder in an overvaluation of the plant. Many other methods of stock-watering are possible. A common one is to allow the plant to run down; *i.e.* to fail to make proper repairs, while retaining its old book value in the balance sheet. A railway may be "skinned" in this way, by diverting to dividends what should be paid to a depreciation account. This operation, however, is not commonly called stock-watering, but mismanagement.

It is sometimes said that stock-watering is not wrong, as long as all the terms and conditions are known. This is much like saying that lying is not wrong, provided everybody knows that it is lying; for a false balance sheet is only one form of a false statement, and, ordinarily, a false statement is made with intent to deceive. The object may be, for instance, to mislead intending bondholders by making them believe that there is a larger security for their loans than actually exists. We see here one reason why honest men often *under*value their assets. They prefer, if there is any error in their valuations, that the error shall be against themselves rather than in their favor; in other words, that their representations as to financial strength shall be well within the truth. Yet it not infrequently happens that undervaluations of assets may, like overvaluations, serve the purposes of dishonesty, — to "bear" the speculative market, for instance.

Many attempts have been made to prevent the frauds which result from stock-watering. For instance, the State or National governments compel publicity of accounts in the case of insurance companies, national banks, and interstate railways. The stock exchanges require similar publicity in regard to "listed" securities. Any company whose securities are listed on the New York Stock Exchange must publish its assets and liabilities at stated intervals. But this rule is too general to be very effective. In some cases the law requires the entire nominal capital to be paid into the company, in cash or securities at their market value, as in the case of national banks.[1]

[1] Revised Statutes, § 5140 (Act June 3, 1864, § 13).

§ 9

The original capital of a concern may therefore be either increased or decreased. In the course of its fluctuations it may sometimes shrink to zero. If it sinks below zero we have insolvency, — the condition in which assets fall short of liabilities. The capital-balance is intended to prevent this very calamity; that is, it is for the express purpose of guaranteeing the value of the other liabilities.

These other liabilities represent, for the most part, fixed blocks of property carved out, as it were, of the assets, and which the merchant or company has agreed to keep intact at all hazards. The fortunes of business will naturally cause the whole volume of assets to vary in value, but all this "slack" ought properly to be taken up or given out by the capital, surplus, and undivided profits. Capital thus acts as a buffer to keep the liabilities from overtaking the assets. It is the "margin" put up by those most interested in an enterprise, as a guarantee to others who advance their capital to it. The amount of capital-balance necessary to make a business reasonably safe will differ with circumstances. A capital-balance equal to five per cent of the liabilities may, in one kind of business, such as mortgage companies, be perfectly adequate, whereas fifty per cent may be required in another kind. Much depends on how likely the assets are to shrink and how much; and much, likewise, on the character of the liabilities. If the assets have stability of value, less capital will be required than if they consist of speculative securities.

The risk of insolvency is, then, the chance that the assets may shrink below the liabilities. This risk is the greater, the more shrinkable the assets, and the less the margin of capital-value between assets and liabilities. The subject lends itself to mathematical and statistical treatment; but to work out the quantitative relations would lead us far afield; it would require much statistical material, and its analysis by the mathematics of chances.

§ 10

Insolvency may exist for a time without being known; there may be no legal bankruptcy. Legal bankruptcy exists as soon as there is a legal declaration of inability to meet obligations. This may not be true insolvency. For instance, the assets may exceed the liabilities, but the cash assets at the particular time may be less than the cash liabilities due at that time. This condition we may call pseudo-insolvency. In such a case, a little forbearance on the part of creditors may be all that is necessary to prevent financial shipwreck.

A wise merchant, however, will not only avoid insolvency, but also pseudo-insolvency; that is, he will not only keep his assets in excess of his liabilities by a safe margin, but will also see that his assets are invested in the right form so as to enable him to cancel each claim at the time and in the manner agreed upon.

From this point of view there are three chief forms of assets, — cash assets, quick assets, and slow assets. A cash asset is property in actual money, or what is acceptable in place of money. A quick asset is one which may be exchanged for cash in a relatively short time, as, for instance, call loans, short-time loans, and other marketable securities. A slow asset is one which can be exchanged for cash only in a relatively long time, as real estate, office fixtures, and manufacturers' equipment. The skill of a good business man consists in properly marshaling these various constituents of his assets.

§ 11

When we speak of the assets falling short of the liabilities, we refer only to those assets which are included in the balance sheet. There may be, outside of the company, private means of stockholders adequate to meet the debts of a company, but unavailable. In fact, in the case of a joint stock company, there is express provision for "limited liability," so that the only assets which can be considered in determining solvency are those on the balance sheet of the company. However, in some cases, as in the case of national banks, the stockholders are liable for double the amount of the capital. In the case of a partnership, on the other hand, the partners are liable for almost all of their private property, so that the individual member of the firm has always to reckon w th a contingent liability to the creditors of the firm.

Originally, before business was separated from private life, all of a debtor's assets, even including his own person, were regarded as pledged to the payment of a debt. The attitude of the law and public opinion toward this matter has changed greatly. Only a few generations ago an insolvent debtor was imprisoned, the theory being that insolvency was a crime. When intentional, or due to gross negligence, it is; but when due to the ordinary chances of business it is not. To put a debtor in prison did not of course help him to pay his debts. When this practical point was admitted, special bankruptcy acts were passed to relieve insolvency if very widespread, as after a panic. Such acts were at first merely temporary, and regarded as justified only under extraordinary circumstances. To-day, however, laws exist by which a bankrupt may be discharged free of further liability, and without the necessity of any special legislation. The Ray Act in the United States, under which our present system of bankruptcy has been worked out, was passed as late as 1898. In some places, as in France, the older view of limited liability still prevails; but the English and American system is not only sounder in practice, as shown by its results in encouraging legitimate enterprise, but is also based on sounder theory, for it recognizes the fact that the creditor is a risk-taker. This has always been and is necessarily the case, however much the debtor may try to safeguard his creditors' interests. The capital of a company exists, as we have seen, for the purpose of minimizing this risk, but it cannot eliminate it altogether.

§ 12

The principle that a creditor of a concern is a risk-taker has two important corollaries. The first is that, when bankruptcy occurs, though the nominal liabilities exceed the assets, their actual value does not. We may say that so far as their actual value is concerned, the value of the liabilities of a company can never be greater than the assets, for they derive their value from these assets. A company which can pay only fifty cents on the dollar must have its obligations classified as "bad debts," worth only half their nominal amount. This fact does not, of course, justify the intentional repudiation of debts. Some states of the United States have, it is true, attempted to reduce the burden of their debt by offering to buy up their own bonds at their market price, when this price was below par, owing to a lack of confidence in their ultimate redemption. Such an operation is evidently a species of repudiation.

On the other hand, we must not regard it as an unforgivable sin for the *bona fide* bankrupt not to pay his debts in full. So long as the creditor understands in advance the nature of the risk he is taking, he must abide by the result. Nowadays, in the case of investments in large corporations, this is perfectly well understood. Many railroads have been bonded for almost their entire cost, the bondholder realizing fully that he could obtain nothing unless the road was a success. This participation in risk is particularly evident in the case of income bonds, which specifically pay interest only so long as the road's income is adequate.

The principle that the true value of the liabilities is derived from the assets and can never exceed them may seem to have an exception in the case of a person who succeeds in borrowing money "without capital." It is clear, however, that if we employ the term "wealth" in its larger sense, a person who is really good for his debt is himself assets to that extent. His present value must in the estimation of his creditors be at least equal to the discounted value of his debt-paying power; otherwise he could not borrow. It follows that his liability, being only part of the discounted value of his debt-paying power, cannot exceed his assets.

The second corollary, from the principle that all securities imply risk, is that the distinction between stockholders and bondholders is chiefly one of degree, and may be bridged over by intermediate forms. Preferred stock and income bonds amount to very nearly the same thing. The preferred stockholder is elevated above the common stockholder, and resembles a bondholder in that he is assigned a certain fixed amount of the earnings before any accrue to the common stockholder. The income bondbolder, on the other hand, is depressed below the other bondholders, and resembles a stockholder in that he will not be paid until the ordinary bondholders have been satisfied. The chief remaining differences between these two forms of security are that the stock confers voting power, while the bond does not; and that the bond has a due date for final extinguishment, while the stock continues until the company is "wound up."

The distinction between the different classes of creditors of a concern is still further swept away in some cases where there is no capital stock, as in that of a mutual insurance company. Here the policy holders, instead of being creditors for fixed sums due them from the company, as are the bondholders of a joint stock concern, themselves assume the risk of the business and also take whatever chance there may be of profit. They are, as it were, both stockholders and creditors. In the accounts of a mutual company there will be almost no outside creditors. In such companies, therefore, bankruptcy would seem to be impossible; but as their debts for death claims are for specific sums, they may be forced into liquidation, if unable to obtain these sums by remitting dividends or by assessments.

§ 13

When bankruptcy occurs, the claims of creditors are settled in one of three ways: through an agreement of "composition," by which the creditor agrees to take what he can get and excuse the debtor for the difference; through an assignment by the debtor of his assets to his creditors; or through foreclosure by the holder of some obligation.

The final result of bankruptcy will be either liquidation, by which the business assets are sold and distributed and the business wound up; or reorganization, by which the business is continued and the liabilities are entirely changed in character. In the case of companies with large fixed capital, as, for instance, railroads, reorganization is the usual result, and the old bondholders often become the stockholders, the old stockholders surrendering their rights altogether. While this reorganization is being effected, the affairs of the company are administered by a receiver appointed by the bankruptcy court. He calls in all the stock and bonds, and issues temporary receiver's certificates. These in turn are exchanged for the new securities when ready. However, the bondholder seldom wishes to assume his right of control and become a stockholder, and is usually offered instead the option of cash or some new security similar in kind to that which he held before, but less in amount. He is apt to accept one of these alternatives, realizing that to foreclose and take possession is likely to be more troublesome, and, in the end, less advantageous. Thus the losses of the old company are "written off," and the reorganized company starts afresh with a clean set of books. The change is simply a change in the forms of ownership of wealth and in the individual owners.

§ 14

The bankruptcy of one firm often causes the bankruptcy of another. The interdependence between firms may be clearly seen in the following table, where the liability of one person is represented by the asset of another, thus: —

PERSON A

Assets		Liabilities	
Miscellaneous	$100,000	Note to B	$50,000
		Capital	50,000
	$100,000		$100,000

PERSON B

Assets		Liabilities	
A's note	$50,000	Note to C et al.	$40,000
Miscellaneous	20,000	Capital	30,000
	$70,000		$70,000

PERSON C

Assets		Liabilities	
Note of B	$20,000	Bills to D et al.	$10,000
Miscellaneous	20,000	Capital	30,000
	$40,000		$40,000

PERSON D

Assets		Liabilities	
Due from C	$5000	Miscellaneous	$9000
Miscellaneous	4000		
	$9000		$9000

Now suppose A fails, for the reason that his assets unexpectedly shrink to $10,000, that is, become $90,000 less than they were before. Then the value of the liabilities shrinks $90,000. This wipes out all of A's capital of $50,000, and takes $40,000 from the value of the rest of his liability, which was a note to B. B gets, therefore, only $10,000 out of a claim of $50,000 or only 20 cents on the dollar. In B's account this note of $50,000 must now be scaled down as a bad asset worth only $10,000 instead of $50,000; that is, B's assets shrink $40,000. A's loss is thus enough to wipe out all of B's capital of $30,000, and pare down the value of his other liabilities by $10,000, so that B can now pay only $30,000 out of the $40,000 he owes. In other words, he is able to pay only 75 cents on the dollar. Next comes C, who has $20,000 invested in B's note. He gets only 75 cents on the dollar, so that this asset, nominally worth $20,000, is found to be worth only $15,000, and his loss is only $5000. This loss is not enough to wipe out all his capital, but only reduces it from $30,000 to $25,000, so that C remains solvent. Consequently D, who owns C's bills for $5000, will lose nothing. The force of the catastrophe has been spent. It ruined A and B and injured C, but stopped short of D.

From this example we may see that the statistics of bankruptcies are often misleading. Thus, it is usual for the statistician to sum up the liabilities of all bankrupt firms. But in case the various firms are connected, as in the above example, the total sum lost is not as great as though the same amount of bankruptcy occurred in independent firms. In the preceding example the only loss is $90,000, all in A's assets. But there would appear to be a loss of $90,000 in A's account, one of $40,000 in B's account, and one of $5000 in C's, or $135,000 in all. This misleading result is evidently due to counting parts of the loss twice and three times.

Failures are sometimes due to a false fear of calamity, a shock to business *confidence*. This will cause a shrinkage of values in several ways. For instance, it will induce creditors to demand payment and refuse renewals of bills. Forced liquidation and contraction of credit are the result. No physical capital is destroyed, but the form of ownership is violently disturbed, and often the management, being transferred from stockholders to bondholders, is turned from competent to incompetent hands. Above all, the expectations of the future are changed and confused. Plans are given up, orders are countermanded, and trade is stopped. Assets, representing as they do the value of future expectations, suffer sudden and heavy reductions.

§ 15

Briefly summarizing this chapter we may say that a person who has liabilities is, in a sense, a trustee. He *holds* more than he owns. He holds all his assets; he owns only the margin between these and his liabilities. His responsibility for the liabilities requires that he should keep his own margin of capital comparatively safe. But there is always risk of losing his margin and becoming insolvent. This risk, whether large or small, is necessarily assumed by his creditors, and its existence should be recognized in law as well as in business practice. The record of the relations which at any time exist between assets, liabilities, and the margin of capital separating them constitutes what we have called the "capital accounts."

CHAPTER VI

CAPITAL SUMMATION

§ 1

THE interdependence of the balance sheets of different firms or companies which has been revealed by the communication of bankruptcies exists, of course, irrespective of bankruptcies. It exists wherever any item enters two accounts, in one as asset and in the other as liability. In fact, every liability item in a balance sheet implies the existence of an equal asset in some other balance sheet, for every debtor implies a creditor. Consequently every negative term in one balance sheet is offset by a corresponding positive term in some other. The converse, however, does not follow, namely, that every asset implies a liability.

When we attempt to sum up the it ms in the balance sheets of various persons, the positive and negative elements may be canceled out by pairs or couples. This method of cancellation may be called the method of couples. Each debt or liability between any two persons whose accounts are included, being a liability to one and an asset to the other, constitutes a couple or pair of equal and opposite items. We have already noted another way in which liabilities may be canceled against assets, namely, by subtracting the liabilities in any capital account from the assets in the same account. This method may be called the method of balances, since for each individual account liabilities are deducted from assets and the net balance is taken. Both methods must, of course, lead to the same result.

CAPITAL SUMMATION

The two methods may be illustrated by the balance sheets of three persons, say X, Y, and Z:—

Person X

Assets		Liabilities	
Z's note	$30,000 A	Mortgage held by Y	$50,000 b
Residence	70,000	(Capital balance	70,000)
R.R. shares	20,000		
	$120,000		$120,000

Person Y

Assets		Liabilities	
X's mortgage	$50,000 B	Debt to Z	$40,000 c
Personal effects	20,000	(Capital balance	40,000)
R.R. shares	10,000		
	$80,000		$80,000

Person Z

Assets		Liabilities	
Y's debt	$40,000 C	Debt to X	$30,000 a
Farm	50,000	(Capital balance	80,000)
R.R. bonds	20,000		
	$110,000		$110,000

The items which appear twice, once as a liability of one man and again as an asset of another, are indicated by the same letter. Thus, "A" in X's assets is matched by the equal and opposite item "a" in Z's liabilities. The method of couples thus consists simply in omitting these pairs of items and entering those which remain. These, in the present case, are all assets.

The results of summing up the capital accounts by the two methods are shown in the following tables:—

Method of Balances		Method of Couples	
X's capital	$70,000	Residence	$70,000
Y's capital	40,000	Personal effects	20,000
Z's capital	80,000	Farm	50,000
		R.R. shares	30,000
		R.R. bonds	20,000
	$190,000		$190,000

The totals are the same by both methods, but the method of balances shows the share of this total capital which is owned by each individual, while the method of couples shows the various items of capital-goods of which this total is composed, namely, residence, personal effects, farm and railroad shares and bonds.

§ 2

It is well to note here the distinction between the accounting of *real* persons and of *fictitious* persons. For a real person, the assets may be and usually are in excess of the liabilities, and the difference is the capital-balance of that person. This capital is not to be regarded as a liability, but as a balance or difference between the liabilities and the assets. For a fictitious person, on the other hand, as for instance a corporation or partnership, the liabilities are always *exactly equal* to the assets; for the balancing item called capital is as truly an obligation from the fictitious person to the real stockholders, as any of the other liabilities. A fictitious person, in fact, is a mere bookkeeping dummy, holding certain assets and owing *all* of them out again to real persons. Bookkeepers, it is true, apply the same methods in both cases, but they do so by regarding the accounts even of a real person as relating to a fictitious entity for bookkeeping purposes. One's business self and one's real self are separated. Thus if X's business shows a balance in X's favor of $10,000, he enters this as a liability item in his business accounts and considers his "business" as owing him this sum. There is no objection to such a procedure. But we must remember that when we say that "X's business" owes X $10,000, we imply that the real X in his own accounts holds a claim of that amount against his "business." In other words, we are compelled, in order to be consistent, to open a separate account for X and carry forward the $10,000 balance to the opposite side, thus: —

X's Business

Assets		Liabilities	
Miscellaneous . . .	$50,000	Due to others . . .	$40,000
		Due to X	10,000
	$50,000		$50,000

X's Self

Assets	
Due from "X's business" . .	$10,000

In the second account there is no counterbalancing liability. For real persons, then, assets and liabilities are not equal. If they were, the summation of their balance sheets would yield simply zero! If we would avoid this absurdity, we must either omit the capital-balance from the liabilities side, or if for the moment we place it there, we must, as in the above example, carry it forward to the opposite side of another account, which amounts to the same thing in the end.

§ 3

With this preliminary explanation, let us now introduce into our summation the capital accounts of the railroad whose stocks and bonds are included among the assets of persons X, Y, and Z. For simplicity, we shall suppose that these three persons are the only persons interested in the road. The balance sheet of the railroad company will accordingly appear as follows: —

Railroad Co.

Assets		Liabilities		
Railway	$50,000	Bonds (held by Z) . .		$20,000
		Capital stock		
		(held by X)	$20,000	
		(held by Y)	10,000	30,000
	$50,000			$50,000

Now if we combine this sheet with the preceding we shall see that its inclusion does not affect the results which were obtained by the method of balances before the railroad was introduced into the discussion. The totals will stand as follows: —

X's capital balance	$ 70,000
Y's capital balance	40,000
Z's capital balance	80,000
R.R. Co.'s capital balance	000
	$190,000

When we apply the method of couples, however, we find that the inclusion of the railway company's capital account will affect the items in the final sum. The stocks and bonds, as assets of X, Y, and Z, will now pair off with the corresponding liabilities of the railroad company and their place will be taken by the concrete railroad itself, as follows: —

METHOD OF COUPLES

Residence	$ 70,000
Personal Effects	20,000
Farm	50,000
Railway	50,000
	$190,000

The appearance of the capital inventory is thus changed. Formerly, the items of property-rights in it included *part* rights, as stocks and bonds; now they consist only of *complete* property-rights The items still consist, strictly speaking, solely of property rights — the right to the residence, the right to the farm, etc. But, since the complete right to any article of wealth is best expressed in terms of the article of wealth itself, instead of the long phrase, the "right to a residence," we merely use "residence." The property no longer veils the wealth beneath it, and the inventory, which before was called an inventory of *property*-capital, is now also an inventory of *wealth*-capital.

Such a result is sure to follow when we combine capital accounts, provided we combine enough of them to supply, for every liability item, its counterpart asset, and for every asset which has one, its counterpart liability. The assets which have no counterparts are what we have called *complete* rights to wealth, or "fee simples"; those which have them are the *partial* rights to wealth. The reason is that every article of concrete wealth is to be regarded as owned in "fee simple" *by some one*, even if we have to set up a fictitious person as dummy for that very purpose. Hence every part right to that wealth will necessarily appear as a liability on the opposite side of that person's account, and again as an asset on the account of some other person. Thus, if two brothers own a farm in equal shares, the farm *as a whole* is regarded as owned by the partnership person called "Smith Brothers." The balance sheet of this fictitious person will show as assets the farm and as liabilities the "undivided half-interest" of each brother, and these same items enter the individual accounts of the brothers as assets.

To follow out capital summations thus requires the inclusion of many fictitious persons, for it is often only the fictitious persons who hold the complete rights to articles of wealth. Locomotives and railway stations, for instance, are owned by corporations, not individuals. In fact, these fictitious persons — partnerships, corporations, trusts, municipalities, associations, and the like — are formed for the express purpose of holding large aggregations of concrete wealth and parceling out its ownership among a larger number of real persons.

If, then, we suppose balance sheets so constructed as to include the whole world of real and fictitious persons, with entries in them for every asset and liability, even public parks and streets, household furniture, persons themselves, and other possessions not ordinarily accounted for in practice, it is evident that we shall obtain, by the method of balances, a complete account of the distribution of capital-value among real persons; and, by the method of couples, a complete list of the articles of actual wealth thus owned. On this list there will be no stocks, bonds, mortgages, notes, or other part rights, but only land, buildings and other land improvements, commodities and real persons. In other words, we arrive again at the proposition of Chapter III, that wealth underlies and corresponds to property.

§ 4

Among other part-rights in real wealth we find what is called "credit." There has been much discussion as to the nature of credit; whether, in particular, credit is to be regarded as a "part of capital." It has been claimed that, from the merchant's point of view, credit is capital because it enables a business man to enlarge his business. In this view it is capital, though it is borrowed capital. MacLeod specifically includes credit under capital. Professor J. Shield Nicholson says that credit is a sort of revenue capital,[1] but that "strictly and taking only material (productive) capital, this would involve counting the same elements twice over." We see, from our study of capital accounts, how to avoid such double counting. That part of a man's so-called capital which is borrowed should not enter his books as his capital at all, being but a manifestation of the fact that the total capital of the community which he in part owns is also owned in part by others. Indeed, the phenomenon of credit means nothing more nor less than a specific form of divided ownership of wealth. Credit merely enables one man temporarily to control more wealth or property than he owns, that is, some part of the wealth or property of others. This occurs generally on the theory that he can use it to better advantage than the real owner.

[1] Palgrave's *Dictionary of Political Economy*, Vol. I, p. 452.

It is therefore a cardinal error to regard credit as increasing capital by the amount of that credit. Indirectly, credit may result in an increase of capital, through stimulating trade and production and by getting the management of capital into the right hands and its ownership into the most effective form; but the amount of any such increase of capital thus indirectly produced bears no necessary relation to the amount of the credit itself. If capital is increased, the credit does not *constitute* the increase, but merely represents a part ownership in the final total, after all the increments have been counted in.

§ 5

A great deal of confusion in legislation and writing could be avoided if the two methods of summing up capital were distinguished and their interrelations recognized. In taxation, the two methods are often confused. A chief problem of efficient taxation is how to tax all property once, and none of it more than once. There are two solutions: One is to tax the amount owned by each real person in a list which expresses the method of balances; this method seeks out the real *owners* or part owners of wealth. The other is to tax the actual concrete wealth in a list which expresses the method of couples; this method seeks out the real wealth owned. At present the two are much confused. Legislators too often fail to perceive that under the first, or *owner*-method, corporations should not be taxed, for they are not true owners; and that under the second, or *wealth*-method, bonds, stocks, and other part-rights to wealth should not be taxed, for these are sufficiently included when the actual railways and other wealth are taxed, which these securities represent.

It is not claimed, of course, that a complete system of taxation can be worked out merely by choosing one of the two forms of taxes just indicated. We are here only concerned in pointing out that the distinction between the two should be observed and that where one is applied the other cannot also be applied without duplicating the tax.

The failure to distinguish clearly the methods of balances and couples also manifests itself in the form of fallacious statistics of capital. Statistics of railway capital have been compiled in which the value of all railway property is obtained by adding up the assets of the railways, regardless of the fact that many of these assets consist in stocks and bonds of other railways.

We should therefore distinguish carefully the two methods for the summation of capital, — one the method of balances, which exhibits capital as owned by different individuals, and the other the method of couples, which exhibits capital as consisting of different concrete instruments. The one relates to the owner, the other to the things owned. They do not conflict, but present the same facts in different aspects.

PART II. INCOME

CHAPTER VII. INCOME
CHAPTER VIII. INCOME ACCOUNTS
CHAPTER IX. INCOME SUMMATION
CHAPTER X. PSYCHIC INCOME

CHAPTER VII

INCOME

§ 1

INCOME has already been defined as a *flow* through a *period* of time and not, like capital, as a *fund* at an instant of time, and as consisting of *abstract services* and not, like capital, of *concrete wealth*. The income from any instrument is thus the flow of services rendered by that instrument. The income of a community is the total flow of services from all its instruments. The income of an individual is the total flow of services yielded to him from his property. Before attempting to elaborate or even to justify this definition, we have first to examine the erroneous concepts of income now current. The present chapter is devoted to such an examination.

It is no exaggeration to say that at present the state of economic opinion on this important subject is deplorably confused and conflicting. Many writers fail to construct any definition whatever, either because they find the task too difficult, or because they deem the concept too obvious to require definition. And those who do set themselves the task of reaching a working concept of income do not find it an easy one; and authors often confess dissatisfaction with their own results.

The definitions which are given are usually vague.[1] Their authors, often able and distinguished, and keenly alive to the difficulties of the subject, seem to take refuge

[1] For a collection of conflicting definitions see Appendix to Chap. VII, § 1.

in an obscure and ambiguous phraseology.[1] Were it not for an instinctive feeling that there exists a definite income-concept, the repeated failure to formulate it might lead one to conclude that it is not susceptible of any exact and rigorous definition, and that the best course is to abandon its search as futile. Kleinwächter, who wrote a book especially devoted to this subject, specifically takes this course. He states that there is no useful concept of income.[2] His idea is that, originally, merchants attempted to keep a record of their transactions by counting the money which they received and disbursed, and that, in consequence of this, arose the "illusory" notion that through some such record the complete economic standing of an individual or firm could be expressed. He observes, that such a complete picture could not be obtained by recording merely the incomings and outgoings of money, but should include likewise the incomings and outgoings of every other kind of wealth.[3] A complete record, he states, would alone cover the required ground. So-called statistics of income are, he maintains, merely a makeshift for such a record.[4]

But why should the possibility of a concept of income be rejected because it does not reveal a "complete" picture of an individual's economic condition? On the same plea we might also reject the possibility of a concept of capital.

---

[1] *E.g.* F. Y. Edgeworth, Palgrave's *Dictionary of Political Economy*, article, "Income," Vol. II, p. 374:—
"Income may be defined as the wealth, measured in money, which is *at the disposal of* an individual, or a community, per year or other unit of time." (The italics are the present writer's.) This formulation is adopted by N. G. Pierson, *Principles of Economics*, London (Macmillan), 1902, p. 76.

[2] *Das Einkommen und seine Verteilung*, Leipzig, 1896, p. 11.

[3] *Op. cit.*, p. 14.

[4] The present writer at one time also expressed these doubts (*Economic Journal*, December, 1896, pp. 553, 554). By aid of the criticisms of Cannan and Edgeworth, the conclusions here stated were reached. These were first outlined in "Senses of Capital," *Economic Journal*, June, 1897, and in "The Rôle of Capital in Economic Theory," *Economic Journal*, December, 1897.

A good definition should always conform to two tests: it must be useful for scientific analysis; and it must harmonize with popular and instinctive usage. We shall see that the usual definitions of income fail in one or both of these requisites. Many fail to lend themselves to scientific analysis by committing the fallacy of double counting, others by confusing income and capital, while almost all fail to harmonize with popular usage by making out income larger or smaller than common sense would dictate.

Like most familiar notions, the notion of income seems to the uninitiated clear enough without definition. But pitfalls which are unseen are for that very reason all the more dangerous. We shall point out a few of them by criticising, not the specific definitions of particular authors, but the general concepts of income which the reader is likely, more or less unconsciously, to have acquired.

§ 2

The concept of income which is the most common is that of "money-income." A business man's "money-income" means to him the money receipts from his business, less the money expenses of obtaining them. As applied to commercial affairs, this concept is nearly adequate, and in fact it coincides, as a special case, with the concept of income which we have adopted; for the services which a man's business capital yields him usually consist exclusively of bringing him money, and the disservices which it causes him, of taking money from him. Thus the net value of its services to him, or difference between the value of the services and disservices, is simply the difference between the money brought in and the money taken away from him by his business.

But while the concept of "money-income" is correct so far as it goes, it is far fom exhausting the complete income concept. As soon as we pass outside of commercial circles, we find cases in which money-receipts are evidently only a part of all receipts and money-costs only a part of all costs. In primitive communities, and even in highly organized communities, the income of many persons consists partly in the acquisition of goods other than money. The clergyman receives, besides his salary, the use of a parsonage; and domestic servants receive, besides their wages, their food and lodging. Again, many goods considered as constituting income are not acquired by exchange at all, but produced by the individual himself. It is usually recognized that a farmer's income includes not only what he gets in money by sale and barter, but what he obtains "in kind," — the products of his farm consumed by his own family.

On the other side of the ledger there are many costs which are not in money form, namely, sacrifices of commodities and labor in the process of acquisition. The farmer's crops cost him labor as well as wages. Again, he may not pay money for his seed and fertilizer, but sacrifice for these some of the products of his farm instead.

While the acknowledged existence of non-monetary receipts and costs is of itself a sufficient proof of the inadequacy of the money-income idea, there is the further objection that money-income itself exists, so far as it has any existence, merely for the purpose of purchasing other goods. The laborer's wages are not his "real wages," but the means to them. He transforms his money-wages into food, clothing, housing, and other uses. These, and not the money which buys them, constitute his real income. If we acknowledge this, we are led away from money-income to another concept common in economic literature, but still inadequate, namely, "real income."

§ 3

"Real income" has been defined in various ways, and, like income in general, is often not defined at all. So far as it has any recognized meaning, it may perhaps be expressed in the phrase "*enjoyable commodities and services.*" This concept is certainly more adequate than that of money-income; for it includes the supplementary elements which we found lacking under the head of money-income, such as the clergyman's use of a parsonage, the servant's board and lodging, and the farmer's produce for his own consumption. It is also less superficial than the concept of money-income; for it recognizes that money is only an intermediary, and seeks to discover the real elements for which that money-income stands.

But the definition errs in two particulars: first, instead of making income consist simply and consistently of one kind of element, services, it attempts to include with this element the totally incongruous element, commodities; and, secondly, it unnecessarily restricts itself to *enjoyable* elements; for, though enjoyable elements are, in the last analysis, the final income of society or of an individual, the fact that they are should constitute the end of our reasonings and not the beginning. We shall now take up these two errors in order.

That the two elements — "commodities" and "services" — form a heterogeneous combination is evident from the fact that one is concrete wealth and the other, abstract use of that wealth. To bring about homogeneity we could exclude uses altogether and confine "income" to concrete commodities; or we could exclude commodities altogether and restrict the term wholly to uses. The latter alternative, which is the solution offered in the present book, seems never to have occurred to those who have written on the subject. The former alternative is quite untenable and has been instinctively discarded. Instead of either alternative, the course which has actually been pursued has been the eclectic makeshift of including some commodities and the services or uses of others, and even sometimes both the commodities and the uses of these very commodities.

The choice of the commodities to be included has usually fallen on the less durable varieties, such as food, fuel, and clothing, while the objects the uses of which have been included have been the more durable instruments, such as dwelling-houses. In the case of intermediate types, such as carriages, furniture, and musical instruments, no fixed rule seems to have been observed. Some economists are inclined to regard a newly acquired piano as a part of real income, others to regard the music which comes from it as the real income, while still others apparently regard both the piano and its music as real income. Evidently such a patchwork of arbitrarily selected elements is incapable of furnishing any consistent, reliable, and logical theory of income.

§ 4

The only true method, in our view, is to regard uniformly as income the *service* of a dwelling to its owner (shelter or money rental), the *service* of a piano (music), and the service of food (nourishment); and in the same uniform manner to exclude alike from the category of income the dwelling, the piano, and even the food. These are capital, not income; and the instant we include any such concrete wealth under the head of income, that instant we begin to confuse capital and income. The newly purchased or newly constructed house is not an element of income, but of capital. The income appears afterward in the services the house yields its owner, — the shelter it affords through subsequent years or the bringing in of a money rent to its owner. In like manner the newly acquired piano and loaf of bread are not income, but capital. Their income follows later in the form of piano music and nourishment.

No reason has ever been given why the short-lived bread should be treated differently from the long-lived dwelling. The use of the bread is just as distinct from the bread as the use of the dwelling is distinct from the dwelling. The difference between the case of the bread and that of the dwelling is purely one of degree. The uses of the bread follow the acquisition of the bread almost instantly, whereas the uses of the dwelling are not completely ended until many years after the dwelling is acquired. From this difference in time comes a corresponding difference in value. The value of the use of the bread is practically identical with the value of the bread. A man will give ten cents to-day for a loaf if he expects its use (consumption) to-morrow to be worth ten cents. The value of the dwelling, however, will be less than the value of its prospective uses, owing to the fact that these uses are so remote in the future. If the dwelling is expected to last fifty years, and its shelter to be worth $1000 a year, this $50,000 worth of shelter will not by any means be worth $50,000 in advance, but only, say, $15,000. This "capitalized" value of the expected uses of the dwelling will be the value of the dwelling. In short, the bread and its uses are practically contemporaneous and equal in value, whereas the dwelling and its uses are widely diverse in both particulars. Consequently it has not seemed worth while to economists to distinguish between the bread and its uses; whereas they could not help distinguishing between the dwelling and its uses.

But in science, logical distinctions are inexorable, and their violation always brings retribution. It may be said in truth that if economists had been scrupulous enough to distinguish a loaf of bread from its uses, they would have escaped most of the confusions which have so long enveloped the theory of income. Having once chosen as the income element the food instead of its use, economists have proceeded to do the same in the case of clothing and other moderately durable commodities. Naturally they have not known where to cease calling the concrete instrument income and begin calling its use income instead. In their hesitation they have in some cases ended by including both. By so doing they commit the fallacy of double counting. This fallacy they escape only in the case of the very durable instruments, such as the dwelling, and the very perishable instruments, such as the bread. The dwelling is too evidently not income ever to be so regarded, and, as to bread, one of the two elements—its use—is overlooked altogether. But it is felt that intermediate types, like the piano, are as fairly entitled to be called income, when acquired, as the bread, and that their services are as fairly entitled to be called income as are the services of the dwelling. Consequently both are deemed income. But a piano valued at $500 is so valued because this sum is the capitalized value of the future expected uses which, let us say, are $600, distributed over the lifetime of the instrument. Consequently if, when the piano is first purchased, it is entered as real income to the extent of $500, and then later its subsequent services in providing its owner with music are also counted as income to the extent of $600, it is clear that there has been double (though successive) counting. The services of the piano have been counted as income in anticipation as well as in realization.

Yet this error, in one form or another, is not infrequently committed. It is virtually in this way that Cannan[1] and others regard "savings" as income in the year in which the savings are accumulated, although the interest upon those savings will be counted as income in subsequent years. The nature of the fallacy is seen as soon as we translate from money to other instruments. If a man saves up money and purchases an automobile, it is clearly double counting to call the automobile thus obtained "real income," and then include its subsequent uses in the real income of ensuing years. It does not matter

[1] *Elementary Political Economy*, London, 1888, pp. 58, 59. The fallacy of including savings in income will be treated at greater length in Chap. XIV. The reader who believes that savings ought to be regarded as income is asked to stay judgment until he has finished Chap. XIV.

how durable the instrument; it is always double counting to include the instrument and its uses. The savings may be invested in land or in confectionery. The only true income is the use of the land or the use of the confectionery. To include also the value of the land or the value of the confectionery is to count as income the capitalization of income.

§ 5

Economists have been more or less aware of the pitfall of double counting, but not of the reason for it. They have therefore attempted to avoid it, not by excluding all commodities from the income concept and restricting it to services, but by specifically excluding from income certain groups of commodities. Naturally, they have been at a loss to formulate a satisfactory and logical principle for this exclusion. Some of them have no better suggestion to offer than that all "large" or "unusual" acquisitions should be ruled out, and that only those commodities which come into a man's possession in a "regular" stream shall be entitled to the name income. This makeshift has received much currency among German writers. To be sure, it serves the purpose of excluding from income such obviously inappropriate elements as bequests and gifts of large fortunes. It is clear that when a well-known millionaire recently fell heir to seventy millions, this did not constitute his income for the year in which he received it, but that it merely constituted the principal or capital from which he would receive income in subsequent years. But the reason that it is improper to call this suddenly acquired fortune income is not that it was large, nor that it was sudden, but that it consisted of rights to concrete wealth — factories, ships, railways, and dwellings. These things are not under any circumstances income, but yield income through future uses. It is idle to call income "regular"; for we all know that it is irregular.

Another but very similar attempt to escape the difficulties of double counting and of confusing capital and income is to specify, not that income must in a vague way be "regular," but that it must be such as to leave unimpaired the capital which yields it.[1] Such a definition has the merit of connecting income with capital as its source, but it merely shifts the pretended attribute of uniformity from the income itself to its parent capital. In actual fact it is seldom true either that income flows uniformly or that capital remains at a constant level. To stipulate such uniformity as a necessary limitation of income is to define, not the actual irregular income which exists in fact, but an ideal standard which we set up for reference. It cannot be denied that the term "income" is sometimes used in the sense of such an ideal instead of in the sense of actual income; and we shall follow this usage so far as to call such an ideal by the name of "standard income." What we insist on is that such standard income is not, and must not be confused with, the actual income which a man receives from his capital. It is simply the income which he *would* receive if he chose to keep his capital unimpaired and unincreased. If a man has his capital invested in the form of a house which yields him rent, this actual rent, less any actual expenses for repairs, taxes, etc., is his income from that house, even though the house may be depreciating in value. The ideal or standard income which the house might yield without depreciation will be somewhat lower than this actual income, the difference being what is called amortization.

This is not the place to discuss amortization and the relations subsisting between standard and real income. These topics will be fully discussed in Chapter XIV. We are at present concerned with actual, not ideal, income; so

---

[1] This specification is characteristic of Hermann, Schmoller, and many others. See Kleinwächter, *Das Einkommen und seine Verteilung*, pp. 22–23.

far as popular usage goes, it gives its sanction to the use of the term "income" in the one sense quite as much as in the other, though usually with very little intelligent discrimination between the two. For instance, a life annuity from an insurance company, or a pension from a government, is universally recognized as "income." Yet this income trenches on the capital which produces it, eating it up year by year until, at the end of its allotted period, it is entirely exhausted. Let us suppose that the annuity is one of $1000 a year for twenty years. Reckoning interest at five per cent, such an annuity is worth, by the actuaries' tables, $12,462. That is, the annuitant could sell his annuity, on a five per cent basis, for $12,462 in ready money. But this $12,462 invested at five per cent would bring in, without impairing the principal, not $1000 a year, but only $623.10. If then he actually gets $1000 he is trenching on his capital the first year to the extent of $376.90. Yet we regard him, and very properly too, as having a true *income* of $1000 a year.

If it were true that income could never trench on capital, we could not reckon a laboring man's wages as income without first deducting a premium or sinking fund sufficient to provide for the continuance of this income after the destruction by death of the laborer. If the annuitant or laborer should *actually* set aside such an annual sum as to maintain the capital value of his property unimpaired, we should be quite justified in considering the net sum, and not the gross sum, as income. The $1000 annuitant who pays $376.90 annually into a sinking fund is getting only $623.10 annually, not $1000, for an income, and the laboring man who pays an insurance premium reduces his income by that amount. It surely makes a difference whether these "sinking funds" or "premiums" are actually set aside or merely reckoned. To reckon what one *ought* to save in order to maintain capital is not to save it, and a definition of income which depends upon an ideal reckoning instead of a real payment is to that extent inadequate.

§ 6

We have now seen how the fatal inclusion of concrete wealth by the side of abstract services as a part of income has led economists into two errors, — one the confusion of capital with income, and the other the fallacy of double counting. We now proceed to consider the other mistake in the ordinary concept of real income, namely, that due to the needless restriction introduced by the term "enjoyable." Real income, we were told, consists of "enjoyable commodities and services." We have thus far succeeded in eliminating "commodities" from this formula; we now proceed to show that we may also eliminate "enjoyable," and leave the very simple formula: Income consists of *services*.

It is quite true that when we put together all the elements which go to make up the total income of a community or of an individual, and deduct all the negative elements, or outgoes, we shall find that there are *then* left solely enjoyable services. But the various elements which are thus combined — the income from factories, mines, farms, and other instruments or groups of instruments — do *not* all consist of enjoyable services. Most of them consist of intermediate services preparatory to enjoyable services. How these intermediate services cancel themselves out in the final summation will form the subject of a future chapter. At present we are merely concerned in pointing out that any adequate concept of income must leave room for these intermediate services, *i.e.* for the income rendered by a factory or a bank as well as that yielded by a dwelling or a pleasure yacht. We have already had occasion to note the inadequacy of that concept of income which restricts it to the yielding of money; we now need to observe the inadequacy of that concept which goes to the opposite extreme and leaves money income out of account altogether. Having found "money income" insufficient for their purposes, economists have conceived of "real income." But by making real income consist of "enjoyable" elements, they have excluded money income altogether. Some of them more or less avowedly retain both concepts, but they do not show how to coördinate them nor how to include them both under a more general income-concept. In their minds the two seem to stand totally disconnected, except that, in a partial and incomplete way, real income is thought of as that for which money income is spent.

§ 7

The ordinary concepts of income fail to conform to any consistent scheme whatever. In consequence, among other needless distinctions, are those which have been drawn between social and individual income.

Social income has usually been conceived as the "net product" of society, — not in the sense of the net difference between services and disservices, but in a sense which includes commodities. No consistent method of reckoning this net product has been furnished. It is clear that we cannot include all products. Some are only too evidently new capital, such as newly constructed railways, steamships, tunnels, bridges, and buildings and would not be included by most persons in social income. Others must certainly be omitted to avoid duplication in our reckoning. If we were to include the wheat crop of the farmer, the flour of the miller, and the bread of the baker, we would be counting the same thing three times over, — once for each of three successive processes. Some economists have sought to avoid this repetition, either by excluding the production and consumption of raw materials, or, if these are included, by not including the whole value of the finished product, but only the increment of value over that of the raw materials.

"We must be careful not to count the same thing twice. If we have counted a carpet at its full value, we have already counted the values of the yarn and the labour that were used in making it; and these must not be counted again. But if the carpet is cleaned by domestic servants or at steam scouring works, the value of the labour spent in cleaning it must be counted separately; for otherwise the results of this labour would be altogether omitted from the inventory of those newly-produced commodities and conveniences which constitute the real income of the country."[1]

These reservations are entirely correct; but they furnish no general means of avoiding double counting. For instance, are fuel and labor to be deducted in the same way as raw materials? Some writers have gone so far as to claim that, just as the cost of feeding work animals must be deducted from the value of the work they do, so the cost of supporting laborers must be deducted from the value of their product.[2] If this view were correct, it would seem that the laborer could not share at all in the distribution of the social income, since all that comes to him is deducted!

A similar question as to deductions arises in the oft-cited case where one profession is more disagreeable or irksome than another. Should any deduction be made from the income of the hangman, for instance, to equalize his net income with the net income of a more desirable calling?

When social income is called "net product," the same question arises which was met with in the case of individual income, viz., whether by "product" is meant concrete wealth, or services, or both. In our own theory, "services" are taken, but the usual concepts adopt wealth, or both wealth and services. According to them, part of the income of society consists of new wealth, such as factories, sihps, and dwellings, while the services of these new creations

[1] Marshall, *Principles of Economics*, Vol. I, p. 150.
[2] *E.g.* "Report of Committee on a Common Measure of Value in Direct Taxation," *Report of British Association for Advancement of Science*, 1878, p. 220.

figure as income in future years. We have already observed that to count a new dwelling or piano as income this year, and its use as income in succeeding years, is a species of double counting as well as a confusion of capital and income. Both of these errors are repeated in any concept of social income which includes at once additions to the world's wealth, and the income which this very wealth subsequently yields.

§ 8

When a wrong road is once taken, it almost inevitably happens that it leads those who follow it further and further astray. Economists, having selected a wrong idea of income to start with, naturally found it so ill suited to their purposes that, in each problem to which they attempted to apply it, some special interpretation or amendment became necessary, until, instead of one concept, they became possessed of a miscellaneous assortment[1] of concepts! They have been compelled not only to dissociate money-income and real-income, but also to dissociate the income of the individual and the income of society. When it is understood that the entire and only contribution to the income stream which any given instrument of capital can make consists in the services which that instrument renders, it will be found that all subsidiary meanings of income are simply incomes from particular instruments or groups of instruments. If the instrument in question is a private carriage, the services which it brings forth, as events desirable to its owner, are the acts of conveying him from one place to another. These are primary or *natural*-income. If the instrument is a public carriage, the services which it brings forth, as events desirable to its owner, are the payments of fares. These are *money*-income.[2] If the group of

[1] The reader who cares to study them in detail will find a collection of definitions in the Appendix to Chapter VII.

[2] It should be borne in mind that the income is not the money itself, which is a concrete *commodity*, but the *bringing in* of the money, which is an abstract *service*.

instruments is the entire group of instruments constituting the entire capital of a community, the net total of their services and disservices is the entire income of the community. This is *social* income. If the group be the entire property of an individual — the rights which he owns, complete or partial, in instruments — the net total of the services and disservices to which he is thus entitled constitutes his income. This is *individual* income.

In science, the chief test of a definition is its adaptability to analysis. Judged by this test, none of the current concepts of income which we have passed in review can claim to be adequate; for we have found them subject to the confusions of capital and income, and of double counting. A secondary test is that a working definition should also fit into, or rather, give clear and consistent outlines to the vague notions of income which we find ready made in the actual world of business and accounts.

Of our own concept of income, as consisting exclusively of services, we shall endeavor to show that it includes the commercial bookkeeper's concept of "money income"; that it is coextensive with the popular notions of income, including what those notions include and excluding what they exclude; that it affords a place for the usage by which sinking funds are reckoned and justifies the phrase "living beyond income"; that it avoids double counting automatically and without the necessity for the exercise of judgment in each special case; that it makes capital and income strictly correlative but never in danger of being confused; and last, but not least, that it lends itself readily to economic analysis and serves as a foundation for the theory of interest.

The concept of income to be elaborated is similar to several which have been put forward by other writers. It is almost identical with that of Edwin Cannan;[1] it

---

[1] See *History of the Theory of Production and Distribution; Elementary Political Economy;* and "What is Capital?" *Economic Journal,* 1897.

also harmonizes with what Professor Marshall [1] calls the "usance" of wealth, and with the psychological concepts of income in President Hadley's *Economics*,[2] in Professor Flux's *Economic Principles*,[3] and in Professor Fetter's *Principles of Economics*.[4] Finally, it harmonizes more closely than at first glance might be supposed, with the etymological and popular meaning of income. Income from any source is what comes in from that source. The income from any capital is what that capital brings in to its owner, no matter what may be the form of benefit brought in. If the capital serves to bring in money, the income is "money-income." If it serves to bring in crops or products, as does a self-supporting farm, the income is of another form. If it serves to bring in enjoyable comforts, as does a dwelling house, the income is of a still different form. But in all cases, the essential fact is that the capital performs service, — accomplishes something desired.

As this usage makes income include all money-income, it cannot be maintained that it conflicts with commercial usage. It may be objected by the unreflecting that by including non-monetary elements it includes too much; but many — often all — of the non-monetary benefits conferred by capital are recognized as income by economists, as well as by such men of affairs as have studied the subject with care. A business man who had bought a yacht remarked: "It's a good investment, and I get my dividends every Saturday afternoon when I take a sail in it." And the writer has never had any difficulty in persuading other business men of the propriety of such usage. In fact, without an enjoyable use in prospect, money-income itself would have no existence or meaning. A house could

---

[1] See *Principles of Economics*, 3d ed. (Macmillan), Vol. I, p. 156. A part of this passage is quoted in Appendix to Chap. VII. See also Carver's *Distribution of Wealth* (New York, Macmillan, 1904), p. 123.
[2] Chap. I.   [3] p. 17.   [4] pp. 43, 571.

never command a money rent to the landlord if it did not also yield shelter to the tenant, and even from the standpoint of the landlord the receipt of the money only intervenes as a medium for payment of his own rent and other expenses of living, in other words for securing *his enjoyable* income.

Income is, then, a very general concept. It consists of services rendered by capital. We have seen that under it are included several special concepts: *Social income, individual income, money income, natural income,* and *enjoyable income.* We shall soon see that the *net* income of society or of an individual consists wholly of enjoyable income. This is because the non-enjoyable elements of income, such, for example, as money-income, are all exactly offset by equal items of outgo. But the non-enjoyable elements are none the less a part in the grand total, and, in fact, by far the greater part. The money-income of ordinary bookkeeping forms the bulk of any true inventory of income; but its significance cannot be understood until its counterpart in *outgo* is also taken into account, nor until, in fact, a complete picture of *all* elements of income is brought before the mind's eye. To present this picture will be the object of the next three chapters.

CHAPTER VIII

INCOME ACCOUNTS

§ 1

THE income of our capital, then, is simply that which it does for us. Whether it brings us money or other return does not matter; the flow of its *services* is its income. These services of wealth, as was previously explained, consist of any desirable events which occur by means of that wealth or any undesirable events prevented.

Services exist in infinite variety. All work done by human beings, all the operations of industry, all the transactions of commerce, are services, and enter into income accounts. A bird's-eye view of this busy planet would reveal wealth — real estate, commodities, and human beings, — ceaselessly at work performing services. Land, men, and implements are changing land, seed, and live stock into grain, beef, lumber, and steel. Manufacturing plants are converting raw materials into flour, furniture, cloth, and implements. In domestic establishments we find the services of cooking, warming, cleaning, and sheltering. Agriculture, mining, transportation, and commerce are simply names that we give to the group of services performed by farm, mine, railroad, and business capital.

A *disservice* is a negative service. It is an undesirable event occasioned, or a desirable one prevented, by means of an article of wealth. A flow of disservices or negative income is called *outgo*. It does not matter whether the outgo occasioned by an article consists in depriving the owner of money or in some other evil. If the outgo is in monetary form it is called *expense;* if it is in the form of human exertion it is called *labor.* It includes all of what economists have called *cost, i.e.* labor, trouble, expense, and sacrifices of all kinds.

An instrument very seldom yields services without involving some disservices. A dwelling house, for instance, not only gives off services called shelter, but also occasions disservices in the form of labor (or expense) for renewals, painting, cleaning, caretaking, insurance, and taxes. Any disagreeable event occasioned by that house is a disservice, just as any agreeable event is a service. Again, while a saddle horse performs services in giving its owner a daily ride, it performs disservices in being stabled, fed, and shod. A farmer gets services out of his land when it yields him crops; but to get these services he has to put fertilizer, seed, labor, and expense into that land. A railway performs a vast service of transportation, hauling passengers and commodities, but it requires a prodigious amount of coal, supplies, and labor to keep it going.

Disservices are not essential to the idea of wealth; an article of wealth sometimes offers services without any disservices. When disservices exist they are usually overbalanced, in the estimation of the owner, by prospective services. As soon as the disservices of an article of wealth preponderate, in the estmation of its owner, over the services, it is regarded as "more trouble than it is worth," is cast aside and ceases to be wealth. In the meantime such articles, if regarded as owned at all, constitute a sort of wealth of negative utility, — Jevons calls them "discommodities." They are never of great importance and need receive no special attention. The chief examples of such articles are garbage, ashes, sewage, carrion, rubbish, and waste.

It has already been observed that services and disservices, like wealth, are measured in two ways — in quantity and value — and that the quantity of each service is measured in its own special unit. The quantity of the services of a gardener is often measured by the number of hours he works; the services of a windmill, by the number of gallons of water pumped. Quantities of services (or disservices) are thus, like instruments of wealth, very heterogeneous and are incapable of being combined in a single sum. To obtain a homogeneous mass of value, we must multiply the quantity of services (or disservices) by their several prices.

Income and outgo, then, like capital, are used in two senses: *income-services* (as well as outgo-disservices) and *income-value* (as well as outgo-value). Hereafter, when the terms "income" or "outgo" are used alone, the value sense will be understood.

The value of any individual service or disservice constitutes an *element* of income or outgo. The value of all the services flowing from an article of wealth through any period, that is, the sum of all the elements of income, is called its *gross* income. The excess of the gross income over the outgo, in other words, the algebraic or net sum of all elements of income and outgo, is the *net income*. If, instead of an excess, there is a deficiency, it is called *net outgo*. Net income is of far more importance, both in practice and in theory, than gross income. Gross income may often be measured in more than one way, according as the elements of which it is composed are considered with or without accompanying offsets; but the sum called net income will be the same in either case.

§ 2

Income (or outgo) always implies (1) capital as the source, and (2) an owner of capital as the beneficiary. Mr. Smith's income from his farm implies that the farm yields the income and that Mr. Smith receives it. In this book we shall need to consider income chiefly in its relation to the capital yielding it rather than in its relation to the owner receiving it.[1] This twofold aspect of income is expressed in accounts by regarding the farm as "in account with" its owner. All income from it to him is placed on one side of the ledger and is said to be "credited" to the farm, while its outgo is, in like manner, "debited." A credit item, then, signifies income which is yielded by a given capital, and a debit item signifies outgo which it occasions. The terms refer respectively to positive and negative elements in the income and outgo accounts of that capital.

We are now in a position to apply the foregoing definitions to income accounts. We begin by imagining a "house and lot" as an article of wealth or capital, and shall first consider its income and outgo during the period of the calendar year 1900. The income which this capital brings in to its owner may be either a money rental or the services of shelter for himself and family. In either case the income may be *measured* in money, although in the case of occupancy by the owner this measurement requires a special appraisement. We shall suppose that the house was built many years ago and in 1900 is nearly worn out. It yields an income worth $1000 a year. Against this income there are offsets in the form of repairs, taxes, etc.; for these payments are "undesirable events" occasioned by the house and lot. We have, then, the following "income account":

INCOME FOR HOUSE AND LOT DURING YEAR 1900

Income		Outgo	
Use of house and lot	$1000	Repairs	$200
		Taxes	100
		Insurance	100
	$1000		$400

The net income is therefore $600.

[1] The terms income and outgo are somewhat unfortunate, as, etymologically, they suggest the relation to the owner Smith rather than to its source, the farm. Smith's *in*come is the farm's "*out*come" or "yield" (in German, *ertrag*). Similarly, when the farmer

Next year we may suppose that the house is found to have rotted beams, is condemned, and must be abandoned or torn down. Its services are ended, but the land is still good and the owner can build a new house. This operation consumes, let us say, the first six months of the year 1901, so that during that period there is no income, but only outgo. During the second half of the year the house is occupied and its use is valued at $600. In the first six months not only did the "house and lot" fail to yield any income, but on the contrary occasioned an expense. The *cost of production* of the house was a disservice; for this was an "undesirable event" occasioned by the house and lot. It was withstood only for the sake of future services which it would bring in its wake. It was not itself a desirable event. When we say, then, that any event is undesirable, we make abstraction of future compensations. All disservices are "necessary evils"; they lead to good, but are themselves evils.

We have, then, the following account: —

Income for House and Lot during Year 1901

Income		*Outgo*	
Use of house and lot (six months)	$600	Expense of building house	$10,000
		Taxes	100
	$600		$10,100

During this year, then, the house yields a net outgo of $9500. This adverse balance will be more than made up in the years which follow. For the year 1902 we may have the following: —

puts fertilizers on his land, this, his *outgo*, is the farm's *ingo*. But, although we shall be largely concerned with income and outgo in relation to capital as their source, and might therefore logically employ the terms outcome and ingo, it seems preferable, for reasons of usage, to retain the usual terms, income and outgo.

Income for House and Lot during Year 1902

	Income		Outgo
Use	$1200	Repairs	$ 50
		Taxes	150
	$1200		$200
Net income	$1000		

Let us suppose that these figures remain about the same for forty-nine years, and give $50,000 net income during that time, which cancels the excess in cost for 1901 of $9500 and leaves a large margin besides, the nature of which, as interest, need not here be considered. Then a second time the house is worn out and has to be rebuilt. The same cycle is repeated, one year of excess of cost being offset by forty-nine years of excess of income.

§ 3

It will be observed that the cost of reconstructing the house was entered in the accounts in exactly the same way as repairs or other "current" costs. There may seem to be objection to such a proceeding in the thought that reconstruction appears to be not a part of "running expense" but a "capital cost," and belongs, not to income accounts, but to capital accounts. It is true that the *value of the new house* must be entered on the capital balance sheet, but the *cost of producing it* belongs properly to income accounts. The former represents *wealth;* the latter represents *disservices*. The former relates to an instant of time (which may be any instant from the time it is begun till the time when it ceases to exist); the latter relates to a *period* of time (which may be all or any part of the time during which the labor and other sacrifices occasioned by the house occur). A house is quite distinct from the series of sacrifices by which it was fashioned. The confusion between the two is natural in view of the practice of bookkeepers in often entering capital at its "cost value." In fact it is sometimes said that "liabilities represent money received by a company, and assets, how it has been expended." But this is not strictly true. Since its market value depends on its suitability to the uses to which it is put, not on the money sunk in its construction, the house on which was expended $10,000 for construction may be worth more or less than $10,000. In this case the income account should contain $10,000 on the outgo side, and the capital account should contain a larger or smaller figure.[1]

And yet it is undoubtedly true that we instinctively object to entering the cost of building the house in its income-and-outgo account; and we express this objection by calling this cost a "capital cost," rather than a part of running expenses. By so classing it we mean that it does not recur, or, at any rate, only at long intervals. On this basis Wagner and others have erroneously claimed that income and outgo should be confined to "regular" items. At first glance this seems feasible because, in actual practice, an extraordinary expense in a given year, like the cost of constructing a house, does not usually reduce the owner's net income for that year by that amount. He will generally contrive to avoid such a result by offsetting the extraordinary expense of the house by a correspondingly extraordinary income from some other source, such as a depreciation fund. It is evident that the house owner

[1] Even in the normal case the value of the house, as is well known, is not exactly equal to the cost expended in construction, but to that amount *plus interest*. A house which costs $10,000, expended through six months, ought to be worth a few hundred dollars more than this sum at the time of completion; otherwise the man who expended those $10,000, and at completion has only $10,000 worth of house to show for it, has evidently received no interest on his money. The relation between the value of capital, and its cost, and interest, will form a subject to be taken up in a later chapter, where the common error that accrued, but unpaid, interest is itself a cost will also be discussed.

who has had the foresight to set aside annually throughout the period of existence of the house a small deposit in a savings bank, may derive therefrom, when the time for rebuilding arrives, a large sum of money, the receipt of which is just as properly an element of income as its expenditure for rebuilding is an element of outgo. The great *outgo* for rebuilding is then offset by a great *income* from the savings bank account, so that the *combined* net income from the two sources — depreciation fund and house — will be approximately zero and the total net income of the individual will be affected little or not at all. The depreciation fund, therefore, does not prevent, but merely offsets the large negative balance in the income account from the "house and lot" considered by itself. The combined income from the *two* sources taken together will be negligible, but that from the *one* source, the "house and lot," will fluctuate. In figures, from this single source, the net income is evidently $+\$1000$ a year for each of forty-nine years, and $-\$9500$ for the fiftieth year. It is misleading to say that the $1000 is "gross" income from which must be deducted the depreciation fund or "amortization" supposed to be laid aside each year against the cost of rebuilding. Merely to *suppose* a depreciation fund is not to have one. It is quite true that the $1000 income which the house yields during each of forty-nine years is more than the income which would have been left after an annual payment into a depreciation fund had actually been made; but an income which simply might have been is only an *ideal* standard. Confusing the actual and the ideal is one of the commonest fallacies in this field. The *actual* net income of the house and lot is alone the object of our present study, and this actual income, in the example we are supposing, is $1000 each year for forty-nine years. While this sum is in excess of the ideal standard income during each of these forty-nine years, this overplus is atoned for by the sudden and large deficiency every fiftieth year.

§ 4

Such irregularity of income may be avoided, not only by a depreciation fund, but by other devices, for instance, by paying for the house in installments, by borrowing money to defray cost and mortgaging the house, or by selling other property. Another method of steadying income — and one which ought to set at rest any remaining qualms which the reader may feel at the procedure, which has been adopted, of entering cost of new construction under "outgo" — applies when the same owner possesses so many of the articles in question that the reconstruction of one or another of them must occur at short intervals. Consider, for instance, the case of a building and loan association which has fifty houses, each built in a different year and each of which lasts fifty years, so that the houses have to be rebuilt at the rate of one every year. In the accounts of such an association the expense side should include the cost of new construction as a regular annual item, thus: —

BUILDING AND LOAN ASSOCIATION

Fifty houses (with land) 1900

Income		Outgo	
Rents of 49 houses at $1000 a year	$49,000	Construction of one new house	$10,000
Rent of one house for part of the year in which it is constructed	500	Repairs on 49 houses	4,900
		Taxes	5,000
	$49,500		$19,900

Net income $29,600

We have here a net annual income of $29,600, which continues year after year without interruption. The irregularity of income which we found in the case of a single house ceases when the larger number is taken. But if it is proper to regard the cost of reconstructing the houses as outgo in the case of a large number of houses, it must be equally proper to regard it as outgo in the case of each single house; for the income account of the total mass of the community's capital is simply the combined accounts of the individual elements. We cannot consistently do otherwise than regard all costs, whether recurrent or not, as outgo.

In actual business there are usually many articles of the same kind, so that it is seldom necessary to reckon the net income from each individual article. Such articles may be conveniently lumped together. This we have just seen in the case of the houses of the loan association. As another example we may take the stock-in-trade of a merchant. This stock yields him income, not, as in the case of the house, by rent, but by sale; the difference between rent and sale being simply that rent consists of a series of contributions to income, whereas sale consists only of one. A stock of stoves, just as a stock of houses, yields income which is the sum of the net incomes from its individual constituents. But the stove dealer would find the bookkeeping very troublesome were he to reckon in a separate account the net income from each individual stove which he buys and sells. He reaches the same final result for his stock as a whole (or rather, for each specific category of articles in his stock) by taking from his gross receipts obtained by selling stoves the year's cost of replenishing his stock, the rent of his warehouse, salaries of clerks, and other outgo. Were he to arrive at this result by applying the same process to each individual stove, the individual results would, of course, vary widely; for a stove left over from last year (and therefore free from any item of cost in this year's accounts), if sold this year, would give a large net income, while another stove, bought this year, but not sold until next, would only have debit items in this year's account. But the sum of these irregular incomes from individual parts of the merchant's stock will give a steady income for the whole.

Any merchant's stock that rapidly changes the individual elements of which it is constituted is most conveniently treated as a whole. To use Professor Clark's admirable simile, it is like Niagara Falls, which remains a waterfall, although consisting each day of entirely different drops of water. The stock of a butcher, grocer, or fruiterer consists of rapidly changing elements, but remains as a whole relatively unchanged. Though it would be logically sound, it would be foolish and impracticable to keep an income and outgo account for each individual leg of mutton or box of figs. The tendency to-day, however, is distinctly toward a more detailed accounting. Some business firms, by means of modern card indices, keep a careful record for each separate *variety* of commodity dealt with, if not for each individual article in that variety. The important thing to observe is that the net income of the entire group is simply the difference between the sums of the incomes and outgoes of the elementary units which constitute that group. The very item which, for the elementary unit, constitutes "capital" cost, and which, for that unit, occurs but once, becomes, for the group, the regular cost of replenishing, and recurs annually. From the explanations and illustrations which have been given, it is clear that consistency and logic must assign to every cost, whether large or small, regular or irregular, a place as an element of outgo in the income-and-outgo accounts.

§ 5

Whether or not the irregularities of income from individual articles of wealth are smoothed away in the total, the combined income, even from a large group of articles, is not necessarily an absolutely steady flow. We usually strive to make it so to some extent; but we do not always succeed, nor do we even always try. When income does vary, the method of measuring which has been given will unerringly register that variation automatically. The method is not, of course, restricted to a group of articles of the same kind, like the fifty houses of the building and loan association or the stock of stoves of the stove dealer. It applies to any stock of miscellaneous articles, and even to the entire stock of wealth of a community or the world. The net income from any such group is simply the sum of the net incomes of the various articles of wealth in existence at all the points of time within the period for which that income is reckoned.

In like manner may be obtained the income from any collection of *property rights* as capital. This application of income-and-outgo accounts occurs especially in the case of an individual. For we then find that the sources of income consist largely, not of capital-wealth, but of capital-property, — partial rights to wealth, such as bonds, stocks, and mortgages. But the introduction of the idea of property as distinct from that of wealth involves no new difficulties; for we have seen that property is only another aspect of wealth, and represents simply rights to some of the services of wealth. Thus in respect to partnership rights, each partner in the firm of Smith & Jones, farmers, receives half the income of the *farm*. The same principle applies in respect to shares, bonds, or other forms of property. Business men are accustomed to say that a railway bond yields or earns so much income. But this merely means that the *railway* behind this bond yields income, a specified share of which belongs to the bondholder. Thus the true source of the services which flow to the property holder is the concrete wealth; his property-right merely specifies such portion of those services as are his. The income of a stockholder, for instance, consists of all the benefits he receives from being a stockholder, less all the sacrifices. Usually, for him, both benefits and sacrifices accrue in monetary form. His income from his stock is usually the receipt of dividends.

The total net income of a person is, then, the sum of

the net incomes from each individual article of property which he holds within the time interval considered.

§ 6

To illustrate this, let us consider the case of a lawyer living in a rented house, but owning the furniture. We shall assume, for simplicity, that his property is grouped under the following nine heads: (1) stocks and bonds, (2) lease of house (including not only the privilege of occupancy but also the obligation to pay rent), (3) furniture of house, (4) other household supplies, especially food, (5) money and bank account, (6) claim on servants (including not only the claim on their work but also the obligation to pay wages), (7) like claims on, coupled with obligations from, office clerks, (8) his own person, (9) "etc." We shall take, as the time interval, a period of a month.

During the month, the stocks and bonds bring in checks aggregating $2,000 and the lawyer buys new securities to the extent of $500. His total net income, therefore, during this particular month from this particular group of property rights is $1500. Under his lease he enjoys a month's use of a house, this use being regarded by him as worth, let us say, exactly what it costs, or $100 a month. Since the lease yields him $100 worth of shelter and costs him $100 in money, it leaves no net income. His furniture yields him comfort worth $50, from which cost of repairs, etc., amounting to $30, has to be deducted, leaving a balance of $20. His stock of food and similar supplies yields him the board of himself and family for the month, worth $150; but the cost of replenishing this stock and the services of cook and waitress in preparing and serving it absorb, let us say, all of this sum, leaving for the month no net income from the pantry's stock.

The next source of income (or outgo) is "cash." By this is meant the stock of property which includes money on hand and money on deposit in bank. To find how much income or outgo comes from "cash" we need only follow the well-established usage of bookkeepers which regards a stock of cash as though it were a gold mine which, consequently, is to be *credited* with all the gold or cash which comes *out* of it, and *debited* with all that goes *into* it. This usage often puzzles the novice, but its correctness is undoubted and it harmonizes with our definition of services and disservices. For the services or desirable events which come from one's stock of cash — the events, in fact, for the sake of which that stock of cash exists — are the furnishing of money from time to time; the disservices, or the undesirable events occasioned by that stock of cash, are the absorption by it of money from time to time. In other words, my purse *serves* me whenever it pays my bills; it *costs* me whenever I, so to speak, pay its bills. In this respect it is precisely similar to any other stock of wealth. A bin of coal *serves* its owner when it renders him fuel; it *costs* him when it has to be filled. The cost may be the sacrifice of money, of labor, or of coal taken from some other store of coal. In the case before us, the income from "cash," or all the payments the lawyer takes out of his pocket-book or check book, amounts, let us say, to $3780, whereas the outgo to "cash" — all sums paid to it — amounts to $4000, leaving $220 as a net outgo.

The claim on the servants, like the lease of the house, involves an obligation to pay as well as a right to receive. We shall suppose that the servants render services during the month worth $100, and also cost $100 in wages, leaving no net balance. Similarly the office clerks cost $500 in wages and yield $500 worth of assistance to the lawyer in the preparation of his cases.

The man himself receives from his practice during the month $2000. But his office and professional expenses amount to $500 and leave a balance of $1500. The class called "etc." comprises all sources of income not otherwise included, such as clothing, watches, jewelry, and other articles of wealth or property not contained in the other categories. For simplicity we shall suppose that the income and outgo connected with "etc." are equal to each other, and amount to $2500.

The total income of this man is therefore as follows: —

Income		Outgo		Net Income
				Profit and Loss
By stocks and bonds (money)	$2000	To stocks and bonds (money)	$ 500	+ $1500
By lease right (shelter)	100	To lease right (money)	100	00
By furniture (use)	50	To furniture (money)	30	+ 20
		To food (money (50) and work of servants (100)		
By food (use)	150	ants (100)	150	00
By "cash" (money)	3780	To "cash" (money)	4000	− 220
By servants (services)	100	To servants (money)	100	00
By clerks (personal assistance)	500	To clerks (money)	500	00
		To self (assistance of clerks) (money)	500	+ 1500
By self (money)	2000			
By "etc." (direct uses)	2500	To "etc." (money)	2500	00
		Total net income		+$2800

These accounts may be simplified in various ways, and without any sacrifice of logical completeness. If we are interested only in the total net income, and not in the share which each item of property contributes to this total, we may omit several items which in the above accounting stand on both sides. For instance, the cooking and serving food was debited to the stock of food and credited to the servants. At first sight it may appear that the wages of cook and waitress are entered as debit both to "servants" and to "food" and that double counting has occurred. But the debit to food was not servants' wages but servants' *work*.

A little consideration will show that if we credit the servants with the services of cooking and waiting, and debit them with wages as a distinct item, we must debit the food with their services of cooking and waiting. If we prefer to drop out these services both from the credit side of the servants' account and the debit side of the food account, we are then at liberty to omit the category of servants entirely, and to leave only the charge of their wages against the food. There are endless admissible modifications of the accounting here described, many of which have practical advantages, but the preceding is presented as a complete and detailed record of all income and outgo arranged by sources.

§ 7

In complete accounting we must not omit the negative items of property, or liabilities. The same principles apply here as for positive items, or assets. Items which are negative are such because they yield negative income, or outgo. If the lawyer whose accounts we have followed is in debt, the payments on his debt (whether "interest" or "principal") which he makes during the time-interval considered are outgo. On the other hand, if a debt is contracted during the time-interval considered, its proceeds are for that period an addition to gross income.

Thus an income-and-outgo account may always be completely formed by recording the values of the services and disservices occasioned by all the articles of capital under consideration. In the case of an individual these articles of capital are his assets and his liabilities. No other items than the services and disservices mentioned can properly find a place in the accounts. We have already warned the reader against the fallacy of deducting from income any depletion of capital; he should also be warned against the opposite fallacy of adding to income any savings of capital. This fallacy is so common and so subtle that its discussion will be postponed to Chapter XIV, where it may receive the attention it deserves. We content ourselves at present with a preliminary illustration. A savings bank depositor is sometimes thought to draw income from his deposit when the interest "accumulates." This is an error. He draws income when, and only when, he draws money out of the bank; he suffers outgo when, and only when, he puts money into it. If he merely lets his deposit accumulate, he derives no income and suffers no outgo. There is no effect on income. What does occur is increase of capital. He cannot have his cake and eat it too. If we make the fiction that the man who allows his savings to accumulate virtually receives the interest, we must, to be consistent, also make the fiction that he redeposits it. If the teller hands over the interest across the counter, the depositor's account certainly yields up "income" to him, but if he hands it back it must, in consistency, be charged as "outgo," and the net result on his income is simply a cancellation. This procedure reveals clearly the fact that the accumulation is not income.

§ 8

The method of accounting employed in the preceding lawyer's account is, of course, not the only, nor is it the usual, method. It is the method, however, which shows the shares of the total income attributable to each individual source. In practice, the minor sources of income are neglected. The income and outgo of one's "cash" almost balance in the long run, and the same is true of the lease, the servants' contracts, and the household supplies. One's furniture probably yields a larger net income than is commonly realized, but even this is usually a small element in the total. It is only in case the lawyer lives in his own house that a serious correction would need to be made on this account. In this case, his shelter is not offset by any rent payment, and enters the accounts as pure income.

Practically, therefore, the lawyer's income is obtained by taking from the above table only the two principal items, the income from investments and the income from his professional work. Each of these is $1500, so that according to this approximate accounting the net income is $3000. Another and more common method of approximating an income account is to record simply *money* receipts and disbursements, in other words, to record only the items of the preceding account under "cash." The lawyer's cash account book would present an appearance like the following: —

Receipts		*Disbursements*	
From stocks and bonds	$2000	Investments, in stocks and bonds	$ 500
From personal labor	2000	Rent	100
		Furniture repairs	30
		Cost of food	50
		Servants	100
		Clerk hire	500
		"Etc."	2500
	$4000		$3780

This leaves a cash balance of $220, which is to be added, at the end of the month, to the cash on hand at the beginning. This *balance* does not here indicate the net income of the lawyer, as did the balance in the completer accounting which preceded. The net income of the lawyer, in the incomplete and makeshift accounting now under consideration, is, so far as it is represented at all, shown in the *total* cash receipts less certain makeshift corrections. The justification of such accounting, so far as any exists, is that most income, from whatever source, passes through the cash drawer.

It will be noticed that the receipts side of the above account, $4000, greatly exceeds the true net income, $2800, shown in the previous accounting. Instinctively any one using such mere money accounting feels the need of making *some* deductions from the total money receipts. He also instinctively feels that not all of the disbursements should be thus deducted; otherwise little or nothing would remain. The ordinary makeshift is to deduct the "business expenses," — the $500 invested in stocks and bonds and the $500 for clerk hire. The remainder will then be $3000, which is, for practical purposes, a sufficiently close approximation to the true net income of $2800.

Practically, therefore, either money receipts (less "business" expenses) or the sum of the net incomes from securities and labor, are good makeshifts for true income. But even from a practical point of view they will not always serve, while as a matter of strict theory they are always wrong. They could be right only under the condition that *all* income, from whatever source, flowed through the cash drawer. If it were true that the net income from stocks and bonds, the net income from the lawyer's practice, and, in like manner, the net income from every other source flowed into the cash drawer, while, on the other hand, the flow out of that drawer consisted exclusively of expenditures for each and every satisfaction as it occurred, then the flow of money through the cash drawer would serve as a true measure of income, and the cash drawer might be called a sort of income *meter*. The flow into it would be money income and the eventual satisfactions obtained from it would be real income. The two would then also have the relation usually ascribed to them by economists. This case is practically realized in the case of a *rentier*, who simply receives money from investments and spends it for immediate satisfactions, renting, let us say, not only a dwelling but its furniture as well, so that practically no part of his income can reach him except by passing through the money stage. But few people are in exactly this position, so that not all income passes through the meter. Some passes around it, as, for instance, the shelter derived from a man's own house or the comforts from his own furniture, and hence will not be registered by the meter at all. On the other hand, some passes through it not toward direct satisfactions but toward some "business" expenditure likely later on to repour cash through the money meter and hence to cause it to register too much. Thus it happens that the money meter sometimes fails to register and sometimes registers twice. It is therefore only a rough and imperfect instrument for measuring net income.

§ 9

When we turn from real to fictitious persons, we find, for income accounts, as for capital accounts, that the two sides necessarily balance exactly. A corporation, as an entity distinct from its stockholders, cannot enjoy income or suffer outgo. All the income not devoted to other expenses is absorbed in paying dividends. A railway company, for instance, has an income account as follows:—

INCOME ACCOUNT OF RAILROAD CORPORATION FOR YEAR

Income		Outgo	
By passenger and freight service	$1,246,147	To operating expenses	$800,000
		To interest to bondholders	100,000
		To dividends to stockholders	200,000
		To surplus applied to (1) purchase of land	140,000
		(2) cash in treasury	6,147
	$1,246,147		$1,246,147

In these accounts we see that the gross income from all sources was $1,246,147, of which $800,000 disappeared for running expenses, $100,000 for paying bondholders, and $200,000 for paying stockholders, leaving a balancing item of $146,147. But this balance is likewise expended, $140,000 of it being outgo for new land, and the small odd sum

$6147 being put into the safes of the company or deposited in bank. Even this last operation is a true outgo; for a cash drawer and a bank account are, as we have seen, always debited with what is put into them. There remains, therefore, no final balance for the abstraction called the "company." Just as, in the capital accounts, the company's excess of assets over liabilities to other than stockholders constitutes the true liability to the stockholders themselves, so, in income accounts, any excess of income over outgo to other purposes than dividends paid to stockholders constitutes a true outgo for the benefit of those stockholders.

§ 10

We see, then, that the guiding principle for the construction of the income account, either of real or fictitious persons, is simply to make a complete list of the services and disservices which flow from each and every item of the assets and liabilities. This simple relation between capital and income accounts is commonly obscured by the fact that it is not practically convenient to include in one's *capital* accounts certain items of assets and liabilities, although their services and disservices are entered in the *income* account. This is true, in particular, of one's own person, and such claims as are coupled with equal obligations, as leases and contracts with laborers. These are not and, from a purely practical point of view, ought not to be entered in the capital account; but much of the income and outgo from them, such as wages and rent, are entered in the income account. In respect of income accounts the use of one's dwelling is omitted, as well as the unpaid-for services and disservices of human beings. A shopkeeper usually keeps a punctilious record of the work of his employees, but seldom any of his own personal work. If he owns the building he occupies, he will not usually include its use in his accounts. In private life he seldom or never includes in his accounts the use of furniture.

Our present object, however, is to show, not the methods of practical bookkeeping, but merely the application of economic principles to such bookkeeping. The chief object is to find the philosophical basis of accounting. Careful examination shows that accounting is at bottom not a mere makeshift but a complete, consistent, and logical system. When thus conceived and understood it will be seen to be of importance, not alone to the accountant but also to the economist. For his purposes, the only method of constructing income and outgo accounts which is philosophically correct, and which can serve as a basis for economic analysis, is the method by which are recorded, for each article of capital, the values of all its services and disservices. These services and disservices are of many kinds. Sometimes they consist of money payments, sometimes of productive operations, and sometimes of enjoyable elements. These all enter the accounts on the same footing, but in the next chapter we shall see that after being thus entered, the items may be so combined that all except the enjoyable elements will cancel among themselves.

CHAPTER IX

INCOME SUMMATION

§ 1

We have now seen how to reckon the income of either a real or a fictitious person. By combining the net incomes of all persons, the net income of society may be obtained. As we have seen, fictitious persons have no net income, and would therefore not affect such a method of summation. Another way to obtain the total social income is by adding together the net incomes from each individual article of concrete capital, regardless of its ownership. In such a summation no partial property-rights, such as stocks and bonds, would appear. Instead we would only find actual railways, mills, refineries, and other concrete capital. For instance, the net income earned by the Southern Pacific Railroad, considered as an aggregate of roadbed, terminals, rolling stock, and other existing instruments, would be taken. This would not be the income of the Southern Pacific Railroad *Company*, for, as we have seen, the company, as such, has no net income. Nor would it be the income of the stockholders of the company, for this constitutes only a part of the earnings of the road. Nor would it be exactly the sum of the incomes of the stockholders and bondholders, inasmuch as the company may earn income from other sources than the railroad itself, as, for instance, through leases of other roads and shares held in other companies, none of which income is produced by the railway. It would be simply the difference between the total value of the services of transportation rendered by the railroad and the value of the disservices occasioned by it, whether through cost of operation, repairs, renewals, or betterments.

The two ways of obtaining the total social income which have just been outlined — (1) by summing the net incomes of individual persons as *owners*, and (2) by summing the net incomes from individual articles of wealth as *sources* — may be illustrated by supposing two ledgers to be opened containing the income for a given community, one ledger being devoted to each way. Each page of Ledger No. 1 would be devoted to the income-account of a particular individual, stating in detail, in two columns, the items of income and outgo in the minute manner already shown. In Ledger No. 2 likewise each page would be devoted to the income-account of a particular article of wealth. The first ledger would represent, therefore, the distribution of income among different persons in the community. The summary of such a ledger, arranged according to the magnitude of the incomes, would give us the "distribution curve" of incomes shown by Professor Pareto.[1]

Let us suppose, for the sake of illustration, that the following is such a summary for the United States: —

DISTRIBUTION LEDGER No. 1

	Net Income for 1900
15,000 millionaire families	$ 2,000,000,000
100,000 families, incomes ranging from $10,000 to $50,000	3,000,000,000
1,000,000 families, incomes $1000 to $10,000	5,000,000,000
20,000,000 families below $1000	10,000,000,000
	$20,000,000,000

The second ledger would show the same total income, but distributed according to the source which produced it. We may suppose a summary of Ledger No. 2 to be as follows: —

[1] See his *Cours d'Économie Politique*, Lausanne, 1897, Vol. II, pp. 299–345.

INCOME SUMMATION

Distribution Ledger No. 2

	Net Income for 1900
From land	$ 2,000,000,000
" buildings	2,000,000,000
" railways and tramways	1,000,000,000
" factories	1,000,000,000
" persons	13,000,000,000
" etc.	1,000,000,000
	$20,000,000,000

§ 2

Both these ledgers would be constructed by combining a number of separate net incomes, each one of which was the balance remaining after deducting the outgo from the gross income of the particular group of capital considered. In other words, both ledgers would be constructed — to adopt the phrase which was employed under capital accounts — by the "method of balances."

But there is also a second method of summing incomes, — the "method of couples." Just as the same item in capital accounts is both asset and liability, according to the point of view, and is, therefore, self-canceling, so the same item in income accounts is both service and disservice, and is, therefore, also self-canceling. The reader may, in fact, have felt that, in many of the examples cited, what we called disservices seemed to him to be services. He may have asked himself, Why should we call rebuilding a house a disservice? When a carpenter and his tools repair it, do we not credit him and them with services? Is not any production a service? Are not, then, repairs placed on the wrong side of the ledger? In answer it may be said that when a carpenter with his plane, hammer, and saw helps to rebuild a house, we have to consider two groups of capital. One group, the carpenter and tools, is acting on the other group, the house. The *carpenter and tools* used in the process certainly perform a service, but the *house* does not. Considered as occasioned by the *house*, the repairs are disservices. The house absorbs or soaks up these costs, promising to compensate for them by better service later on. The renailing of loose shingles is certainly not what the house is for, but is only a necessary evil. On the part of the hammer, however, these same events are services. The service called "nailing" is credited to the hammer. Therefore the repairing of the house is at once a service and a disservice.

Such double-faced events require a special name. We may christen them *interactions* between two instruments or groups of instruments. Alternative names are interacting services, intermediate, or preparatory services, coupled services, or simply "couples." They underlie what business men call "double entry bookkeeping."

An interaction, then, is a service of the acting instrument, a disservice of the instrument acted on. There can never arise the slightest doubt as to when it is to be regarded as positive and when negative. The definitions of service and disservice settle this question in each case, by referring it to the desire of a human being, viz. the owner of the service or disservice. As he desires that the house should *not* occasion repairs, these repairs are disservices of the house; as he desires that the tools *should* occasion repairs, they are services of those tools. The hammer exists for and derives its value from its prospective services in renailing shingles. The house does not exist for nor derive its value from the renailing of its shingles; on the contrary, the prospect of that event detracts from its value.

The example given is typical of the general relations between interacting instruments. The mental picture we should construct is that of two distinct groups of capital. Group A acts on group B for the benefit of the latter. Whatever the nature of this interaction, A is credited with it and B debited. The credit and debit are equal and simultaneous, the only result of the interaction being that, in consequence of it, B is enabled at some later time to yield more income.

Interactions are essentially identical with what were discussed a generation ago under the title "productive services." But inasmuch as the name "productive services" is not a very happy one, and its use has been so confused and has engendered so many verbal quibbles, it seems advisable not to revive it. The essential fact that these "productive services" were two-faced — negative as well as positive — was always overlooked, and there remained no other characteristic which could give the phrase a definite and scientific meaning.

Interactions constitute the great majority of the elements which enter into income and outgo accounts. The only services which are not merely the positive side of interactions are mental satisfactions — desirable conscious experiences — often miscalled "consumption"; and the only disservices which are not the negative side of interactions are pains or "labor." But these are only the outer fringes of the economic fabric. Between them is a connective network of productive processes and commercial transactions, every fiber of which has two sides, a positive side of services and a negative side of disservices.

§ 3

The interactions between two articles or groups of articles may, of course, consist either in causing or preventing changes or events. The events or changes which are caused or prevented are of three chief kinds, — changes of form of wealth, changes of position, and changes of ownership; or, transformation, transportation, and transfer. We shall take these up in order.

What is here called transformation of wealth is practically identical with what is usually understood by "production" or "productive processes."[1] By the transformation of wealth, or the changes produced in its form, is meant the changes of relative position of its parts. Weav-

---

[1] Cf. Marshall, *Principles of Economics*, 3d ed., p. 132.

ing, for instance, is the transformation of yarn into cloth by a rearrangement in the relative position of the warp and woof. Spinning, likewise, consists of moving, stretching, and twisting fibers into yarn; sewing, of changing the position of thread so that it may hold cloth together; and so with carding, wool-sorting, shearing, and all the other operations which constitute the manufacture of fabrics.

All manufacture and agriculture consist simply of a series of transformations of wealth, and each transformation is two-faced. On the part of the *transformed* instrument (or instruments) the transformation is a disservice; on the part of the *transforming* instrument (or instruments) it is a service. We have seen that when a carpenter and his tools transform a house, *i.e.* build or repair it, he and his tools are credited and the house is debited. The same is true when the painter decorates it or the janitor cleans it. When a cobbler transforms leather into shoes, he is performing services; the shoes at each stage are occasioning disservices, or costs. When a bootblack transforms dirty shoes into clean and polished ones, he likewise is rendering services, and the shoes, disservices. In like manner, a loom which produces cloth out of yarn is to be credited with this operation as income, while the stock of cloth receiving the product of the loom is to be debited with the very same item as part of its outgo or "cost of production."

Again, land renders a service in producing wheat. On the part of the wheat, however, this is a disservice. Wheat production is a service of land, a disservice of wheat. If we consider a farm as pouring its crop into the stock of wheat of a granary, the entry of wheat from farm to wheat stock is credited to the farm as its service and debited to the wheat stock as its disservice.

Sometimes, as has been said, the interaction consists not in causing a change, but in preventing one. A warehouse renders its service as a means of storing bales of cotton, *i.e.* protecting them from the elements. This storage is, however, on the part of the stock of cotton, an element of outgo or expense.

As has already been intimated, there may be, and usually are, more articles than one in either or both of the two interacting capitals. Plowing, or the transformation of land into a furrowed form, is performed by a plow, a horse, and a man. The plowing is a cost debited to the land on the one hand, and at the same time a service credited to the group of capital consisting of the plow, horse, and man on the other. We are not here concerned with the problem of how much should be placed to the credit of each cooperating agent, but merely with the fact that the sum total of the three is equal to the debit for the land.

The principle is not altered if one or more of the transforming agents perishes and another comes for the first time into existence in the transformation. Bread-baking is a transformation debited to the bread and credited to the cook, the range, the flour, and the fuel, of which the last two perish as soon as they perform their services. Agents which disappear in the transformation but reappear, in whole or in part, in the product are called "raw materials." The production of cloth from yarn is a transformation effected by means, not only of the loom, but also of a number of other agents, and among them the yarn itself. The cost of weaving includes as cost the consumption of raw material, yarn, and this consumption of yarn, on the part of the yarn itself, is not cost or disservice, but service. It is the event for which the yarn had existed. When cloth is turned into clothes this transformation is a service to be credited to the cloth, and a disservice to be debited to the clothes. All raw materials yield services as they are converted into finished products. Their conversion is, however, always outgo on the part of those products.

In this way, when an article passes through various stages of production, it is often an arbitrary matter whether we designate those stages by different names or not. A "sapling" grows into a "tree." We may, if we choose, consider the sapling as one category and the tree as another. In this case the "sapling" performs a service at the moment it becomes a "tree," just as the "tree" performs one later when it, in turn, becomes "lumber"; but no effect on social income is produced, because, if we credit the sapling with the value of the tree, we must debit the tree with the cost of the sapling. Likewise we may arbitrarily designate the moment when a "calf" becomes a "cow," or when "new" wine becomes "old," without disturbing the income accounts of society; for such events are always two-faced and cancel themselves out in the total. We may, in fact, mark any stage whatever in the course of production by an arbitrary line, and regard the passage across this line as a service on the part of the capital on one side of the line and a disservice on the part of the capital on the other side.

§ 4

The second class of interactions is transportation, or the change in place of wealth. It is a very thin line which separates this class from the preceding class. Transforming or producing wealth consists of changing the position of its parts relatively to each other; transporting wealth is changing the position of that wealth as a whole. But "part" and "whole" are themselves loose and relative terms. Bookbinding is a transformation or production of wealth; it assembles the paper, leather, thread, and paste into a whole book. Delivering books to a library is transportation. Yet the library is, in a sense, a whole; and to assemble books into a classified and organized library is to make a whole out of parts. The distinction between transformation and transportation is thus merely one of convenience. Many writers prefer to include them both under "production." We prefer to include them under the less ambiguous and more inclusive rubric "interactions," and our object here is not to emphasize their difference, but their similarity. The same principle of equal and opposite services applies to both. When merchandise is changed from one warehouse to another, the first warehouse is credited with the change and the second debited. The warehouse which has rendered up the merchandise has done a service; that which has received it has done a disservice. A banker who takes money from his vault and puts it in his till will, if he keeps separate accounts for the two, credit the vault and debit the till. When wheat is imported from Canada, that nation is credited and the United States is debited with the value of the operation. We may, as in the case of continuous productive processes, divide up transportation districts by any arbitrary lines, and consider the passage of any articles across those lines as an interaction.

§ 5

The third class of interactions is the change of ownership of wealth or property. This has been called *transfer*. Transfers usually occur in pairs, and involve two objects transferred in opposite directions between two owners. This double transfer, we have called an exchange. Since an exchange consists of two transfers, and since a transfer is a species of interaction and as such is self-canceling, every exchange is self-canceling and cannot of itself contribute anything to the total income of society.[1] When a bookseller, for instance, sells a book, he credits his stock with the fact that it has brought in money, and the customer debits his library to the same amount.

[1] The exchange does not duplicate income, but merely shuffles it about. It may and does put services of wealth where they are most needed, and thus results in a more effective use of income, just as credit and other forms of the divided ownership of wealth may make a more effective ownership of capital. In both these cases there is an increase of "total utility." This needs to be considered in its proper place, but it must not stand in the way of our canceling the *values* of assets and liabilities or of services and disservices. These values, as is well known, are connected, not with total utilities, but with marginal utilities.

These two items constitute the transfer between the stock of books of the dealer and the stock of books of the customer. The remaining two items constitute a transfer between the stocks of cash of the two men; the dealer debits his " cash " and the customer credits his.

When therefore an article of wealth changes hands, it occasions an element of income to the seller and an element of outgo to the purchaser, and therefore no income at all to society. The effect of canceling these items — the credit item of the seller and the debit item of the purchaser — is to free the income account of that article from all entanglements with exchange, to wipe out all money income, and to leave exposed to view what we have called the *natural* income of the article. Thus, books yield their natural income, not when the book dealer sells them, but when the reader peruses them. The sale is a mere preparatory service, a credit item to the book dealer and a debit item to the buyer. The fact of bookselling adds nothing to the income of society, but the reading of the book does. Again, a forest of trees yields no natural income, until the trees are felled and pass into then ext stage of logs. The owner of the forest may, to be sure, "realize" on the forest long before it is ready to be cut, by simply selling it to another; and to him the forest has then yielded income; but, as the purchaser has suffered an equal outgo, the forest has as yet yielded nothing to society.

The principle that an article of capital yields, to society, no income except its natural income, is not altered when its ownership is divided nor when the part rights are bought and sold. Adam Smith regarded a rented house as bearing income in the form of rent, but a house occupied by the owner as bearing no income at all. The truth is nearly the reverse. Both houses yield income, and both incomes are of the same kind, viz. shelter. The *rent* of the rented house is, for society, not income at all. It is income to the landlord but outgo to the tenant, — outgo which he is willing to suffer solely because of the shelter he receives. This shelter alone remains as the income from the house after the rent transaction is canceled out between the two parties concerned. The shelter-income is the essential and abiding item, and without it there could be no rent-income to the landlord.

Again, a railway yields as its income solely the natural one of transporting goods and passengers. Its owners sell this transportation service for money and regard the railway simply as a money maker; but to the shippers and passengers this same money is an expense and exactly offsets the railway's money earnings. Of the three items — money income of the road, money outgo of its patrons, and transportation — the first two mutually cancel and leave only the third, transportation, as the real contribution of the railway to the sum total of income.

We see, then, that the method of couples, applied to buyer and seller, denudes all capital of its so-called "money-income," and lays bare the only income it can really produce, the natural income. We see that capital is not a money-making machine, but that its income to society is simply its services of production, transportation, and gratification. The income from the farm is the yielding of its crops; from the mine, the production of its ore; from the factory, its transformation of raw into finished products; from commercial capital, its passage of goods from producer to consumer; from articles in consumers' hands, their enjoyment or so-called "consumption."

Similar principles apply to *outgo*, no part of which, for society, exists in money form. The great bulk of what merchants call "cost of production," expense, or outgo, consists of money costs which carry with them their own cancellation. For manufacturers, merchants, and other business men, almost every outgo is an expense, *i.e.* consists of a money payment. Such money payments are for wages, raw materials, rent, and interest charges. Now all these outgoes are incomes for other people. The wages are the earnings of labor; the payment for raw material is received by some other manufacturer; the rent by the landlord; the interest charges by the creditor.

§ 6

Not only do exchange transactions completely cancel themselves out in reckoning total income, but the great majority of the natural services of capital do so also. Even these natural uses of capital consist, for the most part, of "interactions," — they are transformations or transportations of wealth. These intermediate stages are merely preparatory to the final use or so-called "consumption" of wealth, and, after the interactions have been canceled out, do not enter as items either on the income or outgo side of the social balance sheet.

In order to show the effect of canceling out the equal and opposite items entering into every interaction throughout the productive processes, let us observe the various stages of production which begin with the forest above referred to. The product of the forest, its gross income, is the series of events called the *turning out of logs*. This log-production is a mere preparatory service, a credit item to the forest and a debit item to the stock of logs of the saw mill, to which they next pass. As the sawmill turns its logs into lumber, the lumber yard is debited with the production of lumber, and the sawmill is credited with its share in this transformation.

Intermediate categories may, of course, be created, and we may follow, in like manner, the further transformation, transportation, and exchange to the end of the stages of production, or rather, to the ends; for these stages split up and form several streams flowing in different directions. To indicate merely one of these streams, let us suppose that the lumber which goes out from the yard is used in repairing a certain warehouse. The warehouse is used for storing cloth; the cloth goes from the warehouse to the tailor; the tailor converts the cloth into suits for his customers; and his customers receive and wear those suits. In this series, all the intermediate services cancel out in "couples" and leave as the only uncanceled element, or final fringe of services, the use of clothes in consumers' hands.

Should we stop our accounts, however, at earlier points in the series, the uncanceled fringe will be not consumers' services, but the positive side of intermediate services or interactions. The negative side will not appear, as it belongs to later stages in the series. This will all be clear, if we put the matter in figures, stage by stage. The following are the items for the logging camp above mentioned, in the accounts of its owner: —

INCOME ACCOUNT FOR LOGGING CAMP FOR YEAR 1900

Income	Outgo
Production of logs $50,000	(Omitted)

The gross income from the logging camp, considered by itself, and without any deductions for expenses, is here seen to consist in the production of $50,000 worth of logs. If, however, we combine the logging camp with the sawmill, we shall have accounts like the following, in which, to avoid irrelevant complications, no account is taken of any expenses which are not interactions between the groups of capital considered: —

INCOME ACCOUNT FOR LOGGING CAMP AND SAWMILL FOR 1900

Capital Source	Income	Outgo
Logging camp	Yielding logs to sawmill . . . $50,000	
Sawmill	Yielding lumber to lumber yard $60,000	Receiving logs from camp . $50,000

In this case, canceling the two log items we have left only the lumber item; *i.e.* the income from the combined logging camp and sawmill consists only of the production of lumber, its final product. The transfer of logs from one department to the other no longer appears. This transfer is like the taking of money from one pocket and putting it in another, as is particularly evident in case the logging camp and sawmill are combined under the same management.

Extending the same principles to the entire series, we have the accounts as given on the opposite page.

It should be noted that these entries relate not to successive but to *simultaneous* events; that all the items refer to a fixed period of time; that is to say, we are not following the fortunes of the original logs through succeeding stages, but comparing the simultaneous operations of the series of groups of instruments.

If we successively cancel items pair by pair by offsetting any item on the right side by the item in the line *above* it on the left side, we shall find, if we stop after the first two cancellations, that the net income from logging camp, sawmill, and lumber yard, consists only of the production of retail lumber, $70,000; it does not include either the transfer of logs or the transfer of wholesale lumber. In like manner, if we proceed one stage further, that is, if we stop our cancellations, at the end of the first four interactions, the production of retail lumber no longer appears as an element of income; and so on, step by step to the end, when the only surviving item will be the "wear" of the suits.

It is, of course, true that in any actual accounts there will be numerous other items than those which have been exhibited in this simple chainlike fashion. Were it worth while, we might insert these additional entries of income and outgo elements. Most of them would consist of the positive or negative side of an interaction, and if we were to introduce its mate, the opposite aspect of the same transac-

Income Account for a Specified Series of Instruments for the Year 1900

Capital Source	Income		Outgo	
Logging camp	Yielding logs to sawmill	$50,000	Receiving logs from logging camp	$50,000
Sawmill	Yielding lumber to lumber yard	60,000	Receiving lumber from sawmill	60,000
Lumber yard	Yielding lumber to warehouse	70,000	Receiving lumber from lumber yard	70,000
Warehouse	Warehouse shelter to cloth	80,000		
Stock of cloth in warehouse	Yielding cloth to tailor	90,000	Shelter from warehouse	80,000
Stock of cloth of tailor	Yielding suits to customers	100,000	Receiving cloth from stock	90,000
Stock of clothes of customers	Yielding "wear"	110,000	Receiving suits from tailor	100,000

tion, it would be necessary to include still other accounts. If we should follow up all such leads we should soon have an intricate network of related accounts. But the same principle of the interaction as a self-effacing element would apply. The only items of outgo which are not the negative sides of interactions will be the items of subjective labor and trouble. These alone will finally remain as uncanceled elements of outgo.

§ 7

The table given will throw light on the question, Of what does income consist? The question is not a thoroughly definite one. If we ask instead, Of what does the income *from a particular group of capital* consist? we shall make it definite. Whether the production of logs is income or not depends upon the point of view. It is income from the first link of capital (logging camp) in our series; it is not income from the first two links combined, for in the second link it occurs as outgo. Likewise, the use of the warehouse is true income with respect to the first four links or groups of capital, but is no longer income when the fifth is included.

We see, therefore, that the income from any group of capital does not consist in any degree of the *interactions* taking place within it, but only of the final or outer fringe of services performed by the group. As the group is enlarged, this particular outer fringe disappears by being joined to the next part of the economic fabric, and another fringe, still more remote, appears. The question naturally arises, When is the economic fabric complete, and has it any final outer fringe? But this question must be deferred for the present.

Nor do we yet inquire what relations exist between the two sides of the same account, say the expense to the sawmill for logs and its income from sawn lumber. In the illustrative tables the latter is entered as greater than the former, and this is normally the case, if the capital of the sawmill remains constant. At present, however, we are not concerned with the effects of income and outgo on capital, but only with the summation of income.

§ 8

The method of couples, then, is useful in showing of what elements income consists in any given case. The method of balances, on the other hand, exhibits the amount of income contributed from each article of capital as its source. The two methods, as applied to the example just given, are as follows: —

Method of Balances

Capital	Income	Outgo	Net Income
Logging camp	$ 50,000 −	. . . .	= + $50,000
Sawmill	60,000 −	$50,000	= + 10,000
Lumber yard	70,000 −	60,000	= + 10,000
Warehouse	80,000 −	70,000	= + 10,000
Stock of cloth in warehouse	90,000 −	80,000	= + 10,000
Stock of cloth of tailor	100,000 −	90,000	= + 10,000
Stock of clothes of customers	110,000 −	100,000	= + 10,000
			$110,000

Method of Couples

Income	Outgo
~~50,000~~	
~~60,000~~	~~50,000~~
~~70,000~~	~~60,000~~
~~80,000~~	~~70,000~~
~~90,000~~	~~80,000~~
~~100,000~~	~~90,000~~
110,000	~~100,000~~

The two methods — balances and couples — show the same result, but from different points of view. By means of the method of balances we are enabled to see what part of the final net income is contributed by each of the articles in the group. By means of the method of couples, we are enabled to see of what the net income *from the entire group* of articles consists; canceling by the oblique lines, we have left but one item, $110,000, representing the "wear" of the suits. The two methods must not be confused. When we find by the method of couples that the net income of $110,000 consists exclusively of the use of suits of clothes, this does not imply that this net income is all due to the stock of clothes. To discover to what it is due, recourse must be had to the method of balances. We thereby see that only $10,000 of it is due to the stock of clothes, the remainder being due to the other capital instruments in the table and most of all ($50,000) to the logging camp. Combining the results of *both* methods, we may state that the total net income from the specified group of instruments *consists* of $110,000 worth of "wear" of suits and that this is *due* partly to the stock of clothes and partly to other capital.

The two methods, that of balances and that of couples, correspond in a general way to the two methods for canceling liabilities and assets in capital accounts. The method of balances gave, it will be remembered, the amount of capital belonging to each individual; the method of couples showed of what elements the total capital consisted.

§ 9

We have now followed the cancellations to which interactions lead, whether they be interactions of exchange or production. The case of exchange, however, needs further consideration. Since every exchange consists of two transfers, and every transfer of two items, a credit and a debit, the exchange evidently consists of four items in all, two of which are credits and two, debits. These four may be paired off in two ways, only one of which has thus far been mentioned. They stand, as it were, at the four corners of a square, as in the following scheme, which shows the credits and debits involved when goods worth $2 are sold. The dealer credits his stock of goods and debits his "cash," while the buyer does the opposite.

	Stock of Goods	Stock of Cash
Seller	+ $2	− $2
Buyer	− $2	+ $2

The two transfers into which any exchange may be resolved are represented by the two *columns* of the table. But an exchange may also be resolved into two pairs of items represented by the two *lines* of the table. The items in the same horizontal line record the part taken in the exchange by one of the two exchangers. This pair of items constitutes his *transaction*, while the remaining pair constitutes, in like manner, the transaction of the other party to the exchange. The term "transaction," though somewhat vague in ordinary use, appears well suited to express the share in an exchange of one of the two who participate in it.

Every exchange, then, consists of four items, and may be resolved either into two transfers (one for each property exchanged) or into two transactions (one for each exchanger). The first resolution has been considered; we proceed now to the second, and enter the subject of "double-entry bookkeeping."

By double entry is meant the record of every double-faced event pertaining to a particular person, whether it be a transaction of that person with another or an interaction between the various categories of capital within his own possession. Double-entry book-keeping is most perfectly illustrated in the case of a fictitious person. The following account represents the entries during a given year for a dry goods company. In this account we observe that every item on the income side is balanced by an equal and opposite item on the outgo side. All items thus paired are represented by the same letters, the capitals being used for positive items and the small letters for negative.

INCOME AND OUTGO OF DRY GOODS COMPANY, FOR YEAR 1906

Capital Source	Income	Outgo
Stock of Goods	By goods sold. $10,000 A	To goods bought . $5,000 c To work of selling . 1,500 h To storage . 1,000 g
Cash	By cash taken out for:— rent . . . $1,200 B purchases . . 5,000 C wages . . . 1,600 D interest payment . . . 800 E profits . . . 2,000 F	To cash received from sales $10,000 a
Store Lease	By storage service $1,000 G	To rent paid $1,200 b
Rights to and obligations from employees	By clerk work . $1,500 H	To clerk hire $1,600 d
Bonded debt		To interest paid . . $800 e
Capital stock		To profits paid . . $2,000 f

Let us consider the first item of capital, the stock of goods. This yields to the company as its gross income the money obtained from sales, amounting to $10,000 ($A$). The payment of this money into the cash drawer becomes a debit item (a) on the part of the stock of cash. Reversely, when the rent is paid the lease of the store is debited with $1200 ($b$), and the stock of cash which yields this value of income is credited (B). In like manner all the transactions involving a payment or receipt of cash are entered on one side with respect to the cash, and on the opposite side with respect to some other capital source. The category of the capital source called "rights to and obligations from employees" yields a certain amount of clerical work and other services appraised at $1500. This item credited (H) to the above-named source is here debited (h) to the stock of goods, to sell which requires the services of these employees. It may be that it should be debited to the store which they clean, or to some other article of capital on which they do work; but in any case it must be debited under some head or heads.

It will be seen that among the other items of capital which are sources of income or outgo are the bonds and stocks of the company. The bonds absorb $800 of interest, and the capital-stock, which is a residual claim on the company, absorbs any surplus of cash which it is decided to distribute in dividends.

The two sides of the account of such a fictitious person necessarily balance. It cannot be otherwise, even if the company accumulates its profit instead of paying it to the shareholders; for, as has been seen, the money thus received is debited to the cash account.

In practical accounting, the items would usually be simplified somewhat. It would not ordinarily be worth while to make an appraisement of the value of the *use* of the warehouse for storage as distinct from the storage *charge*, nor of the value of the *work* performed by the employees as distinct from the *wages* paid them. In the above accounts we have purposely distinguished these magnitudes, estimating the storage benefit as $1000 though the rent paid for it is $1200, and estimating the work done by employees as worth $1500 though their wages were $1600. If, instead, we estimate the storage benefit at the rent figure and the employees' work at the wages figure, our accounts would contain four items of $1200 and four of $1600. Of these, two of each might well be, and in practice usually are, dispensed with. These are the pair of items "storage service" (*G* and *g*) and the pair "clerk work" (*H* and *h*). Omitting these, which are both appraised items, there will be left only cash transactions. These may be further simplified by dispensing with the two categories called "store lease" and "rights to and obligations from employees," by placing the rent (*b*) and the wages (*d*) under the head of "stock of goods." In other words, we charge the expenses for rent and wages directly against the goods stored and cared for instead of, as in the table, charging against them "storage service" and "work of selling." There is no difficulty in recognizing the resulting accounts as those employed in ordinary bookkeeping. Occasionally the more elaborate accounting is necessary, as when a very old lease, like some still in force in London, requires only a nominal rent charge compared with the benefits conferred.

§ 10

In the case of real persons, however, the two sides do not balance, for the accounts do not consist solely of double entries. To show this, let us recur to the accounts of the lawyer considered in Chapter VIII. The table on the opposite page reproduces those accounts, with some of the items given in greater detail.

In these accounts, as in the previous ones, we have indicated the like items on opposite sides by like letters, the positive being represented by capitals and the negative by small letters. We observe that, as in the corporation accounts, many of the items will " pair." But, unlike the corporation accounts, the present accounts contain a residue of items which *will not pair*. The letters representing these unpaired items are designated by being inclosed in square brackets. They show that [*B*], [*C*], [*D*], [*O*] — the shelter of the house, use of furniture, use of food, use of

INCOME AND OUTGO OF LAWYER

Capital Source	Income		Outgo	
Stocks and Bonds	Money received from S. & B.	$2000 [A]	Money invested	$500 e
Lease right	Shelter	$100 [B]	Money rent paid	$100 f
Furniture	Use of furniture	$50 [C]	Money cost of repairs	$30 g
Food	Use of food	$150 [D]	Money cost of food	$50 h
			Work of servants	100 l
"Cash"	Paid out for bonds	$500 E	Money from stocks and bonds	$2000 a
	Paid out for rent	100 F	Money from practice	2000 n
	Paid out for repairs to furniture	30 G		
	Paid out for food	50 H		
	Paid out for servants' wages	100 I		
	Paid out for clerk hire	500 J		
	Paid out for "etc."	2500 K		
Servant contracts	Work on food	$100 L	Money wages	$100 i
Clerk contracts	Personal assistance	$500 M	Clerk hire	$500 j
Self	Fees in practice	$2000 N	Assistance of clerks	$500 m
Etc.	Uses of clothes, jewelry, theater, and other direct uses	$2500 [O]	Money cost of clothes, etc.	$2500 k

Summary:
- Shelter $100
- Use of furniture . . 50
- Use of food 150
- Uses of "Etc." . . . 2500
- Net income $2800

clothes, jewelry, etc.—constitute a kind of income which does not appear elsewhere as outgo.

§ 11

We found, when studying the accounts of *instruments*, the chain of productive services of the lumber camp, etc., that there always remains some outer fringe of uncanceled income produced by the capitalistic machine. We have now reached this same kind of outer fringe in studying the accounts of *persons*, provided they are real persons. This outer fringe consists of what economists have usually called "consumption." All other services are merely preparatory to such services, and pass themselves on from one category of capital to another. Thus the income from investments, being deposited in bank, is outgo with respect to the bank account; the bank account yields income by paying for stocks and bonds, food, etc., but in each case the same item enters as outgo with respect to these or other categories of capital. In all these cases the individual receives no income which is not at the same time outgo. It is only as he consumes the food, wears the clothes, or uses the furniture that he receives income.

The question still remains whether the fringe we have reached is the final outer fringe, or whether we must not proceed one step further and regard the final services just mentioned as merely interactions between a man's external wealth and his own body. This question will be discussed in the following chapter. We are content here to leave the chains of services at the point where they reach the person of the recipient.

CHAPTER X

PSYCHIC INCOME

§ 1

THE stage at which, in the previous chapter, we left income may be called the stage of final objective services. In other words, it is the stage at which the wealth of the objective world at last acts upon the person of the recipient of income. This final income is that for which the economist is usually in search, and is that which the ordinary statistics of workingmen's budgets represent. It is clear from what has been said, that in this final net income all interactions between articles of external wealth drop out, — all the transformations of production, such as the operations of mining, agriculture, and industry, all the operations of transportation, and all business transactions or exchanges. For, in all such cases, the debits and credits inevitably occur in pairs of equal and opposite items. The only items which survive are the final personal uses of wealth, ordinarily called "consumption." Let us rather call them *enjoyable objective services*. The main sorts of enjoyable objective services are the following: services of nourishment, services of housing and warming, services of clothing and personal adornment, services of personal attendance, services of amusement, instruction, and recreation, services of gratification of vanity.

§ 2

It is usually recognized by economists that we must not stop at the stage of this objective income.[1] There is one more step before the process is complete. Indeed, no

---
[1] See Fetter's *Principles of Economics*, New York, 1904, Chap. VI.

objective services are of significance to man except as they are preparatory to subjective satisfactions.

The final *subjective* services come through the human body. No agent outside the body can yield them. All that persons or things outside of man can do is to stimulate his bodily organism. Even what are called services of amusement or instruction cannot directly amuse or instruct the mind; they can only affect the body. An instructive book, for instance, renders its service simply and solely by reflecting light into the eye of the reader. It is necessary that these stimuli on the optic nerve should be transmitted through the nervous system before any mental instruction takes place. So a piano can of itself produce no sensations of tone. It merely produces external vibrations, which, through the ear and auditory nerve, ultimately result in sensation. All sound, sight, taste, smell, touch, come about through reactions of the nervous system to external stimuli. A man who receives a Turkish bath has received enjoyable income in the objective sense, but all the services of the water, towels, attendants, and other coöperating agencies, while credited to them, must, if we treat man himself as capital, be regarded as debited to him. They result simply in cleaning and stimulating his skin. They are income from outside agencies absorbed by his body in order that he may later experience pleasant sensations or avoid unpleasant ones, through the enjoyment of health. Similarly the use of clothing and shelter prevents the occurrence of the sensation of cold, but their immediate objective service is simply in hindering the dissipation of heat from the body. They are disservices with reference to the body, just as similar care and protection of a horse are disservices with reference to it.

When medicine is taken, it may, from the objective standpoint, be counted as a part of income, just as food, clothing, and other ordinary items. But it is clear that the services of medicine are (or are supposed to be) the repairing of the body, and, although credited to the medicine, should be debited to the body, just as the services of a carpenter are credited to him but debited to the house which he mends. So the services of a dentist, far from producing any immediate satisfactions, have for the moment quite an opposite effect, but result later in better service of one's own teeth. They are credited to the dentist, but debited to the body. The "consumption," or use of food, though it is a service of the food, is a disservice of the body; for food stands in the same relation to the body as fuel to a furnace or repairs to a house. The final income consists of the subjective satisfaction of appetite and the other satisfactions which the intake of food enables the body to yield to the mind. These include not simply the immediate gratification of the palate, but the promotion of pleasant sensations or the avoidance of unpleasant ones later on. In other words, the consumption of food, by preserving health and maintaining life, enables the body to yield better and longer-continued income to the mind in future years, just as the repairs on a house enable it to yield shelter a long time after the repairs are made.

§ 3

These and other illustrations will show that, if we include the body as a transforming instrument, while we must credit with their respective services all these outside agencies, such as food, clothing, dwelling, furniture, ornaments, and other articles which, as it were, bombard a man's sensory system, we must also at the same time debit the body with these same items. In this case the only surviving credit items after these equal debits and credits are canceled are the resulting final satisfactions in the human mind. In other words, in order that the external world should become effective to man, the human body must be considered as the last transforming instrument. Just as there is a gradual transformation of services through the farm, flour mill, and bakery, so is there a final transformation within the human body itself. It is a sort of factory, the products of which are the only final uncanceled income of the consumer. In a complete view of productive processes, the human machine is no more to be left out of consideration than machines which handle the wheat in its prior stages.

All objective income, therefore, is entirely erased or negatived as soon as we apply our accounting to the body of the recipient. The services of which that income consists empty out, as it were, their quota into the human body, but the ultimate result is not finally received until it emerges in the stream of consciousness.

We define subjective income, then, as the stream of consciousness of any human being. All his conscious life, from his birth to his death, constitutes his subjective income. Sensations, thoughts, feelings, volitions, and all psychical events, in fact, are a part of this income stream. All these conscious experiences which are desirable are positive items of income, or services; all which are undesirable are negative items, or disservices. We have avoided expressly the statement that subjective income consists of pleasure, or of pleasure minus pain. These terms have been too loosely used by economists, and such use has involved them in unnecessary controversy with psychologists. It is better to avoid such disputes, and content ourselves with the simple statement that subjective events which are desirable are services, and those which are undesirable are disservices. This statement conforms to the definition of services and disservices originally given, and does not commit us to any psychological theory of pleasure or pain. Some psychologists would maintain that pain, to an ascetic, may be just as much an object of desire as pleasure.[1]

---

[1] For instance, of the founder of the Sacred Heart Order, we read that, —

"Her love of pain and suffering was insatiable. . . . 'Nothing

Nor is it necessary to take sides in the controversies regarding the relations between mind and body. We are not concerned with cause and effect, but with means and end, and, whatever may be the causation of mental states, the human body is certainly the means by which the good from external wealth is finally communicated to the consciousness of the owner.

§ 4

The two kinds of final income, the physical and the psychical, or the objective and subjective, are both legitimate in their proper spheres. Usually the physical and psychical income are equal to each other in value. A loaf of bread which yields ten cents' worth of services presumably gives ten cents' worth of immediate satisfaction. When one enjoys a musical concert worth one dollar, it does not matter whether we say that the services of the musicians in producing vibrations are worth one dollar, or the enjoyment which these vibrations occasion in the mind is worth this sum. When rent is paid for a house, this is generally taken to measure also the subjective comfort obtained through it.

Nevertheless, there are several points at which the valuations of subjective and objective income are different, and three of these are sufficiently important to emphasize.

The first case is that in which the transformation within the body takes a long time. Here the two species of income do not correspond. For instance, the instruction received by an apprentice in preparation for his trade is a service rendered to him in the training of his body in manual dexterity, in order that, a few years later, this manual dexterity may increase his income-earning power. Ap-

---

but pain,' she continually said in her letters, 'makes my life supportable.'" Bougand, *Hist. de la bienheureuse Marguerite Marie*, Paris, 1894, pp. 171, 265. Cf. also pp. 386, 387. Quoted from William James, *Varieties of Religious Experience*, 1902, p. 310.

prenticeship is, as it were, an investment in the body, to be returned at a later time (with interest), just as the planting of a tree is an investment in the tree in order that its fruit may be secured in later years. At the time of tree planting there is no net income, for the work credited the tree planter is debited the tree; it is only when in after years the tree bears fruit or other product that any return is obtained from the planting. Similarly, the work of teaching the apprentice should be credited to the teacher and debited to the apprentice's body; the final satisfactions will not come until the acquired knowledge becomes effective. All this can be faithfully recorded only in the complete accounting which includes subjective income.

The same principles apply to any training or education for a profession. When a young man studies law, medicine, journalism, music, or prepares for any other profession, he is investing in his own person, with the hope that the sums thus invested may ultimately be returned to him (with interest). The same is true of physical training. Many of the most successful men are those who, like President Roosevelt, in early life saw the wisdom of developing a strong body, and in consequence have increased their productive power in mature years.

§ 5

The second point at which subjective and objective income diverges is found in occupations whose special gratification or irksomeness renders their return in psychical income widely different from their return in objective income. This is frequent in conditions of labor. Properly speaking, objective income takes no account of the toil of the laborer. The workingman who earns $2 a day earns double the objective income of one who earns $1 a day. Yet if the work of the former is difficult, loathsome, or dangerous, it may well be that many would prefer the nominally smaller income rather than endure these disadvantages. These facts have often puzzled economists, and the question has been asked whether any allowance should be made for disagreeable trades, such as that of the hangman, and whether it is fair to say that a workingman who earns $500 a year by the sweat of his brow really gets as much as a capitalist who receives an effortless $500 from stocks and bonds. The answer to these questions is now evident. So far as objective income is concerned, no allowance should be made. That is, the returns to the laborer are all to be counted gross and not net, no deduction being made on account of so-called "mental anguish" or painful feelings. Objective income stops at the threshold of the laborer's body. It does not follow beyond this point and include what the body communicates to the mind.[1]

But, by passing to subjective income, we avoid some of the manifest unfairness in the usual statistical comparisons which contrast a capitalist's income with that of a laborer, or contrast with each other the incomes of various laborers, some of whose tasks are difficult and others easy. To obtain one's net income we must subtract from the subjective satisfactions the subjective efforts of attainment. A laborer who receives $2 a day may work so hard for it as to justify a deduction of $1.50 for the effort, whereas the laborer who receives $1 a day may possibly need to deduct only 25 cents. The nominally $2 man would then be receiving a net income of only 50 cents a day, whereas the nominally $1 man would be receiving one worth 75

---

[1] The only way in which a man's person contributes to such objective income is, as has been implied in our illustrative accounts, through the work he performs upon external objects, in order that these may, in turn, yield back service to him. Objective income thus includes all the results of his own bodily exertions so far as they come to him *via* these outside agencies. A farmer, for instance, sows wheat, which is sold and yields him income. The farmer's services here start a circuitous process which is transmitted through the farm, the crops, the wheat, the proceeds from selling the wheat, the enjoyable commodities purchased with these proceeds, and finally his own person again, to which those commodities minister.

cents. Again, in the comparison between the capitalist's and laborer's income, we ought to say that the laborer who receives $500 a year, with an expenditure of effort appraised at $250, is only receiving one half as great an income as the capitalist who obtains, during the same period, dividends and interest to the extent of $500, with no effort whatever.

It may be asked how an appraisement of labor is possible. From a practical or statistical standpoint the appraisement is difficult, if not impossible. Yet certain data are obtainable. A servant applying for work asks not simply in regard to the wages, but in regard to the difficulty of the work, and will consent to do extra or disagreeable tasks only on condition of a definite increase in wages. In this case we may say that the increase in wages which is necessary to procure the consent of the laborer represents subjectively, to him or her, the increased difficulty of the work. In like manner, a government employee who has at any time the option of retiring on half-pay may, at the point when he decides to retire, be said to regard the difficulty of his work as equal in his estimation to half of the income he receives for it.

In general we may say that the proper method of appraising the disagreeable element involved in one's work is to deduct from the gross income that sum which the worker would be willing to sacrifice were it possible for him so to avoid the disagreeable element. That is, he is supposed to imagine an alternative condition, considered as an equivalent in his mind to the actual conditions under which he works, but which differs from them in two particulars: in being free from the labor or pain of toil; and being deprived of a certain amount of its earnings or rewards. If, for instance, the laborer who obtains $2 a day for eight hours' work estimates that this would be to him the equivalent of $1.50 without labor, he has virtually made a deduction of 50 cents a day for the irksomeness of his work.

§ 6

We have reached a convenient place in which to emphasize a point of great importance, but one which is seldom understood. This is, that most of what is called "cost of production" is, in the last analysis, not cost at all. We have found, in using the method of couples, that every objective item of cost is also an item of income, and that in the final total, *no objective items of outgo survive cancellation.* This principle holds true whether we stop our accounts at the bodily threshold, confining them to a record of objective income, or extend them to include the body, thus yielding a record of psychic income. Those who have been accustomed to construct their theories of political economy on the assumption that "cost of production" is an essential and ultimate item, may do well to reflect carefully on this proposition. It means that *in a comprehensive view of production there is no cost of production in its objective sense at all.* All of what is ordinarily called cost is really cost only with respect to certain accounts; it is always also income with respect to other accounts. This is true, for instance, of the cost of raw materials. It costs flour to produce bread, but all that the flour costs to the baker is income to the miller. The same is true of wages. The employer counts his pay roll as cost of production, but the laborer counts it as earnings.

Glimpses of the fact that all objective costs are always also objective income, and therefore disappear in the final summation, are occasionally found in the books, especially those on land and interest, although the points of view have been variable and uncertain. There have been long discussions as to whether rent enters into cost of production. The question has by many been negatively answered.[1] Böhm-Bawerk has also maintained that interest was not

---

[1] See the interesting remarks of Jevons in the preface to his *Theory of Political Economy*, 3d ed., 1888, p. xlvii.

an element in the cost of production. From what has been said it is evident that every rent and interest payment, while it is a cost to the payer, is income to the payee. The total objective income of society consists wholly of *positive* items, such as the use of food and furniture, the shelter from houses, and the other direct services of wealth. There are no negative items in the account of social income which survive in the form of "costs of production."

When we turn, however, to subjective income, we find the case somewhat different. Including the human organism as capital acted upon by the outer world and itself acting upon the inner world of consciousness, we not only carry the uncanceled fringe of services one step further and obtain as net income the subjective satisfactions from the use of food, clothing, furniture, dwelling, etc., but we find it necessary to include also the subjective efforts put forth by human beings in order that these satisfactions may accrue.

Thus, to revert to the income account of the lawyer. We found that his net income consisted of the use of house $100, use of furniture $50, use of food $150, and other uses $2500, making a total of $2800. But if we include the lawyer's own person in our accounts, we should have to enter, in addition to all the previous items of income, the following: —

Capital Source	Income		Outgo	
Self	*Satisfactions from shelter*	100 [P]	Shelter	100 b
	Satisfactions from use of furniture	50 [Q]	Use of furniture	50 c
	Satisfactions from use of food	150 [R]	Consumption of food	150 d
	Satisfactions from other uses	2500 [S]	Other uses	2500 o
			Labor sacrifice	500 [t]

Some of these additional items are subjective and some objective; the former are distinguished by italics. It is evident that the objective items, here debited to the person of the recipient, have all equal and opposite counterparts in the accounts as given in Chapter IX, §10. These same items were there entered as credits and constituted the "uncanceled fringe" of final *objective* income. They were designated as [B], [C], [D], [O]. Now, however, after the introduction of the new items, they cancel with the debits of like letters, b, c, d, o; but another uncanceled fringe appears, namely, [P], [Q], [R], [S], which items are wholly subjective. These we have, for convenience, entered at the same figures as their objective prototypes. Their sum is therefore also $2800. But there also appears a subjective labor cost, [t], of $500 to express the personal labor and pain of the lawyer in his work. The result is that his net subjective income is not equal to the objective income of $2800, but is only $2300.

When we have reached this final stage in our inquiries, therefore, we find the only ultimate item of cost to be labor cost, or, if the term "labor" be not itself sufficiently broad, labor, anxiety, trouble, annoyance, and all the other subjective experiences of an undesirable nature which are necessary in order that the experiences of an agreeable nature may be secured.[1] In a sense, therefore, the socialists are quite right when they say that labor is the only true cost of production, although some of the conclusions which they deduce from this proposition are not justifiable.

§ 7

The third discrepancy between subjective and objective income is due to the fact that certain agreeable and disagreeable experiences are due directly to the character of

[1] It may be well here to emphasize the distinction between work and labor which has been so well drawn by Professor J. B. Clark. The work performed consists of the services rendered, and is positive; the labor consists of the efforts of performing those services and is negative. The work is objective; the labor is subjective. Properly speaking, an employer does not pay a man for his labor, but for his work.

the body itself. A large part of our *subjective* income is due to our condition of health or disease. A man with a good constitution has a more agreeable stream of consciousness, or subjective income, than one without. The pains and sufferings of illness here find a place in the complete accounts of income and outgo. It is evident that the wealthy man who confessed that he would exchange all his millions for a young and vigorous body may be the recipient of a large objective income, but not enjoy as much subjective income as Walt Whitman, who had scarcely a dollar in the world.

That these subjective items are by no means to be despised by the economist, who has far too long busied himself with a study of the superficial objective phenomena, is evident when we consider that a healthy body is absolutely essential for receiving and enjoying the income from external wealth. The man who is short-sighted enough to lose his health in the pursuit of what he calls wealth will soon be spending all of this sort of wealth to regain health; and we need only visit the health resorts of Colorado and California to be struck with the number of cases of business men who have found themselves in this predicament. Economists, by fixing attention exclusively on physical phenomena, leave out of account the most essential element of all, the vigor of human life. The true "wealth of nations" is the health of its individuals. A nation consisting of weak, sickly, and short-lived individuals is poor compared with a nation whose inhabitants are of the opposite type. Hence it is that the devices of modern hygiene, sanitation, and preventive medicine, which tend to increase human working power and enjoying power, are of greater economic import than many of the luxurious and enervating devices commonly connoted by "wealth."

We see, then, that subjective income means simply one's whole conscious life. Every item of it comes *via* the body of the person.

§ 8

As to the measurement of the items entering into this psychic stream, the same principles apply which have already been laid down for the measurement of other magnitudes. First, all like events are measured by simple counting. Secondly, so far as it is possible, a valuation in terms of money is placed on them, as on objective services. To accomplish this appraisement it is only necessary for the individual to answer the question what money is he willing to pay for any enjoyment brought about by means of external wealth, such as a box of sweets or a cigar. If the event is one which cannot be connected with purchasable commodities, it is necessary to imagine an exchange, even when actual exchange is impossible.

We have now followed the method of couples from the balance sheet for a particular article of capital, or group of articles, to the entire capital goods of an individual or of society. The result has been inevitably to lead us to a consideration of the psychic stream of events as final income, all the agreeable items being on the credit side and the disagreeable ones on the debit side. But the methods which have been given also enable us to stop at any earlier point. There are two such earlier points which are convenient and logical. The final objective income is one; the other has its existence only in a highly developed civilization like the one now existing in western Europe and America, and consists of the familiar "money income" of an individual, that is, his money receipts from all capital sources, less his money outgo to them. The income of a person reckoned by these three methods will ordinarily be very similar, though in theory, and sometimes in practice, it may differ widely. As long as we understand the various kinds of income, and the relations between them, we are at liberty to consider any one of them as "income" in its proper place. But we can scarcely understand any one without having had at least some view of both of the others.

§ 9

Having completed our survey of the summation of the elements of income, we may properly pause to classify these items. They fall naturally into three groups. The first group includes those items of income which are positive and not negative, that is, the agreeable experiences of subjective income, for these, as we have seen, are the only final uncanceled positive items. The second group includes items which are negative but not positive, namely, disagreeable psychical experiences, and consists of two classes: (1) the labor and trouble which are sacrificed for the sake of procuring income through objective channels, in other words, the toil of the producer; and (2) the disagreeable impressions produced in one's consciousness by an abnormal state of the body, as aches, pains, and all sorts of illness, but which are not, like toil, voluntarily incurred for the sake of future return. The third group includes what we have called interactions, or items which are at once positive and negative, according to the point of view. Both of the first two groups are entirely subjective, and the last is entirely objective. The third group, interactions, constitutes by far the bulk of the items entering into income accounts, and includes all of those which enter into practical bookkeeping. It may be subdivided into two groups: (1) interactions outside of the human body, and (2) interactions between external wealth and the human body, or what have been called "final objective services." The following scheme shows further subdivisions: —

PSYCHIC INCOME

Services
- Pure services (subjective)
- Pure disservices (subjective)
  - labor (cost of production)
  - pains and other discomforts
- Interactions
  - between objective wealth and body of owner (final objective services)
    - nutrition
    - clothing
    - housing
    - amusements
    - instruction
    - etc.
  - between objective articles
    - production
      - agricultural
      - manufacturing
    - transportation
    - commerce
    - etc.
      - advertising
      - organizing
      - indemnifying
      - etc.

PART III. CAPITAL AND INCOME

CHAPTER XI. FOUR INCOME-CAPITAL RATIOS
CHAPTER XII. CONCEPT OF RATE OF INTEREST
CHAPTER XIII. VALUE OF CAPITAL
CHAPTER XIV. EARNINGS AND INCOME
CHAPTER XV. INCOME AND CAPITAL ACCOUNTS
CHAPTER XVI. THE RISK ELEMENT

CHAPTER XI

FOUR INCOME-CAPITAL RATIOS

§ 1

WE have now learned what capital and income are and how each is measured. We have seen that capital is not to be confined to any particular part or kind of wealth, but that it applies to any or all wealth existing at an instant of time, or to property-rights in that wealth, or to the values of that wealth or of those property-rights. We have seen that income is not restricted to money income, nor does it consist of a flow of commodities, nor is it a composite of commodities and services, nor is it necessarily regular in its receipt, nor must it necessarily be such as to leave capital unimpaired; but that it consists simply of the services of wealth, and that, analogously to capital, income may be measured either by the mere quantity of the various services rendered, or by their value. We have seen that in the summation both of capital-value and of income-value there are two methods available for canceling positive and negative items called the "method of balances" and the "method of couples." By the method of balances the negative items in any individual account are deducted from the positive items in the same account, and the difference, or balance, shows the net capital (or income, as the case may be) with which that account deals, whether this be the net capital (or income) of a particular owner, or of a particular article or group of articles of capital. The method of couples, on the other hand, cancels items in pairs and is founded on the fact that, as to capital, every liability relation has a credit as well as a debit side, and that, as to income, every interaction is at once a service and a disservice.

We observed that the method of couples, fully carried out, reveals respectively wherein capital and income ultimately consist. We have seen that such a summation, applied to capital, gradually obliterates all partial rights, such as stocks and bonds, and leaves as the final result the concrete capital wealth of a community; and that when the method of couples is applied to income accounts, the "interactions" involved disappear, leaving an uncanceled outer fringe of services and disservices. If the method is continued as far as possible in the world of objective services, it leaves simply the direct or final services of objective wealth as they affect the human organism; while, if the method is pushed one step further, it leaves, as the final income stream, simply the pleasant and unpleasant experiences of human consciousness. We found as one result of our study that so-called cost of production has no existence as an element of the objective income stream, and that, therefore, the only costs of production which are not also elements of income are the subjective labor and trouble of those engaged in that production.

We have seen that capital and income are in many respects analogous, and are strictly correlative; that all capital yields income and that all income flows from capital — at least when the term "capital" is used in its broader sense, which includes human beings. The old proposition of the economists, therefore, that capital is that wealth which yields income, is correct, although the idea that such a statement is restrictive, and applicable only to certain kinds of wealth, is incorrect.

§ 2

Since capital and income are so intimately related, it becomes necessary to examine in detail what their relations are. The chief relations between capital and income are represented by four ratios. As we have seen, both capital and income may be measured either in quantity or value. It follows that the relation of income to the capital which bears it takes four different forms, according as the income and the capital are measured in one or the other of these two ways. These four forms of the income-to-capital ratio follow:—

(1) The ratio of the *quantity* of services per unit of time to the *quantity* of capital which yields those services may be called the *physical productivity* of capital. Thus, if 10 acres of land yield, in a certain year, 60 bushels of wheat, the ratio of income to the capital may be expressed as 6 bushels per acre per year. This is its physical productivity. In like manner, if 10 looms will weave 500 yards of cloth in a day, the ratio of services to the quantity of capital, or the physical productivity of the looms, is 50 yards per machine per day.

(2) The ratio of the *value* of the income from capital to the *quantity* of the capital may be called the *value productivity*. Thus, if 10 acres of land yield a net return worth $200 a year, the value productivity is $20 per acre per year. This is what has ordinarily been called the rent of land. The same principles apply to the rent of a dwelling or of any other article of capital. Another example of value productivity is found in the wages of the laborer.

(3) The ratio of the *quantity* of services rendered by capital to the *value* of the capital may be called its *physical return*. Thus, if $100 worth of capital applied to land in the form, say, of agricultural implements adds to the yield of the land one bushel, the physical return of this capital is $\frac{1}{100}$ of a bushel per year per dollar invested. Such a concept of physical return is familiar to students of classical economics under the head of "doses" of capital applied to land.

(4) The ratio of the *value* of services to the *value* of the capital yielding them may be called the *value return*. Thus,

if a house worth $10,000 yields in any given year a net rent of $1000, the value return is ten per cent per year. An important case of value return is evidently the rate of interest.

Thus we have four ratios: —

1. $\dfrac{\text{Quantity of services per unit of time,}}{\text{quantity of capital,}} =$ physical productivity.
2. $\dfrac{\text{Value of services per unit of time,}}{\text{quantity of capital,}} =$ value productivity.
3. $\dfrac{\text{Quantity of services per unit of time,}}{\text{value of capital,}} =$ physical return.
4. $\dfrac{\text{Value of services per unit of time,}}{\text{value of capital,}} =$ value return.

These four magnitudes must be carefully distinguished. They are, as mathematicians say, of different "dimensions."[1] This fact is suggested in the four following phrases, which may be taken as typical: —

1. Bushels per acre per year.
2. Dollars per acre per year.
3. Bushels per dollar per year.
4. Dollars per dollar per year.

§ 3

The failure to keep these four magnitudes clearly distinguished has already led to a great many confusions in economic science. The spurious distinction between rent as the income from "land" and interest as the income from "capital" is a case in point.[2] From this confusion comes the notion that land differs from "capital" in that there is a margin of cultivation for the former and none for the

---

[1] For a mathematical statement, see Appendix to Chap. XI.

[2] The error is fully exposed in Cannan's "What is Capital?" *Economic Journal*, June, 1897, pp. 283–284, and in Fetter's "The Relations between Rent and Interest," a paper presented before the American Economic Association, December, 1903. See also Hicks's *Lectures on Economics*, Cincinnati, 1901, p. 228, and the present writer's "Rôle of Capital in Economic Theory," *Economic Journal*, December, 1897, p. 524, and "Precedents for Defining Capital," *Quarterly Journal of Economics*, May, 1904.

latter; and that, whereas different qualities of *land* bear different rents, representing the difference in advantage between a particular grade of land and no-rent land, all parts of *capital* bear the same rate of interest. These errors come from unconsciously regarding the land in terms of quantity and the so-called "capital" in terms of value; in other words, from considering the income from land in the sense of *value productivity*, but that from capital in the very different sense of *value return*. If, in making our comparisons, we abide consistently by either one of these ratios, the imagined distinction between rent and interest and between land and capital will vanish. It is quite true that the value productivity of land differs with different grades of land; but it is equally true that the value productivity of machinery, or of any other element of capital, so varies. New, high-grade, and efficient machinery bears exactly the same relation to machinery which is out of date and inefficient that fertile land bears to sterile. Similarly, different persons have different degrees of productivity, some having high and others low earning power. It was on this basis, in fact, that Francis Walker applied the Ricardian theory of rent to the explanation of entrepreneur's profits.

On the other hand, if we fix our attention on value return, we find it indeed true that the value return called the rate of interest on "capital" (however narrowly capital may be conceived) is uniform, but we find it equally true that the value return on land is also uniform; for land which yields a high rent will have a correspondingly high value, and, in consequence, the ratio of the rental to the value will be exactly the same as for lower grades.

Other examples of confusion might be cited. We find some of them in the cruder theories of interest. The "naïve" productivity theory,[1] for instance, confuses phys-

[1] See Böhm-Bawerk, *Capital and Interest,* English translation, 1888, pp. 120-141.

ical productivity and value return, and attempts to deduce the rate of interest from mere physical productivity, which is impossible.

§ 4

In this book we are concerned chiefly with the fourth relation, value return, or the ratio of the value of income to the value of capital.

The fundamental principle which applies here is that the value of capital at any instant is derived from the value of the future income which that capital is expected to yield. The expected services may, of course, not be the actual services. In our ignorance of the future we fix our present valuations on the basis of what we expect the future to be.

The principle of present worth is of fundamental importance in the theory of value and prices. It means that the value of any article of wealth or property is dependent alone on the future, not the past. The principle has been imperfectly stated as follows: "The value of any article is not determined by its cost of production, but by its uses." But the costs of production are disservices, and these, if they be *future*, enter into value on precisely the same terms as uses or services. They are discounted as are services. For instance, the value of the Panama Canal to-day is dependent upon the future expected services, taken in connection with the expected cost of completion. If these *future* elements be given, the value of the canal will be the same whether *past* cost was large or small, or nothing at all. Of course, the future expected cost for completing the canal is less than if some of the work had not been done already, so that the greater the past cost has been, the less the future cost will be, and hence the greater the value of the canal at present.

Thus normally the value of capital will vary with the past cost of production. Moreover, the experience of the past enables us to make a better estimate as to future cost.

But, however determined, it is the estimated future cost alone which enters into the calculation of present value. All of these principles are well illustrated in the case of the canal. After some $300,000,000 had been sunk in the enterprise, the proprietors were willing to sell out for only $40,000,000. To them, therefore, it was worth less than it had cost. The effect of the work already done on the canal was certainly to lessen the labors of the present possessors, but it also at the same time opened their eyes to the magnitude of the task still before them; hence the reduction in value to correspond to the new forecast of the future.

No one will dispute that the buyer of any article of capital will value it for its expected services to him, and that "at the margin" of his purchases, the price he will pay is the equivalent to him of those expected services, or, in other words, is their "present worth," their "discounted value" or "capitalized value." But some doubt may be felt regarding the professional seller. As to him, he is simply a speculator as to the possible demand. He sells for what he can get, affixing whatever price he believes will, in the end, profit him most, sometimes making out of the transaction more than his costs of acquisition, sometimes less, usually, or normally, covering those costs plus interest on them for the time elapsing between their occurrence and the sale.

The same principle applies all the way back in the production processes. The labor expended is staked (either by the laborer or entrepreneur) in anticipation of the prices which the buyers will be willing to pay. If these anticipated prices are not expected to cover the value of the labor and other costs plus the interest upon them, the result will be that the labor and other costs will not be expended. Hence by trial and error the labor and other costs will, under normal conditions, gradually be fitted to the prices.

When prices find this normal level at which costs plus interest are covered, it is not because the past costs of production have determined prices in advance, but because the sellers have been good speculators as to what prices would be. If they had foreseen that prices would not cover costs and interest on costs, they would have refrained from production entirely, while if they had foreseen the opposite condition, that of large profits, competition would have tended to reduce these profits to the usual dimensions.

We see, then, that although prices bear a normal relation to past costs, this relation does not always hold true; and that, whether it holds true or not, the costs do not predetermine the prices except in the sense that the producers have skillfully adapted the stocks available now, and those to be available at succeeding points of time, to the expected demand for them.

It is not our purpose in the present book, however, to emphasize these principles, for they belong properly to the theory of prices. We merely premise them in order to proceed to the study of the relation between capital-value and income-value, that is, of what we have called "value-return."

CHAPTER XII

CONCEPT OF RATE OF INTEREST

§ 1

From the last chapter we obtained the concept of value-return. This may be explicitly defined as the ratio of the value of the income which flows from a specified capital during a specified interval of time, to the value of that capital at a specified point of time. Thus, if on January 1, 1900, a capital is worth $10,000, and during the year 1900 this capital yields an income worth $500, the value-return is five per cent per annum for that year. If the income is perpetual and flows at a uniform rate, the value-return is called the *rate of interest* realized on the capital. In other words, the rate of interest is, briefly stated, the ratio between income and capital. As business men say, the rate of interest is the "price of money," or the "price of capital." This very common usage is based on the thought that any capital sum is the equivalent of some annuity. The usage has been needlessly condemned by economists on the ground that a different meaning should be assigned to the expression "price of money," viz. its "purchasing power" over goods in general. But the objection is not well founded, for it is evident that "purchasing power" includes not only purchasing power over a stock of goods but also purchasing power over a flow of *income*. If $100 will buy a perpetual annuity of $6 a year in Japan, while in England it will buy one of only $3 a year, the purchasing power of capital *over income* is six per cent in Japan, and only half as much in England. A millionaire in the first country will be able to command an income of $60,000 without trenching on his capital, whereas in England he can get but $30,000, and will, therefore, be just half as wealthy in actual income.

§ 2

The rate of interest has many meanings, and since the concept is so vital to our study, we shall specify carefully, in the present chapter, what these various meanings are. The meaning implied in the previous section postulates the existence of a perpetual annuity, *i.e.* a uniform and perpetual flow of income. Although such an annuity does not actually exist, it is often convenient to employ it as a vehicle of thought. Suppose $10,000 to-day will secure a perpetual annuity of $400 per year *payable annually*, the first payment accruing *one year* from the day of purchase; then the rate of interest is said to be four per cent per annum *payable annually;* that is, the rate of interest (when the interest is payable annually) is the ratio between the rate of flow of a perpetual annuity and its equivalent in present capital.

In case the income accrues *semi-annually* the case is slightly different. Let $10,000 to-day yield a perpetual annuity of $400 a year in semi-annual payments of $200 each, the first payment being due six months from date. Then the rate of interest is said to be four per cent per annum payable *semi-annually*.

That these four-per-cent rates are not equivalent to each other is well recognized in practice, and can be made evident in various ways. The holder of the semi-annual annuity has a slight advantage over the holder of the annual annuity, because he receives half of each year's income six months earlier. He may, in fact, convert his income of $200 twice a year into an income of $404 once a year; for in six months, besides receiving his first installment of $200, he may receive $10,000, by selling his annuity. He may then reinvest the entire $10,200 on the original terms, 4 per cent payable semi-annually, and hence obtain a perpetual annuity of $408, in semi-annual installments of $204. In six months more, or one year from the original investment, he may realize $204 of income and $10,200 of "principal," or $10,404 in all. Of this he may reinvest the original $10,000, retaining $404. From this point onward he may repeat the same annual cycles of sales and reinvestments, and, therefore, receive $404 net, payable once a year. He is, consequently, better off by $4 a year, than the holder of an annuity of $400 a year, payable annually. In other words, a rate of interest of 4 per cent per annum, if the income is payable semi-annually, is equivalent to a rate of interest of 4.04 per cent per annum, if the income is payable annually.

The same reasoning may be applied when the income accrues at quarterly or any other intervals.[1]

By subdividing the time of payment indefinitely, we may pass from an income obtained in installments to a continuous flow of income. The idea of a uniform and perpetual stream of income is nearly realized in certain cases, as in the West, where water rights are sometimes bought in the form of a "miner's inch" — a perpetual flow through a square inch opening under a head of six inches. Let us suppose that the water is worth $100 a year. If the right to such a perpetual and uniform flow can be bought for $2000, the rate of interest is five per cent "reckoned continuously."

We thus reach the conclusion that there are various senses of the rate of interest, according to the frequency of payment, namely, —

The rate of interest per annum, income payable annually.
The rate of interest per annum, income payable semi-annually.
The rate of interest per annum, income payable quarterly.
The rate of interest per annum, income payable at other intervals.
The rate of interest per annum, income payable continuously.

The last named, while it is the least familiar in practice, is in some respects the most natural, and lends itself the most

[1] See Appendix to Chap. XII, § 1.

readily to mathematical transformations. The first, on the other hand, is the most frequently used in practical computations.

§ 3

We have considered the rate of interest as the price of capital in terms of income. If we consider reciprocally the price of income in terms of capital, we shall have what is called the "rate of capitalization." It is measured in years, namely, the number of years during which there would flow an amount of income equal to the capital. Thus, if $25,000 will buy a perpetual annuity of $1000 a year, the rate of capitalization is "twenty-five years' purchase." The concept of "years' purchase" is common in England as applied to land rents. It is evidently interconvertible with the rate of interest. A rate of interest of four per cent indicates a "years' purchase" or rate of capitalization of twenty-five years. A rate of interest of two per cent indicates a rate of capitalization of fifty years. The rate of capitalization has thus as many meanings as the rate of interest, according as the income is payable annually, semi-annually, quarterly, etc., or continuously.

§ 4

The concepts of interest which have been given depend upon the concept of a perpetual annuity. But they can be made to apply also to terminable annuities. Thus, $10,000 may yield at four per cent an income of $400 a year for ten years, at the expiration of which time the $10,000, or the "original loan," is returned. In such a case the loan may evidently be regarded as a *purchase and resale* of a perpetual annuity. A perpetual annuity of $400 is, for the price of $10,000, diverted to the lender's benefit, and at the end of ten years is restored to the borrower for the same sum.

We may regard in this light even short-time loans. Thus,

SEC. 4] CONCEPT OF RATE OF INTEREST 195

if a man borrows $100 to-day and agrees to pay it back with interest at 4% in one year, we may conceive of him as having sold a perpetual annuity of $4 a year for $100, and at the same time as having bound himself to buy it back for $100 at the end of one year. The combined result of these operations amounts to an exchange of $100 this year for $104 next year. It is possible to use such a simple exchange between this year's and next year's money, as the basis of an entirely new definition of the rate of interest, and one which is independent of the idea of an annuity. When $100 to-day is exchanged for $104 next year, the ratio of exchange between the two sums is $\frac{104}{100}$. This ratio is not, of course, itself the rate of interest; the rate of interest is the excess, or premium, of $\frac{104}{100}$, above unity. In other words, the rate of interest is the premium, or "agio," above par of this year's dollars in terms of next year's dollars.

Such a concept of interest may be called the *premium* concept, whereas the concept hitherto employed, or the price of capital in terms of an annuity, may be called the *price* concept of the rate of interest. To say that the rate of interest in the *price* sense is four per cent means that the price of $100 of capital is $4 of income per annum *forever*. To say that the rate of interest in the *premium* sense is four per cent means that the price of $100 of one year's goods is $104 of the next year's goods.

The premium concept of the rate of interest has been so much emphasized, notably by Böhm-Bawerk, that it seems advisable to repeat briefly, with respect to it, the distinctions as to annual, semi-annual, quarterly, etc., reckoning. Let us suppose that $100 to-day is worth $102 six months hence. The rate of interest in the premium sense is here 2 per cent for the six months' interval, and is said to be "4 per cent per annum *payable or reckoned semi-annually*." It will be evident, however, that this is a little higher rate than 4 per cent per annum *reckoned annually*. Let us suppose that at the end of six months, at which time

$102 is due, the debt is renewed for another six months at the same rate. It is evident that the $102 will then, by "compounding," amount to $102 × 1.02, or $104.04. The interest then, at the end of a year, instead of being $4, is $4.04. In other words, 4 per cent interest reckoned half-yearly is equivalent to 4.04 per cent reckoned yearly, as was also the case under the price concept of the rate of interest. In the same way we may consider quarterly or other intervals for compounding. At the limit, the interval for compounding may be reduced to an instant.[1]

We have then two methods of defining interest. In both of them the time element is prominent. Before passing on we should here remark that the *time* element enters not only as referring to the times of payment but also to the time of contract. A rate of interest implies not only the two points of time between which the goods for exchange are available, but also the point at which the decision to exchange them is made. It would be quite possible, for instance, to agree in the year 1900 to exchange $1000 in the year 1901 for a given sum or series of sums returnable at still later dates. In this case the rate of interest for this exchange *appertains to the year* 1900, although execution of the contract does not begin until a year later and is not concluded until later still. These conditions have often been overlooked in treating statistics of the rate of interest.

§ 5

We have defined the rate of interest both in the "price" and the "premium" sense. The question now arises whether these two concepts are interchangeable. Under certain conditions they are, and under others they are not. Cases in which the two are interchangeable are shown in the following propositions.

[1] For the mathematical relations involved, see Appendix to Chap. XII, § 2.

CONCEPT OF RATE OF INTEREST

(1) If the rate of interest, in the sense of a premium on this year's goods in terms of next year's goods, is the same year after year forever, then the rate of interest considered as the price of capital in terms of a perpetual annuity will be equal to it.

A numerical example will make this clear. We shall suppose that the rate of interest is four per cent in the premium sense, *i.e.* that $100 at any moment during the period under consideration will buy $104 to be paid one year later. We are to show that as a consequence $100 will necessarily buy an annuity of $4 a year forever. Let us suppose, then, the premium rate being 4 per cent, that $100 is spent for $104, to be repaid one year later. Of this $104, when it is received at the end of the year, the investor reinvests $100. By our hypothesis of an unchanged interest rate, this $100 will bring, at the end of the second year, another $104, of which in turn $100 is reinvested; and so on indefinitely. By continually reinvesting, he obtains for his original $100, $4 a year indefinitely and $100 deferred indefinitely. If the process is perpetual, the $100 is deferred to infinity, and has no present value. Hence the original $100 obtains simply a perpetual annuity of $4 a year, and the rate of interest in the price sense is therefore also 4 per cent, which was to have been proved.[1]

It is evident that this reasoning may all be put in general terms, and that it applies equally to interest reckoned semi-annually, quarterly, etc., and continuously.

(2) Conversely, if a given rate of interest in the *price* sense holds good to-day, next year, two years later, and so on indefinitely, then the rate of interest in the *premium* sense will be equal to it.

This also may be readily shown by an example. If $100 will buy $4 a year forever, the first $4 being due one year

---

[1] An alternative proof consists in obtaining the present value of each successive item of income and adding the results. This process is exemplified in the next chapter in obtaining the capital-value of a perpetual annuity.

hence, the buyer of such an annuity at the end of one year may, immediately upon the receipt of his first $4, sell out his rights. By hypothesis they will bring $100. Consequently, he receives $104 in all for his $100 a year ago. He has thus virtually exchanged $100 one year for $104 the year after. That is, the *premium* rate of interest for this year is also 4 per cent.

We see, then, that if the rate of interest in either of the two senses — price or premium — remains constant, the rate in the other sense will also remain constant and equal to the former.

It is clear that the same reasoning applies to interest reckoned for any period of time, — semi-annually, quarterly, continuously.

§ 6

But if the rate of interest does *not* remain constant, its two senses of price and premium are no longer interchangeable. Thus, suppose that the rate is 4 per cent in the premium sense for the first year, but 3 per cent for the second year and for all succeeding years. This means that $100 to-day will buy $104 next year, and that $100 next year will buy $103 the year after. Then $100 to-day will evidently not buy $4 a year forever, nor $3, but an intermediate amount, approximately $3.03, so that the rate of interest in the price sense is 3.03 per cent.[1]

Again, suppose that the rate of interest in the price sense is 4 per cent this year, but 3 per cent next year. This means that $100 to-day will buy $4 a year forever, and that $100 next year will then buy $3 a year forever. Then $100 to-day will not buy $104 next year, nor $103, but 137\frac{1}{3}$. That is, the rate of interest in the premium sense is 37$\frac{1}{3}$ per cent.[2] Thus a very *slight* change in the *price* rate of interest implies a *great* change in the *premium* rate of in-

---

[1] See Appendix to Chap. XII, § 3.
[2] See Appendix to Chap. XII, § 4.

terest. This goes to explain why, in the actual market, the rate of interest for short-time loans fluctuates so much more widely than the rate of interest on long-time investments. It is scarcely necessary to exhibit statistics to show this, though they are easily obtained by comparing the fluctuations in the rate of interest on short-term and long-term loans, in the United States or in England.

We see, then, that the two concepts of interest rate, though definitely related,[1] are not always interchangeable.

§ 7

There is yet another device for indicating the terms of time exchanges. Besides the rates of interest and their reciprocals, the ratios of capitalization, there is the *rate of discount*. We have seen that if $104 due one year hence will buy $100 of present goods, then $\frac{104}{100}$ is the rate of exchange between the two times and exceeds unity or par by $\frac{4}{100}$, the rate of interest. The rate of exchange between the two times, when taken in the opposite direction, is $\frac{100}{104}$ and this is *less* than unity or par by $\frac{4}{104}$. This deficiency, which amounts to 3.9 per cent, is called the rate of discount. The number representing the rate of discount is always slightly less than that representing the corresponding rate of interest.[2] The rate of discount is practically employed only for short-time loans, usually less than a year, in which cases it better serves the purposes of rapid computation.

§ 8

The present chapter may be briefly summarized as follows: —

First, the rate of interest is a special case of "value-return," and may be approached from either of two standpoints, according as we consider it the price of capital in

[1] See Appendix to Chap. XII, § 5.
[2] For further discussion of the rate of discount, see Appendix to Chap. XII, §§ 6, 7.

terms of a perpetual annuity, or the premium on the price of this year's goods in terms of next year's goods. These two definitions of the rate of interest we have found to be interchangeable when either one of them is assumed to be invariable; but when this condition is not fulfilled the two are not interchangeable.

Secondly, not only does the rate of interest have the two distinct meanings which have been given, but each meaning is subject to various interpretations, according as the interest is payable or reckoned annually, semi-annually, quarterly, etc., or continuously.

Thirdly, as alternatives to the rate of interest we may employ the rate of discount and the rate of capitalization. Both of these magnitudes also apply either in the price sense or the premium sense. Furthermore, like the rate of interest, they apply somewhat differently according as the reckoning is annual, semi-annual, quarterly, etc., or continuous.

The following table illustrates the various magnitudes which have been considered:[1] —

EQUIVALENT RATES OF INTEREST, DISCOUNT, AND CAPITALIZATION

	A Rate of Interest	B Rate of Discount	C Reciprocal of A, or Rate of Capitalization	D Reciprocal of B
Reckoned annually	4.00%	3.85%	25.0 yrs.	26.0 yrs.
Reckoned semi-annually	3.96%	3.88%	25.3 yrs.	25.8 yrs.
Reckoned quarterly	3.94%	3.90%	25.4 yrs.	25.6 yrs.
Reckoned continuously	3.92%	3.92%	25.6 yrs.	25.6 yrs.

Since the sixteen magnitudes in this table may be taken either in the price or the premium sense, and since, when in-

[1] For their mathematical "dimensions," see Appendix to Chap. XII, § 8.

constancy enters, the two senses will involve two unequal magnitudes, we have here represented or implied thirty-two possible magnitudes. The means for expressing time exchanges between goods of the same kind thus present an embarrassing variety. But since it is easy to proceed from any one of them to all the others, it is evident that we need not, in general, employ more than one. The one which is practically the simplest, and which, therefore, we shall hereafter employ in this book is: *the rate of interest per annum reckoned annually and considered as a premium on the goods of one year compared with those of the year following.*

CHAPTER XIII

VALUE OF CAPITAL

§ 1

Having found what constitutes a rate of interest, we are now enabled to pursue our study of the relation between capital and income. We found in Chapter XI that these relations are of four kinds, according to whether the income and the capital are measured in quantity or in value. The fourth of these, "value-return," brought us to the concept of a rate of interest.

The rate of interest acts as a link between income-value and capital-value, and by means of this link it is possible to derive from any given income-value its capital-value, *i.e.* to "capitalize" income.

To do this, we assume that the expected income is foreknown with certainty, and that the rate of interest (in the sense of an annual premium) is foreknown, and also that it is constant during successive years. With these provisos it is very simple to derive the capital-value of the income to be yielded by any article of wealth or item of property; in other words, to derive the value of that wealth or property. That value is simply the present worth of the future income from the specified capital. This is true whether the income accrues continuously or discontinuously; whether it is uniform or fluctuating; whether the installments of income are few or infinite in number.

We begin by considering the simplest case, that, namely, in which the future income consists of a single item accruing at a definite instant of time. If, for instance, one holds a property right by virtue of which he will receive, at the end of one year, the sum of $104, the present value of this right, if the rate of interest is 4 per cent, will be $100. If the property is the right to $1 one year hence, its present value is evidently $\frac{1}{1.04}$ or $0.962, and if the sum to which the property entitles the owner is any other amount than $1, its present value is simply that amount divided by 1.04 or multiplied by .962. Thus the present value of $432 due in one year is $\frac{432}{1.04}$, or 432 × .962, which is $416.[1]

If the future sum is due in two years, and the rate of interest is still 4 per cent, it is evident that $1 to-day is the present value of $1.04 next year, which in turn (by compounding) will then be the present value of $1.04 × 1.04 (*i. e.* [1.04]^2, or $1.082) at the end of the second year. The $1.082 is called the "amount" of $1 at the end of two years, and $1.04 is the "amount" of $1 in one year.

Similarly, in three years $(1.04)^3$ is the "amount" or sum worth $1 in present value; and so on for any number of years. These results show what $1 to-day is worth at the end of any number of years. And conversely, from them it is easy to see what $1 due at the end of any number of years is worth to-day. We have already seen that the present worth of $1 due in one year is $\frac{1}{1.04}$, or $0.962. Similarly, the present value of $1 due at the end of two, three, etc., years is respectively $\frac{1}{(1.04)^2}$, $\frac{1}{(1.04)^3}$, etc.[2] Knowing the present value of $1, we may evidently find that of any other sum by simple proportion.

To illustrate these results geometrically, let us represent time by horizontal lines, and the value of the capital by vertical lines; then the curve $A\ A'\ A''\ A'''$, as shown in Figure 1, will exhibit the relative values at any two instants, exchangeable on the basis of a given rate of interest, compounded annually.

The point B represents the present instant; B', the in-

---

[1] For the general mathematical treatment, see Appendix to Chap. XIII, § 1.

[2] For a mathematical formulation, see Appendix to Chap. XIII, § 2.

stant a year hence; B'', that two years hence; B''', three years hence; and $B^{(t)}$, t years hence. AB represents any present value, $A'B'$ the "amount" of this sum one year hence, $A''B''$ the "amount" two years hence, etc. Consequently, AB also represents the present value of $A'B'$ due one year hence, or of $A''B''$ due two years hence, or of $A^{(t)}B^{(t)}$ due t years hence. The curve $AA^{(t)}$ is an "exponential curve," this being the name given to a curve which ascends in geo-

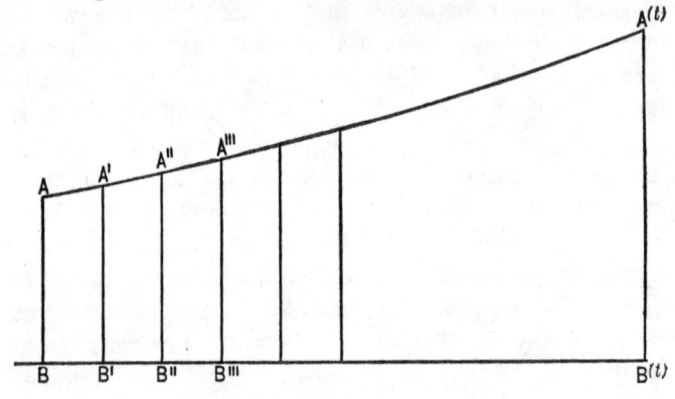

Fig. 1.

metrical progression, *i.e.* ascends so that the successive vertical lines, AB, $A'B'$, $A''B''$, and $A'''B'''$ (ordinates), taken at equal intervals, increase in length at a uniform ratio. We shall, however, for economic purposes, christen this curve the "discount curve."

§ 2

The principles which have been explained for obtaining the present value of a single future sum apply to many commercial transactions, especially to the valuation of bank assets, which exist largely in the form of "discount paper," or short-time loans of other kinds. The principles also apply, though in combination with those of risk and foreign exchange, to that form of property called "bills of exchange." Still another application is to wealth which is in course of trade and of which, therefore, the only service to the owner consists in its sale. It is on this principle that a dealer reckons the value of his stock, by discounting its selling price for the time which will probably elapse before it is sold — deducting, of course, the prospective expense of selling, discounted in like manner. Similarly, the value of any article of wealth reckoned when that wealth is in course of construction is the present value of what it will bring when completed, less the present value of the cost of completion. For instance, the maker of an automobile will appraise it, at any of its stages in course of construction, as worth the discounted value of its probable return when subsequently finished and sold, less the discounted value of the costs of construction and selling which still remain. Of course, the element of risk cannot, in such cases, be overlooked; but its consideration belongs to a later chapter.

Another application of these principles of capitalization is to goods in transit. A cargo leaving Sydney for Liverpool is worth the discounted value of what it will fetch in Liverpool, less the discounted value of the cost of carrying it there. Other classical examples are wine, the value of which is the present worth of what it will be when "mellow" and ready for consumption; and young forests, which are worth the discounted value of the lumber they will ultimately form. In Germany and some other countries, such appraisement of forests is now worked out with considerable precision.

§ 3

It seldom happens, however, that there is one item only of income or outgo earned by an article of capital. The items are unusually numerous. Perpetual annuities, for instance, form an important class, in which these items recur in equal amounts and during equal intervals forever. We have already seen, in the last chapter, that if a person owns the right to $1 a year payable at annual intervals forever, its present value, reckoned at four per cent, is $\frac{1}{.04}$, or $25. If his annuity is $2 per year, its present value is evidently double this, or $50; and if it is any other sum, its present value is found by multiplying in the same way. Thus, an annuity of $17 is worth $\frac{17}{.04}$. In other words, the value of a perpetual annuity is found by dividing the annual income by the rate of interest,[1] or, what amounts to the same thing, by multiplying the income by the rate of capitalization, also called the number of years' purchase. This proposition, however, serves to determine only that capital-value which an annuity possesses at its inception (*i.e.* one year before the first installment) or at any other point taken one year in advance of the first of the installments to be included in the calculation. The value of the annuity, taken *immediately before* any installment of income falls due, is evidently greater than the above, by the amount of that installment. Thus, if the rate of interest is four per cent, a perpetual annuity of $4 a year, of which the first payment falls due one year hence, is worth $100 to-day, and is also worth this same sum at any instant immediately *following* the payment of an installment. But next year, immediately *before* the first payment becomes due, it will be worth $104. At any intermediate point between the present when it is worth $100 and a year hence when it is worth $104, it will be worth an intermediate amount, determined by the discount curve; for its value will always be the discounted value of the $104, which could be realized on it at the time of the next interest payment. As soon as this payment has passed by, the value will drop to $100 again, after which it will gradually ascend as before, and so on, following a series of curves like the teeth of a saw, as shown in Figure 2. In this diagram, the value of the annuity is represented by suc-

---

[1] For a mathematical statement, see Appendix to Chap. XIII, § 3.

cessive vertical lines, four units in height, each representing $4, and situated one unit of time apart.[1]

If the annuity is "deferred," *i.e.* does not begin till some future time, its present value is the discounted value of

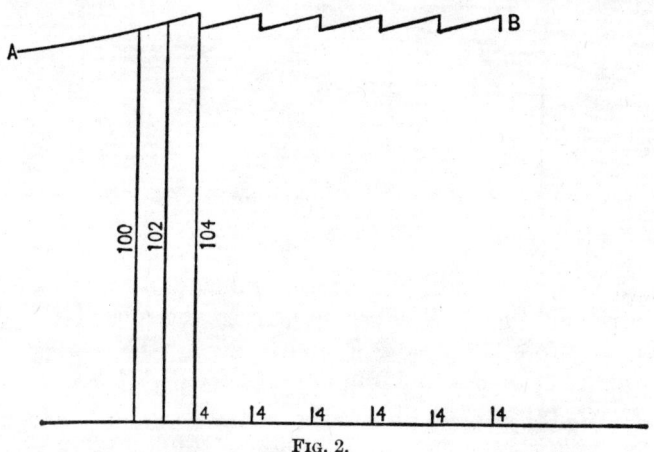

Fig. 2.

that value it will possess when it *does* begin. Thus, interest being four per cent, while $100 is the value of a $4 annuity beginning to-day (by which, as we have seen, is meant that its first installment falls due one year from to-day), the present value of an annuity deferred one year later will be only $\frac{100}{1.04}$, or $96.15, and the present value of an annuity deferred five years is $\frac{100}{(1.04)^5}$, or $92.46. The value of the annuity at any time before its inception at the point A is shown by the height at any point of the discount curve through A.

In the preceding discussion, the income, which is supposed to accrue in installments, is represented by separate successive vertical *lines*. But when the income is supposed to flow continuously, it becomes necessary to represent it by an *area*. In the "area" method, time is still

[1] For further discussion of the effect of reckoning interest for different time-intervals, see Appendix to Chap. XIII, § 4.

represented by horizontal lines, and vertical lines or ordinates are employed — not to represent income, but *rate* of income. Thus, in Figure 3, AC is the rate of income flowing at the instant A, and BD is the rate at the instant B.

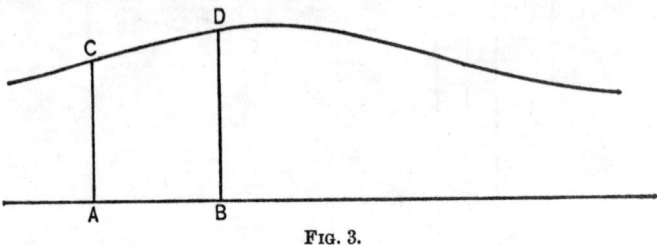

Fig. 3.

As a consequence, the income which flows through any period of time, AB, is represented by the area $ABDC$. It is therefore the time AB multiplied by the *average* rate. In the case of a uniform flow of income, CD reduces to a horizontal straight line. The area method will hereafter be used wherever continuous income is in question.[1]

§ 4

Actual examples of true perpetual annuities cannot be said to exist; but for practical purposes, some government "rentes" are perpetual annuities, also railway leases for 999 years. While the capital value of a perpetual annuity of $4 a year, capitalized at 4 per cent, is $100, that of an annuity of $4 a year for 50 years is $85, for 75 years is $94, for 100 years $98, and for 200 years $99.96. It will be seen, therefore, that for any ordinary rate of interest, an annuity extending a century or more is practically equal in value to a perpetual annuity.

Among non-monetary examples may be cited as perpetual annuities the before-mentioned water rights in the West. These are often sold by the miner's inch, *i.e.* a theoretically perpetual flow of $1\frac{1}{5}$ cubic feet per minute,

---

[1] For a fuller statement of the area method, as related to the line method, see Appendix to Chap. XIII, § 5.

which is supposed to be the rate at which water will flow through an aperture of one square inch with a "head" of six inches. The "first" inches are often so sure to continue as to be guaranteed. Again, if we overlook the element of risk, the hares in joint stock companies often exemplify perpetual annuities.

Turning from capital proper y to capital wealth, we find in land an approximate example of capital yielding a perpetual annuity. Land is often capitalized on the basis of a perpetual and uniform income, in the form of crops or other uses. It is then valued at a certain number of years' purchase. These so-called "natural and indestructible powers of the soil," however, which such a calculation assumes, do not always exist, and when they do exist, do not always yield a perpetual annuity. Mines and quarries become exhausted, while much land yields an irregular, increasing, or decreasing income stream.

§ 5

We turn now from perpetual to terminable annuities. Suppose that a man possesses a ten-year annuity of $100 a year. This means that he has the right to receive ten annual payments of $100 each, the first falling due one year from the present moment. It is clear that such an annuity differs from a perpetual one by lacking the infinite succession of payments after the ten years are past. In short, the terminable annuity is simply a perpetual annuity dated to-day, less a perpetual annuity deferred ten years. Therefore, the present value of the terminable annuity is simply the difference between the present value of the two perpetual annuities. Of these two perpetual annuities, the present value of the one which begins immediately, interest being four per cent, is $2500, and that of the one which is deferred ten years is $\frac{2500}{(1.04)^{10}}$, or $1689. Their difference is $2500 - $1689 or 811. Now such a difference as this, *i.e.* the difference between any particular sum (as $2500) and its discounted value for any time, is called the *total discount* on that sum. We may, therefore, express our result by saying that the present value of a terminable annuity is the total discount on a perpetual annuity of the same annual amount beginning when the terminable one ends.[1]

If the terminable annuity is itself deferred, its present value is the discounted value of its value reckoned at inception.

§ 6

Terminable annuities are sometimes employed by insurance companies and governments, but are otherwise comparatively rare as specific forms of property rights. Approximate cases, however, of such income exist in the case of many, if not most, durable articles of wealth. Thus, a machine yields a series of services of fairly uniform value for a fairly fixed term of years, and the same may be true of a house or other building, a ship, the rolling stock and other equipment of a railroad, etc. Such terminable income is also exemplified in many kinds of land, in the case of mines and quarries, peat beds and other tracts whose yield brings exhaustion. The state of Nevada presents an example of a large area of land which once yielded large incomes, but to-day is quite or nearly unproductive. It is evident, however, that in all these cases risk is an important factor in determining capital-value. This factor is for the present excluded from consideration.

As the date for the termination of the annuity approaches, the total discount diminishes; hence, the capital-value of the terminable annuity diminishes. The decrease of capital-value is what is sometimes known as "wear and tear"; namely, the depreciation of an article due to the fact that the services left for it to render gradually diminish. The approaching cessation of services may or may not be due to physical wear, so that the expression "wear and tear" is a

---

[1] For a mathematical presentation of this proposition, see Appendix to Chap. XIII, §§ 6, 7.

misnomer. We can imagine an article which suffers no material change, and of which the services will nevertheless last only a limited period. On the Atlantic coast the fishermen sometimes construct temporary platforms which are pretty sure to disappear in the September gales. It is evident that the value of such a property will decrease rapidly as the end of the fishing season approaches, without this decrease being due in the least to any physical deterioration. The "World's Fair" buildings at St. Louis depreciated, during the brief period of the fair, from $15,000,000, which was first paid for their construction, to $386,000, for which they were sold after they had served the purpose for which they were built. In like manner, a small wooden bridge, which is to be supplanted by a larger and better structure near by, will decrease in value rapidly as the time approaches for the other structure to divert its traffic, without any corresponding physical deterioration. Examples are common enough of productive instruments losing their value, because of its being known that better devices are soon to displace them. "Wear and tear," therefore, is a phrase which we must use only in a metaphorical sense. Even when the wear and tear take place because of physical deterioration, this deterioration acts upon the value only in so far as it decreases or terminates the flow of income, and not because of a physical change in the capital which bears this income.[1] The value of the capital depends exclusively on the income from it, and not directly upon its physical condition.

§ 7

Having considered the case of a terminable annuity, we turn to the case of a bond, which entitles the holder not only to a terminable annuity, but also to a single deferred sum called the "principal." Thus, a so-called "five

[1] Cf. Böhm-Bawerk, *Positive Theory of Capital,* English translation, 1891, p. 347.

per cent, ten-year, $100 bond" means the right to receive an annuity of $5 a year for ten years, and, in addition, $100 at the end of the ten years.

If the rate of interest is five per cent, and one buys a bond which entitles him to an annual income of $5 a year for ten years and $100 returnable at the end of this period, it is evident that the purchase price of the bond must be $100. In this case the $5 of annual income is the interest on the purchase price, and the sum of $100 which is to be received at maturity is equal to the originally invested capital or "principal." For these reasons such a bond is called a five per cent bond, the annual installments of income are called "interest," and the final payment of $100 is called "principal."

But more often than not the bond is not sold at par; consequently all of the three terms just mentioned are misnomers. If the bond is sold above par the rate of interest is not five per cent, but less than five per cent, so that it is only nominally a "five per cent bond"; the $5 annually received is only nominally "interest"; and the $100 returnable at the end is only nominally "principal."

In order to obtain the capital-value of a so-called five per cent bond when the market rate of interest is four per cent (*i.e.* when the bond is sold on a four per cent basis), we need simply to add together the present values (reckoned at four per cent) of the ten payments of $5 and of the final payment of $100. We may consider these items as consisting of (1) a ten-year annuity of $5 a year, and (2) a sum of $100 deferred ten years. Both of these we can easily find from the explanations already given.

It has been explained[1] that the present value of a ten-year annuity is the "total discount" on the capitalized value of a corresponding perpetual annuity beginning when the terminable annuity ceases. Now a perpetual annuity of $5 is worth, if interest is four per cent, $\frac{5}{.04}$, or $125.[2]

---

[1] See § 5, *supra*.   [2] See § 3, *supra*.

A perpetual annuity beginning in ten years will thus be worth \$125 — *in ten years*. To-day, therefore, it is worth, by discounting at four per cent, $\frac{125}{(1.04)^{10}}$, or \$84.45. The "total discount" is, therefore, \$125 less \$84.45, or \$40.55. We need to add to this the other element in the bond, namely, the present value of the so-called "principal" of \$100 due in ten years. Discounted at four per cent, this is worth $\frac{100}{(1.04)^{10}}$, or \$67.56. Combining our two figures we have, for the value of the bond, \$40.55 + \$67.56, or \$108.11.

We find, therefore, that a so-called five per cent bond yields the investor four per cent if it is bought at $108\frac{11}{100}$. In like manner it could be shown that it will yield him six per cent, if bought at \$92.50.[1]

In general a bond sells at par when the annual income, or nominal "interest," is equal to the true interest on the principal; it sells above par if the annual income (nominal interest) is greater than the interest on the principal; and below par if it is less.

In a similar way we may calculate the value of a bond in cases where the installments of income, or nominal interest, are semi-annual and the rate of interest is reckoned semi-annually, and in the case of more frequent intervals, as well as in the limiting case of continuous payment.[2]

Elaborate tables have been constructed, called "bond value books," calculated on the foregoing principles, which are used by brokers for showing the value of bonds under different circumstances. The tables are usually employed, however, for the converse problem, to find the rate of interest "realized" when a bond is bought at a given price. The following is an abridgment of these tables, for (so-called) three per cent, four per cent, and five per cent bonds. The prices of the bonds in all cases are the prices taken

[1] For a mathematical statement, see Appendix to Chap. XIII, § 8; for an alternative method of calculating the value of a bond and one which gives the "premium" separately, see Appendix to Chap. XIII, § 9.

[2] For mathematical statement, see Appendix to Chap. XIII, § 10.

Rates of Interest

(reckoned semi-annually) realized on a bond (with semi-annual coupons) known as a *"Three per cent bond"*

Price	Years to Maturity							
	1	2	3	5	10	20	30	50
120						1.8	2.1	2.3
110					1.9	2.4	2.5	2.6
105			1.3	2.0	2.4	2.7	2.8	2.8
103		1.5	2.0	2.4	2.7	2.8	2.9	2.9
102		2.0	2.3	2.6	2.8	2.9	2.9	2.9
101	2.0	2.5	2.7	2.8	2.9	2.9	2.9	3.0
100	3.0	3.0	3.0	3.0	3.0	3.0	3.0	3.0
99	4.0	3.5	3.4	3.2	3.1	3.1	3.1	3.0
98	5.1	4.1	3.7	3.4	3.2	3.1	3.1	3.1
97	6.1	4.6	4.1	3.7	3.4	3.2	3.2	3.1
95	8.3	5.7	4.8	4.1	3.6	3.3	3.3	3.2
90		8.6	6.7	5.3	4.2	3.7	3.6	3.4
80				7.9	5.7	4.5	4.2	3.9
70					7.3	5.5	4.9	4.5

Ditto for a *"Four per cent bond"*

Price	Years to Maturity							
	1	2	3	5	10	20	30	50
130						2.2	2.6	2.9
120					1.8	2.7	3.0	3.2
110				1.9	2.8	3.3	3.5	3.6
105		1.5	2.3	2.9	3.4	3.7	3.7	3.8
103		2.5	3.0	3.3	3.6	3.8	3.8	3.9
102	2.0	3.0	3.3	3.6	3.8	3.9	3.9	3.9
101	3.0	3.5	3.6	3.8	3.9	3.9	3.9	4.0
100	4.0	4.0	4.0	4.0	4.0	4.0	4.0	4.0
99	5.0	4.5	4.4	4.2	4.1	4.1	4.1	4.1
98	6.1	5.1	4.7	4.5	4.3	4.2	4.1	4.1
97	7.2	5.6	5.1	4.7	4.4	4.2	4.2	4.1
95	9.4	6.7	5.8	5.2	4.6	4.4	4.3	4.2
90		9.6	7.8	6.4	5.3	4.8	4.6	4.5
80				9.1	6.8	5.7	5.6	5.1

Rates of Interest

(reckoned semi-annually) realized on a bond (with semi-annual coupons) known as a *"Five per cent bond"*

Price	Years to Maturity							
	1	2	3	5	10	20	30	50
140						2.5	3.0	3.4
130					1.7	3.0	3.4	3.7
120					2.7	3.6	3.9	4.1
110			1.6	2.8	3.8	4.3	4.4	4.5
105		2.4	3.2	3.9	4.4	4.6	4.7	4.7
103	2.0	3.4	3.9	4.3	4.6	4.8	4.8	4.8
102	3.0	4.0	4.3	4.6	4.8	4.8	4.9	4.9
101	4.0	4.5	4.6	4.8	4.9	4.9	4.9	5.0
100	5.0	5.0	5.0	5.0	5.0	5.0	5.0	5.0
99	6.1	5.5	5.4	5.2	5.1	5.1	5.1	5.1
98	7.1	6.1	5.7	5.5	5.3	5.2	5.1	5.1
97	8.2	6.6	6.1	5.7	5.4	5.2	5.2	5.2
95		7.7	6.9	6.2	5.7	5.4	5.3	5.3
90			8.9	7.4	6.4	5.9	5.7	5.6
80					7.9	6.9	6.5	6.3

immediately after an installment of income. They are what business men call "ex-interest" prices, *i.e.* are devoid of accrued interest. To use the tables when we have given the price at any time between two installments of income, it is necessary first to "strip" this price of the interest accrued since the last installment of income.

It may be asked, Where is the line of demarcation between what are nominally "principal" and "interest"? The answer is: None at all of any logical importance. In our calculations all the items receivable from the bond, including the principal when paid, have been treated on the same basis. They are, with respect to the bond, its true "income." The so-called "principal" is usually regarded as a repayment of the original investment. Approximately, the original investment and final "principal" are equal. But whether equal or not they are distinct.

The original investment is the discounted value of expected receipts; the final "returned" principal is simply one (the largest one) of those receipts. The only difference between this large receipt and the other smaller ones is that, usually, it is employed differently when received. It is usually reinvested in other long-time securities, whereas the smaller items of income, the so-called "interest," are spent for articles of shorter duration, and, thereby, soon converted into true "final income." The "principal" and "interest," therefore, while both are income with reference to the bond considered by itself, are apt to lead to different results when followed into the final transformations of purchase and sale, by the debit and credit cancellations previously expounded. If we suppose a five per cent bond to be always sold on a five per cent basis, and the principal to be always reinvested in the same kind of security, it is evident, in relation to the *whole* series of operations, *including the reinvestment,* that the principal, though income, is immediately canceled by reinvestment as outgo. In other words, whenever it appears as income from one bond, it immediately disappears again as outgo for another; consequently the owner is virtually in possession of a perpetual annuity of $5 a year. It is with a view to such an operation that the final payment of $100 on a bond is instinctively regarded on a different footing from the other payments called "interest." It is called "principal" on the theory that it is to be reinvested in order to continue the annuity of $5. It thus in theory represents capital, whereas the other payments represent only income. But we see now that both are income received from the bond as a source of income, although either may, by reinvestment, be put into capital. That one of them is usually put back into capital and the other not, is a matter of subsequent history and does not affect the immediate study of the bond itself.

Even when the "principal" received at the maturity of

the bond is reinvested, it may be that it is not equal to the original investment, nor, therefore, to the capital-value of the bond at any time before maturity. This equality would hold true only in case the bond is always kept at par. When it is worth more or less than par the capital-value is more or less than the "principal," and for this reason, if for no other, the capital-value should not be confounded with the "principal."

In order to determine whether or not a nominally five per cent bond really yields five per cent, we must refer to the price at which it sells, and while there is no necessity to abandon the terminology by which "principal" and "interest" are used with reference to bonds, these terms are undoubtedly misnomers and their existence is responsible for considerable confusion. For instance, insurance companies have recently been offering their policy holders an option between the receipt at the death of the insured of a definite insurance of $1300, or of a "five per cent gold bond" for $1000. The gold bond has seemed, to many policy holders, a tempting form of investment because of the "high rate of interest," — five per cent; but it is evident that such a bond, considered as the equivalent of $1300 in cash, is on a lower basis than five per cent.

§ 8

Hitherto we have considered only four special cases of capitalizing income, viz. (1) the capital-value of a single income item; (2) the capital-value of a perpetual annuity; (3) the capital-value of an annuity terminable in a definite number of years; and (4) the capital-value of a bond. But it is clear that the items of income from any property may occur in many other forms, may last for any length of time, and may be distributed through this time in any manner whatever. Let us, therefore, consider the general case in which any random series of income items, AB, $A'B'$, $A''B''$, $A'''B'''$, are received, as shown in Figure 4. The capital-value of this series at the point of time O is found by adding together the present value of the separate items. The best way to exhibit this is to begin at the *last* income payment, $A'''B'''$. Just after this last installment, of course, the property is valueless; that is, its capital-value is zero. Just *before* this installment the capital-value is equal to the installment itself, and is represented by $A'''B'''$. At

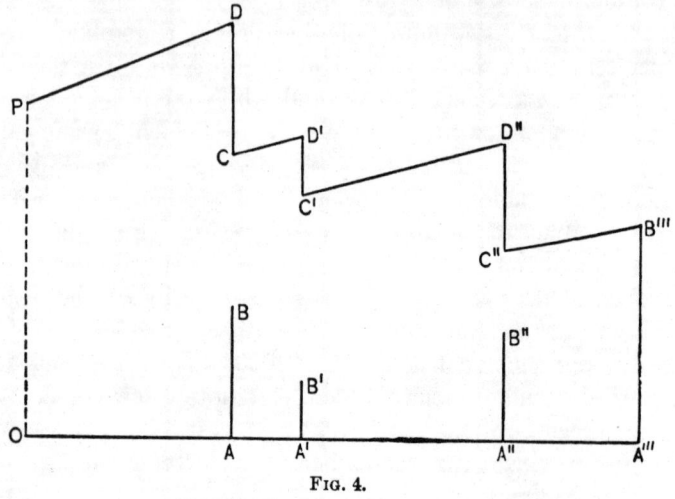

Fig. 4.

any time in the interval between this installment of income and the next preceding installment, the value will evidently be found by following the discount curve $B'''C''$, C'' being vertically over A''. The height $A''C''$ is, therefore, the capital-value of the property just after the payment $A''B''$. Its capital-value just *before* this payment is found by adding the vertical line $C''D''$, equal to the installment of income $A''B''$. From D'' in turn we proceed backward along the discount curve $D''C'$ to C', at which point $A'C'$ represents the capital-value of the property just after the installment $A'B'$. To this is added, if we pass back an instant, an amount $C'D'$ equal to the installment $A'B'$. The result is $A'D'$, the capital-value just before said installment. From D', in turn, the capital-value descends along the discount curve to C, where CD, equal to AB, is added, and from D we proceed finally by discount curve to P, vertically over O. OP is, therefore, the capital-value of the property at the "present" instant, and its value at any succeeding instant is shown by following the course of the broken line $PDCD'C''D''C'''B'''A'''$.[1] This curve must descend to zero

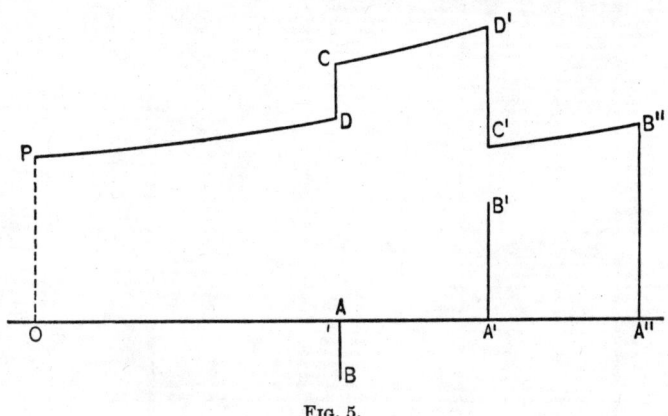

Fig. 5.

finally, when the income is exhausted, and it usually shows a tendency to decrease before this last payment is reached.

If, in a series of income items, a negative one occurs, it is only necessary to reverse the capital curve, as shown in Figure 5, where the first installment, AB, is outgo instead of income. The curve PB'' evidently represents the behavior of capital-value, rising suddenly as the outgo AB is passed and falling when the income $A'B'$ is received, and so on to the end.

We may, if we choose, trace the history of the value of a security from the time immediately before its purchase, and consider the purchase price itself as an outgo. If this price

[1] For the mathematical formula for the capital-value of any series of income installments, see Appendix to Chap. XIII, § 11.

is exactly equal to the discounted value of the succeeding income, it is evident that the value immediately before its purchase must be exactly zero. Thus in Figure 6 let OM be the purchase price, and equal to OA, which is the capital-value immediately after purchase. The capital-value immediately *before* purchase is, therefore, zero, and the entire capital curve is the line $OABCDEFH$, which starts

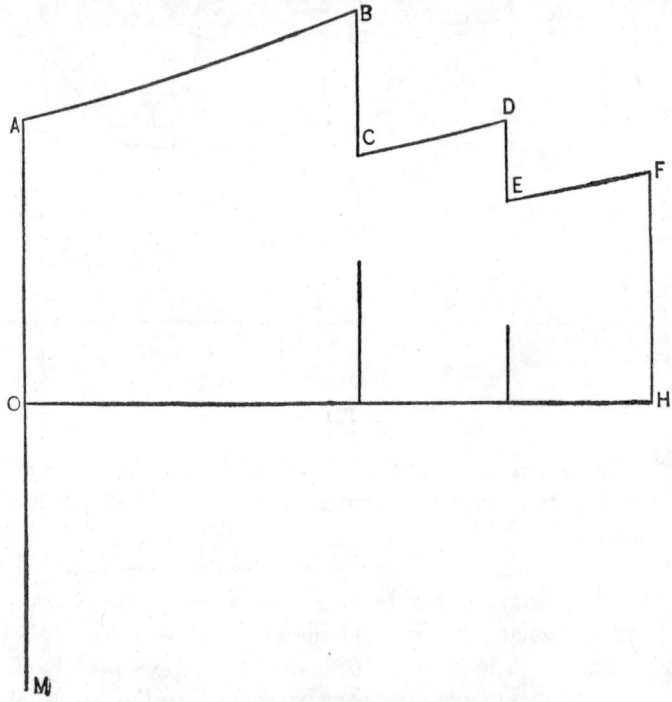

Fig. 6.

at zero and ends at zero, but is above the zero line at all intermediate intervals. This represents the normal history of any capital instrument if bought at a "fair price."

If the flow of income is continuous, we may obtain the capital-value approximately by dividing the continuous income stream into arbitrary installment sand discounting each installment separately.[1]

The value of the income stream has heretofore been always reckoned in advance of its occurrence; that is, we have discounted income to obtain *present* value. We may, however, consider an income as paid for at the close of the period, in which case we have to deal with its "accumulated" value or its "amount."[2]

§ 9

Thus far we have considered the possibility of but *one* income stream from any given capital wealth. But it often happens that, with one capital instrument, there is a choice between various income streams. Land may be used for grazing, agriculture, building, or recreation purposes. Tools may be employed in a variety of ways, and the same is true of innumerable articles of wealth, particularly when taken in combination. What determines the choice of the series of uses to which any given instrument may be put? Evidently that series of uses or income stream will be selected which yields the maximum present value. Thus, if land used for grazing purposes will yield a net service of $1000 a year forever, and interest is taken at four per cent, its value for grazing purposes is evidently $25,000. If, in like manner, the capital-value for some other use, say for growing wheat, is $20,000, it is clear that the land will be employed for grazing rather than for growing wheat.

Sometimes the two series of uses to which land or other wealth may be put differ, not only in their amount, but in their time of beginning or ending. In a city, for instance, land may be used either for present dwelling or for future business-purposes, and it often becomes a question which use is the more valuable. In case the city is growing

[1] For a fuller statement, see Appendix to Chap. XIII, § 12.
[2] For discussion, and for formulæ for the capital-value of any income, discontinuous or continuous, see Appendix to Chap. XIII, § 13.

rapidly, it may happen that in certain quarters, although the present use for dwelling purposes is more important, in a few years the locality will cease to be a residence quarter and the land will be needed for business purposes. In such cases, it may "pay" to keep the land out of present use entirely and reserve it until the city has grown so as to make it profitable to erect a business block. If the land were now encumbered with a dwelling, either the possibility of its subsequent use for business purposes would be cut off, or the profit from its conversion to those purposes would be impaired by the prior destruction and waste of the dwelling. Under such circumstances it would usually happen that speculators would buy up and hold the land. The manner in which the gain presents itself to them is simply as a prospective rise in value from the growth of the city; they therefore buy the land to sell it later at a higher price. Such a speculator is commonly regarded as keeping land "out of use." He is, however, only *deferring* the use, and, if he has foresight, is no more to be condemned than the wise speculator on the wheat exchange, whose work, as is well known, operates to conserve the supply of wheat. The speculator thus tends to bring about the best utilization of the land in the sense that, out of several alternative income streams which the land might be made to yield, that one is selected which possesses for him the maximum present value. In general it is probable that the best uses of the land for the public also are found in this way. The latter conclusion does not, however, absolutely follow from the former, since the "best" uses are not necessarily those which have the greatest market value; but those who would prevent all land speculation will at least need to adduce other arguments than that speculation "keeps land out of use," before they have proven their case; for wise land speculation means simply the discriminating choice, out of a number of uses, of that use or series of uses which affords to-day the greatest present value.

It should be observed that if the rate of interest is raised, the relative advantages of the two uses in the example given might be quite different. In this case it might pay to put up the dwelling rather than wait for the business block; for the holder of the land, as he expresses it, could not afford to "lose his interest" when it is at so high a rate.

§ 10

Thus far we have considered the capital-value only of individual articles of wealth. The same reasoning applies to a group of articles of wealth. An important case is that of a merchant's stock. In this case we may prefer to capitalize the stock as a whole rather than to take the sum of the capitalizations of its separate elements. The net income from the stock is found by subtracting from the gross income all the outgo, including, besides the cost of replenishing the stock, the other costs of the business, — clerk hire, rent, and even an allowance for the work of the merchant himself, unless he is a mere "silent partner." If the net income is supposed to remain constant forever, the capital value of the stock will, of course, be found by dividing the net income by the rate of interest. In this case the rate of interest must be taken for the proper installment interval. If the goods are supposed to be continuously bought and sold, the rate to be employed is the "rate of interest per annum reckoned continuously."[1]

§ 11

We conclude, therefore, that the value of any capital-good, either of wealth or of property-rights, assuming that all future income is foreknown, is the discounted value of that income, and consequently that, as time goes on, the value of that capital will oscillate, rising gradually during intervals between installments along a "discount curve,"

[1] For a mathematical statement in this connection, see Appendix to Chap. XIII, § 14.

as the future income approaches, and falling suddenly as the installments are successively passed by and acting in a contrary manner before and after an outgo. This oscillation of capital-value ends finally at zero, when the life or service of the article or group is ended. It also often begins at zero, when the instrument or group is one that is newly acquired or produced. These changes constitute, as it were, a sort of life history of capital-value.[1]

It may seem to some readers that there is an exception to the rule that the value of capital is the discounted value of its expected income, in the case where the income which might be received from the capital is indefinitely postponed. This is the case in which the "principal" accumulates at compound interest so that no "interest" is withdrawn. If a person has a deposit of $1000 in a savings bank and leaves it there to accumulate at 4 per cent until it amounts to double that sum, which will happen in about eighteen years, the $1000 does not appear to him to be the discounted value of any income. If he thinks of it as the discounted value of anything at all, it will be of the $2000 of capital which he expects to own at the end of eighteen years. It is perfectly true that the capital-value of $1000 is the discounted value of the future capital-value of $2000; but the latter capital-value is itself the discounted value either of some subsequent *income*, or, in turn, of a capital still further deferred, and so on indefinitely. Actual income is hoped for *sometime*, even if it be not for a million years. The present $1000 is the discounted value of that ultimate income, however far distant. A perpetual accumulation is, humanly speaking, out of the question. But if such perpetual accumulation be regarded for the moment as possible, it may still be interpreted as a perpetual postponement of possible income; so that even in this case the $1000 may

---

[1] For mention of the case where the rate of interest changes and its changes are foreknown, see Appendix to Chap. XIII, § 15.

still be regarded as the discounted value of an income which is indefinitely postponed, but indefinitely great. Of course, such a limiting case is of purely theoretical interest. The prodigious sums which result from the reckoning of compound interest always surprise those who have never made such computations. One dollar put at compound interest at 4 per cent would amount, in one century, to $50, in a second century to $2500, in a third century to $125,000, in a fourth century to $6,500,000, in a fifth century to $325,000,000, and in a sixth century to $16,000,000,000. Beyond this the figures are almost unthinkable in magnitude.[1]

Yet we have few instances in which any one has endeavored to set aside even one dollar for the benefit of posterity six centuries removed! There is too much reluctance to build for the remote future, even though the attainable results are enormous. Benjamin Franklin, at his death in 1790, left £1000 to the town of Boston and the same sum to Philadelphia, with the proviso that it should accumulate for a hundred years, at the end of which time he calculated that at 5 per cent it would amount to £131,000. In the case of the Boston gift, it actually amounted, at the end of the century, to $400,000, and has since accumulated to about $600,000. The sum received by the city of Philadelphia has not increased nearly as fast.

Another interesting case of accumulation is that of the Lowell Institute in Boston, which was founded by a bequest of $200,000 in 1838, with the condition that 10 per cent of the income from it should be reinvested and added to the principal. The peculiarity of this provision is that it applies in perpetuity. There is, therefore, theoretically no limit to the future accumulation thus made possible. The fund, after sixty-seven years, amounts already to $1,100,000.

It must be remembered however that practically even a

[1] For a geometrical representation, see Appendix to Chap. XIII, § 16.

small sum, such as $1000, if allowed to accumulate, let us say, at 4 per cent for 1000 years, could never actually attain the theoretical magnitude. This is evident from the fact that the theoretical sum would then amount to over $100,000,000,000,000,000, which is so far in excess of the total value of capital on this planet, as to be out of the range of possibility. The reason the sum would fail to accumulate as fast as theoretically required, aside from fortuitous losses, lies in the reduction of the rate of interest which the very accumulation would bring about. The administrators of such a fund, as the centuries passed by, would find it increasingly difficult to obtain fields in which to invest it, and their effort so to invest would have the same effect in reducing the rate of interest realized on the investments as is now felt by the national banks in their pressure to buy government bonds.

CHAPTER XIV

EARNINGS AND INCOME

§ 1

In the last chapter it was shown that, perfect foresight being assumed, the value of any capital good is derived from its future income by discounting the value of that income. It now remains to compare the capital-value thus derived with the expected income-value on which it depends.

It is evident at the outset that the capital-value is less than the total expected income; for the discounted value of any future sum is necessarily less than that sum itself. This fact is illustrated in the third and fourth columns of the following table of capital and income in the cases of five typical articles: —

Capital	Net Income per Year	Total Income	Capital-value (Int. at 5%)	Capital-value (Int. at 2½%)
Land	$1000 per year forever	Infinite	$20,000.00	$40,000.00
House	$1000 per year for 50 years	$50,000.00	18,300.00	28,400.00
Horse	$100 per year for 6 years	600.00	508.00	551.00
Suit of clothes	$20 1st year; $10 2d year	30.00	28.00	29.00
Loaf of bread	$36.50 per year, for 1 day	.10	.10	.10

In this table we observe that the value of the land, when interest is at 5 per cent, is $20,000, whereas the total income to be expected from it is infinitely greater; that the value of the house when interest is at the same rate is $18,300, whereas the total income to be expected from it is about three times as much, or $50,000; that the value of the horse is a little over $500, whereas the total expected income is about $100 more, or $600; that the value of the suit of clothes is $28, whereas its total income is $30, of which $20 accrues the first year and $10, the second; and, finally, that the capital-value of the loaf of bread is 10 cents and the income expected from it is also 10 cents. In this limiting case there is practically no diminution on account of the interval of time to elapse between the time of valuing the instrument and the time of receiving its services, for the reason that this time is too brief.

From the table we see clearly one reason that certain articles have been identified with income and others not. Bread has practically the same capital-value as income-value, so that, if a person were not accustomed to fine distinctions, he might think it unnecessary to discriminate between the 10 cents which is the value of the *use* of the bread, and which is, therefore, *income*, and the 10 cents which is the value of the bread itself, and which is, therefore, capital. There is almost as much danger of such confusion in the case of clothing; for there is only a slight difference between the $30 which is the value of the use of the suit, and is therefore income, and the $28 which is the value of the suit, and is therefore capital. But as we pass to the more enduring articles, there emerges so wide a difference between the value of the use of an instrument and the value of the instrument itself, that there is no difficulty in distinguishing between them. Accordingly we usually find in treatises on economics some distinction between the value of the use of a house ($50,000 in the foregoing table) and the value of the house itself ($18,300 in the table). But if the distinction is valid in one case it is valid in the others. The consequence of disregarding it we have already seen in Chapter VII.

§ 2

If the rate of interest is not 5 per cent, but $2\frac{1}{2}$ per cent, there will result great differences in the capital-values. The consequences are seen in the last column of the table. But the effect on capital-values wrought by thus cutting the rate of interest in two will be different for each of the five different articles. The more enduring ones will be affected the most. When the rate of interest is halved the value of the land will be doubled, rising from $20,000 to $40,000, but the value of the house will rise by only about 60 per cent, *i.e.* from $18,300 to $28,400; the value of the horse will rise only 10 per cent, *i.e.* from $508 to $551; the value of the suit will rise only from $28 to $29; and, finally, the value of the loaf of bread will not rise at all, but will remain at 10 cents. We see in these five types of articles that the sensitiveness of capital-value to a change in the rate of interest is the greater the more enduring the income.

In general, also, this sensitiveness is the greater the more remote the periods of time at which the income is concentrated. For instance, if the total income is $100, and is all concentrated at a point of time fifty years distant, its capital-value, when the rate of interest is 5 per cent, is $8.72, but it becomes $29.09 when the rate of interest is reduced to $2\frac{1}{2}$ per cent. That is, the rate of interest being halved, the capital-value is more than trebled. If the same income of $100 were to be due only one year from date, the change from 5 per cent to $2\frac{1}{2}$ per cent in the rate of interest would elevate the capital-value only from $95 to $97.50.

§ 3

Thus far we have been concerned only with *total* income, in relation to capital-value; we now consider the *rate* of income per year in relation to capital-value. This ratio has already been called the rate of "value-return."

In accordance with previous explanations the sequence

of calculating the rate of value-return is as follows: A specified property entitles the owner to a future series of income items which is assumed to be definitely foreknown. These items are all discounted by means of a specified rate of interest. The sum of the discounted values constitutes the capital-value of the property. This capital-value, at any time, taken as divisor and the income per year taken as a dividend gives the rate of value-return as quotient.

It must be steadily borne in mind that the value of the capital which forms the divisor is not a fictitious book value, nor the value as indicated by the sum of money originally invested, but is simply the discounted value, at the specified time, of the expected income subsequent to that time. We should at the outset rid our minds of the bogey of an unvarying "principal" perpetually existing somewhere in a debt or other property. The only value entity we have to deal with is the value of the property considered, which is the discounted value of the expected income, and which therefore is continually changing. When capital is for the present yielding no income, as, for instance, vacant land, it nevertheless is expected *sometime* to yield income, and it is the discounted value of this remote income which alone constitutes the present value of the land. It is true that a speculator may prize the land simply because he thinks he can sell it later to some one else, and to him it may seem that its value is independent of any future income, and depends only on the future capital-value at which he expects to sell. But it is clear that this future capital-value is itself the discounted value of the income which the then purchaser will expect. Or, if he too be a speculator, and his valuation, like his predecessor's, depends on a resale, the dependence on future income is merely again postponed to the time when some purchaser shall buy the land for the income it will yield. This ultimate expected income gives the basis for all prior capital valuations. Were there no expectation of any future income — or, at least, the expectation that there would be an expectation of it — there could be no capital-value. Capital-value, independent of expected income, is impossible.

§ 4

The first proposition to be emphasized as to the rate of value-return is that it is not necessarily equal to the rate of interest, but may be either greater or less than that rate, and to any degree.

Let us take, for example, the case of the house which we assumed would endure just fifty years, giving throughout that period a shelter-service worth, after actual expenses are deducted, $1000 annually. We saw that its value, computed by discounting this fifty-year annuity on a 5 per cent basis, is $18,300. It therefore yields the first year a rate of value-return on its capital-value of $\frac{1000}{18,300}$, or 5.4 per cent. At the end of ten years its value, found by discounting the income still remaining, will be $17,200. It will therefore then be yielding a value-return of $\frac{1000}{17,200}$ per year, or 5.8 per cent. At the end of thirty years, in like manner, it will be worth $12,500 and yielding $\frac{1000}{12,500}$, or 8 per cent. Again, the suit of clothes which will last two years, and gives services worth $20 the first year and $10 the second, has a value at the start of about $28, and at the end of the first year of about $9.50. The value-return the first year is therefore $\frac{20}{28}$, or 71.4 per cent, and the second year $\frac{10}{9.50}$, or over 100 per cent. The loaf of bread has a value of 10 cents. It yields 10 cents' worth of income in a day, which is at the rate of $36.50 per year; consequently its value-return is $\frac{36.50}{.10}$, or a rate of 36,500 per cent per annum (interest reckoned daily or "continuously").

In these examples the value-return exceeds the rate of interest. Reversely, it is possible for the value-return on capital to be less than the rate of interest. If, for instance, forest land with small trees is bought, it may be that no product can be obtained until the end of ten years. We may suppose that then the yield is worth $1000 a year during the ensuing (second) decade, after which it will be worth $2000 a year forever. It may be shown that the present value of the forest, reckoned on a five per cent basis, is about $20,000. This would be the discounted value of an annuity of $1000 a year, whose commencement is deferred ten years from the date of investment, and which then runs ten years, plus the discounted value of a perpetual annuity of $2000 a year beginning twenty years in the future. On the five per cent basis, the forest will, in ten years from the present, be worth about $32,000 (this being the discounted value of an immediate ten-year annuity of $1000 followed by a perpetuity of $2000). Twenty years from the present, the forest will be worth $40,000 (this being the discounted value of $2000 a year forever). The forest land therefore rises gradually in value from $20,000 to $32,000 in the first decade, during which no income is realized, and continues to rise, though less rapidly, to $40,000 in the second decade, during which there is realized the comparatively small income of $1000 a year. The rate of return, therefore, at the beginning, being the quotient of the income realized divided by the capital, is $\frac{0}{20,000}$, or zero. The rate of return evidently remains zero throughout the first decade. At the beginning of the second decade the rate is evidently $\frac{1000}{32,000}$, or 3.1 per cent; at the beginning of the third decade it is $\frac{2,000}{40,000}$, or 5 per cent. We see, therefore, that in this case the rate of value-return gradually rises from zero to a height equal to the rate of interest.

There may even be a negative rate of return. A colt, for instance, may occasion more trouble than it is worth for the first year, and produce a net expense or disservice of $20. Thereafter it may render a net income of $10 during the second year, $20 during each year from the third to the tenth inclusive, and $10 a year the next five years, after which it dies. Supposing, as our preliminary hypothesis obliges us to do, that all these are definitely foreseen at the start, the colt would be worth the discounted value (at 5 per cent) of all these, or about $135. It will therefore yield during the first year a return of $\frac{-20}{135}$, or − 15 per cent. The value-return for the second year, reckoned on its capital-value taken at the beginning of that year, is $\frac{10}{161}$, or 6 per cent; on the third year $\frac{20}{159}$, or 13 per cent, on the fifteenth year about $\frac{10}{10}$, or 100 per cent. The entire series may be seen from the following table: —

	INCOME DURING YEAR	CAPITAL-VALUE AT BEGINNING OF YEAR	RATE OF RETURN
1st year	− $20	$134	− 15%
2d year	10	161	6
3d year	20	159	13
4th year	20	146	14
5th year	20	134	15
6th year	20	121	17
7th year	20	107	19
8th year	20	92	22
9th year	20	76	26
10th year	20	60	34
11th year	10	43	23
12th year	10	35	28
13th year	10	27	37
14th year	10	19	54
15th year	10	10 −	100 +

From the foregoing examples it is evident that a property which yields 5 per cent to the investor may yield in individual years either more or less than 5 per cent. The dwelling house yielded more than 5 per cent for 50 years, and then ceased to yield income. The forest yielded less than 5 per cent for 20 years, and thereafter yielded 5 per cent on its value at that time. The colt yielded rates rising from − 15 per cent in the first year to 100 per cent in the fifteenth year, and then zero forever after.

At this juncture, however, the business reader may feel disposed to object. He will point out that in our tables the house is represented as yielding 5.4 per cent the first year instead of 5 per cent, by neglecting depreciation, and that, contrariwise, the forest was represented as yielding in the eleventh year 3.1 per cent instead of 5 per cent, by neglecting appreciation. For it is true that the house, worth $18,300 at the beginning of the year, must, under the given conditions, depreciate $85 during the year; and the objector will maintain that this ought to be deducted from the $1000 received from the house, in order to obtain the true "net earnings." The deduction leaves $915, which is just 5 per cent on the capital of $18,300. According to this calculation, therefore, the house really returns, not 5.4 per cent, but only 5 per cent. And, applying the same line of reasoning to the case of the forest, the objector might insist that the forest increased in value just enough to make up the difference between the 3.1 per cent, which was given as the rate of value-return at the beginning of the second decade, and the 5 per cent to which it would seem to be entitled.

These calculations are correct. But they do not militate against the treatment of value-return which has been given. They merely bring into relief a distinction between income which is *realized* by the investor and income which is *earned* by the capital. Realized income is the value of the actual services secured from the capital; earned income is found by adding to realized income the increase of capital-value, or deducting from it the decrease. We may designate them briefly simply as *income* and *earnings*.

To illustrate this distinction and to show its importance, let us consider a four per cent $1000 bond, the interest on which is payable annually. From what was shown in the previous chapter it is clear that (if the bond is valued on a four per cent basis) the value of the bond will oscillate between $1000 and $1040, rising gradually from the former to the latter between interest payments and falling back suddenly as each payment is made. The *income* is simply the payment of $40 at the end of each year. Even our objector will not deny this. During the entire year up to the very end there is no income at all; yet the bond "earns" about $10 each quarter, in the form of an increase in the value of the bond. These earnings are simply equal to the interest on the capital. And so in general, when we assume that income is definitely foreknown, earnings will equal the interest on the capital. It is, therefore, to earnings that accountants instinctively give their main attention. But they err grievously when they attempt to spirit away realized income and put earned income in its place. Realized income plays the more important rôle, for on it depend all the other elements, — capital-value, value-return, depreciation, and even earnings themselves. To take the case of the house, the first and primary fact is that it promises to yield $1000 a year for fifty years. This income series being given, it is possible to obtain its capital-value by the discounting process; its value-return, by division of income by capital; its depreciation, by comparing its capital values at successive dates; and its earnings, by deducting depreciation from realized income. Unless the realized income be given at the start, all these calculations are impossible. Earnings could not serve as our starting point, for earnings cannot be calculated except by the aid of depreciation, depreciation cannot be calculated except from capital-value, and capital-value cannot be calculated except from expected realized income.

Moreover, the fundamental proposition of the last chapter, that capital-value is the discounted value of expected income, will cease to hold true, if by income we mean earnings. Thus, the house has a capital-value of $18,300, which is the discounted value of its realized income of

$1000 a year for 20 years, discounted at 5 per cent. But it is not true that $18,300 is the discounted value of the earnings of the house, for the earnings are all less than $1000, beginning at $918 a year and dwindling each year until the fifty years have expired; and clearly the discounted value of fifty annual items each less than $1000 must be less than the discounted value of fifty annual items of $1000 each.

Since, then, earned income cannot be derived without assuming realized income, and since capital-value has been shown to be the present value of the latter, and not of the former, it is clear that realized income is the more fundamental concept of the two.

§ 5

But so persistent is the accountant's instinct to put aside realized income in favor of earnings that we need to point out in detail the confusions which arise, unless income and earnings are carefully distinguished. We first observe that, under the given conditions of foreknowledge, earnings and interest are equal. Now if interest is at 5 per cent, a capital of $1000 invested in whatever form — land, houses, horses, securities, or anything else — though it is said to earn 5 per cent, does not necessarily receive an income each year of $50. The $1000 means the present value, discounted at 5 per cent, of some expected income stream; but that income stream may take any one of an indefinite number of forms; such, for instance, as a perpetual annuity of $50 a year, as in the case of land; or a terminable annuity of $100 a year for 14 years; or an income of $25 a year for 10 years followed by an income of $167.50 a year for 10 years. All of these are inter-equivalent, and when discounted at 5 per cent, each of them represents a capital of $1000.

Of all these possible forms of income it is usual to take the perpetual annuity as the *standard* income (earnings) and to compare other incomes with it. Consider, for instance, the possessor of a property yielding $100 a year for 14 years. He will, if he discounts this income at 5 per cent, value that property at $1000. He thinks of himself as possessing $1000 "invested in" that property. From it he gets the income of $100 a year for 14 years. But he knows that he might sell this property for $1000 and reinvest in another property yielding the standard $50 a year forever. Contrasting with the standard income of $50 a year forever which he *might* receive, the income of $100 a year for 14 years which he *does* receive, we observe that at first his income is double the earned or standard income, being $100 instead of $50. The excess of $50, however, is compensated for by a reduction of $50 in the capital-value of his property, for at the end of the first year the value of his property will be the discounted value of $100 a year for thirteen (instead of fourteen) years, which, if interest is still reckoned at 5 per cent, is $950. And so it is in general that the owner of $1000 invested at 5 per cent can obtain a higher income than the standard $50 only at the cost of trenching on capital to the extent of the excess.

Suppose, on the contrary, that the $1000 is invested at 5 per cent, but in such a form as to yield at first less than $50, *e.g.* in a form which yields the above-mentioned income of $25 a year for 10 years, followed by $167.50 a year for 10 years. In that case, during the first year the owner receives only $25 instead of $50, which is the earned or "standard" income. But the deficiency of $25 in his income is made up by an augmentation of his capital by that amount.

The principle is perfectly general, and perhaps too familiar to require a rigorous demonstration, though there is no difficulty in framing one. We may therefore state: —

(1) When a property yields a specified foreknown income, and is valued by discounting that income according to a specified rate of interest, if the income realized is equal to

the income earned (and hence equal to the rate of interest), the value of the capital will remain at a uniform level.

(2) If realized income exceeds earned income, the value of the capital will be decreased by the amount of the excess.

(3) If realized income is less than earned income, the value of the capital will be increased by the deficiency.

These principles hold true whether the period for reckoning or compounding interest is a year, half year, quarter, or any other period, or shrinks to the vanishing point in the case of continuous interest. A slight modification or qualification in the statement of these principles is, however, necessary when, instead of there being a rate of interest which remains the same year after year, there is a succession of different rates.[1]

Expressed in a single sentence, the general principle connecting realized and earned income is that they differ by the appreciation or depreciation of capital. It is thus possible to describe earned income as realized income less depreciation of capital, or else as realized income plus appreciation of capital. We may therefore state anew the fallacy of confusing realized income with earned income: the fallacy consists in reckoning depreciation of capital as a part of outgo, or appreciation of capital as a part of income. This usage is difficult to combat, for with many it has become habitual. To expose the fallacy completely will be our object during the remainder of this chapter.

§ 6

We may at the outset emphasize a fact already mentioned in Chapter VII; namely, that this popular and erroneous usage is not consistently adhered to. A pension is an income the capital-value of which is continually diminish-

---

[1] The case is discussed in the Appendix to Chap. XIV, § 1. For practical purposes, however, this is a refinement into which we seldom need to enter.

ing. Yet even popular usage seldom or never deducts this depreciation from the pension to obtain the "true" income; and the reason we instinctively include (as we ought) the whole of such a pension in income, is that the depreciation is not actually offset. In ordinary business, on the other hand, we are accustomed to deduct depreciation, because this is usually offset by actual payments into a depreciation fund. Even in this case the depreciation is not *itself* an expense; but there is a concomitant expense approximately equal to it, in the form of payments into the depreciation fund. It thus makes all the difference in the world whether the depreciation fund is actually maintained, or merely reckoned. If a depreciation fund is actually maintained, the expense of maintaining it serves to reduce realized income so as to make it coincide with earned income. In such a case, therefore, the ideal earned income becomes realized in actual fact.

Assuming a fixed rate of interest, the depreciation fund may be defined as a fund formed by accumulating that part of income which must be turned back into capital in order to maintain the value of capital at a fixed level. A depreciation fund is thus made from annual contributions equal to the excess of realized income above earned income. If, instead of an excess, there is a deficiency, the contributions to the depreciation fund become negative, that is, instead of a certain quantity of income being converted into capital, a certain quantity of capital must be converted into income.

Geometrically, a depreciation fund is very simply represented. In Figure 7 let the income consist of the items a, a', a'', a''', a^{iv}, etc. The capitalized value of this income stream is AB. The interest on AB is represented by the height AC, so that the standard income would be represented by a series of annual lines of the height of the dotted line CD. The excess of the lines a, a', a'', etc., above the dotted line CD therefore represents the contributions to the depreciation fund. Where there is a deficiency, as in the case of a''', the contribution to the depreciation fund is negative; that is, for that particular time, instead of some of the income being reinvested, some of the capital is used as income, to prevent income from falling below the uniform level prescribed for it. The same

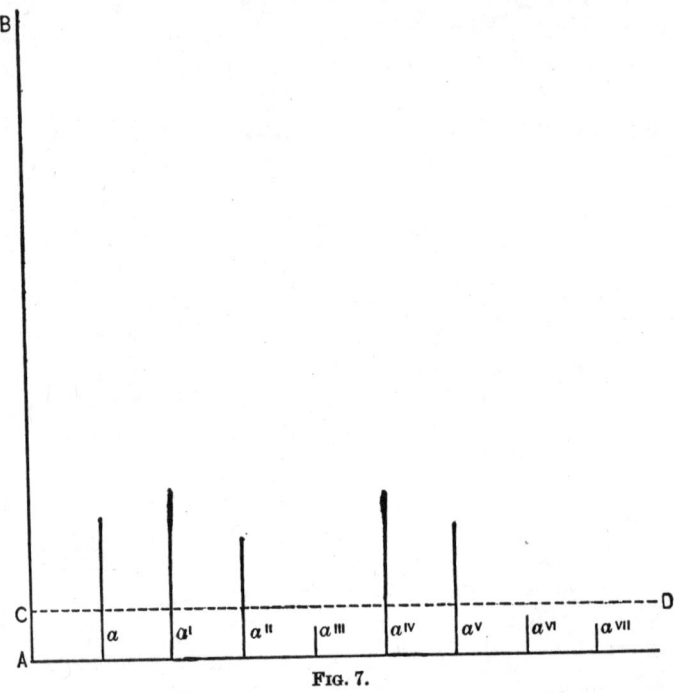

Fig. 7.

principles apply in case the income is a continuous flow, as shown in Figure 8. Here the earned income is represented by the elevation of the straight line CD, and the realized income by that of the curved line EF; the depreciation fund is formed from the successive differences between these elevations. Thus, if $1000 of capital is invested on a 4 per cent basis, but so that the returns are not $40, but $70 a year for twenty-two years, the annual contribution to the depreciation fund is evidently $30. For at the end of the first year, before the income is received, the capital-value will, under the supposed conditions, become not $1070, but only $1040. The first item of income, $70, is then received. This being deducted from $1040 leaves $970, which is $30 short of the original

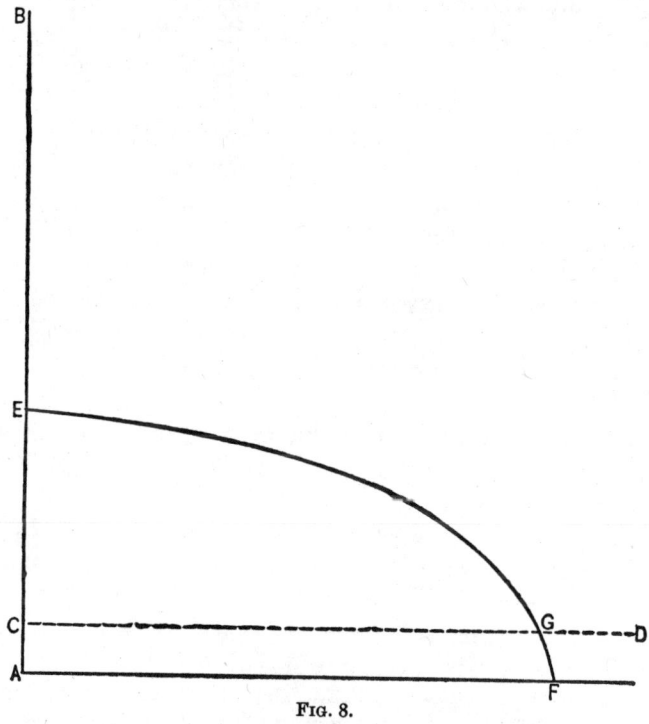

Fig. 8.

capital-value. Consequently it is necessary to restore $30 to the capital, in order to bring it up to the original level of $1000.

It will evidently make no difference whether the income items are reinvested simply as additions to the original capital, or invested at the same rate of interest in some other form of capital. The owner of depreciating machinery may offset that depreciation by investing annually in a few new machines, or by annually buying investment securities. The latter type of investment is usually thought of when the phrase "depreciation fund" is used. If the owner of the machines follows this procedure, then instead of the original capital being maintained at a fixed level, it is continually decreasing, while the depreciation fund is continually increasing in such a manner that the value of the two together — the machinery and the depreciation fund — remains constant. Consequently, at the end of the income term, when the value of the original capital, the machinery, is entirely exhausted, the value of the depreciation fund in securities will have exactly taken its place. This fact is sometimes employed in the definition of a depreciation fund. The fund is then described as formed of a succession of payments out of income, such that if each be accumulated at compound interest the total will equal the original capital at the end of the entire income term.

The most common application of a depreciation fund is to a bond which does not sell at par. For instance, a $100 five per cent bond, when interest is 4 per cent, will, if it has 20 years to run, sell at $115. The interest at 4 per cent on this capital is $4.60, which shows that the depreciation fund, being the difference between the income and the interest, is $5 minus $4.60, or 40 cents. This item of 40 cents should annually be saved out of the income and reinvested at 4 per cent, in order that at the end there may still remain a capital of $115. If the last installment of income from the bond, $105, is treated as an income like the previous items, the depreciation fund is, in the last year, $105 minus $4.60, or $100.40; that is, besides the 40 cents annually there should be reinvested, at the end of the term of the bond, the $100 of so-called "principal." Thus we again reach the reason that the $100 of the last payment is regarded as "principal" or "capital" and not "income." It is simply that this $100 is always supposed to enter into the depreciation fund, that is, to be reinvested and not *retained* as income. In case the bond is sold at par (*i.e.* if it yields an income equal to the market rate of interest), there is no depreciation fund except the "principal" itself at the end, when the last item of realized income ($105) exceeds the earned income of $5 by $100. This excess, being reinvested at the same rate, 5 per cent, will secure the continuance of the same income.

The operation of the depreciation fund presupposes that it is possible to invest the small differences each year in such a manner as to accumulate at compound interest at the rate which the original capital is earning. Such is not always the case, especially with articles of wealth, like land, machinery, and so forth. In case two different rates of interest are involved, one for computing the capital-value of the given income, and another for compounding the annual savings put into the depreciation fund, the calculation of the depreciation fund will, of course, be more complex.[1]

§ 7

In close relation to a depreciation fund is the "sinking fund" employed by governments as a means of meeting large obligations — in particular of meeting the "principal" of public debts. Needless obscurity has enveloped the "sinking fund," especially since the intricate but fallacious theories of Price and Pitt.

The annual contribution to the *depreciation* fund was the difference between the income actually experienced and an ideal *perpetual* annuity of the same present value. A *sinking* fund, however, is formed from the difference between income (or more commonly outgo) actually expe-

[1] The reader is referred to the *Institute of Actuaries' Text-book*, Part I, London (Layton), 1901, where this and other problems in annuities are fully dealt with.

rienced and an ideal *terminable* annuity of the same present value. A government has to meet a series of expenses connected with its bonded debt. These expenses constitute, let us say, a stream of outgo lasting ten years, and consisting of nine equal payments — nominally "interest" — and one much larger payment, exceeding the others by the amount of the so-called "principal." The sinking fund is merely a device for equalizing all ten payments. If the actual payments are $5000 a year for nine years and $105,000 in the tenth year (as is the case of 10-year "five per cent" bonds), the ideal 10-year annuity equivalent to this series would, on a 4 per cent basis, be $13,329. The government, therefore, if it would pay off its debt, or rather provide for it in ten equal installments, must during each of the first nine years, besides paying the $5000 to its creditors, pay into the sinking fund $8329. In the tenth year the process is reversed, and the entire $100,000 then accumulated in the sinking fund is taken to pay the $100,000 of "principal." Hence, as applied to bonded debts, the sinking fund may be defined as formed by accumulating an annual sum during a specified period, such that its amount will just suffice to extinguish a given sum at the end of that period.

§ 8

Depreciation and sinking funds are not the only devices by which uneven income streams may be, as it were, smoothed out. Many other devices may be employed. For instance, a person engaging in an unusual expense, such as that of building a house, will not allow this expense to seriously interrupt the even flow of his income, but will provide for it by some correspondingly unusual item of income. He may sell other property, for instance railway shares; the unusual sum he realizes on the sale will then offset the unusual outgo for the dwelling. Or, he may mortgage his dwelling and the land on which it stands, and pay the debt off gradually — sell a claim upon the dwelling itself instead of selling some property distinct from the dwelling. Or again, he may make an arrangement at the outset to pay for the house in installments.

All of these methods of maintaining more or less regularity of income merely shift the burden of an unusual expense from one person to another. The first method, by which the purchaser of the house raises the necessary money by selling other property, shifts to the buyer of that property an expense equal to that which he himself seeks, for the time, to avoid. The second method, that of mortgage, presupposes a money lender who is ready to supply the necessary funds. The money lender is in this case the one who, for the time, shoulders the burden. The third method, payment by installment, implies that the builder (or some other party) advances the cost of the dwelling. In other words, the person who attempts to smooth out his own income does so by throwing his irregularities on some one else, usually a banker or broker.

To society as a whole such purely shifting devices are inapplicable, for society can find no outside party on whom to shift the fluctuations. There is, however, a method by which society's income may be more or less standardized. This is by assorting and combining the various instruments of capital wealth so that the various income streams may mutually compensate. For instance, if a community owns iron mines, it has a form of property which, for a time, probably yields more than the standard income. By the nature of the case, every bucketful of ore reduces the amount which the mine can yield in future. The mine is, in fact, a sort of terminable annuity. After it is exhausted there will be no further returns. The capital-value of the mine will therefore continually decrease. On the other hand, forest land which is covered with young saplings will not begin to yield much income for many years. The income from this capital is therefore tempo-

246 NATURE OF CAPITAL AND INCOME [Chap. XIV

rarily below the standard. A community which owns both mine and timber land will consequently find that the increase and decrease will offset each other, so that its income will be more nearly standard than if it merely possessed either one without the other.

§ 9

The last-named method is applied to the case of capital which consists of a large number of instruments in different stages of production or consumption. If a weaving mill is equipped with 20 looms of the same degree of wear, the value of this plant will evidently depreciate and a depreciation fund may be necessary. But if the 20 looms are evenly distributed throughout the different stages of wear, and if, for convenience, we assume that one loom wears

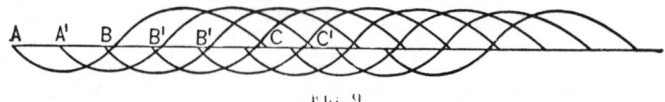

Fig. 9.

out each year, no depreciation fund will be necessary. The replacement of one loom annually is equivalent to such a depreciation fund, and the capital is thereby maintained at a constant level.

Any income stream whatever, even if its component parts are very irregular, will, if these parts are renewed at frequent and regular intervals, necessarily produce in total a uniform or standard income. Let ABC (Figure 9) represent an income stream which at first is negative and afterward positive, such, for instance, as is occasioned by first constructing and then using a machine. Let an exactly similar income stream $A'B'C'$ begin a short time later, as at A', and so on indefinitely, at equal intervals. It is evident that after we have reached the point C at which our first income stream ends, we have a fairly uniform income and outgo, the income at any point consisting of the sum of the ordinates above the base line AC', and the outgo of the sum of the ordinates below.

This case brings into juxtaposition two different points of view from which the interest on capital may be considered. Professor J. B. Clark conceives of interest as the net difference between the rate of total income and rate of total outgo at any point, and compares this net return with the capital-value as it exists at that point. This concept treats the outgo or cost of production as simultaneous with the income, that is, it takes into consideration any small section of the curves in Figure 9 contained between any two vertical lines a short interval apart. Professor Böhm-Bawerk, on the other hand, always thinks of cost of production as preceding income. He fixes his attention on the elementary income stream ABC, and contrasts the outgo or cost between A and B with the later income between B and C. These two points of view are evidently quite reconcilable, though their authors do not seem to have realized the fact. Each carries his own special point of view throughout his treatment of capital and interest. Professor Böhm-Bawerk regards interest as an agio, or premium, found by contrasting the positive income return between B and C with the investment or outgo between A and B, whereas Professor Clark regards interest as the ratio between a perpetual, uniform flow of income and the capital-value of the entire stock. In short, Böhm-Bawerk has in mind what we have called in the previous chapter the premium concept of interest, and Clark, the price concept of interest.

§ 10

We have seen that earned income is often only an ideal standard, and not to be confused with actually realized income. Yet the confusion is common. Even Edwin Cannan, who is usually a safe guide, makes an error at this point. He states in his *Elementary Political Economy*: [1] —

"If a man has a cellar of port wine, or a plantation of trees, the annual increment of the value of these things is evidently part of his annual income. If he likes to spend it, he can do so without decreasing his property. If he does not choose to spend it, he is engaged in a form of saving and is thereby adding to his property."

And again, in "What is Capital?" [2] he states, "The income is divided into two parts, (1) the increase of the capital, and (2) the things enjoyed."

That "saving" or increase of capital is *not* income coordinately with ordinary income is evident from the fact that this item is never discounted in making up capital-value. As we have seen, one of the fundamental characteristics of income is that it is the desirable event which occurs by means of wealth, and for the sake of which, consequently, that wealth is valued. This definition implies that every item of income is discounted in order to obtain its contribution to capital-value. The mere increase or decrease of capital-value, on the other hand, is never thus discounted. Suppose, for instance, with interest at 4 per cent, that a man buys an annuity of $4 a year, which does not begin at once but is deferred one year. Since this annuity will be worth $100 one year hence, its present value will be about $96, which, during the ensuing year, will gradually increase to $100. If this increase of value of (about) $4 is itself to be called income, it should be treated like every other item of income, and should be discounted. But this is absurd. The discounted value of $4 would be $3.85, which, if added to the $96, would require that the entire value of the property to-day should be $99.85, or practically the same as a year later instead of $4 less as is actually the case. In other words, the hypothesis which counts an increase of value as income is self-destructive; for if the increment *is* income, it must

[1] p. 59.   [2] *Economic Journal*, Vol. VII, 1897, p. 284.

be discounted, but, if discounted, it is practically abolished. Clearly, then, increase of capital is not income in the sense that it can be discounted in addition to other items of income. If it is income at all, it is income in a very peculiar sense, and nothing but confusion can result from having to consider two kinds of income so widely divergent that whereas one is discounted to obtain capital-value, the other is not.

We have seen that the increase of capital is at the expense of income. It is occasioned by and is equal to the deficiency of realized compared with standard income. With this in mind, Edwin Cannan's definition of income could be stated as realized income plus the deficiency between realized and earned income. But this is earned income, not realized income.

§ 11

To put the matter in a practical light, let us imagine the case of three brothers, each of whom inherits the same fortune, say, $10,000. Let us assume that interest is 5 per cent. The first brother invests his $10,000 in an annual annuity of $500 a year forever. The second puts his in trust to accumulate at 5 per cent for fourteen years, at which time, having doubled in value, it is to be invested in a perpetual annuity of $1000 a year. The third, being of the spendthrift type, buys an annuity of $2000 a year for (nearly) six years.

According to the theory here advocated, the first has a perpetual income of $500 a year; the second has *no* income for 14 years, and thereafter an income of $1000; the third has an income of $2000 a year for 6 years and thereafter none at all. This mode of viewing the matter also squares with ordinary business reckoning.

On the other hand, according to the theory which regards increase of capital as income, although the income from the first would be the same as we have reckoned it, that of the second and third would be quite different: the income of the second would be $500 the first year, for during that year his capital increases from $10,000 to $10,500; it would be $525 the second year, during which his capital increases again from $10,500 to $11,025, and so on, until in 15 years he is receiving an income of $1000 a year. The third brother, during the first year, uses $2000; but as his interest is only $500 he is forced to take $1500 out of capital. This is, in our view, true realized income. But according to the theory which we are criticising, this depreciation of $1500 would have to be deducted from the $2000 which the spendthrift actually enjoys, in order to compute his net income. The net income would thus be only $500, or the interest on his original capital. At the beginning of the second year, this spendthrift brother would possess a capital of $8500, the "income" of which would, by the same theory, be 5 per cent on $8500, or only $425. Following similar reasoning to the end we find that the so-called "income" would progressively diminish until, in the sixth year, it would be only $90. The capital then having been entirely destroyed, no income would remain. It would appear from all this that the spendthrift had received from the original $10,000, during the six years of its life, a very small income, steadily diminishing from $500 to zero, the sum total being only $1695. Was it for such an "income" that he invested $10,000?

§ 12

If we suppose an income tax laid on the three brothers, we shall find that, according to the different interpretations which we give to the term "income," the results will be startlingly different. If the income be taken in its true sense, namely, as those items whose capital-value is the $10,000 with which the three brothers started, then an income tax of 10 per cent will yield from the first brother $50 a year; from the second, nothing for 14 years, after

Sec. 12]   EARNINGS AND INCOME   251

which it will yield $100 a year; and from the third, $200 a year for 6 years [1] and nothing thereafter. The burden of the three taxes on these three brothers will under these conditions be exactly equal, when the three are compared by means of their present values. Each brother could "compound" for his taxes (that is, could pay a fixed sum in advance in lieu of the annual sums) at the same cost, namely, $1000; for $1000 is the sum in present cash which is equivalent respectively to $50 a year forever; to $100 a year beginning 14 years hence; and to $200 a year for 6 years. But turning now to the spurious interpretation of income as the value of uses *plus* the accumulation of capital, or the value of uses *less* the depreciation of capital, we find that the three brothers would be very unequally taxed. The first would, as before, pay $50 a year indefinitely. But the second who "saves" for 14 years, will be compelled

SECOND BROTHER

	CAPITAL	SO-CALLED "INCOME"	TAX THEREON	TRUE INCOME	TAX THEREON
At beginning . .	$10,000				
In 1 year . . .	10,500	$500	$50.00	nil	nil
In 2 years . . .	11,025	525	52.50	nil	nil
In 3 years . . .	11,576	551	55.10	nil	nil
In 4 years . . .	12,155	579	57.90	nil	nil
In 5 years . . .	12,763	608	60.80	nil	nil
In 6 years . . .	13,401	638	63.80	nil	nil
In 7 years . . .	14,071	670	67.00	nil	nil
In 8 years . . .	14,775	704	70.40	nil	nil
In 9 years . . .	15,513	738	73.80	nil	nil
In 10 years . . .	16,289	776	77.60	nil	nil
In 11 years . . .	17,103	816	81.60	nil	nil
In 12 years . . .	17,959	856	85.60	nil	nil
In 13 years . . .	18,856	897	89.70	nil	nil
In 14 years . . .	19,799	943	94.30	nil	nil
In 14½ years . . .	20,000			nil	nil
Thereafter . . .	20,000	1000	100.00	$1000	$100

[1] Or, to be exact, $200 a year for 5 years and $180 in the last year, inasmuch as the capital will be exhausted in a little *less* than 6 years.

to pay an annually increasing tax on this saving for the 14 years of postponement, and then a tax on the income from these same savings in which his annuity is to consist. His first year's savings will be $500 and will be taxed $50. During the second year his capital grows from $10,500 to $11,025, making an increase of $525, the tax on which is $52.50, and so on, as shown in the preceding table.

The third brother, under such a tax, will fare as shown below:—

THIRD BROTHER

	CAPITAL	SO-CALLED "INCOME"	TAX THEREON	TRUE INCOME	TAX THEREON
At beginning	$10,000				
In 1 year	8,500	$500	$50.00	$2,000	$200
In 2 years	6,930	425	42.50	2,000	200
In 3 years	5,270	340	34.00	2,000	200
In 4 years	3,530	260	26.00	2,000	200
In 5 years	1,710	180	18.00	2,000	200
In 6 years	nil	90	9.00	1,800	180
Thereafter	nil	nil	nil	nil	nil

When we compare the burden of the various taxes imposed on so-called "income," we shall find that the first brother could "compound" for his taxes, as before, by a cash payment of $1000. The second brother, however, would need to pay $1714. For he would have to pay $1000 as the present value of the tax of $100 a year beginning in 14 years, and in addition, $714 as the present value of the series of taxes on his savings, namely, $50, $52.50, etc. And the third brother, though the least provident of all, could compound for only $157.73, this being the present value of the six small tax payments which he would have to make, namely, $50, $42.50, $34, $26, $18, and $9.[1]

[1] In the foregoing calculation it was assumed that the tax did not itself affect the value of the "income" on which the tax is laid. But this would be untrue of "income" which includes the increment of capital. For the discussion of this point, see Appendix to Chap. XIV, § 2.

Instead, therefore, of having a burden of taxes on the three brothers, all of which have an equal present value of $1000, we find the unequal burdens of $1000, $1714, and $157.73. Such a system of taxation is clearly unjust and discourages the saver, while it encourages the spendthrift. The spendthrift virtually has some of his taxes remitted to him, whereas the saver is made the victim of that too frequent concomitant of fallacious economic theory, — double taxation; for he is first taxed 15 years on his accumulation of capital ($10,000 in all), and thereafter is taxed again on the income which he derives from that same accumulation.

And yet this procedure is very common in practice. It amounts to taxing, not the *income* actually flowing from capital, but its "earnings" or the interest upon the capital. It is familiar in the "general property tax" in the United States. Under it such wealth as temporarily unproductive land is taxed, though it bears no income except the purely constructive income of its annual rise in value. To some extent also the British income tax is an instance of the same fallacy.

§ 13

In the example which has been given we have supposed each brother to be possessed of a fixed and definite annuity. We have considered the effect of an income tax on these properties, according to the incorrect interpretation of "income." It often if not usually happens, however, that the owner of a property may use it in any one of many ways, and thus derive from it any one of many income streams. We have seen in the previous chapter that the choice between the different methods of using the property will depend on the question, Which source of income possesses the greatest present value? An income tax laid according to the correct idea of income would not disturb the comparative merits of these different income streams; but if income be interpreted to include savings, the tax would disturb them greatly. The effect of such a tax as was illustrated in the example of the three brothers would be to discourage the uses of capital which involve waiting. In fact, this discouraging effect is well recognized and applauded by the single-tax advocates, although they overlook the inequities involved. According to them, it is right to discourage waiting, and no speculation in real estate such as was described in a previous chapter should be permitted. They would tax all increase of value of land in the manner just described. Perhaps the most harmful case of such a system of taxation is that of forest land. Forestry advocates have long been aware of the baleful effect of the taxation of growing forests, producing, as it does, wasteful and premature cutting, and have attempted to secure a reduction or remission of such taxes. But the persistent belief that the annual increment of value of such forests is income and should be taxed has hitherto prevailed in America, with the natural consequence that the owners of these forests have cut them when they should have allowed them to grow. In Europe, a longer experience in forestry has led, in some cases, to a more rational system. "Baden exempts newly established forests from tax for twenty years (law of 1886). In Austria they are exempt for twenty-five years (law of 1869). In France three-fourths of the land tax is remitted for thirty years."[1] Even a small tax, when laid on forest land which will yield no timber for fifty years, becomes a very serious drain in the long run.[2]

§ 14

The fallacy which has been exposed is not only a confusion between realized and earned income; it is also a confusion between income and capital. To regard "sav-

[1] " How shall Forests be Taxed? " by Alfred Gaskill, *Forestry and Irrigation*, April, 1906, p. 173.
[2] Some limitations on the applications of a theoretically correct income tax are mentioned in the Appendix to Chap. XIV, § 3.

ings" as income, is essentially to regard an increase of capital as income. But from what has been said it is clear that he who increases his income must decrease his capital to an equal extent. Capital and income are thus mutually exclusive. One cannot receive the whole standard income, and at the same time secure also an increase of his capital. The truth of this has been instinctively expressed in the adage, "You cannot eat your cake and have it too."

We have learned, then, to distinguish between standard and realized income. The one is ideal, the other actual. The one is that income which, if it were received, would leave the level of capital-value unchanged; the other is that income which is actually received and detached from capital, no matter whether that capital, as a result, is increased or decreased. In short, the one is earned, the other realized.

The two may, of course, coincide, in which case capital-value remains constant. When they do not coincide, the discrepancy measures the increase or decrease of capital-value. This discrepancy may be partially or wholly done away with by means of a depreciation fund or other devices whereby realized income, otherwise irregular, is made regular. But, merely to *reckon* depreciation is not to provide for it. It merely stigmatizes part of realized income as "coming out of capital," but it does not make good the loss of capital nor prevent its becoming a part of realized income. No more does the mere calling of "savings" by the name of income make it realized as income. These two procedures are both attempts to standardize income in thought when it is not standardized in fact. We have seen that they represent a confusion both between capital and income and between income which is merely earned and income which is actually realized, and that they lead to inequitable taxation — double taxation to the saver and remission of taxes to the spendthrift.

CHAPTER XV

CAPITAL AND INCOME ACCOUNTS

§ 1

THE last two chapters have their counterpart in accounting. Correctly kept accounts will show that an abnormal increase of income is always at the expense of capital. In the case of a corporation, the distribution among the stockholders of such excessive income is called "paying dividends out of capital." It is not necessarily or always wrong. A Land Company of California has already been cited as a legitimate case. A case at the opposite extreme would be one in which the dividends are made unusually small in order that the capital may be increased. There is in New York City a company which has never declared any dividends, but has been rolling up a large surplus for years, and whose stock is for this reason much above par.

We have already seen in Chapter VIII, that every item in an income account represents the income or outgo from some item in the capital account. That is, the income account consists merely in a statement of the income and outgo connected with each item of asset or liability, including that class of assets and liabilities which are alike claims and obligations, such as leases and employees' contracts. If the income for each item remains steady or standard, the relation between the capital and income accounts is very simple. In such a case (supposing the rate of interest to be 5 per cent), each item in the capital account will constantly stand at twenty times the amount of the corresponding item in the income account. Let us suppose a factory company operating a plant worth $300,000, which is bonded for $100,000. The remainder, $200,000, will represent the capital and surplus of the company If these valuations represent a true and not simply a fictitious book value, and if the rate of interest be taken at 5 per cent, the fact that the plant is worth $300,000 signifies simply that its earning power is $15,000 a year, of which $5000 goes in interest to the bondholders and $10,000 in dividends to the stockholders. The capital and income accounts of such a firm, doing a steady and uninterrupted business, would repeat themselves in monotonous regularity year after year.

§ 2

If now we suppose that the repairs and replacement of the plant do not occur in equal amounts each year, but that it is necessary, at long intervals, to make large, special, or extraordinary repairs; there will occur during the intermediate years "depreciations" of the plant, and sudden restorations in its value when these special repairs are made. Thus, suppose that during the year 1900, the factory depreciates by $10,000. The capital account at the beginning and end of this year, and the income account during the year, will be given in the following table: —

CAPITAL ACCOUNT AT BEGINNING OF YEAR 1900

Assets		Liabilities	
Factory	$300,000	Bonds	$100,000
		Capital and surplus	200,000
	$300,000		$300,000

CAPITAL ACCOUNT AT END OF YEAR 1900

Assets		Liabilities	
Factory	$290,000	Bonds	$100,000
		Capital and surplus	190,000
	$290,000		$290,000

INCOME ACCOUNT DURING YEAR 1900

Capital Source	Income		Outgo		Net
Factory	Product . $40,000	Running expenses . .	$15,000		+ $25,000
Bonds		Interest . .	5,000		− 5,000
Capital and Surplus		Dividends .	20,000		− 20,000
	$40,000		$40,000		000

From this table we see that the factory yields $25,000; as it is worth only $300,000 (on a 5 per cent basis), by the principles of Chapter XIV, it cannot yield more than $15,000 without depreciating to the extent of the difference ($10,000); but, instead of setting aside something for depreciation, *i.e.* to pay for future repairs, the company has declared larger dividends. Hence, corresponding to the depreciation of $10,000 in the value of the plant there is an excess of $10,000 above the "standard" income received by the stockholders. Instead of $10,000, which is the normal interest on their capital and surplus of $200,000, they receive $20,000. The extra $10,000 above the standard thus corresponds precisely to the depreciation of their property, which accordingly sinks in the course of the year from $200,000 to $190,000.

During the next year we shall suppose that the factory yields again $25,000. Since its value was, at the beginning of the year, $290,000, it cannot, on a 5 per cent basis, yield more than $14,500 without depreciating to the extent of the difference (in this case $25,000 − $14,500, or $10,500). Its value at the end of the year exclusive of improvements is consequently $290,000 − $10,500, or $279,500. We shall suppose that the entire depreciation for the two years, $20,500, is made good by extraordinary repairs to that amount. Since the factory yields only $25,000 and only $20,000 after the bondholders are paid, it will be necessary, in order to meet the $20,500 of repairs to assess the stockholders $500. The accounts will then stand as follows:—

Capital Account at Beginning of Year 1901

Assets		Liabilities	
Factory	$290,000	Bonds	$100,000
		Capital and surplus	190,000
	$290,000		$290,000

Capital Account at End of Year 1901

Assets		Liabilities	
Factory	$300,000	Bonds	$100,000
		Capital and surplus	200,000
	$300,000		$300,000

Income Account during Year 1901

Capital Source	Income		Outgo	Net
Factory Product	$40,000	Running expenses	$15,000 }	+$4500
		Special repairs	20,500 }	
Bonds		Interest	5,000	−5000
Capital and surplus Assessment	500	Dividends	000	+500
	$45,500		$45,500	000

§ 3

Had the repair bill been distributed over the two years, the dividends to the stockholders, instead of being $20,000 the first year and less than nothing the second, would have been $10,000 in each. In order to make their income thus stable and "standard" instead of irregular, it is only necessary to employ a special repair fund. This accumulates for a few years as a separate investment, and is then converted back into the plant itself, which meanwhile will have continued its depreciation. We shall assume that this plan is adopted, beginning with the year 1902, for which the capital and income accounts will be as follows: —

Capital Account at Beginning of Year 1902

Assets		Liabilities	
Factory	$300,000	Bonds	$100,000
		Capital and surplus	200,000
	$300,000		$300,000

Capital Account at End of Year 1902

Assets		Liabilities	
Factory	$290,000	Bonds	$100,000
Repair fund	10,000	Capital and surplus	200,000
	$300,000		$300,000

Income Account during Year 1902

Capital Source	Income		Outgo		Net
Factory	Product . $40,000	Running expenses	. .	$15,000	+$25,000
Repair fund		Investment	.	10,000	− 10,000
Bonds		Interest	. .	5,000	− 5,000
Capital and surplus		Dividends	.	10,000	− 10,000
	$40,000			$40,000	000

Here we see that the value of the plant depreciates by $10,000 as before, but that, to replace the loss, there are $10,000 worth of repair funds invested in, say, stocks and bonds. The consequence of the repair fund is that the value of the assets of the company remains stationary at $300,000; the share of this property which falls to the stockholders also remains at a constant level, namely, $200,000; and the stockholders receive dividends of only $10,000 instead of $20,000, having set aside $10,000 to invest in their repair fund. We may suppose that during the next year the depreciation continues and that the factory yields again $25,000, as we saw in § 2. Since its value was only $290,000, the "earnings" of which are only $14,500, it must have depreciated $10,500. Since the repair fund set aside in the previous year has earned 5 per cent, or $500, the accounts for the year 1903 will now be as follows: —

Capital Account at Beginning of Year 1903

Assets		Liabilities	
Factory	$290,000	Bonds	$100,000
Repair fund	10,000	Capital and surplus	200,000
	$300,000		$300,000

Capital Account at End of Year 1903

Assets		Liabilities	
Factory	$279,500	Bonds	$100,000
Repair fund	20,500	Capital and surplus	200,000
	$300,000		$300,000

Income Account during Year 1903

Capital Source	Income		Outgo		Net
Factory	Product	$40,000	Running expenses	$15,000	+ $25,000
Repair fund	Interest received	500	New investment	10,000	− 10,000
			Interest reinvested	500	
Bonds			Interest	5,000	− 5,000
Capital and surplus			Dividends	10,000	− 10,000
		$40,500		$40,500	000

Here we see that the repair fund has absorbed in outgo another $10,000 of new investment, and that it has yielded an income of $500, which, however, has been immediately reinvested and appears as outgo also. The consequence is that in the capital account at the end of the year, the factory, which has depreciated now to $279,500, has, synchronously with its depreciation, acquired a repair fund enough to bring up the total value of the assets to $300,000. The value to the stockholders, therefore, remains stationary at $200,000, on which amount they have received their standard income of $10,000.

§ 4

During the next year, we shall suppose, the extraordinary repairs again need to be made. Inasmuch as during this year the plant has continued to depreciate, the special repairs will amount, approximately, to $31,500, whereupon the repair fund is sold and the cash employed in actual repairs. The accounts for the year 1904 will then be as follows: —

Capital Account at Beginning of Year 1904

Assets		Liabilities	
Factory	$279,500	Bonds	$100,000
Repair fund	20,500	Capital and surplus	200,000
	$300,000		$300,000

Capital Account at End of Year 1904

Assets		Liabilities	
Factory (exclusive of improvements)	$268,500	Bonds	$100,000
Improvements	31,500	Capital and surplus	200,000
Repair fund	000		
	$300,000		$300,000

Income Account during Year 1904

Capital Source		Income	Outgo		Net
Factory	Product	$40,000	Running expenses	$15,000	−$6,500
			Special repairs	31,500	
Repair fund	Sale of entire fund in Dec.	31,500	New investment	10,000	+21,500
	Interest	1,000	Interest	1,000	
Bonds			Interest	5,000	−5,000
Capital and surplus			Dividends	10,000	−10,000
		$72,500		$72,500	000

Here we see that during the year 1904, the value of the factory at the beginning was $279,500, and at the end, *exclusive of improvements*, $268,500. But the improvements or special repairs amounting to $31,500 have made up the total value of the factory to $300,000. There is at this time no repair fund whatever, as it has all been absorbed in improving the factory. The assets, therefore, amount to $300,000; the property of the stockholders remains stationary as before at $200,000; and their dividends also remain stationary at $10,000. The factory itself during this year does not yield the $25,000 which has regularly appeared as the net income in the previous accounts, for during this year we have to charge to the factory the special repairs of $31,500. The factory itself, therefore, produces a net deficit of $6500, offset by the large proceeds received from the sale of the repair fund of $31,500, which, less the new investment of $10,000 during the year, shows a net return for the year of $21,500. We see, therefore, that the existence of the repair fund to cover depreciation virtually maintains the capital accounts at a constant level, merely changing from year to year the form of the items, but not affecting either the interest of the bondholders or the dividends of the stockholders. In other words, the repair fund acts as a means of *standardizing* the stockholders' income. In ordinary business accounting, such standardizing is regarded as sound policy.

§ 5

Certain exceptions occur, as in the case of mining companies or land companies which necessarily must terminate their operations in the more or less remote future. But even in such instances, the instinct of the accountant toward standard accounting is so strong, that he usually treats the excess or deficiency of real income with relation to standard income in a special manner.

Thus, when a company winds up business, the final distribution of the proceeds is not treated as an ordinary dividend; the most of these proceeds are regarded as capital returned to the stockholders. The "company" therefore goes through the form of paying for the shares of its stockholders and enters what it thus pays over to the stockholders as a cost of purchase instead of as a dividend.

The reverse operations may occur if at any time the stockholders forego their dividends. It is in such a way that a company usually enlarges its capital. It nominally distributes the regular dividends, but allows the stockholders who choose to do so to reinvest them and receive in return new stock certificates.

§ 6

From the foregoing accounts it is clear that the theory of capital and income which has been explained applies practically to the accounting ordinarily employed in business. Such accounting is, in fact, nothing but a method of recording the items of income and their capitalization at different points of time. A merchant's balance sheet is a statement of the prospects of his business. Each item in it represents the discounted value of items which he may expect later to enter in his income account. Rightly interpreted, the capital account merely represents as a whole the *capitalization of expected items in the income account;* the fluctuations of the capital account correspond with the *deviations from the standard income in the items of the income account;* and where there are no such fluctuations, every item of the income account is equal to the standard income from the corresponding items of the capital account.

There are, of course, numerous practical modifications of this general statement to be made when actual accounts are treated. It was shown in Chapter VIII that such modifications are due to a variety of circumstances, such, for instance, as the influence of that important element, risk; the desire of accountants to maintain their capital accounts unchanged from year to year; and the omission from their capital accounts of such two-sided items as leases, employee-contracts, and the like. But none of the exigencies of practice militate in the least against our theory of capital and income accounts. In all cases the income account simply records the values of the services and disservices of articles of property through any given period; and the capital account records the present values of those articles, as resulting at any given instant from the expected values of their services and disservices.

CHAPTER XVI

THE RISK ELEMENT

§ 1

THROUGHOUT the three previous chapters, we have assumed the existence of artificially simple conditions. We have assumed that the entire future history of the capital in question is definitely known in advance; in other words, we have ignored *chance*. The factory which was taken for illustration was supposed to yield definite future income which could be counted upon as a bondholder counts upon his interest. In actual practice, however, every factory or other enterprise offers chances both of gain and loss. How these chances affect capital-value will be discussed in the present chapter.

We have seen that capital-value increases as an anticipated installment of income approaches in time, and diminishes as that installment is reached and passed. These changes in capital-value take place when the future income is regarded as certain. The introduction of the element of *chance* will bring other and even more important changes in capital-value. If we take the history of the prices of stocks and bonds, we shall find it chiefly to consist of a record of changing estimates of futurity, due to what is called chance, rather than of a record of the foreknown approach and detachment of income. Few, if any, future events are entirely free from uncertainty. In fact, property, by its very definition, is simply the right to the chance of future services. A mine owner takes his chances as to what the mine will yield; the owner of an orange plantation in Florida takes risks of winter frosts;

the owner of a farm takes risks as to the effect of sun and rain and other meteorological conditions, as well as risks of the ravages of fire, insects, and other pests. In buying an overcoat a man takes some risk as to its effectiveness in excluding cold, and as to the length of time it will continue to be serviceable. Even what are called "gilt-edged" securities are not entirely free from risk. In a sense, therefore, every owner of property is a risk-taker. Some persons will estimate more highly than others the risks taken. From this fact it might seem that there is a distinction between the actual risk incurred and the estimate which individuals put upon it. But a little consideration will show that this distinction is spurious; for, by the nature of the case, *chance is always an estimate.* Chance is subjective. Although one man's estimate may be better than another's through superior knowledge, intuition, or experience, the best estimate is still only an estimate, not a certainty. In the actual world of events there is no uncertainty. Aside from human opinion, there is no such thing as chance. To an omniscient being, all things are certain.

It must be admitted that this view of chance is not familiar to the ordinary man, nor is it universally accepted by the professed students of chance. Thus, writers like Dr. Venn, adhering to an *objective* theory, regard the chance of an event as the number of times it would occur in the long run, out of the total series of possible occurrences. But no matter how long the "run," the number of times the event actually occurs seldom corresponds exactly with the chance of its occurring. Even in so simple a case as cointossing, 1000 trials will not often give exactly 500 heads and 500 tails. Yet even the "long-run" theorists regard the chances of heads and tails as even. If 600 heads fall and only 400 tails, the odds are not 6 to 4. To this objection the only answer offered by the long-run theorists is that the run is not long enough, that heads and tails are equally probable because the longer the trial is continued the more will the two tend toward equality. But they argue in a circle. It is not necessarily true that the longer the run the more closely will the frequency of the event approach its probability. For example, it is *possible* that though heads and tails have an equal chance, a run of heads may keep up for any given number of times, however long, a million, for instance; or that at first heads and tails may occur with equal frequency and as the experiment proceeds they may diverge more and more from such equality. No student of chance, whatever his theory of the philosophy of chance, would claim that these cases are *impossible*. The most that can be said is that they are extremely *improbable*. The statement, therefore, that the longer the run the more closely will the frequency of the event approach its probability turns out to be "the longer the run the more *probably* will the frequency correspond to the probability." This is true as a proposition and it is in fact known as "Bernoulli's Theorem"; but it cannot be made the basis of a sound definition of probability, for probability would be defined in terms of itself. It states that the probability of heads coming up is the frequency which heads will *probably* approximate in the long run! How else than in terms of probability can we formulate the conditions under which in the long run the coin "will" fall according to its probability? It is precisely at this point that the radical difficulty with the "long-run" theory is seen. It is said that in an athletic contest, the chance of winning is one half when two wrestlers are so nearly mated that in the long run "under precisely the same conditions," each will win in half the contests. If the conditions are, literally speaking, *precisely* the same, then the same result will necessarily follow and the same man will *always* win. It is only as the conditions vary slightly from time to time in their *unknown* elements that there is a change of winner; and the instant the *unknown-*

ness of these elements is introduced into the problem, the observer unconsciously shifts his ground from the "long run" to the true theory of chance.

Chance is, then, an affair of human knowledge or ignorance. According to this — the ignorance — theory, chance is not objective, but subjective. Outside of the mind, chance has no place. If a man holds a coin in his hand and, without letting it be seen, asks his neighbor what the "real" chance is that heads are up, will not the latter reply one half? But as a matter of fact the position of the coin is absolutely determinate. Either heads are up, or tails are up; there is no ambiguity. Without changing the coin, the holder opens his hand. He sees that heads are up. Without disclosing this fact to his neighbor he repeats the question, "What is the chance that heads are up?" Will not the latter still reply, "One half"? *To him*, in his ignorance about the coin, the chances are exactly even; but to the man who holds the coin and whose eye has seen it, there is no uncertainty. He *knows* that heads are up. For *him* the element of chance has vanished because the element of ignorance has vanished. Chance exists only so far as ignorance exists; varies with different persons according to their comparative ignorance of the matter under consideration; and is in fact a measure of ignorance.

Of course the actual statistical record may afford an important and sometimes the only basis for our degree of knowledge and ignorance. Practically it therefore often happens that we derive our estimate of chances from the behavior of events "in the long run." It is thus that the chances of fire, shipwreck, and death are estimated by the insurance companies. But while statistics supply data for the forming of subjective estimates of chances, they do not, themselves, constitute chances; and even when they enter into the problem the insurance examiner does not follow them blindly. He always examines the special circumstances of each case; and his final estimate of the chance that a particular building will burn, a particular ship founder, or a particular person die, is based on all the data available, among which the data supplied by statistics are an important but by no means the sole element.

To apply this idea of chance to an economic example, consider a gold mine. What is the chance that it conceals a rich lead of ore? The ordinary man makes an estimate, based on his experience or inexperience. The geologist has additional knowledge and would make a different estimate. In actual fact, however, gold is either actually there in certain definite quantities, or is totally absent. It is a coin held in nature's closed hand.

§ 2

But, in showing that chance is purely a psychological and not an objective magnitude, we are still far from defining chance as a *mathematical* magnitude. In order to measure chance, it is necessary to state (1) when two chances are equal or unequal; and (2) when one chance bears any given ratio to the other.

The chance of one event is said to be equal to the chance of another in the mind of a particular individual, when that individual has no inclination to believe that one will occur rather than the other. One of the chances is said to exceed the other when the individual is "inclined to believe" that one event will occur rather than the other. The test of the equality of two chances is mere indecision *of opinion* — opinion exactly and evenly balanced.

Next comes the question of the *ratio* of two chances. When it is said that the odds in favor of one event as compared with another are two to one, the meaning is that out of three *equally probable* combinations of conditions, two imply the first event and only one the second. Thus, if there are three cards in a hat, of which it is known that only one will draw a prize, the chance against a person who draws a card from the hat receiving the prize is two to one; for of the three *equally probable* drawings, two are blanks.

In general terms the odds in favor of one event as compared with another are said to be m to n when there are $m + n$ *equally probable* cases in which one or the other of the two events may happen, and among these $m + n$ cases there are m cases such that the first event would happen, and n cases such that the second event would happen. The chance of the first event is then $\frac{m}{m+n}$ and the chance of the second is $\frac{n}{m+n}$. The m and the n cases are, it should be noted, assumed to be mutually exclusive.[1]

Probability is thus not merely an affair of pure mathematics, as is so often imagined. It is, first of all, a matter of concrete human estimate. What are called the mathematics of probability apply only to arrays of equally probable combinations, and consist in calculating the number of these which are favorable or unfavorable to a given event. The mathematics of probability never establish a probability of itself, but always rest on some human estimate of chances which are equal to start with. Like every other branch of applied mathematics, it must depend on having its raw material supplied from without. By mathematics we seem to discover that the chance of throwing double sixes with two dice is one in thirty-six. But this calculation rests on the hypothesis that, in some person's estimation, each die is equally liable to fall on any one of its six faces. Starting with this assumption, it is easy to show that in throwing two dice there are thirty-six equally

[1] It often happens that we cannot divide the field of probability into separate cases all equally probable. In such a case the mind is forced to make an estimate. For instance, the probability of an event may be said to be one third against the field if the estimator's state of opinion toward the field is exactly similar to his state of mind toward another field in which the division into three separate combinations *is* possible and one of them favors the event in question. If the state of mind is similar but less definite, then the chance is " about " one third but not definite.

probable cases and that only one of these will give double sixes. Mathematics could not obtain the result unaided by experience. All that mathematics accomplished with the dice was to derive a result from the assumed conditions of two sets of six equal chances. Whether these assumed conditions existed was a question, not of mathematics, but of concrete opinion. If the dice were known to be "loaded," the case would be materially altered.

§ 3

In order to apply this theory of chance to the valuation of capital, we observe that both the future rate of interest and the future items of income are uncertain. In the problem of capital-valuation, however, the uncertainty in the rate of interest does not always enter, for only present and not future rates are employed at the time at which the valuation of the capital is made. When we call a rate a "present" rate we mean, of course, that the contract or estimate to which it relates is a present contract or estimate. The very fact of valuation implies a known rate or rates at which the valuer is contrasting present and future goods. There may be several "present" rates. Thus if the "present" be the year 1906, we may imagine a whole series of rates of interest holding true in 1906 for such a man; for instance, 4 per cent for a 1-year contract, 6 per cent for a 5-year contract, and 5 per cent for a 15-year contract, all originating at the present moment. All of these rates are fixed and known and hold true in the year 1906, but they do not determine the rates which will hold true for the contracts or estimates of 1907 or 1914.

In valuing capital, therefore, it is not necessary to regard the rate of interest as uncertain except when the rate in question is a future rate.

Let us suppose that in Figure 10 the income AB is due at the end of the time FA, and that the rate of interest is such as to produce the discount curve BE. Then the present value of AB is FE. But the future valuations of AB may not follow the line EB as they would were the rate of interest unchanged. Thus, at a midway point of time, G, the valuation of AB may be only GD, found by means of a higher rate of interest involving the steeper discount curve DB. The history of the value of the property, namely, the right to AB, therefore follows the broken line $ECDB$, abruptly changing from GC to GD, if we suppose G to be

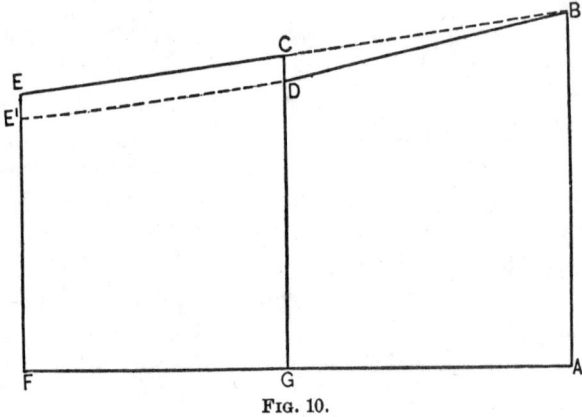

FIG. 10.

the point at which the rate of interest changes unexpectedly from one level to the other. Had the owner of the property foreseen at the start that when the point G was reached the rate of interest would be higher, he would have taken this fact into account in valuing the property at the moment F, and the value would have been FE', found by using the discount curve BDE'. This curve has a slight angle at D, being composed of the curve BD, constructed according to the high rate of interest prevailing at the time G, and the curve $DE,'$ constructed according to the lower rate of interest which applies to the period FG and which was employed in the curve EC. The essential fact, therefore, is that because of the failure to foresee the future rise in the rate of interest, the value of the property is FE, instead of FE', and that the value of the capital will fall, as at CD, or it may be rise, in accordance with successive future adjustments in the rate of interest. Since these readjustments are usually small and gradual, fluctuations in the capital-value will not ordinarily be as great or as abrupt as here represented, but the principle involved will still hold true. We see, therefore, a new cause for the fluctuations in capital-value, namely, unforeseen changes in the rate of interest.

§ 4

There is, however, a more fundamental way in which a change in the rate of interest enters into our calculations, for it will affect the magnitude of the future income items themselves. In the above example it was assumed that the income items were not dependent on the rate of interest. But it often happens that the income items are not elements of what in Chapter VIII we called "final income," but are "interactions"; or, in more practical language, it often happens that the income is to be reinvested. In this case such an item cancels itself out and leaves in its place a series of income items in the future, and the magnitude of the income items in this later series will depend on the rate of interest at which the preliminary "interaction" was reinvested. If the intention in advance is to reinvest, it becomes important not simply to know the present rate of interest, but to forecast the future rate. This enters into the calculations of an investor who holds a 25-year bond at 5 per cent. He will usually regard the final payment as "principal," intending that when it becomes due it shall be reinvested in a similar 25-year bond. He, therefore, is not really buying a 25-year income stream of $5 a year plus $100 at the end of the term, but is buying, let us say, a *50*-year income stream consisting of $5 per year for the first 25 years and an *unknown* amount per year during the second 25 years. In order to forecast what income will be received in the second period, he has to forecast the rate of interest. In other words, although the bond represents nominally a fixed and certain series of income items, yet, in view of the intention to reinvest, it actually represents an income which is quite uncertain after 25 years, because of the uncertainty in the future rate of interest. Such an investor, if he expected the rate of interest at the end of 25 years to be 2 per cent, would, in purchasing the above-mentioned bond, be getting $5 a year for 25 years and $2 a year for the next 25 years. Under these conditions, if he could buy a 50-year bond at 4 per cent, he would prefer to do so. But, if he expected the rate of interest to remain, for each 25-year period, at 5 per cent, he would prefer, rather than invest now in a 50-year bond at 4 per cent, to invest in the 25-year bond at 5 per cent, intending to reinvest at 5 per cent at the expiration of the term. His forecast of what the rate of interest will be in 25 years will thus materially affect the choice of his investments to-day. Those who expect the rate of interest to fall will prefer to invest in long-time securities at the present market rates, even when those rates are less than on securities of shorter time, while those who expect the rate of interest to rise will prefer short-time securities. In the case of insurance companies which are constantly reinvesting, a change in the rate of interest becomes a very serious matter. One of the actuaries of a large company has recently pointed out that such changes in the rate of interest are not uncommonly encountered and are more important for the prosperity of the company than the most unusual changes in the mortality tables. Insurance companies can only roughly take account of the chances, reckoning that the greater the likelihood of a rise, the better the policy of making temporary investments at high rates; and the greater the likelihood of a fall, the better the policy of making permanent investments, even at moderately low rates.

§ 5

The main application of risk to capital valuation is, however, not to the rate of interest, but to the income items themselves. To this application we now address ourselves. Let us begin by considering the case in which the element of discounting is wholly absent. The simplest case is that of ordinary gambling. If one invests in a lottery ticket where there is one chance in ten of drawing a prize of $50, it is evident that the price of the ticket must be considerably less than $50, which is the income it may yield. Mathematicians have called the product of the prize multiplied by its probability, the "mathematical value" of the chance. In the present instance this "mathematical value" will be $50 $\times \frac{1}{10}$, or $5. If a professional gambler should always pay the mathematical value of the chances, he would, in the long run, probably come out about even, as is well known from "Bernoulli's Theorem." Thus, if he continued to try for such $50 prizes, paying each time $5, he would probably win about one time in ten. In a thousand trials, therefore, he might expect to win 100 times, spending $5 each for his 1000 tickets, or $5000, and receiving $50 each for his 100 prizes, or $5000.

But the actual price which one will pay is not necessarily the mathematical value of the chance. It may be higher; it is usually lower. The gambler is usually a person who will pay more than the mathematical value of the chance. At Monte Carlo, the "bank" makes its profit in this way, although its victims know full well that they are paying more than the mathematical value of their chances. The consequence, of course, is ruin to most of them. Fortunately, persons who deliberately gamble are in most communities in the minority. The ordinary man is unwilling to pay even the full mathematical value of the chance. He is reluctant to assume any risks, and is, on the contrary, willing to make sacrifices in order to rid himself of them. Where the gambler would be willing to pay more than $5 for his lottery tickets, the cautious investor would only be induced to buy such tickets for considerably less than $5. To him, the chance of gain is outweighed by the prospect of loss. Rather than risk little in order to obtain large gains, he prefers to sacrifice much in order to avoid large losses. It is this sentiment which gives rise to the phenomenon of insurance.

§ 6

There are three values which apply to an uncertain return: (1) the value which that return would have if the uncertainty could be eliminated, or its *riskless* value; (2) the value which would be attached to it if the investor were willing to pay the product of the income by the chance of obtaining it, or the *mathematical* value; (3) the value which he is actually willing to pay, or the *commercial* value. Thus in the case of the lottery ticket, entitling the holder to the chance of $100, the riskless value is $100; the mathematical value is $5; and the commercial value, more than $5 for the reckless, less for the man of ordinary caution, and just $5 for those of an intermediate temperament.

The ratio of the mathematical to the riskless value may be called the "coefficient of probability." In the supposed case of the lottery ticket this coefficient is $\frac{5}{100}$. The ratio of the commercial to the mathematical value — a ratio which will vary according to the temperament of the individual — may be called the "coefficient of caution." In the case of a man who values his chance at $4, this coefficient would be $\frac{4}{5}$. Given these ratios, we can for a given individual derive the commercial value from the riskless value by multiplying the riskless value by the coefficient of probability and the result by the coefficient of caution, thus: $\$100 \times \frac{5}{100} \times \frac{4}{5} = \$4$. The product of these two ratios is the ratio of the commercial to the riskless value ($\frac{5}{100} \times \frac{4}{5} = \frac{4}{100}$) and may be called the *coefficient of risk*.[1]

The coefficient of caution expresses a feature of individual character as determined partly by nature and partly by environment. In times like the colonial period when lotteries were common, or in places like Monte Carlo, where gamblers congregate, the coefficient of caution is such as to represent an abnormal lack of caution. The opposite extreme is found in the timid investor who hoards money rather than risk its investment in any form. The coefficient of caution also varies with the same individual under different circumstances. Chief among these varying circumstances, as Professor Norton has pointed out, is the amount of capital of which the individual is possessed. The more capital a man possesses, the less is his chance of serious loss in any enterprise involving risk; and for this reason a rich man finds it possible to grow still richer. The rich can well afford to lose millions where the poor could barely afford to lose hundreds. There is less likelihood of ruin to the United States Steel Corporation from its projected investment of $75,000,000 to found a new steel-producing city than there would be to a workingman who makes a " safe " investment of $1000.

§ 7

We are now in a position to apply these principles of probability to the valuation of capital, *i.e.* to the capitalization of uncertain income. The most important classification of investments from a practical point of view is into two categories of safe and unsafe investments. But even in so-called safe investments the element of risk enters. As between bonds and stocks, the latter usually represent the precarious and the former the safe investments; yet in the case of bonds, the receipt of interest and principal is always in some degree a matter of uncertainty.

[1] For a mathematical statement, see Appendix to Chap. XVI, § 1.

Take, for example, a "5 per cent" bond running for 10 years. Let us assume that the market rate of interest is 4 per cent, in the sense that $100 at any time will exchange for $104 *certain* one year later. Under these conditions, the bond ought to sell for $108 (see Chapter XIII). That is, an investor buying this bond at a premium of $8 will in 10 years "make" 4 per cent provided he receives all the sums stipulated. The $108 is the "riskless value" of the bond.

But, while $108 would be the price of the bond were the investor absolutely *sure* of the income items to which it entitles him, he may feel that there is a risk, — for instance, that the probability of any given interest payment is only $\frac{9}{10}$, in which event it is evident that he will not pay $108. We can easily calculate, on the basis of the assumed probability, that what has been called the "mathematical value" of the bond would be $97. This figure is found by multiplying each income item by its coefficient of probability and discounting the result at the market rate of interest, 4 per cent. We assume here that the risk attached to each individual interest and principal payment is independent of that attached to all the others. The probability of receiving each payment is $\frac{9}{10}$, and the risk of its not being received is in each case $\frac{1}{10}$. It is evident that the first payment of $5, due in one year, has at that time a mathematical value of $5 \times \frac{9}{10}$, and the present value, when discounted at 4 per cent, would be $\frac{5 \times \frac{9}{10}}{104}$. If the same expressions be obtained for all the other items of income, and the sum total of the present valuations be found, it is evident that in the result the factor $\frac{9}{10}$ will appear for every individual sum, and that the total will simply be $\frac{9}{10}$ as much as though the element of risk were absent. In other words, the "mathematical value" of the bond will be $\frac{9}{10}$ of its riskless value of $108, or about $97.

But the actual "commercial value" of the bond will

SEC. 8]   THE RISK ELEMENT   279

ordinarily be less than this "mathematical value" of $97. We may suppose it to be $92.50, indicating a coefficient of caution of $\frac{92.50}{97}$. Here, as in the case of the lottery ticket, we have regarded the actual value of the bond as obtained from its riskless value by applying first the probability factor, and second the caution factor, $\frac{92.50}{97}$.

If the probabilities of receiving the individual interest payments were not regarded as independent, the calculations of the mathematical value would differ somewhat from the preceding. Thus, if we suppose that default in one interest payment carried with it, by the terms of the contract, the default in all subsequent interest payments, we should have to apply the theory of probability somewhat differently[1] but the principle would be the same.

§ 8

There is another way, and one which conforms more to ordinary usage, in which the commercial value of the bond may be derived from the riskless value. While the price of the bond will vary inversely with the risk, the rate of interest varies directly with the risk; so that as the value of the bond descends, the corresponding rate of interest will ascend. Thus we have riskless, mathematical, and commercial rates of interest — 4 per cent, 5.4 per cent, and 6 per cent — corresponding respectively with the riskless, mathematical, and commercial values of the bond — $108, $97, $92.50.

The question sometimes arises, where the element of risk thus raises the basis on which the bond is sold, whether the 6 per cent is a true "rate of interest." The question is purely one of definition. Were it possible, it would be simpler to confine the application of the phrase "rate of interest" to an exchange between present and future riskless income. But in this case, it is always exceedingly diffi-

[1] For the consideration of this case, see Appendix to Chap. XVI, § 2.

cult to state what the riskless rate of interest is, since some slight risk attaches to almost every investment. Accordingly it is usual to regard the commercial rate as a true "rate of interest." The best course, therefore, is to recognize all three as rates of interest, distinguishing them, when necessary, as "riskless," "mathematical," and "commercial."

§ 9

When we speak of the riskless value or the riskless rate, we intend by the employment of the word "riskless," to exclude from consideration the chance element entirely — not only the risk of receiving less, but also the chance of receiving more than the specified income. For cases are not wanting in which the mathematical and commercial values of a security are, by reason of the *chance* that it will prove extra-profitable, more than its riskless value. Take, for instance, a $100 share of preferred stock, on which a minimum income of 5 per cent, or $5, is assured. If the true rate of interest be 4 per cent, the value of such stock should be $125. This is the "riskless" value. The mathematical value, however, will be greater, say $150, inasmuch as there is a probability that the holder will receive more than $5 a year, and practically no probability that he will receive less. And the commercial value will be still different, falling, by reason of the caution of the investor, somewhat below the mathematical, say to $130.

Another instance is that of United States government bonds. The national banks which invest in these receive, besides the interest, a special privilege in the form of permission to issue bank notes. This additional benefit may be regarded as a species of additional income, and materially enhances the value of the bonds. For this reason, United States government bonds are not used for investment purposes, except among those in whom the element of caution is unduly strong, but are held for the most part by national banks. It is therefore misleading to cite, as some have done, the rates of interest realized on government bonds as an indication of the true rate of interest. A similar benefit attaches to the bonds of the Credit Foncier in France. These are sold on a very low "basis" because of the chance, connected with them, of winning prizes.

§ 10

In the general case we have to do not simply with the risk of falling below a specified income, nor with the chance of rising above a specified income, but with both. Thus, the dividends from common stock have no fixed minimum as do those from good preferred stock, nor any fixed maximum as do the interest payments from bonds. They may vary, and vary widely, in *either* direction. The amount of variation may be measured with reference to any specified amount selected arbitrarily as a basis of comparison. For instance, in the case of stock which has yielded, in successive years, the following percentages: 5, 5, 6, 5, 5, 4, 5, 7, 5, 3, 4, 5, we may for convenience take 5 per cent to serve for a basis of computation. The stock has yielded 1 per cent or more in excess of this in two cases out of twelve; it has yielded 2 per cent in excess in one case out of twelve; it has fallen short by 1 per cent or more in three cases out of twelve, and fallen short by 2 per cent in one case out of twelve. If these frequencies are our only guide for judging the future, they represent the probabilities of receiving the respective dividends.

On the basis of the foregoing figures it is possible to calculate the "riskless" and the "mathematical" value of the stock, and, if we know the caution factor, it is possible to calculate the "commercial" value also. Thus, the "riskless" value, in this case, signifies that value which the stock would have if it were *certain* to yield the (arbitrarily assumed) 5 per cent forever — never more and never less. The riskless value is therefore simply the capitalized value of a perpetual annuity of $5 per share of $100 face value. If the rate of interest is 4 per cent, the result is $5 divided by 4 per cent, or $125.

To obtain the "mathematical" value we simply add to the riskless value the value of the chance of getting more, and subtract that of the chance of getting less. The chance of getting an additional $1 a year is found by experience, as set forth above, to be two in twelve, or $\frac{1}{6}$ each year. The present value of the right to this chance has therefore a mathematical value $\frac{1}{6}$ as great as though the $1 increment were a certainty. But the certainty of $1 a year would be worth $25. Hence a chance of 1 in 6 of getting $1 a year would be worth mathematically $\frac{1}{6}$ of $25, or 4.16\frac{2}{3}$. In like manner the chance of a second additional dollar is one in twelve and is worth (mathematically) $\frac{1}{12}$ of $25, or 2.08\frac{1}{3}$. These two terms, 4.16\frac{2}{3}$ and 2.08\frac{1}{3}$, are the additive terms sought. The subtractive terms are the mathematical value of the chance of getting $1 less than the $5, and of getting still another $1 less. These chances, being 3 in 12 and 1 in 12 respectively, are worth $\frac{3}{12}$ of $25 and $\frac{1}{12}$ of $25 respectively, or $6.25 and 2.08\frac{1}{3}$. The whole mathematical value is therefore $125 + ($4.16$\frac{2}{3}$ + 2.08\frac{1}{3}$) − ($6.25 + 2.08\frac{1}{3}$), or 122.91\frac{2}{3}$. Applying to this the factor of caution, which, let us say, is $\frac{9}{10}$, we find the commercial value to be $110.63. The three values are thus, approximately: —

"riskless" value $125
"mathematical" value $123
"commercial" value $111

In this manner we may compute the three values in any other case. Usually, however, the chances involved are so indefinite that the reckoning is made only by rule of thumb.

[Sec. 11]

Any further attempt to apply the theory of probability would therefore outrun the exigencies of practice.[1]

§ 11

The practical investor, in order to estimate the influence of probability, attempts to forecast as nearly as possible all the elements which may affect his interests. An example occurs in the *Engineering and Mining Journal* for December 8, 1904. It is there stated that the mine at Cananea, belonging to the Green Consolidated Copper Company, was worth, according to quotations at that time, $30,000,000. This valuation the journal shows might be justified if we suppose the mine to contain a total of 1,040,000,000 pounds of copper which can be mined at the rate of 104,000,000 a year for 10 years, and if we suppose that the price of copper will be 14 cents, and the cost of production 8 cents, to which should be added the expense of refining, selling, commission, etc., making $2\frac{1}{2}$ cents more, or $10\frac{1}{2}$ cents in all. If we make allowance for future economies, this may be called 10 cents, leaving a net profit of 4 cents a pound. On this basis we should obtain a 10-year annuity of $4,160,000 per annum, the present value of which, at 5 per cent, would be $32,000,000. But inasmuch as these forecasts involve great uncertainty, a fair price would be regarded as $30,000,000, the discrepancy between $30,000,000 and $32,000,000 being due to the element of risk, *i.e.* the combined influence of probability and caution. This price represents a basis of $6\frac{1}{2}$ per cent.[2]

[1] Nevertheless it is more than conceivable that the time may come when practical brokers will make use of probability computations in the same way that they now make use of bond tables. The writer's colleague, Professor Norton, has shown this possibility. For a brief statement, see Appendix to Chap. XVI, § 3.

[2] For such properties as mines which rapidly depreciate, brokers often reckon the "basis" in a somewhat different manner, computing the percentage realized to the investor on the supposition that he employs a depreciation fund and reinvests, not at the $6\frac{1}{2}$ per cent just

In forecasting the income from capital, it is thus necessary to forecast all the elements which may influence it and also their variability. These elements are sometimes exceedingly numerous. A stockholder in a railroad, in order to obtain a true idea of the value of his property, must look forward to the traffic of the road, the price which can be charged for this traffic, the cost of operation, involving the amount of labor, fuel, and materials, the prices paid for these items, etc. To forecast any one of these involves, in turn, some knowledge of outside conditions, as the outlook for crops, prices of agricultural products, probabilities of increased trade through connecting lines, increased density of population, possible competition, possible adverse legislation, etc.

§ 12

We now see that the value of capital actually changes through any one of four causes: (1) Through the effect of discount; that is, while no income is being received, the value of the capital will rise along a discount curve. (2) Through the periodic detachment of income; that is, at times when income or outgo occurs, the capital will be directly decreased by the amount of the income and increased by the amount of the outgo reached and passed. (3) Through unexpected changes in the rate of interest; that is, when such changes occur causing revaluations of the future by discounting it at a new rate, the value of the capital will change correspondingly — increasing if the rate of interest falls, and decreasing if it rises. (4) Through unforeseen changes in expected income.

The fourth cause is the one of most practical importance.

mentioned, but at the true or safe rate of interest, 5 per cent. On this calculation the investor would be found to make 10 per cent per annum in addition to the amount set aside for depreciation at 5 per cent, and the "basis" would be called 10 per cent. For the case just mentioned, this 10 per cent realized, with the depreciation fund reinvested at 5 per cent, is equivalent to 6½ per cent realized, with a reinvestment at 6½ per cent.

The market quotations for any product are constantly being changed and revised, not so much through the operation of the first three principles as through the fourth — the constantly changing outlook into the future. Every rumor as to crops, every storm or pest which is known to have destroyed them, changes the expectation of future income. Since the third and fourth causes are both due to lack of foresight, they may be included, if desired, under the common head of "risk."

In Figure 11 the operation of these four causes is represented as occurring successively in the order enumerated. The capital-value first rises along the discount curve AB,

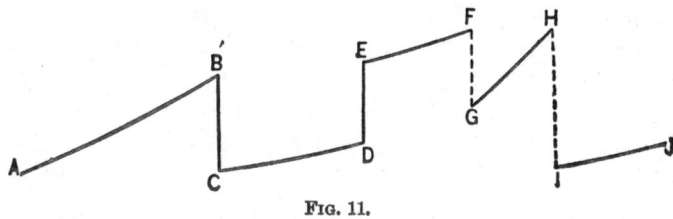

Fig. 11.

constructed according to a particular rate of interest. When the first income coupon, so to speak, BC, is detached, the value falls to C, after which it travels again along the discount curve CD, rising suddenly when a certain expected cost DE has been gotten rid of, then following EF again, whereupon, in consequence of a sudden and unexpected rise in the rate of interest, it falls to G, after which it ascends according to the steeper discount curve GH, and then, in consequence of a change in the estimate of future income, falls again to I, after which it proceeds along another discount curve to J, and so on indefinitely. The changes caused by actual income and outgo, we here represent by the continuous lines BC, DE, etc., and the changes due to a revised estimate of interest and of income we represent by the *dotted* lines FG, HI, etc.

§ 13

The discount curves just employed are assumed to be the same as those employed formerly in the discussion of *certain* prospective income. But, as a matter of fact, chance will have an effect even on discount curves. For the increase of capital-value along a discount curve is due to the approach of expected income, and this approach, in the case of uncertain income, is quite different from what it is in the case of certain income. It is only as the owner has a conviction that he is nearing the time when income will be received, that the capital-value will increase at all. This will be true of dividends for the declaration of which there are definitely appointed times; but if the times for the installments of income are wholly fortuitous, the capital-value will not increase and instead of a discount curve, we shall have a horizontal line. If a piano dealer is asked to value a particular piano in his stock, he will not add interest because it had been in his stock a long time. It is impossible for him to say which individual piano will be sold next, and the mere fact that a particular piano has stood for a long time in his store will offer no assurance that it will be sold earlier than the others. Therefore the value of the piano will not advance with time, but will remain nearly at the wholesale price. In the same way, a stock of money which a man carries as cash does not advance in value by lying in his pocket. For although the services which it will render to its owner are actually approaching, their exact time of occurrence is not known, but is subject to chance. It is chiefly in the case of bonds and stocks, where there are definite times for the occurrence of income, that the actual value ascends strictly along the discount curve. In the case of shares of stock if the stockholder fears that a dividend will be small, the value of the stock will only slowly increase as the time for the dividend approaches. It will follow a discount curve, but one which climbs toward only a slight elevation — enough to represent the commercial value of the uncertain dividend. Then when the amount of the dividend is known, just before it is distributed, the stock (including the right to the impending dividend) will suddenly jump in value. After the dividend is paid, it will again descend and then increase slowly in value until the approach of the next dividend. This will explain the fact which has sometimes been observed, that the value of a dividend-paying stock often remains fairly constant. Normally its course will be somewhat as in Figure 12. The capital-value increases only slowly from A to B, when, with the declaration of a dividend, it immediately jumps to C, and with the distribution of the dividend at D

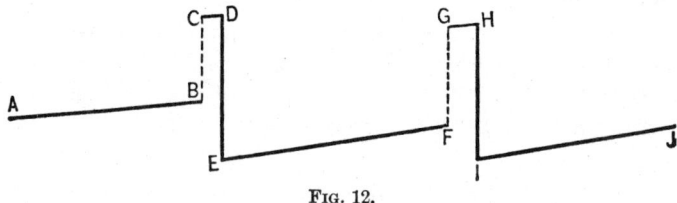

Fig. 12.

descends to E, and so on indefinitely. If we omit the fluctuations between the declarations of dividends and the distributions, the course of the stock remains relatively horizontal, as represented by AB, EF, IJ.

§ 14

The introduction of the element of chance does not greatly affect bookkeeping except to impair somewhat the correspondence between capital accounts and income accounts. This is occasioned by mere changes in the size of the capital items. When revision of capital-value is due to a new estimate of future income, as after a fire, shipwreck, or other calamity, the immediate result is merely to reduce (or, it may be, to increase) the value of the assets. The accountant must "write down" (or up) the assets, and therefore also reduce the balancing item on the other side, called undivided profits, or profit and loss. But the income account is not affected except as the new outlook toward the future may lead to new expenses for reconstruction, or to new income.

§ 15

Business men try not only to estimate the risks which they must encounter and to adjust their accounts accordingly, but they also endeavor to avoid such risks altogether. This follows from the existence of the factor of caution. Where the coefficient of caution is abnormal, amounting to *incaution*, risks are not avoided, but are expressly sought, and the phenomena of gambling and indiscriminate speculation are the result. But in the great majority of men there exists a healthy fear of risks, and in consequence a tendency to avoid or reduce them.

There are five principal ways in which risks may be reduced, viz.: —

1. By increasing guaranties for the performance of contracts;
2. By increasing safeguards against incurring losses;
3. By increasing foresight and thereby diminishing the risks;
4. By insurance, that is, by consolidating risks;
5. By throwing risks into the hands of a special class of speculators.

These will be considered in order.

§ 16

The ownership of capital wealth necessarily involves risk, since the income from it can only be estimated, — never precisely foreknown. But it is possible, by a division of the ownership of capital wealth, for one class of property holders to assume the burden of risks and to *guarantee* to another class a fixed income. This is the primary reason for the separation of securities into two great classes called stocks and bonds. In any large enterprise the stockholders take the risks, and by so doing guarantee to the bondholders a fixed income. As was remarked in a previous chapter, the capital stock acts as a buffer between the liabilities and the assets, which amounts to saying that it guarantees a fixed income to the holders of the liabilities. President Hadley has emphasized the fact that a bondholder "commutes" the precarious income of an enterprise into a fixed annuity and that the system by which one class receives "interest" and another "profits" has its origin in the desire of one class to avoid and the willingness of another to assume risks.[1]

Nevertheless the general relation between creditor and debtor necessarily carries with it a certain amount of risk to the creditor. This risk may be reduced by the deposit of collateral security or endorsement[2] as in the case of bank loans and discounts; by mortgage on real estate, or occasionally on chattels; by legal regulations, as in the case of notes of national banks, and by other methods.

§ 17

The method of guaranties is really a method of *shifting* risks rather than of avoiding them. The second method aims to reduce risk by special safeguards. Some articles

[1] But the "rate of commutation" is not a rate of interest, since any ratio of commutation is necessarily a ratio between two incomes, those respectively of the stockholders and the bondholders, whereas the rate of interest is a ratio of income to capital.

[2] The influence of endorsement in reducing risk is greater than would appear on the surface. Thus, if there is one chance in a hundred that the signer of a note will default, and a like chance for his endorser, both these risks being *independent*, the chance that the bank will lose is the product of these two, or only one chance in ten thousand. Hence, two-name commercial paper is ordinarily a safe security, provided, of course, the names are those of reliable business men, such as have a high "rating" in Bradstreet's or other standard commercial agency.

of wealth exist, in fact, simply for the sake of meeting sudden unforeseen emergencies. This is true, for instance, of fire engines, fire extinguishers, safety appliances on railways, safety valves, and other devices connected with steam engines and machinery, burglar alarms, safety deposit vaults, etc. To a large extent this risk-meeting function applies to almost every stock of wealth. Food in a pantry usually exists beyond *certain* wants in order to provide for *un*certain wants, and when sources of supply are distant, such stores of food need to be large. Especially is this true in the case of armies. Again, a factory will usually have a large reserve stock, both of raw materials and finished products, in order to meet unexpected demands. In like manner, jobbers, wholesalers, and retailers maintain a sufficient stock of goods to meet not only the foreseen, but some of the unforeseen demands of their customers. The function of speculators in grain or other commodities consists largely in conserving the stock of a community as a safeguard against future scarcity. Almost all of what is called the reserve of a bank is used as a safety fund to meet the unforeseen demands of note-holders and depositors, and, in particular, to meet a special "run." These reserves often remain as idle as a fire extinguisher for years or even decades against the hour of need. It is said that there are bars of precious metals in the Bank of England which have lain there undisturbed for two centuries. A large part of the cash carried by an ordinary individual is quite analogous to a bank reserve, being held to meet special emergencies. Some individuals even keep in a separate pocket a special gold piece, lest some day they should become "stranded." It may be said that this risk-meeting function of pocket cash is the chief compensation for the so-called "loss of interest" on the money thus carried. The convenience and security obtained by having an adequate supply is a species of income replacing the income which might be earned were the sum invested. The same principles, from the standpoint of an individual, apply to bank deposits, and thus to the whole volume of the circulating medium.

§ 18

The third method of reducing risks is by increasing knowledge. It has been seen that risk is nothing but an expression of ignorance, and decreases with the progress of science. It may be said that the chief progress now being made industrially consists in lifting the veil which hides the future. The countless trade journals now in use have their special reason for existence in enabling their readers better to forecast the future, by supplying them with data as to past and present conditions, as well as by instructing them in the relations of cause and effect. The government reports of crops, the technical schools and agricultural colleges, all tend in the same direction. Whereas formerly the mine prospector could only guess wildly at the ore "in sight" and the time and cost required to mine it, the graduate of mining schools is now able, through knowledge of geology and metallurgy, to bring these forecasts into some degree of scientific accuracy. And, whereas until recently farming was one of the most uncertain of occupations, it is to-day — thanks to modern scientific agriculture — almost if not quite as amenable to prediction as industry or commerce.

§ 19

We come now to that important means of avoiding and shifting risks, called insurance. Insurance involves the offsetting of one risk by another; that is, the consolidation of a large number of chances whereby relative certainty is, as it were, manufactured out of uncertainty. To illustrate this, let us suppose that 10,000 houses of the same kind are too distant from each other to be destroyed by the same fire, and let us suppose that these houses in the average would be worth $10,000 each were it not for the risk of fire; in other words, that $10,000 is the capitalized value of the services to be rendered by each house, assuming that it lives out its natural life. The value of the total number of houses would then be $100,000,000. This is the "riskless value." It is the capitalized value of the income which the 10,000 houses would bring in, were there no loss by fire. If interest is at 5 per cent, the income which is thus capitalized is $5,000,000 a year. If now we suppose that the annual risk of fire is one chance in 200, there will be about 50 houses annually burned. Reckoning the value thus destroyed at an average of $10,000 for each house, there will be $500,000 annually lost by fire. We must now deduct this from the $5,000,000, which would be the income were it not for fires. We have left $4,500,000, the capitalization of which is only $90,000,000. In other words, the total property of 10,000 houses is worth in "mathematical value" $90,000,000 instead of $100,000,000, the reduction being because of the prospect of fires. If we suppose all of these houses to be owned by one corporation, this mathematical value of $90,000,000 might also be the actual value, for such a corporation could count on about 50 houses burning annually almost as a certainty. Each house would then be worth, on an average, $9000. But if such an individual house is owned by an individual person, this mathematical value would not be its "commercial value," on account of the element of caution. Let us say that the caution coefficient is $\frac{7}{9}$, in which case the house would be worth $7000. In other words, we have $10,000 as the "riskless" value of the house, $9000 as its "mathematical" value, and $7000 as its actual "commercial" value, assuming that there is not as yet insurance. Now if the owner of such a house could secure insurance on a purely mathematical basis of the risk, which, as we have seen, is one half of one per cent, and, therefore, could pay only $50 per annum, in consideration of which the value of his house, if destroyed by fire, is restored to him, it is evident that he has made a good investment; for he is now assured of a house even should a fire occur, and he has, instead of the risk of fire, merely to pay his annual premium of $50 a year, the capitalized value of which is $1000. Consequently, his house is worth $10,000 − $1,000, or $9000.[1]

Such an insurance rate, however, being based on the mathematical or "pure" premiums, would not pay any profit to the companies conducting it. But even a higher insurance would leave a large margin of capital-value saved to the insured. If we suppose a "loading," so that the insurance premium is not $50 but $100, similar reasoning would show that the value of the house when insured would be to the owner $8000 instead of $7000. As long as the loading is not sufficient to absorb *all* the margin between the $7000 and $9000, it will be advantageous to insure.

Between the case of a man owning an individual house, when the element of caution would have a large influence, and that where 10,000 houses are owned by the same corporation, in which case the caution element is almost entirely absent, there are numberless intervening cases. The larger the number of houses owned by one individual or corporation, the less profitable becomes insurance. To express it in the language of the business man, the various risks insure each other. Thus, the North German Lloyd Company finds it profitable not to insure its vessels against shipwreck, because they have so large a fleet that their losses through a period of time can be counted on fairly well in advance.

One effect of insurance on the individual is to steady the income from his property. The owner of the house in question would receive, if it were not insured, a net annual income, after providing for depreciation, of 5 per cent on $10,000, or $500 a year until the house was burned, after

[1] For a mathematical statement, see Appendix to Chap. XVI, § 3.

which he would receive nothing; whereas, if he insures, he receives this $500 income less his premium up to the date of the fire, and afterward the income from the indemnity paid him by the company.

§ 20

The same principles apply to other forms of insurance, as marine insurance, which, by consolidating in an insurance company the risk on a large number of vessels, reduces for the individual even the perils of the sea to relative certainty and regularity; or as steam boiler insurance, which in a similar manner treats the risks of explosion; or as plate-glass insurance, burglar insurance, live stock insurance, hail and cyclone insurance, fidelity insurance, accident insurance, employer's liability insurance, and, above all, life insurance.[1] This form of insurance, like the other forms, tends to steady the income of the beneficiary. If a wife holds insurance on her husband's life, the consequence is that, although what he gives her during his life is somewhat diminished, her income will not suddenly cease at his death. The tendency of insurance here as elsewhere is to make regularity out of irregularity, relative certainty out of relative uncertainty; and where, under the form of insurance contracts, the opposite result follows, the case is not one of true insurance, but tends to become one of gambling. Thus, if a person insures the life of some one in whom he has no financial interest, he is merely gambling on that person's life. Some years ago in Michigan there was an abuse of this type called "graveyard insurance." Speculators went through the form of insuring the lives of certain old persons, in other words of betting on their deaths, a procedure not only vicious as gambling, but calculated also to lead to crime. The same considerations apply to fire insurance, where a person insures a building in which

---

[1] See Appendix to Chap. XVI, § 4.

he is not financially interested, or over-insures one in which he is.[1]

The range to which insurance can apply is always limited; but it is constantly being extended, as business men learn how to bring risks of any kind on to a statistical basis and to apply the theory of probability. At present the total assets of life insurance companies alone in the United States are nearly $3,000,000,000.

§ 21

Where risks cannot be reduced to a statistical basis, and therefore cannot be insured against, recourse is often had to the shifting of the risk into the hands of those who are willing to take it. Such persons are speculators. A speculator is usually one in whom the caution factor is not so pronounced as in the ordinary individual. In extreme cases he tends to become a simple gambler. The distinction between a speculator and a gambler, however, is usually fairly well marked. A gambler seeks and makes risks which it is not necessary to assume, whereas the speculator is one who merely volunteers to assume those risks of business which must inevitably fall somewhere. A speculator is also usually fitted for his work by special knowledge, so that the risk *to him*, owing to superior foresight, is at the outset less than it would be to others. The indiscriminate prejudice against all speculation, which is so often met with, is beside the point; for, were there no speculators, the same risks would have to be borne by those less fitted to bear them. The chief evils of speculation flow from the participation of the general public, who lack the special knowledge, and enter the market in a purely gambling spirit. In addition to suffering the usual evil consequences of gambling, they produce evil consequences for the non-participating public by causing factitious fluctuations

[1] For the moral effects of insurance, see *Insurance and Crime*, by A. C. Campbell, Putnam's, 1902.

in the values of the products or property in which they speculate.

The evils of speculation are particularly acute when, as generally happens with the investing public, the forecasts are not made independently. Were it true that each individual speculator made up his mind independently of every other as to the future course of events, the errors of some would probably be offset by those of others. But, as a matter of fact, the mistakes of the common herd are usually in the same direction. Like sheep, they all follow a single leader. How easily they are led is shown by the effect on the stock market in the year 1904, when Thomas Lawson published scare-head advertisements in the newspapers advising the public to sell certain securities.

A chief cause of crises, panics, runs on banks, etc., is that risks are not independently reckoned, but are a mere matter of imitation. A crisis is a time of general and forced liquidation.[1] In other words, it differs from any other period in two particulars, viz. that the liquidations are more numerous, and that they are for the most part forced upon the debtors by the creditors because of threatened or actual bankruptcy. Neither of these conditions could exist unless there had been at a prior time a general miscalculation of the future. Both creditors and debtors must have made a wrong forecast when their ill-fated agreements were entered into. Hence a crisis is the penalty which must be paid when a previous *general error in prediction* is discovered. Such a general error *may* be due to the coincidence of a number of independent mistakes of individuals; but it almost always *is* due to lack of independence, — to the principle of imitation. The error, whatever it is, when committed by a person of influence, is like an infection; it is caught by hundreds of others and

[1] See Juglar, *Des Crises Commerciales*, Paris, 2d edition, 1889, Chapter I.

transmitted to thousands. A great mob of easily led investors, eagerly searching for "straight tips" which may bring instant wealth, make their mistake in common, and when the mistake is disastrous they try, *en masse*, to escape. A sudden rush of all the passengers on a ferry-boat to one side will produce a "list" in the boat's position, and sometimes cause it to capsize, though the independent movement of the individual passengers will seldom or never produce disaster. So also the sudden general realization of unforeseen danger on the part of the investing public may submerge the craft of credit and those whom it has hitherto borne along in safety. In short, a general crisis bears the relation to individual bankruptcies which a general conflagration bears to individual fires. The key to the study of either crises or conflagrations is the existence, in place of independent hazards, of *interdependent* ones. So far as conflagrations are concerned the principle of interdependence is distinctly recognized by students of fire insurance, and in consequence, each company strives to keep its own fire risks independent of each other, by not having too many in the same locality; but so far as crises are concerned, the principle has not yet been sufficiently emphasized by students of economic history.

The same principle applies to the phenomenon of a run on a bank. The opinions of the bank's solvency are not formed independently but interdependently. A year or more ago the newspapers reported that, a policeman and a crowd of people being collected on the steps of one of the Wilkes-Barre savings banks to escape the rain, two Hungarian depositors who were passing jumped to the conclusion that the bank had been attacked by burglars, and circulated the disturbing news in the Hungarian colony, with the result that when the bank opened for business many depositors made a run upon it.

We see, then, that where speculation is imitative, it is dangerous alike to those who engage in it and to the public.

Where, on the other hand, speculation is based on independent knowledge, its utility is usually enormous. It operates both to *reduce* risk by means of utilizing the special knowledge of speculators, and also to *shift* risk from those who lack this knowledge to those who possess it. The consequence is that normally speculative property will gravitate into the hands of those most able to forecast its true income.

Modern production has been called capitalistic-speculative production, owing to the fact that it is managed by "captains of industry," who are specially fitted at once to forecast and to mould the future within the special realms in which they operate. The industries of transportation and manufacturing particularly are under the lead of an educated and trained speculative class, whose function it is to assume for themselves the main risks, and leave the ordinary investor, who is not so equipped, to coöperate as a mere "lender" or silent partner. Yet it often happens that they betray the confidence placed in them, and continue to throw the burden of risk on those whom they pretend to shield.

§ 22

In the special field more usually known as "speculative," — namely, that in which attempts are made to forecast prices in the great exchange markets, — we find a similar class who are specially trained. These speculators are either "bulls" or "bears"; that is, they speculate either for a rise or a fall. Those who believe that wheat or any other article is likely to rise in value and hence yield more than the "rate of interest," will hold it, or if they do not own it, will buy it or obtain an option on it. Such an option is known as a "call," and is put in force at a later time, at a price fixed in advance and considered low. On the other hand, those who believe that prices will fall will sell out their present holdings, or may sell "short," agreeing to supply such holdings at a later time at a fixed price which they consider high. Such a contract to sell is often made in the form of an option, in which case it is known as a "put."

To show how such contracts will shift risks, a few examples will suffice. A building contractor who had taken a large contract was asked if he were not taking large risks, since he could not foreknow the cost of building. He replied, "No, I am taking no risks at all except on 'labor'; I have made contracts to be supplied with all materials when needed, at fixed prices." Those who made these contracts thus assumed the risk of fluctuation in price in the special materials in which they dealt, relieving the contractor of the necessity of informing himself of the special market conditions for stone, brick, timber, etc., and enabling him to make a closer bid for the contract, inasmuch as there was less need of the element of caution. The public, of course, get the benefit of such a shifting of risk in the form of reduced cost of building. Similar results follow from most other "short" sales. Again, a woolen manufacturer need not carry so large a stock of wool if he can make a contract by which some one will sell short, or agree to supply the wool at fixed prices and at certain dates. He can afford to use up his present stock fearlessly, with the certainty that when it is gone he can obtain a new supply.[1] Without such a contract, he would be under the necessity of carrying a large and idle stock.

An important method of shifting risks is "hedging," whereby a dealer, for instance in transporting wheat, may be relieved of the risk of a change in price. He buys wheat in the West intending to ship it to New York and sell it there at enough to cover cost of transportation and a small profit. In consequence of a sudden fall in price he might find all his profit wiped out; or he might, on the other hand, by a rise in price, make much more than normal profits. But, being of a cautious disposition,

[1] Cf. Hadley, *Economics*, Putnam's, 1896, p. 106.

he prefers an intermediate course, — a small profit which is sure, rather than the chances of both gain and loss. Consequently he "hedges." He enters into some speculative market, knowing that it will move in sympathy with the New York market, and there he "speculates" for a fall, or sells "short." In case the price in New York falls, what he loses on the wheat which he has transported he gains through his speculative short selling. Contrariwise, if the price rises, what he gains on his wheat transported he loses in the speculative market. In other words, he is, as it were, betting on both sides of the market at once, and therefore eliminating all risk, so that he only obtains his normal profit, commission, or percentage on the actual wheat handled, having imposed the burden of risk of speculation on the speculative dealers to whom he sold short.[1]

The effect of hedging on those who engage in it, such as the wheat dealers, is evidently to enable them to work on a smaller margin of profit. In consequence the public receives a benefit in lowered prices. The case is thus very similar to those respectively of the builder and of the woolen manufacturer. Short selling, binding the future to the past, enables the specialist to guarantee to the general public a definite foreseen series of events. The beneficial effect to the public, in saving useless stocks and reserves, in producing more intelligent direction of enterprises, and in encouraging accumulation through greater certainty of its future benefits, is both obvious and great. Risk is one of the direst economic evils, and all of the devices which aid in overcoming it — whether increased guaranties, safeguards, foresight, insurance, or legitimate speculation — represent a great boon to humanity.

[1] See "Speculations on Stock and Produce Exchanges of the United States," by Henry C. Emery, *Publications of American Economic Association*. For the development of insurance-speculation in England, see "The Put and Call," by L. R. Higgins, London, Effingham Wilson, 1902.

PART IV. SUMMARIES

CHAPTER XVII. SUMMARY OF PART III
CHAPTER XVIII. GENERAL SUMMARY
GLOSSARY. SUMMARY OF DEFINITIONS

CHAPTER XVII

SUMMARY OF PART III (CHAPTERS XI–XVI) REPRESENTED BY DIAGRAMS

§ 1

WE have finished our study of the relations between capital-value and income-value and may now pause to summarize them briefly. At the beginning of Part III it was stated that the income from capital wealth consists of whatever service it performs for man; that capital and income may each be measured either in specific quantities of their respective units, or in value; and that consequently there are four ratios between income and capital; namely, (1) the physical productivity of capital, (2) the value productivity, (3) the physical return, and (4) the value-return. Our special theme has been the value-return,—the relation between income-value and capital-value.

We saw that the value of capital wealth is the discounted value of its expected income. The relation between the value of the income and the value of the capital was indicated by diagrams. Income was represented by a series of vertical lines as in Figure 13 (a, a', a'', a'''), the horizontal distances between them representing intervals of time. It was then found possible to represent the capital-value of this income in anticipation, on the assumption that the income could be relied upon with certainty. This representation gave the capital curve,—a broken or toothed curve AB. In this curve, each vertical drop is equal to the corresponding income item shown below it, and the intervening points are connected by discount curves; so that the total capital-value at the time C is represented by the altitude BC.

But this separate representation for capital and for income respectively need not be adhered to, because the capital curve AB alone contains in its vertical teeth all that is necessary to indicate the installments of income; and in the present chapter the main propositions relating to

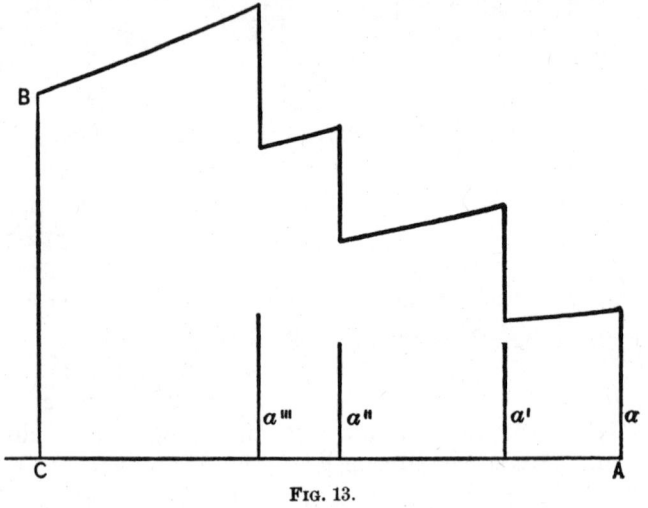

Fig. 13.

capital and income will be restated with the aid of geometrical representations of which this capital curve AB is the type.

§ 2

First of all, such a curve exhibits the fact that the value of any capital is the discounted value of the expected income. In Figure 14 the several discount curves used in previous diagrams are all continued to meet CB. The parts into which CB is thus divided, b, b', b'', b''', will represent respectively the present values of the income items a, a', a'', a'''. This may readily be proved from the nature of the discount curves.

The diagram shows, in the second place (tracing it forward chronologically), that the capital-value alternately rises and falls, rising in anticipation of approaching income and falling as the installments of this income are, like coupons, successively detached from capital. The alternate rise and fall of the capital curve may be equal, each to the other, indicating that the income is "standard"; or the former

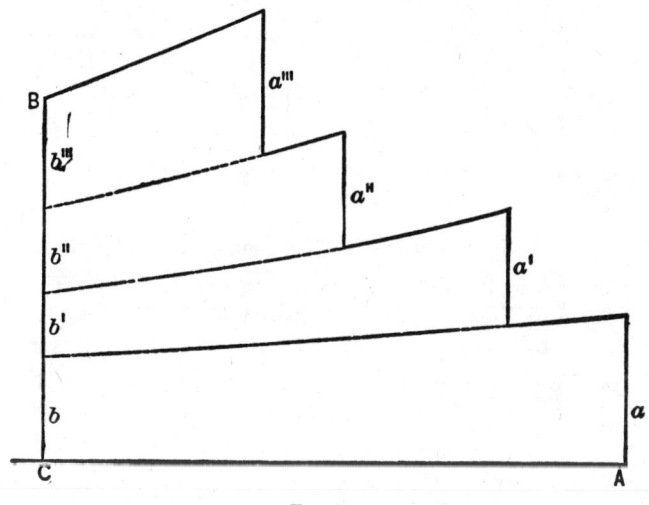

Fig. 14.

or the latter may be the greater, indicating respectively that the income is above or below standard.

If any installment of income is negative — in other words, is not strictly income, but outgo — we need simply to reverse the direction of one of the teeth, as in Figure 15. In this case the capital-value is simply the discounted value of the future income less that of the outgo.

§ 3

As we have seen, if we trace the entire history of a capital curve backward in time from the last installment of income to the beginning of the investment or enterprise, the curve will normally be at the zero point at both ends. This is shown in Figure 16. Such a curve shows the normal cycle of capital-value from the moment when the article of capital is first utilized to the moment when it is ex-

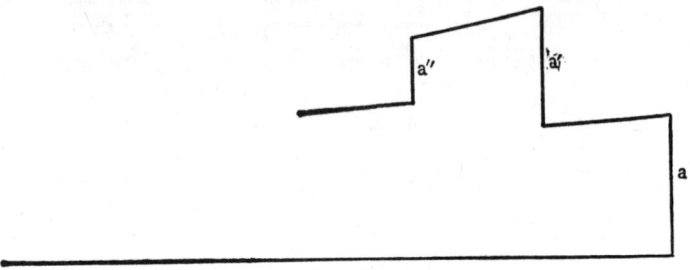

FIG. 15.

hausted. It is "normal" in the sense that the income is just sufficient to compensate for the outlay, no more and no less, and that usually the principal items of outgo all occur in the early part of the cycle, and the principal items of income all accrue in the latter part. In such a

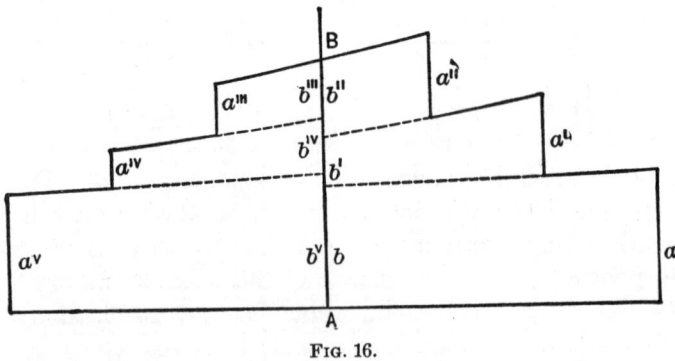

FIG. 16.

normal curve the capital-value (AB in Fig. 16) at any moment may be said to represent two things: first, it represents the *discounted* value of the future expected income (less that of future expected outgo, if any); and, secondly, it represents the *accumulated* value of past outgo (less that of past income, if any). From this it follows that the value of the capital AB is, on the one hand, less than the future total income which it represents, and greater than the past outgo. This capital-value may be regarded as made up of the elements b, b', b''', which are respectively the discounted values of the respective larger magnitudes a, a', a''; and, on the other hand, as made up of

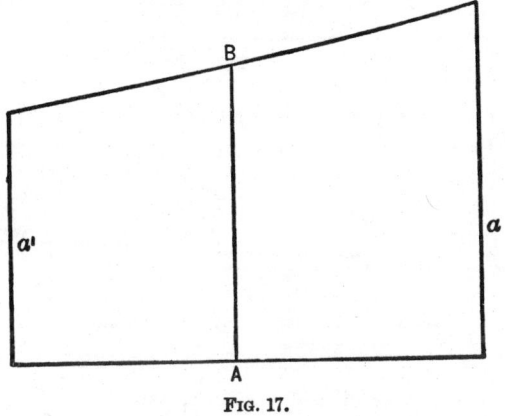

Fig. 17.

b''', b^{iv}, b^{v}, which are the accumulated values of the respective smaller magnitudes a''', a^{iv}, a^{v}. By putting together the elements of which AB is composed, we see, on the one hand, that AB is less than the anticipated income and greater than the past outgo; and consequently, *a fortiori*, that the past outgo is less than the future income. For the sake of simplicity in our illustration, we have chosen a point of time after all the outgo and before any of the income has accrued; but the same principles could be worked out upon such a diagram, no matter what point of time were chosen. In other words, in the normal case the value of any capital is intermediate between the value of its past cost of production or acquisition and the value of its future income.

In the special case in which there is but one item of cost and one item of income, the curve is reduced to that shown in Figure 17, where a is the expected income, and a' the

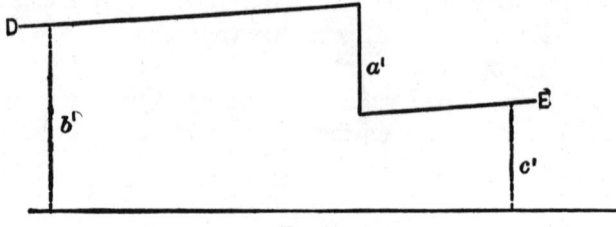

Fig. 18.

past outgo. If the capital-value AB be taken at a point midway between the income and outgo, it evidently fol-

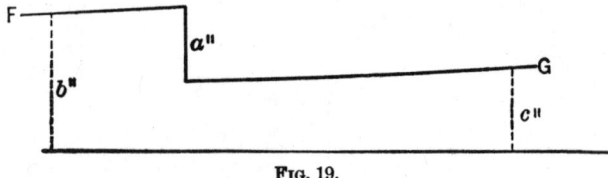

Fig. 19.

lows, by the nature of the discount curve, that the ratio of a' to AB is the same as the ratio of AB to a, or that

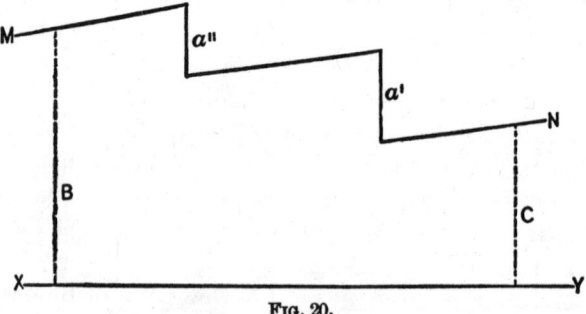

Fig. 20.

AB is the "mean proportional," or "geometric mean," between a and a'. In other words, the normal relation between cost, capital, and return is expressed in the statement that the capital is a mean proportional between its past cost and its future return.

§ 4

Another use which may be made of the diagrammatic representation is to exhibit in a compact manner the summation of both the capital and the income of any given enterprise or community. This may be done simply by

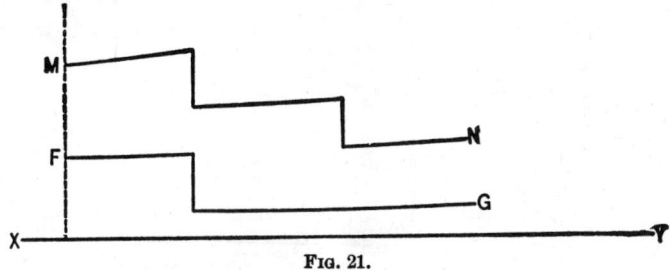

FIG. 21.

adding together the corresponding ordinates or vertical lines in any number of capital curves, representing any number of articles of wealth or property. Let Figure 18, for instance, represent one capital curve, and Figure 19 another. Figure 20, formed by combining Figures 18 and 19, then represents the sum of the capital and income of both. Figure 20 is derived from Figures 18 and 19 in such a manner that the ordinate B is the sum of the individual ordinates b' and b'', and in like manner any other ordinate, C, is the sum of the corresponding individual ordinates c' and c''. From the rule by which Figure 20 is constructed, it is evident that every tooth in the constituent curves, such as a' and a'', will be reproduced in the combined diagram. In Figure 20, therefore, the ordinates represent the combined capital-values at various points, while the two teeth a'' and a' represent the total income accruing in that time interval which includes them. Thus, Figure 20 epitomizes the summation both of capital and income.

But it is not necessary to have three separate diagrams. It is possible to superimpose one of the first two figures upon the other, as shown in Figure 21. In this figure, on the same axis XY is drawn first FG, corresponding to Figure 18 above, and, secondly, at distances above FG corresponding to the ordinates in Figure 19, is drawn the line MN. This line MN contains an apparent tooth or break which does not appear in Figure 19, but this is only for the purpose of preserving at this point the prescribed distance from the line FG. Considered relatively to FG there

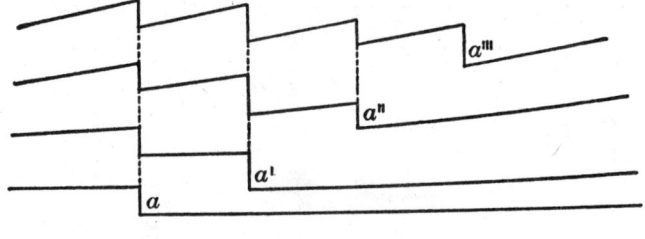

Fig. 22.

is no break. Thus the line MN, measured relatively to FG, takes the place of the constituent curve of Figure 19, and measured relatively to the base line XY it represents the combined curve of Figure 20 for both constituents.

The same method applies where there are any number of constituent capital curves. Thus (Fig. 22), let us draw for our first capital curve one which has an income item a, and superimpose upon it a second capital curve, of which the income item is a', and so on. The capital curve at the top will represent the total of the individual capital curves beneath it, and each belt between — namely, the difference between any two neighboring capital curves — will replace a constituent curve. From the manner of their construction it is clear that the income item a' will be carried forward successively to each of the curves above it, and will be represented by a tooth in the curve at the top, as represented by the dotted lines. Similarly, a', a'', and a''' are transmitted to the top. The final curve at the top thus shows in its separate teeth all the income items contained in the curves of which it is the sum.

§ 5

In case two teeth in separate curves occur at the same instant, the combined curve will, of course, have a large

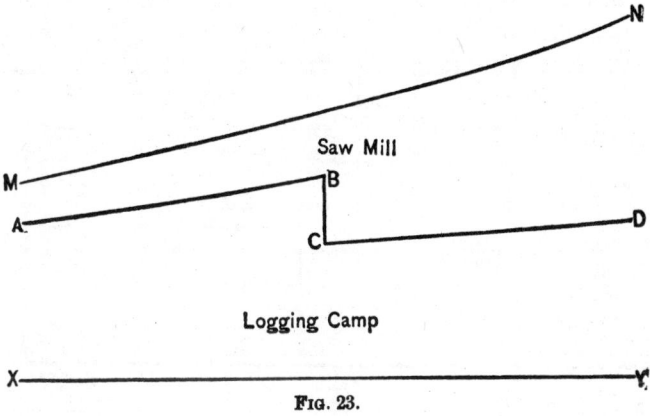

Fig. 23.

tooth equal to their sum. In case one tooth is positive, representing income, and the other is negative, or outgo, the coincidence of these will result in a small tooth equal to their difference, and this difference will be zero if the two items are equal.

The most important case of this kind occurs when there are "interactions." It has been explained that an interaction is an income item for one capital which at the same time is an outgo item for another. If the curves for these two capitals are superimposed, the equal income and outgo items will cancel, and the resulting combined curve will be unbroken at the point representing the time of interaction. This is shown in Figure 23, giving the typical history of lumber operations. Every year a logging camp yields a certain amount of logs, the turning out of which is credited to the camp, but debited to the mill. In the diagram, the space between the base line and the first curve above it represents the capital curve of the logging camp, and the space above this curve represents the capital curve of the sawmill. At the time of the transfer of logs from the one category to the other, there is a corresponding diminution in the capital-value of the logging camp, but an increase in the capital-value of the sawmill.

The characteristic of such an interaction or couple is that it leaves unbroken the upper curve of final summation.

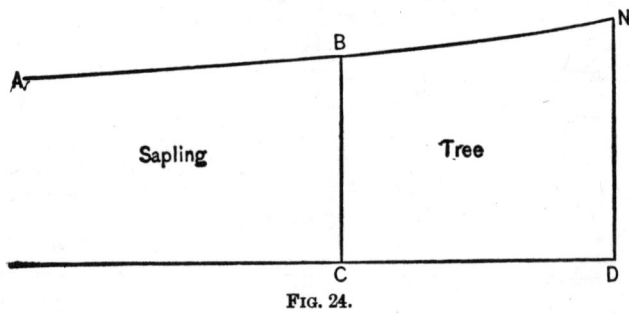

Fig. 24.

There is no carrying forward of teeth, as by the dotted lines in the previous diagram, — or rather, the carrying forward results in a cancellation. The interaction is merely a sacrifice of one capital for the benefit of another, and does not disturb the total.

If the interaction BC is greater than we have represented it in the diagram, so that C is lower and B higher than indicated, the discount curve AB will be nearer coincidence with MN, and CD nearer coincidence with XY. We may suppose a case in which coincidence is reached. This case is represented in Figure 24. Here BC represents such an interaction as occurs when one capital good is completely transformed into another, as when the "sapling" becomes a "tree" at a certain definite point of time. The capital-value of the sapling disappears at *BC*, but there appears in its stead the capital-value of the tree. The change from one to the other is evidently entirely nominal, and it is possible, by drawing any other vertical line than *BC*, to create an "interaction" simply by calling the portion on the two sides of this line by different names.

When, as in Figure 25, a series of curves is constructed and superimposed to represent the income from any specified group of capital instruments, the sum total of the income is evidently represented by the entire series of teeth in the

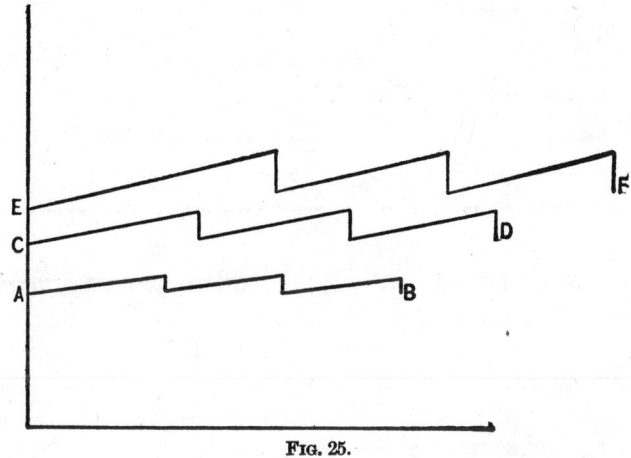

Fig. 25.

top curve. These teeth form a physical picture of the "outer fringe" of services, which was discussed in previous chapters. If in the diagram we omit the uppermost layer of capital, the curve remaining immediately below this layer will then be the outer fringe for the entire series of capital instruments below it. We may proceed step by step in either direction, leaving off an item of capital or taking one on. In every case the outer fringe of teeth will represent the sum total of income for the group of capital represented below it.

In Figure 25 all the teeth below the top layer are represented to be interactions. But if any of them should be final services, they need only be carried forward by dotted lines to the top, as in Figure 26. Or if the capital represented by one layer interacts with the capital represented by a layer two or more removes above it, the connection

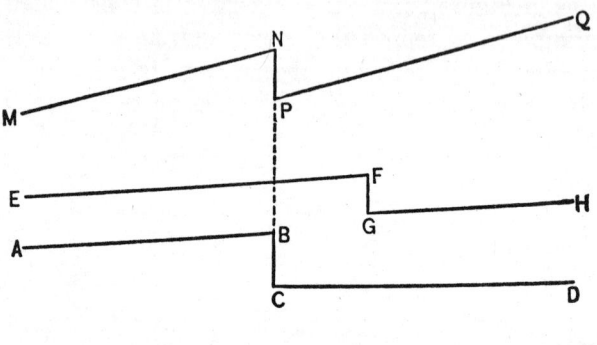

Fig. 26.

will be represented by carrying forward the tooth by dotted lines to the proper stage.

As we are at present interested in the general aspects of the subject, we need not take into account such complications, but may assume, for purposes of exposition, that all capital can be arranged in a single definite series, each member of which acts upon the one above it, and so on to the end. In the actual world, it is usually possible to arrange capital roughly in such an interacting series.

§ 6

Two special applications may be made of the foregoing representation for the summation of capital curves. The first will show the total value of capital property and the total value of income possessed by a particular individual, and the second will show the same condition as to an entire society.

We may suppose a man's capital to be divided into three classes: first, money-paying investments; second, money; third, enjoyable articles purchased by money. We may juxtapose these elements, as in Figure 27.

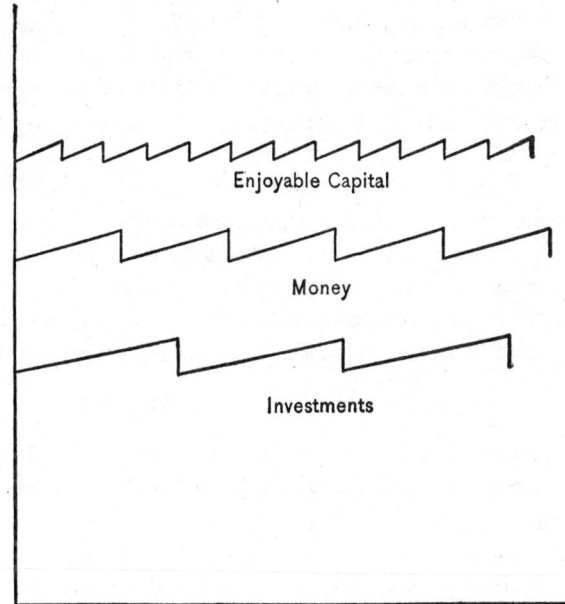

Fig. 27.

Here, whenever an investment pays money, a tooth is produced in the first curve and a transaction takes place between the categories "investments" and "money." By each such transaction the investments are reduced in value by the amount of coupons detached, and the stock of money is increased by the same amount. In like manner, every time money is spent, a transaction takes place between the belt representing money and that representing enjoyable capital. By such transaction the money stock is depleted, and the value of the enjoyable capital increased by the same amount. These operations are therefore self-canceling and are not transmitted to the outer fringe. The total income, therefore, from the entire group of capital, is represented simply by the vertical undulations in the top curve.

By means of this diagram we may see clearly the various meanings of "individual income." The business man usually applies the term to the teeth of the investment curve; the economist to the teeth next above in the money curve, or the teeth above that in the curve representing enjoyable capital. Practically, it does not greatly matter which of the three we select, since usually, for any considerable period of time, all will closely correspond. This must needs be so, unless the stock of money or enjoyable articles is appreciably increasing or decreasing. These exceptional cases have already been discussed in detail, and there is no difficulty in representing them by diagrams.

§ 7

The other application of our diagrammatic summation is to present a fairly complete picture of the total value of capital-wealth and the total value of income of an entire society. In the capital of a community it is not usual to include human beings, and for that reason it is scarcely worth our while to discuss the theoretical questions as to the manner in which they might be included in such a representation. As a matter of fact, the method of capitalizing human beings will vary with the special purpose in view. Our present purpose is chiefly concerned with interactions between man and other capital, and we need practically only to capitalize the money-earning power of the individual. This part of the capital-value of a man we may call "labor power." We then have the total capital of a community consisting of labor power, land, intermediate capital, and enjoyable capital, as in Figure 28. For convenience, and to avoid needless complications, we assume that labor power interacts only with land, land with intermediate capital, and intermediate capital with enjoyable capital. The income from the entire series is represented, as before, by the teeth of the uppermost line.

From this diagram we see that the total income of a community comes through enjoyable goods. The other capital items produce income, but this income is in every case also

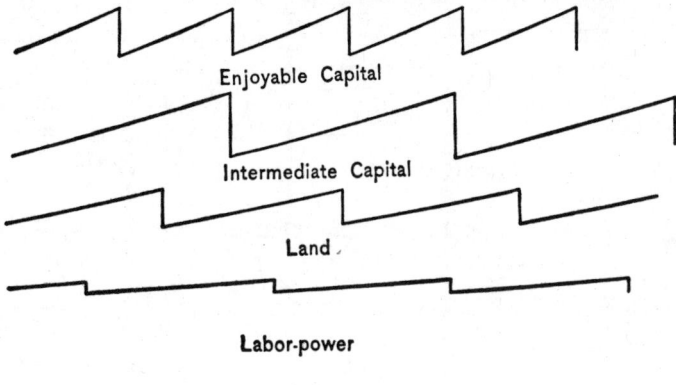

Fig. 28.

an outgo with reference to the layer of capital next above. Many of the fallacious methods of summing income consist virtually in adding together the teeth in the various layers. It is forgotten that the teeth below the top layer are interactions and therefore both positive and negative — positive with reference to the layer below and negative with reference to that above — and that therefore they come into the summation of income only to go out again. Their function in each case is simply to keep up the capital in the layers above. Without their activities these layers above would soon be exhausted, and the income at the top would not continue for long.

§ 8

From this point of view, each interaction may be considered as the discounted value of a certain portion of the items of income from the layer next above. In Figure 29 the interaction a may be taken as the discounted value of the income taken from the layer next above, between the points P and Q. Here we have a geometrical representation of the fact so often insisted upon by Professor Böhm-Bawerk [1] and Professor Taussig,[2] that the production of this year's wool is for next year's (or next month's) yarn, of this year's yarn for next year's cloth, of this year's cloth for next year's clothes, etc.

In tracing the connection between the income items in different layers, we may consider either a cross-section between the different layers, by drawing two vertical lines

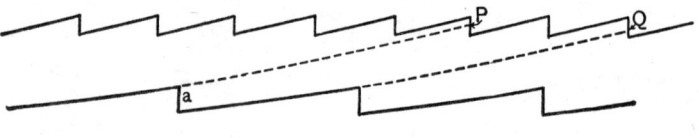

Fig. 29.

separated by a certain interval and noting the intervening income taking place *simultaneously* in the various layers; or we may follow the *successive* time connections involved between one layer and the next. In the treatment which has been given in the previous chapters, the former method was employed. The present diagrammatic representation gives us a bird's-eye view of both. Thus, in Figure 30, representing the logging camp, sawmill, lumber yard, etc., having selected a period represented between the vertical line drawn at A and B, we may either address ourselves to the mutual relations of the various layers there comprised; or we may address ourselves to the income item a, whose

---

[1] *Positive Theory of Capital*, English translation, 1890, pp. 179–189.
[2] *Wages and Capital*, New York (Appleton), 1896, Chapters II, III.

influence traverses the entire section. It is produced by the logging camp; "ripens" into all that income of the sawmill which is comprised between the points P and Q; and this in turn ripens into the income of the lumber yard

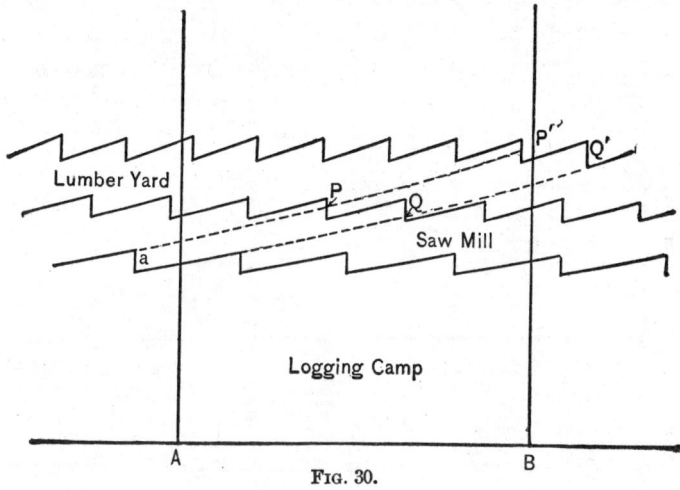

Fig. 30.

comprised between the points P' and Q'. In this way we are virtually following the log as it is transformed in the various processes from tree to lumber.

It is in consideration of such a relation or set of relations that an income item like a was called a "preparatory service." Each such preliminary process of production takes place in anticipation of future resulting processes, and derives its value from them. Combining this principle with the principle that the value of all capital is the discounted value of its expected income, we see that the value of the capital in the lower layers is ultimately dependent on the value of the income in the topmost layer; for the value of that earlier capital is the discounted value of the income it produces, and this income, consisting of interactions or preparatory services, is in turn the discounted value of the services to which it leads, and so on through successive layers to the top, as seen in Figure 31. Here *AB*, the capital-value of the lowest layer, is the discounted value of the income from that layer, namely the teeth *a*, *a′*, *a″*, but this income in turn is the discounted value of the income represented by the teeth intervening between *P* and *Q* from the layer next above, and this income in turn is the discounted value of the income between *P′*

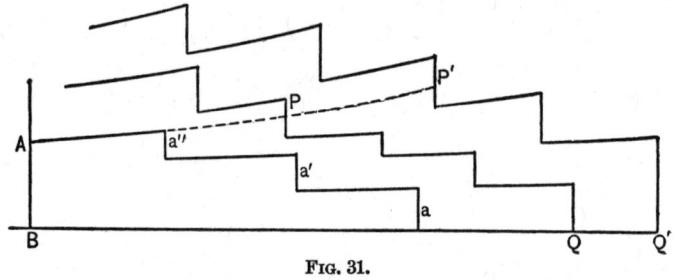

Fig. 31.

and *Q′* on the layer still above. In this representation the curves are shown as all terminating in the base line; but the representation may readily be extended to the case of an income infinitely continued.

§ 9

In Chapter XVI it was shown that certain modifications needed to be introduced into our theory of the determination of capital-value when the element of uncertainty was introduced. We are fresh from the discussion of these, and they need no extended mention here. The main point to be kept in mind is that when the element of chance is taken into account, sudden breaks occur in the capital curve, so that instead of following the simple order previously indicated, beginning at zero and ending at zero, with intermediate teeth alternately rising and falling along the discount curve, it suffers additional interruptions at points where the estimates of future chances are changed.

The most important point in the life history of such a

curve of capital-value is at the beginning. When the element of chance or luck is taken into account, the capital curve is less likely to begin at the zero line. It may begin at some point above; it will not begin at any point below; for if the present value of the chance of gain did not outweigh the present value of the chance of loss, the enterprise would never be undertaken at all. In the great majority of cases, the capital-value at the outset of an enterprise is greater than zero; that is, in the estimation of those who enter into it, the gains will not only pay for the costs with interest, but something in addition, even when the element of chance is included in the discounting operation. At any rate, it is not infrequent that when a new enterprise is started, those who have the first knowledge of the possibilities, and the first opportunity to exploit them, expect returns out of proportion to the ordinary rate of interest and compensation for risk. The only reason this is not more generally true is because of the existence of competition, by which the special advantage of individuals through special knowledge, foresight, etc., is offset by the vigilance of their rivals.

With these points in mind, we observe that the history of the value of any particular article of capital-wealth may be represented as in Figure 32. Starting at A, some point above the zero line, the capital-value rises to B, because, let us say, of the first expenditure involved. From B it proceeds along a discount curve to C. There, through the influence of the risk element, it suddenly drops to D, at which point some new information has reduced the prospect of future gain or increased the risk of future loss. From D in turn it proceeds along the discount curve to E. At this point the cost EF is incurred, but at the same time confidence as to the future receives a shock, and instead of proceeding from F, the curve drops at once to G. Thence it rises gradually and normally to H, when the first income item, HI, is received. This being, let us say, less than was anticipated, it shows that the capital-values had been hitherto too high. Consequently the curve drops to J, and thence proceeds in the manner indicated in the diagram, ending at the zero point P, when the last installment of income OP is received.

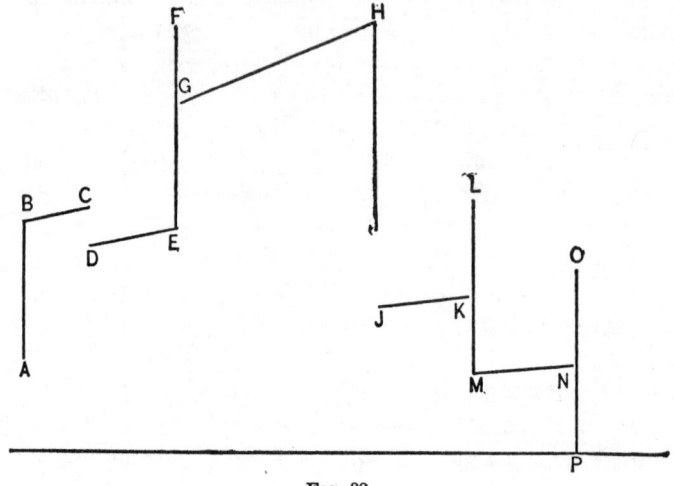

FIG. 32.

In this chapter we have treated income as accruing discontinuously; but it is not difficult, in accordance with the suggestions made in a previous chapter, to extend the principles to apply to the continuous case. It would also be possible, were it worth while, to exhibit, by means of similar diagrammatic representations, numerous propositions other than those already noted. Our object, however, has not been to exploit the diagrams, but merely to use them for a running epitome of the general relations existing between capital and income.

CHAPTER XVIII

GENERAL SUMMARY

§ 1

It has been the endeavor in the preceding chapters to give a definite picture of the mass of capital and its services to man. In such a picture we see man standing in the midst of a physical universe, the events of which affect his life. Over many of these events he can exercise no control or selection; these constitute his natural environment. Over others he exercises selection and control by assuming dominion over part of the physical universe, and fashioning it in new shapes to suit his needs. The parts of the material world which he thus appropriates constitute wealth, whether they remain in their natural state or are "worked up" by him into products to render them more adapted to his needs. This mass of instruments will consist, first, of the appropriated parts of the surface of the earth, of the buildings and structures attached to the soil, and of the movable objects or "commodities" which man possesses and stores in the buildings upon the earth; and, secondly, of the persons of the human population itself,—for these, though they are also the abode of the owner of wealth, are themselves objects owned.

This mass of instruments serves man's purpose in so far as its possession enables him to modify the stream of historical events. By means of land and the modifications which he makes upon it he is enabled to increase and improve the growth of the vegetable and animal kingdoms in such a way as to supply him with food and the materials for constructing other instruments. By means of dwellings and other buildings he is enabled to divert the elements from contact with his body and with the objects of wealth which he stores in them. By means of machinery, tools, and other instruments of production, he is enabled to fashion new instruments to add to his stocks or to take the place of those destroyed or worn out. By means of the final finished products which minister to his more immediate enjoyments, such, for instance, as food, clothing, books, ornaments, he is enabled to consummate the objects for which the entire mass of wealth is produced and kept in existence, namely, the satisfaction of his desires, whether these be for the necessities, the luxuries, the comforts, or the amusements of life. In these and other ways the stock of wealth will modify the course of natural events in ways more or less agreeable to the owner. These changes in the historical stream of events which occur by means of wealth constitute what have been called the services of wealth.

In our picture, therefore, we observe (1) a stock of instruments existing at an instant of time, and (2) a stream of services through time, flowing from this stock of wealth. The stock of wealth is called capital, and its stream of services is called income. The income is the more important concept of the two, for the capital exists merely for the sake of the income, and the ownership of the capital has no other significance than the ownership of possible income from that capital. The division of income between different owners constitutes in reality a division of ownership of the capital which bears the income, and the individual shares constitute what are called property rights.

§ 2

From this it is apparent that property rights and wealth go side by side, and that neither can exist without the other, property signifying merely the sharing of wealth among individuals. When we piece together these shares, we obtain the ownership of all wealth. In like manner, the value of the entire mass of wealth must be taken to mean simply the sum of the values of the individual shares of this ownership. When we attempt to reach this total by combining the shares of individuals, we do so by making a careful record of all "capital accounts." In such a record we find that many items occur in pairs,— negative items of property or "liabilities" in one account and positive items or "assets" in another. By this pairing of items, there will be left as the final sum of property value the value of the entire stock of physical instruments.

Of the services which flow from the stock of capital, it has been seen that the great majority consist merely of "interactions" between one category of capital and another. All that is accomplished by most instruments of capital is to hand over something to other instruments of capital. The great mass of capital—lands, warehouses, railroads, machinery, ships, etc. — exists either for "transportation," that is, for changing the position of wealth from one place to another; or for "production," that is, for changing wealth from one state or form to another; or finally for exchange, the mutual transfer of rights to wealth. In every such operation, the instruments which have wrought the change are said to have rendered a service; and in the income account these instruments are credited with the value of such services; while the instruments which receive the services, and are thus improved in position or condition, are said to have rendered a disservice and are at the same time debited with exactly the same item. When we thus come to put together the entire total of income, all such pairs of items or "interactions" cancel. These double-faced events or interactions constitute the overwhelming mass of items in the actual inventory of income which enter into the accounts of business men. Out of this fact, combined with the fact that every "transaction" is also double-faced, grows, as we have seen, the entire theory of double-entry bookkeeping.

Out of the entire mass of instruments thus acting and reacting upon each other, there finally emerges an uncanceled or net income which does not represent a mere transfer from one category to another *within* the mass, but an actual contribution issuing *from* the mass to the benefit of man, the owner. These final elements are his real income. In the last analysis they consist purely of subjective or psychic satisfactions; that is, of conscious desirable experiences.

§ 3

But these desirable mental experiences occur at the sacrifice of certain undesirable ones, namely, of *efforts*. The subjective efforts put forth for the sake of subjective satisfactions constitute the net or uncanceled elements of outgo. Thus we see that, side by side with the objective income and outgo stream, and as the final result of that stream, there exists its subjective counterpart, namely, the stream of efforts and satisfactions. In the same way, there exists, side by side with the objective mass of capital, the subjective esteem in which this capital is held, namely, what we have called its desirability, or utility. If efforts and satisfactions are called subjective income, desirability or utility should be called subjective capital. The same antithesis of time applies to the subjective as to the objective; desirability is a state of mind at an instant of time; efforts and satisfactions are experiences through a period of time. Desirability stands for anticipated efforts and satisfactions, just as objective capital stands for anticipated services. We thus see in the mind of man a microcosm of the objective economic world, consisting of desires, efforts, and satisfactions, corresponding respectively in the objective world to capital, outgo, and income.

§ 4

For convenience we have used the term "goods" to comprise any one or all of the three categories, — wealth, property, and services. It has been seen that any two goods may be compared in respect to desirability, and if the marginal increments of two groups of goods are equally desirable, those groups are equivalent in value. The interequivalence of goods in this sense may be measured by expressing all goods in terms of any one good, as, for instance, money. When the various goods are thus converted into a common standard, we have a new sense both for capital and income. Capital, instead of consisting of a miscellaneous mass of wealth or property rights, is now taken in the sense of *capital-value;* and income, instead of consisting of a miscellaneous stream of services, some final and some intermediate, some objective and some subjective, will consist of a single homogeneous element, *income-value*.

It is to the relation between capital and income in the value sense that our attention throughout this book has been chiefly devoted. It has been noted that the relation between capital and income, taken in the value sense, is profoundly different from the relation between capital and income when either or both are measured in their various individual units. When capital and value are measured as "quantities," capital may be said to produce income; but when they are measured in "values," we find that it is necessary to reverse this statement, and to say that income produces capital. The manner in which capital-value is produced from income-value is by discounting, and this is done by means of a rate of interest, due attention being given to the fact that future income is always subject more or less to the element of chance. As a consequence of this fundamental discount relation, it follows that the value of capital rises as future income approaches, and falls as that income is reached and passed. It rises or falls with each change in the rate of interest employed in the discount process, and with each change in the estimate of the chance element. If the alternate rise and fall in the value of capital are rhythmic and even, the capital will recur to a constant level, and the income in this case is said to be the *earnings* of capital. The earnings of capital constitute a *standard* with respect to which the actual income in any case may be compared. If the actual income exceeds the standard income, there will be a depreciation of capital, which may be made good, however, by paying back the excess into another fund of capital called the depreciation fund. If, on the contrary, the earnings exceed the actual income, the excess will constitute savings, and will accumulate and be added to the capital.

§ 5

To describe in a few words the nature of capital and income, we may say that those parts of the material universe which at any time are under the dominion of man constitute his capital wealth; its ownership, his capital property; its value, his capital-value; its desirability, his subjective capital. But capital in any of these senses stands for anticipated income, which consists of a stream of services or its value. When values are considered, the causal relation is not from capital to income, but from income to capital; not from present to future, but from future to present; in other words, the value of capital is the discounted value of the expected income. The fluctuations of this capital-value will, chance aside, be equal and opposite to the deviations of "income" from "earnings," whereas, when the influence of chance is included, there will be in addition to these fluctuations still others which mirror the successive changes in the outlook for future income.

GLOSSARY

A Summary of the Definitions used in this Book

Amortization fund. — (See *Fund, depreciation*.)

Amount. — The amount of any given sum at a given time is its equivalent at a later time. Ch. XIII, § 1.

Assets of a person. — His property-rights, including both those which make good his liabilities and those, if any, which are in excess of and free from any liability. (Syn. *Resources*.) Ch. V, § 1.

Balance sheet. — A statement of a person's assets and liabilities. (Syn. *Capital account*.) Ch. V, § 1.

Basis. — The rate of interest yielded by a security when sold at a specified price. Ch. XVI, § 9.

   commercial, of a security. — The basis corresponding to the commercial value of the security. Ch. XVI, § 8.

   mathematical, of a security. — The basis corresponding to the mathematical value of the security. Ch. XVI, § 8.

   riskless, of a security. — The basis corresponding to the riskless value of the security. Ch. XVI, § 8.

Capital. — Abbreviation for *Capital goods*, and *Capital value*. Ch. V, § 1.

   account. — (See *Balance sheet*.) Ch. V, § 1.

   balance. — The difference between the value of the assets in a balance sheet and of the liabilities. (Syn. *Net capital*.)

      The capital balance is measured in three different ways: as the nominal capital (or capitalization), the book value, and the market value of the rights of the shareholders or those whose capital account is considered. Ch. V, § 1.

   book value of. — The sum of the capital, surplus, and undivided profits, *i.e.* the difference in value at any time between the assets and liabilities according to the entries in the capital account. Ch. V, § 4.

   goods. — Capital-wealth or capital-property. Ch. V, § 1.

   as market value of shares. — The market value of the shareholders' rights in a concern. Ch. V, § 4.

   instruments. — (See *Capital wealth*.)

Capital, net. — (See *Capital balance.*) Ch. V, § 3.
    nominal. — The par or face value of the shares in a joint stock company, and hence also the original book value of the difference between assets and liabilities. Ch. V, § 2.
    original. — The capital when the capital account is first opened. It may be measured in two different ways, as nominal capital and paid-up capital. Ch. IV, § 4.
    paid-up. — The amount of original capital of a concern actually paid in by the shareholders. Ch. IV, § 4.
    property. — A stock (or fund) of property existing at an instant of time. Ch. V, § 1.
    wealth. — A stock (or fund) of wealth existing at an instant of time. (Syn. *Capital instruments.*) Ch. V, § 1.
    value. — The value of a stock of wealth or property at an instant. It is found by discounting (or "capitalizing") the value of the income expected from the wealth or property. Ch. V, § 1.
Capitalization. — A. The process of discounting by which expected income is translated into present capital-value. Usually employed only when the income is considered uniform and perpetual, in which case capitalization consists in dividing the rate of income per annum by the rate of interest. Ch. IV, § 6; Ch. XIII, § 1.
    B. The nominal capital of a joint stock company. Ch. V, § 4.
    rate of. — The reciprocal of the rate of interest. (Theoretically also the reciprocal of the rate of discount. Practically this meaning is never used.)
Capitalize. — To capitalize income is to find the capital-value equivalent to that income. Ch. IV, § 6; Ch. XIII, § 1.
Caution, coefficient of. — The ratio of commercial value to mathematical value. Ch. XVI, § 6.
Chance, of any event. — The ratio of the number of cases in which that event may occur to the total possible number of cases, when all the cases are equally probable. Any two cases are equally probable (to any particular person at any particular time) if the person has no inclination to believe one rather than the other to be true. Ch. XVI, § 2. (Syn. *Probability.*)
    commercial value of. — The value which the chance will actually command in the market. It is equal to the mathematical value multiplied by the coefficient of caution, Ch. XVI, § 6.
    mathematical value of. — The product of the value of the prize at stake multiplied by the chance of winning it. Ch. XVI, § 5.
Coefficient, of caution. — The ratio of commercial value to mathematical value. Ch. XVI, § 6.

SUMMARY OF DEFINITIONS 331

Coefficient, of probability. — The ratio of mathematical value to riskless value. Ch. XVI, § 6.

  of risk. — The ratio of commercial value to riskless value; hence the product of the coefficient of caution multiplied by the coefficient of probability. Ch. XVI, § 6.

Commercial basis. — (See *Basis, commercial.*)

  value of a chance. — (See *Chance, commercial value of.*)

Commodities. — Movable instruments not human beings. Ch. I, § 2.

Consumption. — (See *Services, enjoyable objective.*)

Couple. — A liability to a debtor and its counterpart asset to the creditor. Or the service of one instrument acting on another and the counterpart disservice of the second acted on by the first. Ch. VI, § 1; Ch. IX, § 2.

Coupled services. — (See *Couple, Interaction.*)

Depreciation fund. — (See *Fund, depreciation.*)

Desirability of goods (wealth, property, or services). — The intensity of desire, for those goods, of a particular individual at a particular time under particular circumstances. (Syn. *Utility.*) Ch. III, § 2.

  marginal — of a specified aggregate of goods. — Approximate definition: The desirability of one unit more or less of that aggregate, or the difference between the desirability of that aggregate and another aggregate one unit larger or smaller. Ch. III, § 4.

  Exact definition: The limit of the ratio of the increment (or decrement) of desirability to the increment (or decrement) of the aggregate when the last-named increment (or decrement) approaches zero. (Syn. *Marginal utility.*) Appendix to Ch. III, § 1.

  progressive marginal — of a specified aggregate of goods. — The desirability of one unit *more* of that aggregate. (Syn. *Progressive marginal utility.*) Appendix to Ch. III, § 1.

  regressive marginal — of a specified aggregate of goods. — The desirability of one unit *less* of that aggregate. (Syn. *Regressive marginal utility.*) Appendix to Ch. III, § 1.

  total — of an aggregate of goods. — The difference between the desirability of goods which include and of those which exclude that aggregate. (Syn. *Total utility.*) Ch. III, § 4.

Dimension. — The kind or species of any magnitude as indicated by its measurement in terms of other magnitudes. Appendix to Ch. I.

Discount curve. — A curve so constructed that, if one of its ordinates represents any given sum, any later ordinate will represent the "amount" of that sum at a time later by an interval represented by the horizontal distance between the ordinates; and which is consequently also such that any earlier ordinate will represent the "present value" of that sum at a time earlier by an interval represented by the horizontal distance between the ordinates. Ch. XIII, § 1.

Discount, rate of. — The deficiency below unity of the ratio of exchange between the values of present and future goods, taken in relation to the time interval between the two sets of goods. Ch. XII, § 7.

The rate of discount may, like the rate of interest, be reckoned annually, semi-annually, quarterly, or continuously. (It may also, theoretically, be taken in the *price* sense as well as in the sense above, but practically never is.)

total. — The difference between any sum and its discounted or present value.

Discounted value. — (See *Value, present.*)

Disservice. — A negative service. An instrument renders a disservice when, by its means, an undesirable event is promoted or a desirable event prevented. Ch. II, § 2; Ch. VIII, § 1.

Disutility. — Negative utility. (Syn. *Undesirability.*) Ch. III, § 2.

Earnings. — (See *Income, earned.*)

Exchange. — The mutual and voluntary transfer of goods (wealth, property, or services) between two owners, each transfer being in consideration of the other. Ch. I, § 4; Ch. II, § 3.

Expense. — Outgo in the form of money-spending. Ch. VIII, § 1.

Flow. — The quantity of any specified thing undergoing any specified change during any specified period of time. Ch. IV, § 1.

rate of. — The ratio of a flow to its duration. Ch. IV, § 1.

Fund. — A stock of wealth or property or its value. Ch. IV, § 1.

amortization. — (See *Fund, depreciation.*)

depreciation. — A fund formed by accumulating that part of income which must be turned back into capital to maintain the capital-value intact. It may also be defined as formed from the difference between real income and earnings, when that difference is accumulated.

If the income is uniform and runs only for a fixed term, the depreciation fund may also be defined as formed from a succession of equal payments out of income, such that if each be accumulated at compound interest, the total will be equal to the original capital at the end of the income term. (Syn. *Amortization fund.*) Ch. XIV, § 6.

SUMMARY OF DEFINITIONS 333

Fund, sinking. — A fund formed by accumulating the difference between actual income and a terminable annuity which has the same present worth.

As applied to bonded debts it may also be defined as formed by accumulating an annual sum such that its amount will just suffice to equal (or extinguish) a given sum at the end of a given period. Ch. XIV. § 7.

Income. — Abbreviation for *Income services* and *Income value.* Ch. VIII, § 1.

   account. — Statement of specified income and outgo, whether from capital or to a person.

   earned, by any capital. — Income realized plus appreciation of the capital (or minus its depreciation). *I.e.* that income which a given capital can yield *without alteration* in its value. If interest be assumed invariable and all future income foreknown, this definition is equivalent to another, viz. the *uniform and perpetual* income which a given capital might yield; but the equivalence ceases if interest varies (see Appendix to Ch. XIV, § 1) or if future income is unknown. (Syn. *Earnings, Standard income.*) Ch. XIV, § 4.

   enjoyable. — Income which consists of enjoyable services. Ch. VII, § 6.

   gross. — Sum of all positive income elements. Ch. VII, § 1.

   individual. — The income from the entire capital of an individual. Ch. VII, § 7.

   money. — Income which consists of the receipt of money. Ch. VII, § 7; Ch. IX, § 5.

   natural. — Income which consists of services not obtained by exchange. Ch. VII, § 7; Ch. IX, § 5.

   net. — The difference between gross income and outgo. Ch. VIII, § 1.

   psychic. — Agreeable conscious experiences. (Syn. *Subjective income.*) Ch. X, § 3.

   realized, from any capital — Actual income, *i.e.* the value of its actual services.

   services, of any capital. — The flow of services from that capital through a period of time. Ch. VIII, § 1.

   social. — The income from the entire capital of the society. Ch. VII, § 7.

   standard. — (See *Income, earned.*)

   subjective. — (See *Income, psychic.*)

   value, from any capital. — The value of its income-services. Ch. VIII, § 1.

Instrument. — An individual article of wealth. Ch. I, § 1.

Interaction. — An event which is a service of one capital and at the same time a disservice of another. (Syn. *Interacting service, Intermediate service, Preparatory service, Coupled service.*) Ch. IX, § 2.

Interacting services. — (See *Interaction.*)

Intermediate services. — (See *Interaction.*)

Interest. — The product of the rate of interest multiplied by the capital-value. Ch. XIV, § 4.

   nominal. — The stipulated annual payments on a bond or note nominally (but not always in fact) equal to the interest on the "principal." Ch. XIII, § 7.

   rate of. — Many meanings are given below. The standard meaning used in this book is that called "rate of interest in the premium sense reckoned annually."

   rate of. — *In the price sense:* The ratio between the annual rate of a perpetual annuity and the equivalent capital-value. Ch. XII, § 2.

The rate of interest is said to be reckoned *annually* if the annuity is payable in annual installments; it is said to be reckoned *semi-annually*, if the annuity is payable in semi-annual installments; *quarterly*, if in quarterly installments; *continuously*, if payable continuously.

   rate of. — *In the premium sense:* The excess above unity of the rate of exchange between the values of future and present goods taken in relation to the time interval between the two sets of goods. (Syn. *rate of interest in the agio sense.*) Ch. XII, § 4.

The rate of interest is said to be reckoned *annually* if the two sets of goods are one year apart. This is the standard meaning of the "rate of interest" as used in this book. It is said to be reckoned *semi-annually*, if they are a half-year apart; *quarterly*, if three months apart; *continuously*, if infinitesimally apart.

   rate of. — *In agio sense:* (See *in premium sense.*)

   rate of. — *Reckoned annually, semi-annually, quarterly, continuously:* (See under *rate of interest in price sense* and *rate of interest in premium sense.*)

   total. — The difference between any sum and its "amount." Appendix to Ch. XIII, § 7.

Labor. — Outgo in the form of human exertion. Ch. X, § 6.

Land. — Wealth which is part of the earth's surface. Ch. I, § 2.

   improvements. — Wealth constructed upon and attached to land, Ch. I, § 2.

Liabilities of a person. — Amount of obligations due others. Ch. V, § 1.

SUMMARY OF DEFINITIONS   335

Mathematical basis. — (See *Basis, mathematical*.)
value of a chance. — (See *Chance*.)
Method, of balances. — The method of summing capital- or income-accounts which consists in first deducting the sum of the negative items in each from the sum of the positive items, and then adding the "balances" thus obtained. Ch. IX, § 2.
   of couples. — The method of summing capital accounts and income accounts which consists in canceling out the "couples." Ch. IX, § 2.
Outgo. — Negative income. Ch. VIII, § 1.
   net. — Net income, when negative. Ch. VIII, § 1.
Person. — Any owner of property, whether real or fictitious. Ch. II, § 3.
   fictitious. — An imaginary entity (such as a firm or corporation) regarded, for bookkeeping purposes, as holding property for a number of other persons (real or fictitious.) Ch. II, § 2.
   real. — An owner of property who is a living human being.
Price. — A ratio of exchange. Ch. I, § 4.
   money. — The quotient found by dividing the money exchanged for goods by the quantity of the goods themselves. Ch. I, § 4.
Principal. — The final payment on a bond or note, supposed to be (but not always in fact) equal to the original sum "lent." Ch. XIII, § 7.
Preparatory services. — (See *Interaction*.)
Probability. — See *Chance*.
   coefficient of. — The ratio of mathematical value to riskless value. Ch. XVI, § 6.
Production. — (See *Transformation*.)
Productive process. — (See *Transformation*.)
Productivity, physical. — The ratio of the *quantity* of services of capital per unit of time to the *quantity* of the capital. Ch. XI, § 2.
   value. — The ratio of the *value* of services of capital per unit of time to the *quantity* of the capital. Ch. XI, § 2.
Property (or property rights). — Rights to the chance of future services of wealth. Ch. II, § 3.
   right, complete. — The exclusive right to all the services of an instrument. Ch. II, § 10.
   right, partial. — The right to part of the services of an instrument, other parts belonging to other owners. Ch. II, § 10.
Purchase. — An exchange of money for goods. Ch. I, § 4.
Real estate. — Land and land improvements. Ch. I, § 2.
Resources. — (See *Assets*.)

Return, physical. — The ratio of the *quantity* of services of capital to the *value* of the capital. Ch. XI, § 2.
    value. — The ratio of the *value* of services of capital to the *value* of the capital. Ch. XI, § 2.
Risk, coefficient of. — The ratio of commercial value to riskless value. It is equal to the product of the coefficient of probability multiplied by the coefficient of caution. Ch. XVI, § 6.
Riskless basis. — (See *Basis, riskless.*)
    value. — The value which a thing would have if risk were eliminated. Ch. XVI, § 6.
    value of a chance. — (See *Chance.*)
Sale. — An exchange of goods for money. Ch. I, § 4.
Service. — An instrument renders a service when, by its means, a desirable event is promoted or an undesirable event prevented. (Syn. *Use.*) Ch. II, § 2.
Services, coupled. — (See *Interaction.*)
    enjoyable objective. — Services received directly by human beings, and not (like interactions) merely received for human beings by other objective capital. (Syn. (not well chosen) *Consumption.*) Ch. X, § 1.
    intermediate. — (See *Interaction.*)
    preparatory. — (See *Interaction.*)
Sinking fund. — (See *Fund, sinking.*)
Standard income. — (See *Income, earned.*)
Standardize. — To standardize a given income is to convert it into its equivalent *income earned.*
Stock. — The quantity of any specified thing at any instant. (Syn. *Fund.*) Ch. IV, § 1.
Transaction. — That side of an exchange which relates to one of the exchangers; it consists of two items, a credit and a debit. Ch. IX, § 9.
Transfer. — An interaction which is a change of ownership of wealth. Ch. IX, § 3.
Transformation. — An interaction which is a change of form or condition of wealth. (Syn. *Production, Productive process.*) Ch. IX, §§ 2, 3.
Transportation. — An interaction which is a change of place or position of wealth. Ch. IX, §§ 2, 3.
Undesirability. — Negative desirability. (Syn. *Disutility.*) Ch. III, § 2.
Utility of goods. (See *Desirability.*)
Value. — The value of goods (wealth, property, or services) is the product of their quantity multiplied by their price. Ch. I, § 6.

SUMMARY OF DEFINITIONS 337

Value, commercial, of a chance. — (See *Chance.*)
  discounted. — (See *Value, present.*)
  mathematical, of a chance. — (See *Chance.*)
  money. — The quantity of goods multiplied by their money price. Ch. I, § 6.
  present. — The present value of any given future goods is the quantity of present goods which will exchange for those future goods. (Syn. *Present worth, Discounted value.*) Ch. XIII, § 1.
  riskless, of a chance. — (See *Chance.*)
Wealth (in its broader sense). — Material objects owned by human beings. Ch. I, § 1.
  (in its narrower sense). — Material objects owned by human beings and external to their owners. Ch. I, § 2.
  article of. — A single object of wealth. (Syn, *Item of Wealth, Instrument.*) Ch. I, § 1.
  item of. — (See *Wealth, article of.*) Ch. I, § 1.
Worth, present. — (See *Value, present.*)

APPENDICES

APPENDIX TO CHAPTER I
APPENDIX TO CHAPTER III
APPENDIX TO CHAPTER VII
APPENDIX TO CHAPTER XI
APPENDIX TO CHAPTER XII
APPENDIX TO CHAPTER XIII
APPENDIX TO CHAPTER XIV
APPENDIX TO CHAPTER XVI

APPENDIX TO CHAPTER I

§ 1 (TO CH. I, § 7)

Dimensions of Wealth, Price, and Value

What mathematicians call the "dimension" of a magnitude is simply its species or kind, as indicated by its measurement in terms of other magnitudes of the same or different kinds. It is expressed mathematically by a letter or letters. Consider beef, for example. If b represents any given amount of beef, say three hundred pounds, this letter may be taken to indicate its "dimension." The price of beef in terms of wheat is $\frac{w}{b}$, where w stands for the amount of wheat exchangeable for an amount b of beef. The expression $\frac{w}{b}$ (or, as it may be written, wb^{-1}) thus expresses the "dimension" of *price*. It matters not what particular price of beef in terms of wheat is referred to. Every price is of the same form wb^{-1}. Finally, the dimension of the "value" of the beef in terms of wheat is w, for this value is the product of the amount of beef, b, by its price, $\frac{w}{b}$, i.e. $b \times \frac{w}{b} = w$.

That is, the dimension of beef is represented by b,

its price by $$p = \frac{w}{b} = wb^{-1},$$

its value by $$bp = b\frac{w}{b} = w.$$

We thus have a different dimension for each of the three different magnitudes. This fact is expressed in common language, also. We measure cloth in *yards*, the price of cloth in *bushels per yard*, the value of cloth simply in *bushels*. Price and value differ as fundamentally as velocity and distance, which are measured respectively in *feet per second* and plain *feet;* or as density and weight, which are expressed in *pounds per cubic foot* and simply *pounds*.

It may seem at first that these distinctions between the dimension of price, quantity, and value are somewhat strained. It may be claimed that price is simply the value of a unit, and that value is simply the price of the whole quantity. In the same way it is sometimes loosely said that the velocity of a moving body is simply the distance traversed in a unit of time. It is quite true, of course, that the number which expresses the value of a unit of wealth is the same number as that which expresses the price per unit. It is likewise true that the number which expresses velocity is the same as that which expresses the distance which will be traversed in a unit of time. Yet velocity is not distance, and no more is price, value; although practically where the wealth under consideration is or may be regarded as a single unit, it is less necessary to insist on the distinction between value and price. If the price of a "unique" is $25 *per unit*, then its value is also $25. If a farm of 100 acres has a value of $5000, the price of the farm as a single thing, and not as measured in acres, is $5000 *per farm*.

But as soon as we have to deal separately with a single unit and a number of units, we must make a distinction between price and value. That they are not of the same dimension is clear from the fact that the number expressing the price of beef in terms of wheat varies with both the unit of beef and of wheat, while the number expressing the value of beef varies only with the unit of wheat. Thus, if the quantities of beef and wheat which exchange for each other are 300 pounds and 60 bushels respectively, the price and value of the beef in terms of the wheat will be

price of the beef, $\frac{1}{5}$ bu. per lb.
value of the beef, 60 bu.

A change in the unit of measurement for beef will evidently affect only the first of these two numbers. Thus, if the beef is measured in ounces (4800 oz.) instead of in pounds, the numbers become:

price of the beef, $\frac{1}{80}$ bu. per oz.
value of the beef, 60 bu.

On the other hand, a change in the unit for measuring the wheat will affect both numbers. Thus, if wheat is measured in pecks instead of in bushels (while beef is still measured in pounds), the numbers representing price and value will change from $\frac{1}{6}$ and 60 to $\frac{4}{6}$ and 240 respectively, each being magnified fourfold.

We see then that the value and price of beef are similar in that they are similarly affected by a change in the unit of wheat but are different in that they are differently affected by a change in the unit of beef.

It may aid the reader who is unfamiliar with the subject of the dimensionality of magnitudes to indicate a few of its applications to physical science. If l is taken to represent the dimension of length, area will be represented by l^2 and volume by l^3. Consequently, length, area, and volume are said to be respectively of one, two, and three "dimensions," because l, l^2, and l^3, which represent their dimensionalities, have for exponents 1, 2, and 3 respectively. The term "dimension" was originally applied simply to these cases of length, area, and volume. But it soon came to be extended to apply to every sort of mathematical magnitude. The following examples are noted without comment (l stands for length, m for mass, and t for time):—

Velocity, of dimension lt^{-1}, or feet per sec.
Acceleration, " lt^{-2}, or feet per sec. per sec.
Momentum, " mlt^{-1}, or pounds feet per sec.
Force, " mlt^{-2}, or pounds feet per sec. per sec.
Work, " ml^2t^{-2}, or pounds feet feet per sec. per sec.
Horse power, " ml^2t^{-3}, or pounds feet feet per sec. per sec. per sec.

To illustrate the meaning of this table, we observe that the number which represents work (or energy) would be affected by a change in the units of mass, length, and time, as follows: Halving the unit of mass (so that the number representing any mass would be doubled) would double the number representing the work; halving the unit of length (so that the number representing any given length would be doubled) would quadruple the number representing work; halving the unit of time (so that the number representing any given time would be doubled) would quarter the number representing the unit of work.

The idea of "dimension" and its mode of representation are important subjects, for a fuller treatment of which the reader is referred to the article on the subject in Palgrave's *Dictionary of Political Economy*, as well as for its more general applications to J. D. Everett's C.G.S. System of Units, 1891.

APPENDIX TO CHAPTER III

§ 1 (to Ch. III, § 4)

Definition of Marginal Desirability

To express mathematically the marginal utility or desirability of any group of goods, let Δx represent any increment of goods measured in any specified unit, and Δu the desirability of that increment. For instance, if reference is had to a bin of coal containing 15 tons, and if Δx represents an increment of 3 tons, Δu will mean the desirability of those 3 tons, so that $\frac{\Delta u}{\Delta x}$ will represent the *average* desirability per ton of 3 additional tons. If we suppose the increment Δx to be successively decreased to 2 tons, 1 ton, $\frac{1}{2}$ ton, and so on indefinitely, approaching zero as a limit, the expression $\frac{\Delta u}{\Delta x}$ will mean successively the average desirability per ton of 2 additional tons, the desirability of 1 additional ton, the desirability per ton of $\frac{1}{2}$ an additional ton (*i.e.* twice the desirability of that additional half ton), the desirability per ton of $\frac{1}{4}$ an additional ton (*i.e.* four times the desirability of an additional $\frac{1}{4}$ of a ton), etc. The limit of this series will be the desirability *per ton* of an infinitesimal increment of coal, and may be expressed by the fraction $\frac{du}{dx}$. This, which is, as mathematicians say, the differential quotient of desirability, will, assuming continuity, have the same value if, in place of the increment, a decrement were considered; that is, if instead of supposing the owner of the 15 tons to *add* 3 tons, we suppose him to subtract 3 tons.

Then $\frac{\Delta u}{\Delta x}$ would represent the average desirability per ton of this 3 tons subtracted, which would evidently be somewhat greater than the desirability per ton of 3 *additional* tons. But when we substitute for 3 tons, the smaller magnitudes 2 tons, 1 ton, ½ ton, ¼ ton, etc., the resulting value of $\frac{\Delta u}{\Delta x}$, or the desirability *per ton* of this constantly lessening decrement, will become equal, at the limit, to the desirability per ton of the constantly lessening increment. The limit of $\frac{\Delta u}{\Delta x}$ is expressed $\frac{du}{dx}$. The expression $\frac{du}{dx}$ indicates more exactly than could be indicated in the text the true meaning of marginal desirability, and when the article may be indefinitely subdivided, the marginal desirability is the same whether reckoned by increments or decrements. Practically, however, such mathematical subdivision does not always apply, and it may even happen that the desirability of one unit more may be materially different from the desirability of one unit less. For instance, the owner of one piano may esteem it very highly, but a second piano would have almost no desirability. Here the desirability of one unit less is far greater than the desirability of one unit more, owing to the fact that the piano is an indivisible unit, and we can consider no increments or decrements except of whole pianos. In this case instead of one marginal desirability we have two, which may be distinguished as "regressive" and "progressive."

APPENDIX TO CHAPTER VII

§ 1 (TO CH. 7, § 1)

Specimen Definitions of Income

Murray, *English Dictionary on Historical Principles,* **1901.**

Income: 6. *spec*[*ifically*]. That which comes in as the periodical produce of one's work, business, lands, or investments (considered in reference to its amount, and commonly expressed in terms of money); annual or periodical receipts accruing to a person or corporation; revenue. Formerly also in *pl.* = receipts, emoluments, profits; but the plural is now used only in reference to more than one person. (The prevailing sense.) 1601, R. Johnson, *Kingd. & Commun.* (1603) 196. Paying the expense of one yere with the income of another. 1633, Herbert, *Temple, Ch. Porch.* XXVII. Never exceed thy income. 1646, H. Laurence, *Comm. Angells.* 152. Hee hath beene at a great deale of paines and cost; now what are his in-comes? 1652, C. B. Stapylton, *Herodian,* 16. He scraped still and never was content, But studied more his Incomes to augment. 1697, Dryden, *Virg. Georg.* II, 285. No Fields afford So large an Income to the Village Lord. 1789, *Loiterer,* No. 43, 10. Having lived, what is called up to his income, that is, a good deal above it. 1802, *Med. Jrnl.* VIII, 229. Income, in its usual acceptation, is a loose and vague term; it applies equally to gross receipts and to net produce: But when the Legislature had limited it to be synonimous with profits and gains, it became as clear and precise as any other word. 1866, George Eliot, *F. Holt,* ii, I, 76. No, I shan't attack the Church — only the incomes of the bishops, perhaps, to make them eke out the incomes of the poor clergy.

These definitions afford no means of deciding on *net* income. If income is simply what comes in and outgo simply what goes out, and if in any year as much passes out of one's hands as comes in, is the net income zero?

Dr. N. G. Pierson, *Principles of Economics* Trans. by A. A. Wotzel, Vol. I, p. 76. London (Macmillan & Co.), 1902.

By social income we mean the sum-total of economic goods which a nation has at its disposal in a given period of time; the net result of the productive labour of the nation during that time.

Is not its capital "at its disposal" in any period? Is it then income?

Roscher, *Principles of Political Economy* (2d vol., Eng. trans., p. 5), speaking of national wealth, says that gross income consists of, —

"(*a*) Of the raw material newly obtained in the country.

"(*b*) Of imports from foreign countries, including that which is secured by piracy, war booty, contributions, etc.

APPENDIX TO CHAPTER VII

"(c) The increase of values which industry and commerce add to the first two classes up to the time of their final consumption.

"(d) Services in the narrower sense and the produce of capital in use.

"To find the national net income we must deduct the following items:—

"(a) All the material employed in production which yields no immediate satisfaction to any personal want.

"(b) The exports which pay for the imports.

"(c) The wear and tear of productive capital and capital in use."

The method thus illustrated is the method which takes its starting point from the goods. There is another method which takes its starting point from the persons who receive them. By this method the national income is to be calculated as follows:—

"(a) From the net income of all independent private businesses, etc.

"(b) From the net income of the state, of municipalities, corporations and institutions, derived from their own resources.

"(c) Under the former heads must be taken into the account such parts of property as have been immediately consumed and enjoyed.

"(d) Interest on debt must be added only on the side of the creditor and deducted from the income of the debtor."

How is double counting to be avoided if "raw materials produced" (a) are income and also "the produce of capital in use" (d)? "Increase of values" (c) is not income but capital.

Alfred Marshall, *Principles of Economics*, Vol. I, pp. 149, 150. London (Macmillan), 1898.

"Another convenient term is the *usance* of wealth. It *means the whole income* of benefits of every kind which a person derives from the ownership of wealth, whether he uses it as capital or not. Thus it includes the benefits which he gets from the use of his own piano, equally with those which a piano dealer would win by letting out a piano on hire.

"This income is most easily measured when it takes the form of a payment made by a borrower for the use of a loan for, say, a year; it is then expressed as the ratio which that payment bears to the loan, and is called *interest*. But this term is also used more broadly to represent the money equivalent to the whole income which is derived from capital.

* * * * * * *

"Social income may be estimated by adding together the incomes of the individuals in the society in question, whether it be a nation or any larger or smaller group of persons. Everything that is produced in the course of a year, every service rendered, every fresh utility brought about is a part of the national income.

"We must be careful not to count the same thing twice. If we have counted a carpet at its full value, we have already counted the values of the yarn and the labour that were used in making it; and these must not be counted again. But if the carpet is cleaned by domestic servants or at steam scouring works, the value of the labour spent in cleaning it must be counted in separately; for otherwise the results of this labour would be altogether omitted from the inventory of those newly-produced commodities and conveniences which constitute the real income of the country."

"Usance of wealth" is apparently identical with income as explained in this book. "Social income," however, seems at variance with the concept of "usance"; for it includes concrete wealth.

William Smart, *The Distribution of Income*, London (Macmillan), 1899, p. 18.

"In any case, the attempt at classification seems to bring out clearly that there are, conceivably, two ways of computing the real National Income: the one which takes it as the sum of consumption goods plus any additions to capital, the other which takes it as the sum of the services which contribute to the making of them; and that these two are alternatives. Either alternative, however, may be used when different purposes are in view; and the thesis which I put forward is that, while the National Income must be *conceived of* as the total sum of consumption goods, as these and these alone are the means of satisfying the end of economic action, the life of man, it must be *calculated* as the sum of the contributory services."

Includes concrete goods and abstract services.

F. W. Taussig, *Wages and Capital* (Appleton & Co., New York), 1906, p. 36.

"It would seem best, therefore, to let the term capital stand simply for inchoate wealth: for all the possessions that do not yet serve human wants. Tools and machines, factories and warehouses, raw materials and half-finished and nearly finished goods,—these all go together as being not directly conducive to enjoyment; while all forms of finished commodities — food, houses, clothes, ornaments — belong together as enjoyable wealth and as income."

Are houses income?

Henry Rogers Seager, *Introduction to Economics* (Holt & Co., New York), 1904, pp. 163-164.

"The money income is merely the convenient medium by means of which the real income of the community is divided among those entitled to share it. This real income consists of consumable goods for those who spend their entire money incomes, and partly of consumable goods and partly of capital goods for those who save."

As to the inclusion of "savings" under Income, see text of this chapter and the fuller treatment in Chapter XIV.

Charles Jesse Bullock, *Introduction to the Study of Economics*, rev. ed. Boston (Silver, Burdett & Co.), 1900, p. 376.

"In this way the social income for any month or year may be divided into four constituent parts: —

"1. The satisfactions derived from durable consumable goods, the product of past industry, that still remain in the possession of the community and add to its material enjoyments.

"2. The personal services at the disposal of the society during the period for which the income is computed.

"3. The material goods of a consumable character that are the product of the current industry for the period considered.

"4. The producers' goods, or capital, created by the current industry of the period, and available for the production of economic goods during the following periods."

Is double counting avoided; *e.g.* Are material goods to be counted, and then, in addition, the satisfactions from them?

Frank A. Fetter, *The Principles of Economics*, New York (The Century Co.), 1904, pp. 40, 41.

3. "*Objective income consists of the additional sums of goods acquired by individuals or by society during the income period.*

* * * * * * *

4. "*Income in the logical sense must be a net addition, but the term gross income is not without popular and practical meaning.* Gross income is sometimes spoken of in the sense of total receipts, as the total of goods secured; net income is the remainder after deducting expenditures and after replacing the goods employed to secure the income. In order to produce some goods technically, men make use of other goods. While they are storing up a supply of wood or coal it may be looked upon as the income, but they may burn it to help grow hothouse plants. While they gather flowers with one hand, they destroy fuel with the other. Only the net increase in value can be accounted income in the second period. The goods that come into a man's possession in any period are of many sorts: to get some he has destroyed many previously existing goods; while to get others he has not needed to use up the accumulations of the past or to mortgage the future. The one kind is gross, the other net income.

5. "*An income of consumption goods is a part of wealth, but not the whole of it.* The consumption goods, the 'present goods' at the moment available, are the essential part of wealth for the moment's enjoyment. The only essential and immediate conditions of a series of gratifications is a regular series of consumption goods. But many things existing which could be used to secure a gratification are not in fact treated as consumption goods. A crop of corn is not all income. In a time of famine it could be used, but seed-corn was saved from last year, and some must be kept for next year. This is a

part of wealth, but not of 'present goods' as we understand the term."

"Goods" are not income. Increase of value is not income. See text.

Kleinwächter, *Das Einkommen und seine Verteilung*, Leipzig, 1896, pp. 11, 12.

So bestimmt beispielweise das Einkommensteuergesetz für Hamburg vom 26. März, 1886, im Sec. 4:—

"Die Einkommensteuer ist von dem reinen Einkommen oder Erwerb zu entrichten, d. h. allen in Geld oder Geldeswert (etwaige selbstverwohnte Miete, den Wert etwaige freier Wohnung, Naturallieferungen u. s. f. hinzugerechnet) bestehenden Einnahmen des Steuerpflichtigen, ohne Ausnahme, gleichgiltig aus welcher Quelle sie geflossen. . . ."[1]

Ähnlich sagt das sächsische Einkommensteuergesetz vom 2. Juli, 1878, im § 15:—

"Als Einkommen gilt die Summe aller . . . Einnahmen mit Einschluss des Mietwertes der Wohnung im eigenen Hause, sowie des Wertes der zum Haushalt verbrauchten Erzeugnisse der eigenen Wirtschaft. . . ."

Und fast mit denselben Worten, nur etwas minutiöser und genauer, sagt der österreichische Entwurf eines Gesetzes, betreffend die direkten Personalsteuren vom Jahre 1892, im § 195:—

"Als Einkommen gilt die Summe aller in Geld oder Geldeswert bestehenden Einnahmen der einzelnen Steuerpflichtigen mit Einschluss des Mietwertes der Wohnung im eigenen Hause oder sonstiger freier Wohnung, sowie des Wertes der zum Haushalte verbrauchten Erzeugnisse der eigenen Wirtschaft und des eigenen Gewerbebetriebes, sowie sonstiger dem Steuerpflichtigen allenfalls zukommender Naturaleingänge."

Bemerkenswert ist, dass keine dieser Gesetzesstellen die einzelnen Arten oder Zweige oder Bestandteile des Einkommens, die der Steuer unterworfen sein sollen, taxativ aufzählt, sondern dass die in Rede stehenden Gesetze das "Einkommen" ganz allgemein zu definieren bestrebt sind. Und der Tenor ist jedesmal: "Unter Einkommen versteht man *alle in Geld oder*

Geldeswert bestehenden Einnahmen, gleichgiltig aus welcher Quelle sie geflossen." Da nun in unserer heutigen auf der Grundlage des Privateigentums und der Individualwirtschaft aufgebauten Volkswirtschaft
1. alle erdenklichen Sachgüter,
2. alle erdenklichen Nutzungen dieser Sachgüter und
3. alle erdenklichen persönlichen Dienstleistungen um Geld verkauft und gekauft werden können und demgemäss " Geldeswert haben," so ergiebt sich, dass der Gesetzgeber alle materiellen und immateriellen Güter, die in die Wirtschaft des Einzelnen treten, unter den Begriff des Einkommens subsumiert wissen will. . . . Das heisst also mit anderen Worten: der Gesetzgeber definiert den Einkommensbegriff in der nämlichen Weise, wie es oben definiert wurde, und zwar so, dass unter "Einkommen" alle Güter verstanden werden sollen, welche entweder in die eigene Wirtschaft von aussen hereinkommen, oder welche innerhalb der eigenen Wirtschaft neu entstehen, und zwar gleichgiltig ob diese Güter materielle (oder Sach-) Güter, oder ob sie immaterielle Güter (d. i. Nutzungen von Sachgütern oder persönliche Dienstleistungen) sind.

To include in income *all* newly acquired or newly produced goods is clearly to include too much. To restrict income to money receipts is, as shown in the text, to err both in inclusion and exclusion. To require that the income shall be "rein" or "net" without defining the deduction required to make it so is to leave the definition incomplete.

Kleinwächter, *op. cit.*, pp. 22–23.

An dieser Stelle genügt die Bemerkung, dass die HERMANN-SCHMOLLERSCHE Definition oder Auffassung des (Einzel-) Einkommens bis auf den heutigen Tag so ziemlich (die abweichenden Meinungen sollen weiter unten erwähnt werden) die herrschende geblieben ist. HERMANN ("Staatswirtschaftliche Untersuchungen." 2. Aufl., München, 1870, S. 582 u. 583) definiert das (Einzel-) Einkommen wie folgt:

"So wenig jede Ausgabe Verbrauch ist, so wenig ist jede Einnahme Einkommen. Dieses ist vielmehr die Summe der wirtschaftlichen oder Tauschgüter, welche in einer gewissen Zeit zu dem ungeschmälert fortbestehenden Stammgut einer Person neu hinzutreten, die sie daher beliebig verwenden kann.

APPENDIX TO CHAPTER VII 353

Dass es ebensowohl körperlicher als unkörperlicher Natur sein könne, ist klar."

Und im Anschlusse an diese HERMANNSCHE Definition des Einkommens sagt SCHMOLLER ("Die Lehre vom Einkommen u. s. w." in der "Zeitschr. f. d. ges. Staatsw." Jahrg. 1863, Bd. 19, S. 1 ff. speciell S. 19): —

"Einkommen ist . . . also die Summe von wirtschaftlichen Gütern, die ein Subjekt in einer gewissen Zeit zur Befriedigung seiner Bedürfnisse ohne Schmälerung seines Vermögens verwenden kann. Für Jeden sind die Früchte seiner Arbeit und seines Vermögens sein ursprüngliches Einkommen; ein abgeleitetes hat nur der, welcher solche Früchte nicht hat; d. h. nur er lebt vom Einkommen anderer. . . . Zum Einkommen gehören stets auch sämtliche unmittelbar, d. h. ohne Tausch, verbrauchten oder genossenen Früchte der Arbeit und des Vermögens."

The foregoing definitions express in a general way what we have called "earnings" as distinct from "income." They err however by fixing on concrete commodities in place of their services and in some other respects. See text.

In erschöpfender Weise hat ADOLF WAGNER die aus der bisher geschilderten Auffassung entspringenden Einkommensdefinitionen in seiner bekannten "Grundlegung" (1. Aufl., S. 96 u. 97) zusammengefasst, wenn er das Einzelneinkommen definiert wie folgt: —

"Im Einkommen (einzeln in den Einkünften) werden die Einnahmen oder Erträge in Beziehung mit der Person, welche sie empfängt, daher mit dem Wirtschaftssubjekte gebracht. Das Einkommen einer Person umfasst zweierlei: —

"1. Diejenige Summe wirtschaftlicher Güter, welcher derselben in gewissen Perioden . . . regelmässig und daher mit der Fähigkeit der regelmässigen Wiederholung als Reinerträge einer festen Erwerbsquelle neu als Vermögen hinzuwachsen. Dieser Teil des Einkommens einer Person rührt daher aus der Wirtschaftsfürung überhaupt und aus einzelnen wirtschaftlichen Thätigkeiten (Arbeit, Unternehmung) oder aus Eigentums- oder Forderungsrechten inbesondere (Sklaveneigentum, Grundeigentum, Kapitaleigentum, Forderungen aus Kreditgeschäften), endlich aus regelmässigen unentgeltlichen Einnahmen (Almosen, Geschenk) her.

"2. Die Genüsse (Nutzungen) oder selbst nur die Genussmöglichkeiten, welche das Nutzvermögen einer Person nach Abrechnung der dabei stattfindenden Abnutzung und Verkehrswertverminderung periodisch fortdauernd gestattet.

"Das Einkommen einer Person bildet zunächst den Güterfond zur Befriedigung ihrer Bedürfnisse. Seine Erwerbung ist das Mittel zu letzterem Zwecke. Es kann in derselben Periode, in der es erlangt wurde, vollständig verzehrt werden, ohne dass dadurch das frühere Vermögen geschmälert wird. Die Tauschwerthöhe des Einkommens einer Person entscheidet über das Mass der letzterer möglichen dauernden Bedürfnisbefriedigungen, ist daher volkswirtschaftlich von grösster Bedeutung."

The errors in Wagner's definition are the restriction that income must be "regular" and the inclusion of concrete commodities and abstract services, side by side.

Kleinwächter, *op. cit.*, p. 24.

... man heute unter dem Einkommen einer Person versteht:—

alle Guter, welche in die Wirtschaft oder in das Vermögen einer Person treten, und zwar:—

1. gleichgiltig, ob diese Güter von aussen in die eigene Wirtschaft hereinkommen, oder ob sie innerhalb der eigenen Wirtschaft neu entstanden sind, und

2. gleichgiltig, ob diese Güter materieller oder unmaterieller Natur sind.

Allerdings müssen in diese Definition zwei weitere Momente aufgenommen werden, wenn dieselbe die heutige communis opinio der Wissenschaft widerspiegeln soll, zwei Momente, die ich in der "Einleitung" mit Vorbedacht unberücksichtigt gelassen habe, weil sie für den mir dort vorschwebenden Zweck bedeutungslos waren, nämlich:—

1. dass die in Rede stehenden Güter mit einer gewissen Regelmässigkeit in die Wirtschaft oder in das Vermögen der betreffenden Person treten müssen, wenn sie als "Einkommen" gelten sollen, und

2. dass diese Güter nur dann als "Einkommen" aufgefasst

APPENDIX TO CHAPTER VII 355

werden können, wenn sie neu in die Wirtschaft oder in das Vermögen der betreffenden Person treten, d. h. also wenn sie zu dem bisherigen Vermögen der betreffenden Person hinzutreten, oder mit anderen Worten: es liegt umgekehrt kein "Einkommen" vor, wenn Güter in die eigene Wirtschaft hereinfliessen, welche Teile des Stammvermögens dieser Wirtschaft sind, also beispielweise, wenn ausstehende Forderungen zurückgezahlt oder ausgeliehene Vermögenobjekte zurückgestellt werden.

According to Kleinwächter the effort to reach a self-consistent concept of income had led to the inclusion of every element flowing into one's possession whether by exchange from without or by production from within his own establishment, and whether these elements are material or immaterial, so long as we exclude such elements as "irregular" receipts and the return of old debts. The uselessness of such a concept Kleinwächter himself points out.

Robert Meyer, *Handwörterbuch der Staats-Wissenschaften*, Bd. III, Art. Einkommen "Begriff," p. 348.

Die englische liberale Nationalökonomie war von dieser Grundlage aus zu einseitigen Resultaten gelangt, indem sie das Einkommen ganz in der Art verstand, wie die Buchhaltung einer kaufmännischen oder industriellen Unternehmung den Reingewinn ermittelt.

* * * * * * *

Die deutsche Litteratur hat diese Einseitigkeit vermieden, und die bis auf die Gegenwart herrschend gebliebene Hermannsche, von Schmoller ergänzte und vielleicht über Gebühr viel bewunderte Lehre versteht unter Einkommen alle Tauschgüter, die nach vollständiger Herstellung alles Stammvermögens innerhalb des Jahres neu erzeugt und dargeboten werden und zur Befriedigung der Bedürfnisse der Nation dienen mögen (Hermann), oder die Summe der wirtschaftlichen Güter, die ein Subjekt in einer gewissen Zeit zur Befriedigung seiner Bedürfnisse ohne Schmälerung seines Vermögens verwenden kann (Schmoller).

* * * * * * *

In neuerer Zeit ist ein früher als selbstverständlich vorausgesetztes Merkmal auch begrifflich in den Vordergrund gestellt worden: die Wiederkehr, die regelmässige Wiederkehr oder die Fähigkeit der Wiederkehr der das Einkommen bildenden Einnähmen.

* * * * * * *

Förmliche Definitionen des Einkommens werden häufig vermieden, doch sagt die sächsische Einkommensteuer vom 2. Juli, 1878, § 25: Als Einkommen gilt die Summe aller in Geld und Geldeswert bestehenden Einnahmen abzüglich der auf Erlangung, Sicherung und Erhaltung dieser Einnahmen verwandten Ausgaben sowie etwaiger Schuldzinsen, auch insofern diese nicht zu den eben bezeichneten Ausgaben gehören, Ausserordentliche Einnahmen durch Erbschaft und ähnliche Erwerbungen gelten jedoch nicht als steuerpflichtiges Einkommen, sondern als Vermehrung des Stammvermögens. Ganz ähnlich das österreichische G. v. 25. Oktober, 1896, welches jedoch den zweiten Absatz anders gefasst hat: —

"Ausserordentliche Einnahmen aus Erbschaften, Lebenskapitalsversicherungen, Schenkungen und ähnlichen unentgeltlichen Zuwendungen gelten nicht als steuerpflichtiges Einkommen."

These formulations virtually repeat the definitions given above.

Franz Guth, *Die Lehre vom Einkommen in dessen Gesammtzweigen*, Leipzig, 1878, p. 62.

Einkommen ist jede aus einer Quelle, also mit einer gewissen Regelmässigkeit widerkehrende Vermehrung des Vermögens. Der Bezieher Kann es geniessen, verzehren, oder auf irgend einer Art vernichten, ohne seinen Fonds zu schwächen. Lotteriegewinne, precäre Almosen und Geschenke sind daher kein Einkommen, wohl aber sind es Almosen und Geschenke, die sich auf gewisse Titel gründen.

This view is discussed in the text.

APPENDIX TO CHAPTER XI
§ 1 (to Ch. XI, § 2)
Dimensions of Income-capital Ratios

If we indicate time by t and distinguish the quantity and value of services by the letters q and v, and the quantity and value of capital by Q and V, the four ratios mentioned assume the form: —

Physical productivity, $\dfrac{q}{Qt}$, *e.g.* bushels per acre per year.

Value productivity, $\dfrac{v}{Qt}$, *e.g.* dollars per acre per year.

Physical return, $\dfrac{q}{Vt}$, *e.g.* bushels per dollar's worth of capital per year.

Value return, $\dfrac{v}{Vt}$, *e.g.* dollars per dollar (*i.e.* per cent) per year.

APPENDIX TO CHAPTER XII
§ 1 (to Ch. XII, § 2)
Mathematical Relations between Rates, Annually, Semi-annually, etc., when conceived in the Sense of the Price of Capital

If i' represents the rate of interest per annum when the income is payable semi-annually (such as 4 % in the example in the text) and i the rate which would be its equivalent when the income is payable annually (such as 4.04 % in the example), the relation between i' and i is, —

$$i = i' + \frac{i'^2}{4}.$$

To show this we observe that under our hypothesis as to i and i', a capital of \$1 will buy a perpetual income of either i each year, or $\dfrac{i'}{2}$ each six months. Let us suppose, as in the preceding example, in six months the holder of the latter annuity, after receiving his first installment of income, $\dfrac{i'}{2}$, sells out for $1, which he may evidently do if the rate of interest remains unchanged. With his total receipts, $1+\frac{i'}{2}$, he buys a new annuity of the same type. This will evidently yield him $\left(1+\frac{i'}{2}\right)i'$ per annum, payable in semi-annual installments of half that amount, or $\frac{\left(1+\frac{i'}{2}\right)i'}{2}$. At the end of another six months, then, he receives this last-named sum, and, selling his newly bought annuity for its original value of $1+\frac{i'}{2}$, he has in hand a total sum of $1+\frac{i'}{2}+\frac{\left(1+\frac{i'}{2}\right)i'}{2}$. Of this sum he reinvests $1 and retains as income the remainder, or $\frac{i'}{2}+\frac{\left(1+\frac{i'}{2}\right)i'}{2}$.

This sum may evidently be obtained year after year simply by repeating the above process. It constitutes a perpetual annuity, *payable annually*, and its value simplified from the above formula is evidently $i'+\frac{i'^2}{4}$.

Since this is the annual income, payable annually, which $1 of capital will buy, it is by definition, the magnitude we called i; that is, $i = i' + \frac{i'^2}{4}$.

We may in like manner proceed to quarterly payments, in which case we shall find, by analogous reasoning, denoting by i'' the rate of interest per annum payable quarterly, that

$$i = i'' + \frac{3i''^3}{8} + \frac{i''^3}{16} + \frac{i''^4}{256}.$$

§ 2 (TO CH. XII, § 4)

Mathematical Relations between Rates reckoned Annually, Semi-annually, etc., when Rates are conceived as "Premiums." Diagrammatic Representation. Economic Interpretation of e.

In general let i' be the rate of interest per annum reckoned semi-annually. Then the "amount" of $1 in six months is

$1 + \frac{i'}{2}$, and this sum in another six months will "amount" by compound interest to $\left(1 + \frac{i'}{2}\right)^2$, which must be equal to $1 + i$, the "amount" of \$1 in one year at the equivalent rate of interest, i, reckoned annually; i.e.
$$1 + i = \left(1 + \frac{i'}{2}\right)^2$$
or, expanding and reducing,—
$$i = i' + \frac{i'^2}{4},$$
which is the same result obtained before when the rate of interest was regarded as the price of capital.

Similarly, for the interest rate i'', reckoned quarterly, we may prove $1 + i = \left(1 + \frac{i''}{4}\right)^4$, and for the interest rate $i^{(n)}$, reckoned n times a year, $1 + i = \left(1 + \frac{i^{(n)}}{n}\right)^n$.

In other words,
$$\begin{aligned}1 + i &= \left(1 + \frac{i'}{2}\right)^2 \\ &= \left(1 + \frac{i''}{4}\right)^4 \\ &= \left(1 + \frac{i^{(n)}}{n}\right)^n = \left[\left(1 + \frac{i^{(n)}}{n}\right)^{\frac{n}{i^{(n)}}}\right]^{i^{(n)}}\end{aligned}$$

As n increases indefinitely, the last expression approaches a limit. The limit of $i^{(n)}$ is the "rate of interest per annum computed continuously," called δ. The limit of the square bracket is the base of the Napierian system of logarithms called e; for by the definition of e usually given, it is the limit of $\left(1 + \frac{1}{k}\right)^k$, when k is any number increasing indefinitely. Evidently $\frac{n}{i^{(n)}}$ is such a number, for n, by hypothesis, is to be increased indefinitely, and $i^{(n)}$ evidently decreases. Hence at the limit the last formula becomes,
$$1 + i = e^\delta;$$
Or, substituting for e its numerical value,
$$1 + i = (2.7182818)^\delta.$$

Another proof of this formula could be given for the case where the rate of interest is conceived as the price of capital, by following to the limit the method of this **Appendix, § 1** above.

The number e, or 2.7182818, plays almost as important a rôle in mathematics as the number 3.141592, called π, which expresses the ratio of the circumference of a circle to its diameter, but the meaning of e is less familiar to most students. Various definitions and interpretations may be given. To the economist, the most interesting is the following: e is the "amount" of $1 put at compound interest during the "purchase period," the latter being derived on the assumption that the rate of interest is payable continuously.

This proposition is implicitly contained in the demonstration of the equation $1 + i = e^\delta$, as given above. The following is a more explicit statement, with actual illustrative figures:—

If we consider the rate of interest 4%, or $\frac{4}{100}$ payable *annually*, the purchase period is 25 years, or $\frac{100}{4}$, and the amount of $1 put at 4% interest for these 25 years will be $(1 + .04)^{25}$.

If next we take 4% payable *semi-annually*, the amount of $1 during the purchase period of 25 years will be $\left(1 + \frac{.04}{2}\right)^{50}$.

Similarly, the amount of $1 put at interest at 4% payable *quarterly* is $\left(1 + \frac{.04}{4}\right)^{100}$.

And if the interest is reckoned as payable n times a year, the amount is $\left(1 + \frac{.04}{n}\right)^{\frac{n}{.04}}$.

At the limit, we have the amount of $1 at interest at 4% for 25 years when the rate of interest is payable *continuously*. The limit of the above expression, when n is made indefinitely great, is the definition of e.

The distinction between the different rates of interest may be shown by a diagram. In Figure 33, let the curve $B'AB$ represent a "discount curve," any two ordinates of which represent exchangeable goods situated at two corresponding points of time, as a and b, that is, the sum aA of "present" goods will buy the sum bB of goods which lie in the future a time interval ab, beyond the "present." If we take these two points, a and b, a year apart, the rate of interest as reckoned annually is the

APPENDIX TO CHAPTER XII   361

"slope" of the secant AB in relation to the ordinate aA $\left(\dfrac{BH}{AH} \div aA\right)$. Similarly, the slope of the secant AC drawn through points corresponding to times a half year apart, taken in relation to aA, is the rate of interest reckoned semi-annually,

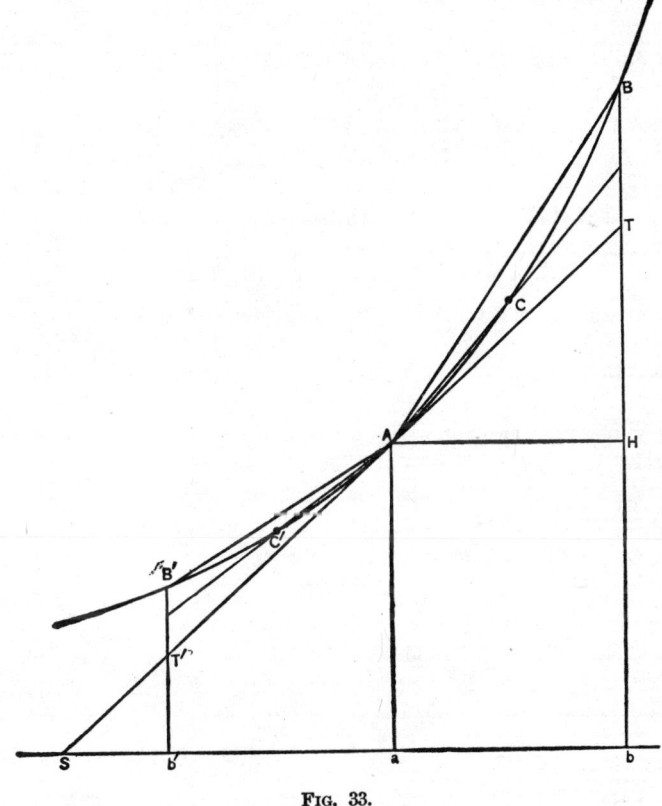

Fig. 33.

and so on. At the limit, the slope of the *tangent* AT (in relation to aA) represents the rate of interest reckoned continuously.

Similarly, the regressive secant, AB', represents the rate of discount, reckoned annually (if ab' represents a year interval),

AC', the rate reckoned semi-annually, and so on until the tangent AT', or AT, is again reached, when the distinction between interest and discount disappears. It is easy to prove (by similar triangles) that the reciprocal of the rate of interest continuously reckoned, in other words the "year's purchase," is represented by aS the subtangent.

§ 3 (to Ch. XII, § 6)

A *Premium* Rate of 4% one Year and 3% Each Year after means a *Price* Rate of 3.03% the First Year.

We have given 4% as the rate of interest (as premium) in the first year, and 3% as the rate for each year thereafter.

Let us suppose that $100 to-day is invested for $104 next year, and that at the end of the year, of this $104, $100 is reinvested. Since thereafter the rate of interest is always 3% in the premium sense, it must be, by proof in the text, also 3% in the price sense. Consequently, the $100 reinvested next year may be used to buy $3 a year forever. The result is that for the $100 to-day the return is $4 next year and $3 each year thereafter. This series of payments is the same as $3 a year forever, together with one extra dollar at the end of the first year. This extra dollar has a present worth (since the interest premium between this year and next year is 4%) of $\frac{1}{1.04}$, or $.96\frac{2}{13}$. If we deduct this present value of the extra dollar from the $100 (which is the present value of the entire series of $4, $3, $3, $3, etc., ad inf.), we have the present value of the series *without* the extra dollar, *i.e.* of $3 a year forever. The remainder is 99.03\frac{11}{13}$. Since, then, this 99.03\frac{11}{13}$ will buy $3 a year forever, the rate of interest in the *price* sense is $3 ÷ 99.03\frac{11}{13}$, or 3.03% approximately. This is the rate at the outset. After the first year it will evidently always be 3%.

§ 4 (to Ch. XII, § 6)

A *Price* Rate of 4% this Year and 3% Each Year after means a *Premium* Rate of $37\frac{1}{2}$% the First Year.

We have given 4% as the rate (in the price sense) for the first year, and 3% as the rate (in the same sense) for each year after.

$100 will to-day buy the right to $4 a year forever, and a year hence this right to $4 annually may be sold on a 3% basis. It will therefore fetch $133.33. The investor will consequently receive in all, at the end of this first year, a total of $4 + $133⅓, or $137⅓. Hence the rate of interest in the sense of a premium will be for that year $37\tfrac{1}{3}\%$. In succeeding years the rate of interest, considered either as a premium or a price, will evidently be 3%.

§ 5 (To Ch. XII, § 6)

Mathematical Relations between the Rates of Interest as a Premium and as a Price

In general, if we let i_1 represent the rate of interest in the premium sense for this year, i_2 for next year, i_3 for the third year, and so on, whereas $j_1, j_2,$ and $j_3,$ etc., represent the rates of interest in the price sense for the same successive years, the following relations between the i's and j's may be proved:—

$$\frac{1}{1+j_1} + \frac{1}{(1+j_1)^2} + \frac{1}{(1+j_1)^3} + \ldots \text{ ad inf.} =$$
$$\frac{1}{1+i_1} + \frac{1}{(1+i_1)(1+i_2)} + \frac{1}{(1+i_1)(1+i_2)(1+i_3)} + \ldots \text{ ad inf.}$$

$$\frac{1}{1+j_2} + \frac{1}{(1+j_2)^2} + \frac{1}{(1+j_2)^3} + \ldots \text{ ad inf.} =$$
$$\frac{1}{1+i_2} + \frac{1}{(1+i_2)(1+i_3)} + \frac{1}{(1+i_2)(1+i_3)(1+i_4)} + \ldots \text{ ad inf.}$$

$$\frac{1}{1+j_3} + \frac{1}{(1+j_3)^2} + \frac{1}{(1+j_3)^3} + \ldots \text{ ad inf.} =$$
$$\frac{1}{1+i_3} + \frac{1}{(1+i_3)(1+i_4)} + \frac{1}{(1+i_3)(1+i_4)(1+i_5)} + \ldots \text{ ad inf.}$$

etc.

These equations may be said to determine j_1, as a peculiar sort of *mean* of the magnitudes $i_1, i_2, i_3, \ldots$ ad inf., and j_2 as a similar mean of $i_2, i_3, i_4, \ldots$ ad inf., etc. Their proof, which is simple, is left to those readers who are interested in mathematics.

The preceding equations express the values of the j's in

terms of i's. The following equations give the i's in terms of the j's: —

$$i_1 = j_1 + \frac{j_1 - j_2}{j_2},$$

$$i_2 = j_2 + \frac{j_2 - j_3}{j_3},$$

$$i_3 = j_3 + \frac{j_3 - j_4}{j_4},$$

etc.

Thus if, as in our example, $j_1 = .04$ and $j_2 = .03$,

$$i_1 = .04 + \frac{.04 - .03}{.03} = .37\tfrac{1}{3}.$$

The proof of these formulæ is also left to the mathematical reader. He will observe that the two sets of equations may be proved independently or either set may be proved and the other set derived from it. To show that either set may be derived from the other, it will be found useful to substitute for the left-hand members of the first set their simpler values as derived by algebra. These are, $\frac{1}{j_1}, \frac{1}{j_2}, \frac{1}{j_3}$, etc. An easy proof of this is found by actually dividing 1 by j_1, etc.

From the formulæ it is clear that if $i_1 = i_2 = i_3 =$, etc., then $j_1 = j_2 = j_3 =$, etc., and that then all the i's = the j's. The converse is also evident.

§ 6 (TO CH. XII, § 7)

Mathematical Relations between the Rates of Interest and Discount

Let V', due one year hence, be the equivalent of V available in the present. Then the rates of interest and discount are expressed respectively by the formulæ: —

$$1 + i = \frac{V'}{V};$$

$$1 - d = \frac{V}{V'}.$$

Whence, by multiplying the two equations together we derive $(1 + i)(1 - d) = 1$, which reduces to $d = i - id$. That is, the number representing the rate of discount equals the number representing the equivalent rate of interest less a small correction, equal to the product of the rates of interest and discount.

The relation between the rates of discount and interest when semi-annually reckoned is analogous to the relation which we found between those annually reckoned. We then have the equations,
$$\frac{V}{V'} = 1 - \frac{d'}{2}$$
and
$$\frac{V'}{V} = 1 - \frac{i'}{2},$$
whence
$$\left(1 - \frac{d'}{2}\right)\left(1 + \frac{i'}{2}\right) = 1.$$

By multiplication and reduction,
$$d' = i' - \frac{i'd'}{2}.$$

We may apply similar reasoning to quarterly-reckoned interest and discount rates.

It follows that
$$\left(1 + \frac{i''}{4}\right)\left(1 - \frac{d''}{4}\right) = 1,$$
or
$$d'' = i'' - \frac{i''d''}{4}.$$

The same reasoning may obviously be applied to reckonings n times a year. We then find,
$$d^{(n)} = i^{(n)} - \frac{i^{(n)}d^{(n)}}{n}.$$

It is evident that if n, the number of parts into which the year is divided, be sufficiently increased, the term $\frac{i^{(n)} d^{(n)}}{n}$ becomes infinitely small, so that, at the limit, the rate of interest and the rate of discount become equal. This rate for continuous reckoning, being the same as the rate of interest for continuous reckoning, is also called δ.

Unlike the rate of interest, the rate of discount is always considered as associated with the exchange of present against future goods, and not with the exchange between capital and income, *i.e.* is taken, not in the "price" sense, but in the "premium" sense (the premium being, in this case, negative). We may, however, to complete our scheme of concepts, construct for ourselves a "rate of discount" in the sense of the price of capital in income. We recur to the fact that the rate of interest, in the price sense, was defined as the ratio of income to capital, when the first installment of income is due at the *end* of the first time-interval. But if the first installment is due at the *beginning*, the ratio of income to capital is no longer the rate of interest, but may be called a sort of rate of discount.

Thus, if $100 will buy a perpetual annuity of $4 a year, the first installment being due *one year hence*, then $104 will buy such a perpetual annuity, the first installment being due *at once*. In the first case, the ratio of income to capital, $\frac{4}{100}$, is called the "rate of interest in the price sense." In the second case, the ratio of income to capital, $\frac{4}{104}$, may be called "the rate of discount in the price sense." The rate of discount in the price sense and the rate of discount in the premium sense are related in a manner strictly analogous to the relation between the rates of interest in the two respective senses.

As is well known, bonds, just before an installment of interest is due, are sold in either of two ways: they may be sold without the interest payment ("ex-interest"), or with the interest payment ("flat"). These two methods are associated respectively with the rate of interest and rate of discount, as just described.

§ 7 (to Ch. XII, § 7)

Mathematical Relations between the Rates of Discount for Different Time Reckonings

The rates of discount for different time reckonings are related in a manner quite analogous to that in which the corresponding rates of interest are related, as shown in this Appendix, § 2. Thus if V to-day will buy W in half a year,

$$\frac{V}{W} = 1 - \frac{d'}{2},$$

and if W will then buy V' in another half year on the same terms,

$$\frac{W}{V'} = 1 - \frac{d'}{2},$$

whence, multiplying, $\quad \dfrac{V}{V'} = \left(1 - \dfrac{d'}{2}\right)^2.$

But $\dfrac{V}{V'} = 1 - d,$

therefore $1 - d = \left(1 - \dfrac{d'}{2}\right)^2,$

and $d = d' - \left(\dfrac{d'}{2}\right)^2,$

from which we see that the discount rate reckoned annually is less than its equivalent reckoned semi-annually. Similar reasoning applies to quarterly and other rates.

§ 8 (TO CH. XII, § 8)

Dimensions of the Rates of Interest, Discount, and Capitalization

The rate of interest in the price sense is of the form $\dfrac{v}{Vt}$, where v represents the part of the perpetual income stream which flows in the time t, and V represents its capital value. Since, in this fraction, v and V are of the same dimension, both being measured in dollars, or else in bushels, or in some other units of same denomination, the dimensionality of the fraction $\dfrac{v}{Vt}$ reduces to $\dfrac{1}{t}$ or t^{-1}.* In like manner, the ratio of capitalization, being the reciprocal of this fraction, or $\dfrac{Vt}{v}$, has the dimensionality t.

These results are recognized in common usage, inasmuch as the rate of interest is so much *per annum*, and the ratio of capitalization is so many *years'* purchase.

The same dimensionality is obtainable from the rate of interest considered as a premium. The rate of interest as a premium is given by the equation $\dfrac{V'}{V} = (1 + ti)$, where V' and V are two exchangeable sums separated by the interval t, usually a fraction of a year, for which the rate of interest is to be reckoned. Thus, if the reckoning is quarterly, t is $\tfrac{1}{4}$. Since V' and V are of the same dimension, $\dfrac{V'}{V}$ is a pure number.

* It is interesting to observe that the dimensionality of this "price of capital" is entirely different from the dimensionality of the price of one kind of goods in terms of another, as shown in the Appendix to Chap. I.

Hence its equal, $1-ti$, is a pure number. Since of this sum, the term 1 is a pure number, the other term, ti, is also a pure number. Hence i must be of a dimension reciprocal to t, i.e. $\frac{1}{t}$, or t^{-1}.

The rate of discount evidently has the same dimensionality as the rate of interest.

APPENDIX TO CHAPTER XIII

§ 1 (to Ch. XIII, § 1)

Formula for Present Value of Sum due in One Year

If the rate of interest be denoted by i, it is evident that $1+i$ due next year is worth $\$1$ to-day,

hence $\$1$ due next year is worth $\frac{1}{1+i}$ to-day,

and any sum V due next year is worth $\frac{V}{1+i}$ to-day,

which is the general formula for the present value of a single sum due at the end of one year.

§ 2 (to Ch. XIII, § 1)

Formula for Present Value of Sum V due at End of Any Time t

In general, it is obvious that $(1+i)^2$ is the amount which, two years hence, has a present value of $\$1$, hence that

$\$1$ due at the end of 2 years is worth to-day $\frac{1}{(1+i)^2}$

and that V due at the end of 2 years is worth to-day $\frac{V}{(1+i)^2}$.

Similarly, V due at the end of 3 years is worth to-day $\frac{V}{(1+i)^3}$

and V due at the end of t years is worth to-day $\frac{V}{(1+i)^t}$.

The last formula is perfectly general. It is not even necessary that t should be an integer. The reader who is mathematically inclined will have no difficulty in proving that the formula applies if the period of time is $3\frac{1}{2}$ years or any other time whatever.

§ 3 (to Ch. XIII, § 3)
Formula for the Present Value of a Perpetual Annuity

The proposition that the present value of a perpetuity is $\frac{a}{i}$ was proved in the preceding chapter. An alternative proof, and the one which is usually given in treatises on annuities, is as follows: Consider a perpetual annuity of $1 per annum; it is required to find the capital value. It is evident from what has preceded that the first payment, $1, being due at the end of a year, has a discounted value at the present time of $\frac{1}{1+i}$; the second has a present worth of $\frac{1}{(1+i)^2}$; the third, $\frac{1}{(1+i)^3}$; and so on indefinitely. Therefore, the present value of the entire series will be, —

$$\frac{1}{1+i} + \frac{1}{(1+i)^2} + \frac{1}{(1+i)^3} + \text{etc., ad inf.}$$

If, for brevity, we substitute v for $\frac{1}{1+i}$, this may be written,

$$v + v^2 + v^3 + \text{ad. inf.,}$$
or
$$v(1 + v^2 + \text{ad. inf.}).$$

Since the series evidently converges, the parenthesis is equal to $\frac{1}{1-v}$, which may be seen by simply dividing 1 by $1-v$. Hence the value of the annuity is, $v\left(\frac{1}{1-v}\right)$, which reduces to $\frac{1}{i}$ if we substitute for v its original value, $\frac{1}{1+i}$. This sum, $\frac{1}{i}$ dollars, is, therefore, the capital-value of an annuity of $1. By proportion, the capital-value of any other annuity a is $\frac{a}{i}$.

§ 4 (to Ch. XIII, § 3)
Formulæ and Diagrams for Capital-value of Annuities payable Annually, Semi-annually, Quarterly, Continuously

In case the annuity accrues semi-annually, the teeth will be finer, but twice as frequent. In Figure 34 we see the behavior of the capitalized annuity if the annuity is payable annually, semi-annually, or quarterly. If the annuity be $4 a year, the teeth drop $4 if payable annually, $2, if semi-annually, and $1, if quarterly. If the frequency of the installments of income be

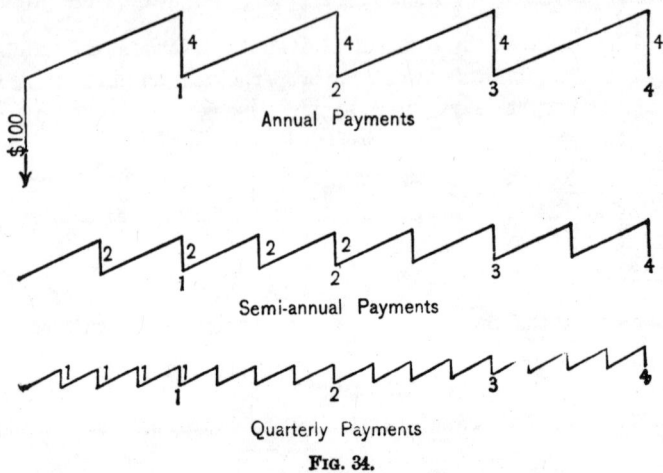

Fig. 34.

indefinitely increased, we reach the limiting case of a continuous income, when the teeth disappear entirely and the value of the annuity remains at a constant level. The value of the annuity of $4 in all these cases, just after any installment of income is received, will be $100, if the rate of interest is 4%, provided the rate is respectively "reckoned annually," semi-annually, and quarterly in the various cases. In the case of continuous income, the value of the annuity of $4 will *always* be $100 if the rate of interest be 4% "reckoned continuously." The same remarks apply, of course, to an annuity of any number of dollars. Its value after each installment is equal to the annual income divided by the rate of interest, or the annual income multiplied by the purchase period.

In order to obtain the formulæ for the value of a perpetuity payable semi-annually, quarterly, or continuously, in terms of i, the rate of interest reckoned annually, we need only to transform $\frac{a}{i'}, \frac{a}{i''}, \frac{a}{\delta}$, by means of the equations in the previous chapter. Thus

APPENDIX TO CHAPTER XIII

the value of an annuity of a dollars per annum payable semi-annually is $\frac{a}{i'}$, which, by substituting for i' its value as derived from the relation between i and i', viz. $1+i = \left(1 + \frac{i'}{2}\right)^2$, or $i' = 2(\sqrt{1+i} - 1)$ becomes $\frac{a}{2(\sqrt{1+i}-1)}$. Similarly, the quarterly annuity becomes $\frac{a}{4(\sqrt[4]{1+i}-1)}$, and the continuous annuity, since $1+i=e^\delta$ or $\delta = \log_e(1+i)$, becomes $\frac{a}{\delta} = \frac{a}{\log_e(1+i)}$. In every case the value just *before* an installment is found by adding that installment to the results just derived; and the value at intervening points by applying the discount curve, *i.e.* dividing the impending value (just before the next installment) by $(1+i)^t$, where t is the time between the present and the time of the next installment.

§ 5 (TO CH. XIII, § 3)

Diagrams for Discontinuous and Continuous Income

If the income installments recur annually, and are $4 each, these installments are represented in the line method by $a, a, a,$

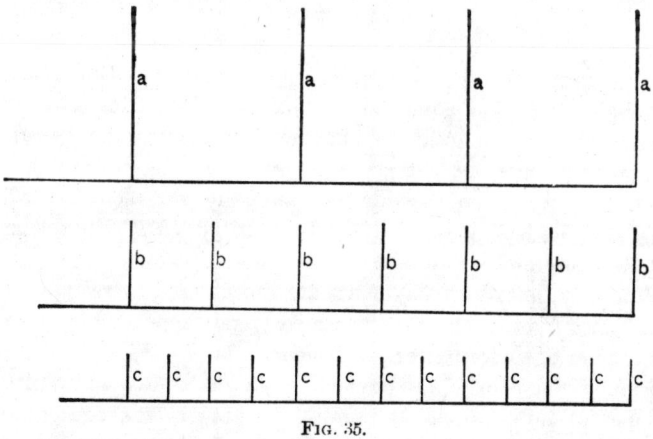

FIG. 35.

in Fig. 35. If they occur semi-annually, in installments of $2 each, they are represented by b, b, b. If they occur quarterly, in installments of $1 each, they are represented by c, c, c, and so on indefinitely, in each case the lines becoming shorter but more numerous. If this process is continued indefinitely, it is clear that continuous income would simply be represented by an infinite number of infinitesimally small lines,— a representation which would be unintelligible. It is for this reason that the area method becomes necessary. To show how it may be used, even for discontinuous income, let a series of annual payments, a, be represented in Figure 36 by the rectangles whose bases are equal to unity and whose altitudes, therefore, are equal to a. The point of time to which each rectangle is referred is taken, for convenience, as the *end* of each year in which it occurs. Thus the rectangle OV refers to the point of time P, and PW to Q. If the payments are semi-annual, we represent them by the areas of

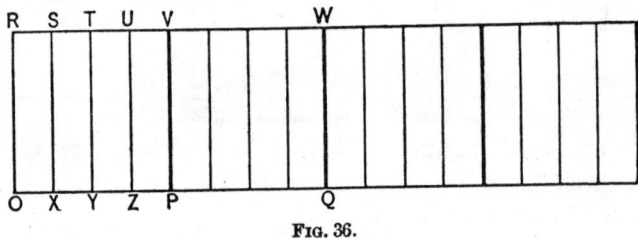

FIG. 36.

the rectangles OT, YV, etc., in the same manner. But as the rectangles are each equal to one half, the altitudes will no longer represent the individual payments, but double those semi-annual payments, *i.e.* the *per annum rate*. Thus, if the annuity is $4 per annum payable semi-annually, the rectangle OT means $2, its base is one half, and its altitude, YT, will not be 2, but 4, the rate per annum.

Similarly, quarterly payments are represented by rectangles OS, XT, YU, etc., whose altitudes will again represent the rate per annum of each quarterly payment.

Finally, for continuous payments, we shall have an infinite number of infinitesimal rectangles, forming in the aggregate the whole figure represented, the altitude of which at any point will be the *rate per annum* at which income is flowing at that point.

APPENDIX TO CHAPTER XIII

By limits we may pass from income which flows at a uniform rate to any income stream. Evidently, therefore, any continuous income-stream may be represented by a curve (Fig. 37) of which the ordinate represents the *per annum rate of flow at any*

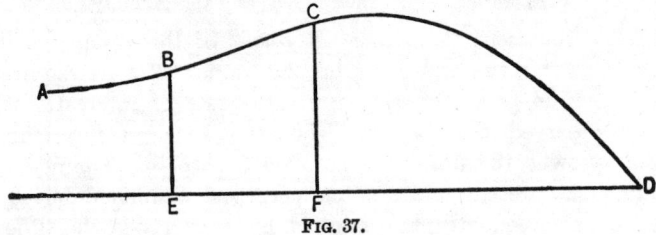

Fig. 37.

point of time, and the area *EC* between any two ordinates *BE* and *CF* represents the total income which flows within the time intercepted between those ordinates.

For the case of uniform flow, the continuous income stream is represented in Figure 38 by the area *OB*. *OA* represents the

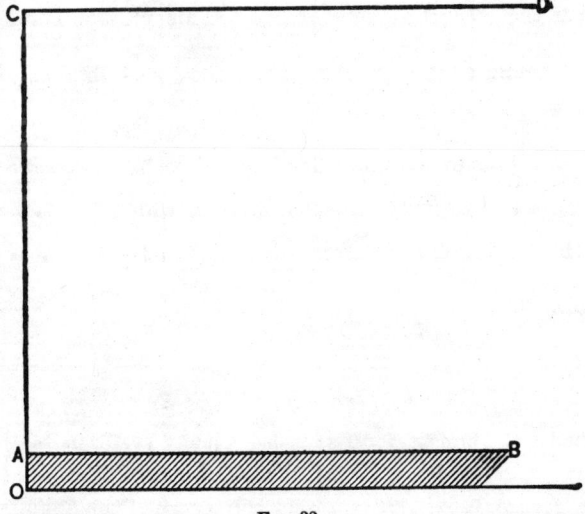

Fig. 38.

rate of income, and *OC* represents the capital-value of this income. This capital-value remains constant, as shown by the horizontal line CD, and the rate of interest (reckoned continuously) is $\dfrac{OA}{OC}$.

§ 6 (to Ch. XIII, § 5)
Formula for Capital-value of a Terminable Annuity

Let a represent the annual payment of the annuity, t its duration or term, and V its present value. We are required to find V in terms of a, t, and i, the rate of interest. We have observed that a man who owns such a terminable annuity owns the difference between a perpetual annuity beginning at present and another perpetual annuity deferred t years. Consequently, the value of his property is the difference between the values of these two; that is, it is equal to the value of a perpetual annuity beginning now, less the present value of a perpetual annuity beginning t years hence. The deferred annuity which begins at the end of t years will, we know, be worth *then* the sum of $\dfrac{a}{i}$, and will be worth *now* whatever is the present value of this $\dfrac{a}{i}$. This present value is of course found simply by discounting the $\dfrac{a}{i}$ just obtained, and is $\dfrac{\frac{a}{i}}{(1+i)^t}$. This expression should therefore be subtracted from the value of the other perpetual annuity which begins now, of which the present value is $\dfrac{a}{i}$. This subtraction gives the formula,
$$\frac{a}{i} - \frac{a}{i(1+i)^t}.$$

§ 7 (to Ch. XIII, § 5)
Discussion of Formulæ for Terminable Annuity by Diagrams. "Total Discount." "Total Interest." Depreciation.

In Figure 39 let AB represent the term t of the annuity, AD the value of a perpetual annuity beginning at the point of time A, and BE the equal value, taken at the end of the term, of a deferred perpetual annuity beginning at that time. Now the

APPENDIX TO CHAPTER XIII 375

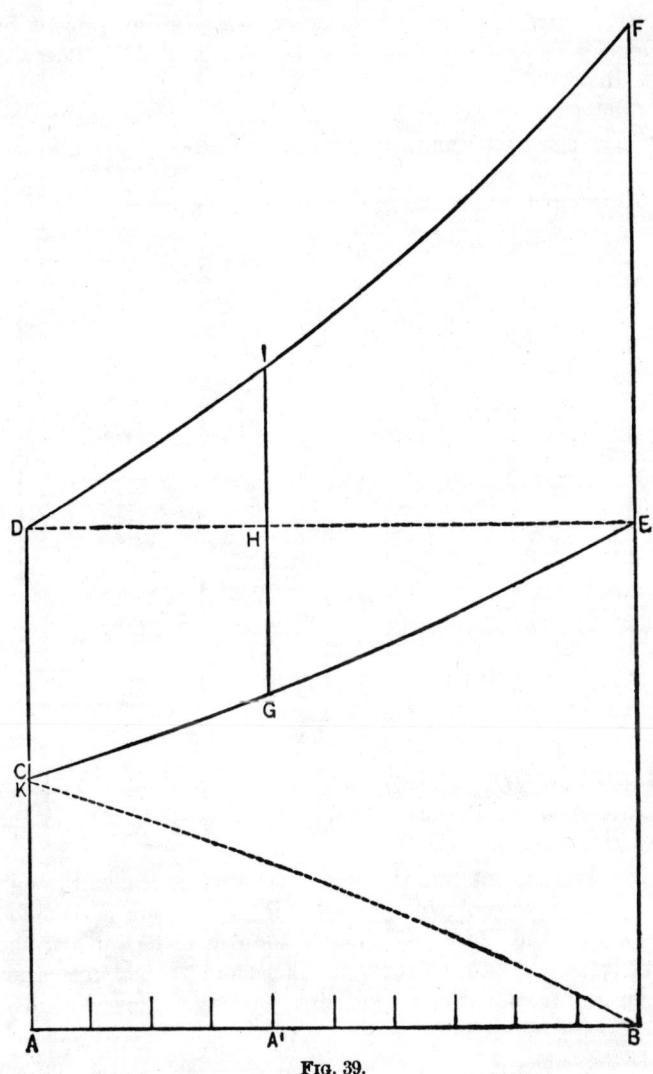

Fig. 39.

present value at time A of the value BE, at time B, is evidently AC, found by drawing the discount curve CE. Therefore the value of the terminable annuity is equal to $AD - AC$, or *DC*, which is the *total discount* on *BE*; *i.e.* the amount by which it is, as Böhm-Bawerk says, "diminished in time perspective."

Similarly, the capital-value of the annuity, taken at any time later A' (just after an installment of income), is equal to the

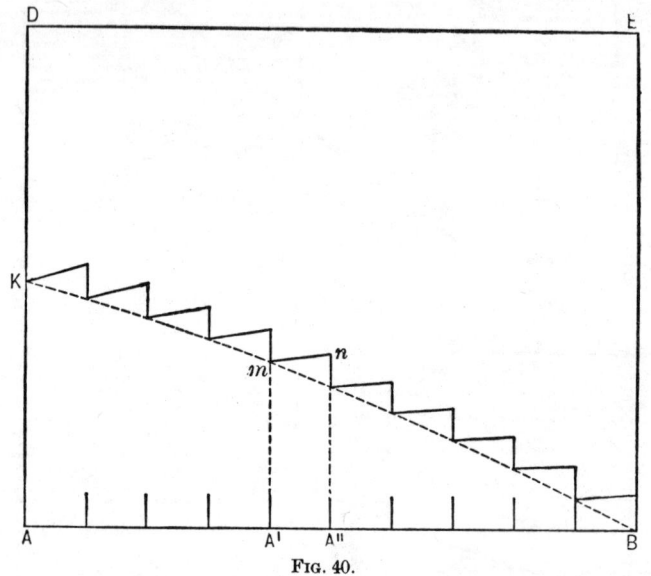

FIG. 40.

smaller sum *GH*. Thus the capital-value gradually decreases in accordance with the distance of the curve *CE* from the line *DE*.

In this representation the discount curve was drawn through *E*. If another is drawn through *D* it may be shown that *EF* is the "amount" of the terminable annuity, or its value at the time it terminates, if we suppose that each individual item is put at interest from its date to the point of time *B*. This "amount," *EF*, is called the "total interest" on that capital in that interval.

In the same way, at any intermediate time just after an installment, *GI* will represent the value of the annuity concentrated at that point, and this value will consist of two parts, *HG*, which is the (discounted) value of the part subsequent to *K*, and *HI*, the (accumulated) value of the part preceding *K*.

APPENDIX TO CHAPTER XIII

The decrease in capital-value of the annuity, which has been represented by the approach of *CE* to the horizontal line *DE* above it, is better represented, however, by inverting *CE* to the position *KB*, in order that the capital-value may be represented, as in our previous examples, by the distance from the

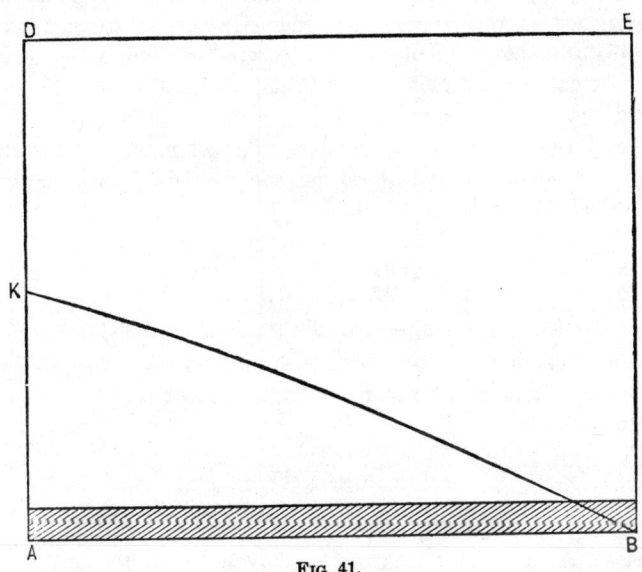

FIG. 41.

horizontal line *AB* below it. This change is accomplished in Figure 40. The value of the annuity taken *after* each installment of income is represented by the ordinate, as mA', of the curve *KB*, and the value just *before* an installment is represented by the ordinate, as nA'', of a point above this curve a distance equal to that installment. The value at intermediate points evidently follows a discount curve, as *mn*, between these two points. The result is that the capital-value will rise and fall according to the steps, or teeth, shown in the diagram.

As the income items become more numerous the teeth become more frequent and smaller, and disappear when the flow of income is continuous, as represented in Figure 41, where the curve KB itself represents the capital-value at *all* points of time.

The formula for the present value (V) of the annuity just after each installment of income is the same, whatever the time intervals between installments. This is strictly true, however, only on the proviso that the rate of interest i is to be understood as reckoned in accordance with the frequency of the installments of income in each case, — semi-annually, quarterly, etc., — instead of annually, as has been hitherto understood.

The formula for the capital-value, V, just before an installment is evidently found by taking the preceding formula for V and adding a. This gives, —

$$\frac{a}{i} - \frac{\frac{a}{i}}{(1+i)^t} + a.$$

At intermediate points the capital-value is equal to the amount just named discounted for the interval elapsed between the point of time considered and the next installment of income.

§ 8 (to Ch. XIII, § 7)

Formulæ for Value of a Bond

To be general, let us suppose a bond, the income from which is a dollars per year, payable annually for t years, at the end of which time, in addition to the final payment a, another larger payment P, called "principal," is paid. We are required to find the present value, V, of these future expected payments for a given rate of interest, i.

The discounted value of the terminable annuity has already been expressed, namely, —

$$\frac{a}{i} - \frac{\frac{a}{i}}{(1+i)^t}.$$

The discounted value of P deferred t years has also been explained and is evidently, —

$$\frac{P}{(1+i)^t}.$$

APPENDIX TO CHAPTER XIII

The sum of these expressions is the value V, which we are seeking. In other words,—

$$V = \frac{a}{i} - \frac{\frac{a}{i}}{(1+i)^t} + \frac{P}{(1+i)^t};$$

or

$$V = \frac{a}{i} + \frac{P - \frac{a}{i}}{(1+i)^t}.$$

Some special cases may be considered. First, if the annual income a is the interest on the "principal" P,—i.e. if $a = Pi$ $\left(\text{or } P = \frac{a}{i}\right)$,—the second term vanishes, as its numerator is evidently zero, and since the first term, $\frac{a}{i}$, is by present hypothesis P, the equation then becomes $V = P$.

Secondly, if a is greater than iP, it may be readily shown that V will be greater than P; and if a is less than iP, that V is less than P.

The formula given is of practical importance, as it enables us to compute the price at which a bond must sell in order to yield a certain rate of interest.

To apply the formula numerically we need only to assign particular values for the magnitudes involved. Let us take the numerical case already considered, where $P = \$100$, $a = \$5$, $i = .04$, and $t = 10$. In this case the formula becomes,—

$$V = \frac{5}{.04} + \frac{100 - \frac{5}{.04}}{(1.04)^{10}},$$

which reduces to 108, as we found before.

Similarly, it may be shown that if bonds are sold on a 6% basis, the price of the bond in question would be $92¼.

We have derived the value of a bond, V, just after a payment of "interest." In this case the bond is said by brokers to be sold "ex-interest." If, on the contrary, it is sold "flat," that is, with interest, its value will evidently be increased by the "interest" a, and will be $V + a$. The price at any time between installments will evidently be $\frac{V+a}{(1+i)^{t''}}$

380   NATURE OF CAPITAL AND INCOME

where V represents the value the bond will have after the next "interest" payment, and t' the time elapsing to that payment. Or, it is $V(1+i)^{t''}$, where V represents the value after the *last* "interest" payment, and t'' the time since said payment. Practically this last formula reduces to $V + Vit''$, which in turn is practically the same as $V + at''$; for a and Vi are practically equal, each being nearly the true interest for one installment period. This is the formula usually employed by brokers, at'' being called the "interest earned" since the last coupon.

§ 9 (to Ch. XIII, § 7)

Alternative Method, whereby the "Premium" in the Price of the Bond is compounded separately

The so-called 5 % bond running for 10 years, which is sold on a basis of 4 %, may be considered as consisting of the following two property rights: (1) the right to *four* dollars a year for 10 years and $100 at maturity, and (2) the right to *one* dollar a year for 10 years. It is evident that the present value of the first property is $100, to which, therefore, we need only to add the value of the second property, namely, the annuity of $1 a year for 10 years. It is therefore the present value of this small annuity, consisting, we may say, of the difference between the real and nominal interest on $100, which constitutes the "premium" on the price of the bond. This present value is $8, and is found in the manner already explained for terminable annuities, being the total discount on $25 at the end of 10 years, $25 being the capital-value of a *perpetual* annuity of $1 a year, when interest is reckoned at 4 %. Consequently, the bond is worth in all $108. This value is represented diagrammatically in Figure 42.

Let AA' represent the 10-year period, with the $5 interest payments shown by the ten vertical lines at unit intervals. $A'B'$ represents the $100 "principal" due in 10 years, and AB represents what the bond would be worth ($100) if the interest payments were $4 instead of $5. To this must therefore be added the present value of $1 a year for 10 years. This is the total discount on $B'C'$ (drawn equal to $25), the capitalization of a perpetual annuity of $1 a year. The total discount on this $25 is shown by the line BD, which is therefore the premium in the selling price of the bond. The total price is $AB + BD = AD$. The price at later dates (taken each just before an installment) is represented by points on

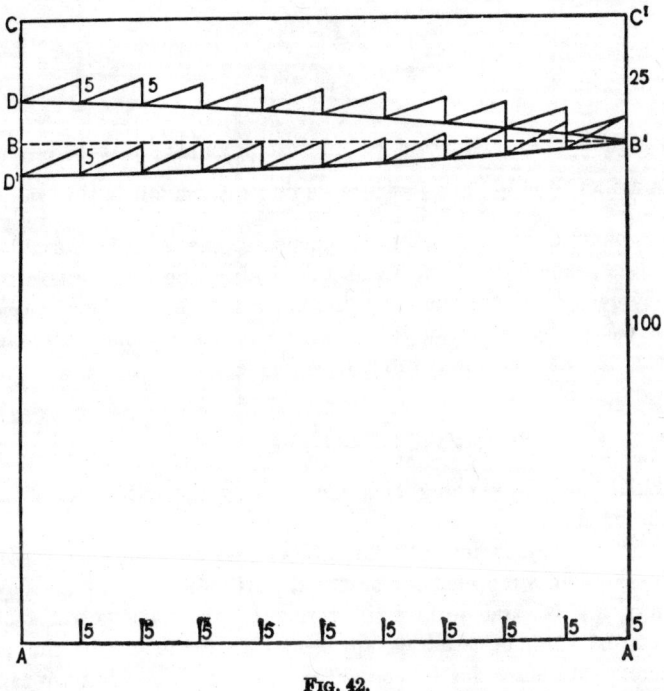

Fig. 42.

the discount curve DB' drawn with reference to CC' as a horizontal axis. Adding at each of these installment points a line equal to $5, we have the value just before interest payments, and connecting the tops of these lines with the preceding interest intervals by discount curves reckoned at 4%, we have a series of teeth representing the normal course of the price of the bond from the present to maturity.

In case a bond is sold at a 6% basis, we have the curve $B'D'$, instead of $B'D$, with the teeth superimposed as before, the tooth curves, however, being in this case on a 6% slope.

§ 10 (to Ch. XIII, § 7)

Formula for a Bond when Interest is reckoned oftener than yearly

The formula in the case of semi-annual income when interest is reckoned semi-annually is evidently,—

$$V = \frac{a}{i'} + \frac{P - \frac{a}{i'}}{\left(1 + \frac{i'}{2}\right)^{2t}},$$

which applies just after an interest payment; just before, it is evidently $V + \frac{a}{2}$; and at intervening intervals it is this value discounted, or for practical purposes, the simple formula, $V + at'$, where V is the value taken after the last "interest" payment, and t the time elapsing since that date. For the case of continuous interest, if we let, as in the previous chapter, δ represent continuous interest, we have,—

$$V = \frac{a}{\delta} + \frac{P - \frac{a}{\delta}}{e^{t\delta}},$$

which formula remains unchanged during the entire period of the bond.

These various formulæ may, of course, be somewhat transformed and simplified for practical purposes. Moreover, they may all be transformed in terms of the various rates of interest. Some actuaries apparently prefer to use, as the interest rate, only the "effective" rate, i, which is what we call the "rate of interest reckoned annually." The preceding formulæ, which employ the semi-annual, quarterly, and other forms of interest rates, may be transformed by substituting their values in terms of i, in accordance with the relations shown in Appendix to Chap. XII, § 2.

§ 11 (to Ch. XIII, § 8)

Formula for Capital-value of Any Series of Income Installments

We may express, in general formulæ, the capital-value of any income stream, as follows: Let $a_1, a_2, a_3,$ represent the successive installments of income accruing at various times dis-

APPENDIX TO CHAPTER XIII

tant from the present instant by the intervals t_1, t_2, t_3, etc., which may be equal or unequal, whole or fractional, or even positive or negative according as the income is in the future or in the past. Let i represent the rate of interest. The present value of such an income stream will be,—

$$V = \frac{a_1}{(1+i)^{t_1}} + \frac{a_2}{(1+i)^{t_2}} + \frac{a_3}{(1+i)^{t_3}} +, \text{etc.}$$

Or, in briefer notation,

$$V = \sum \frac{a}{(1+i)^t},$$

where Σ is taken in its usual sense of the summation of the series of terms of the type of that following it.

§ 12 (TO CH. XIII, § 8)
Diagram and Formula for deriving Capital-value from a given Continuous Income Stream

For any income stream flowing continuously, and represented in Figure 43 by the area below MN, the capital-value will be represented by the curve NO. The ordinate of the income stream at any point, as RS, represents the *rate* of its flow at that point, and any area, as $RSS''R''$, represents its total flow through the period RR''. The ordinates of the curve NO will represent the capital-value of this income stream. NO is constructed from N backward as follows: the curve begins at N on the income stream and is generated by a point moving in such a manner that at any position O its direction of motion is the resultant of two tendencies. To represent these two tendencies we draw through O the discount curve OP. Tangent to this curve we draw OH so as to meet the line QH drawn vertically and distant to the left one unit from OK. OH represents one of the two tendencies mentioned, that due to discounting the future. OK drawn vertically up from and equal to RS, the rate of income at that time, represents the other tendency. The resultant, OQ, drawn according to the principle of the parallelogram of forces, will represent the actual direction in which the curve will be moving at the point O. In other words, a point moving under the influence of two forces, OK and OH, will generate the required curve NO.

In order to show that this is a correct representation let us first take the case of semi-annual income. RR'' represents one year; Rr represents half a year. Draw the ordinate rh. From h draw vertically upward hq to represent a half-year's installment of income, that is, half of Rs. To avoid complicating the figure, hq is omitted; were it drawn, q would lie on the line OQ'. Then, according to our previous representation, the capital-value will follow the curve Ohq, which forms a "tooth." The line Oq is therefore a line drawn through the top points of two neighboring teeth. Its direction is a first approximation to

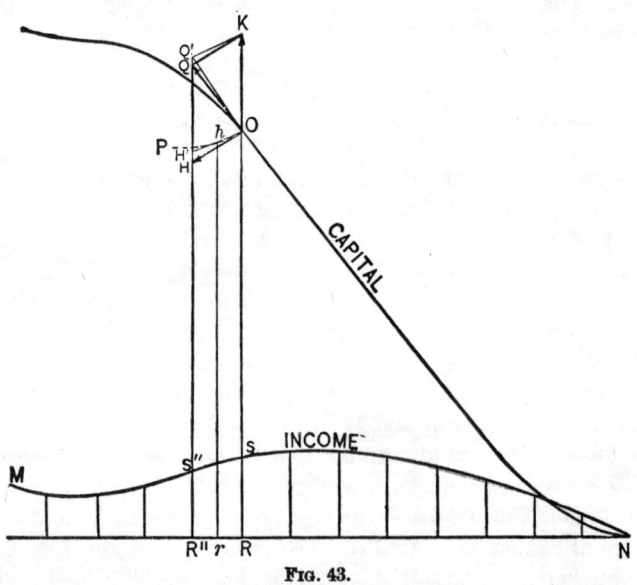

Fig. 43.

the direction OQ of the curve for the continuous case. This direction Oq is the diagonal of a parallelogram formed by producing Oh to meet the ordinate from R'' in H', producing Oq to Q' and completing the parallelogram.

Since $H'Q'$ is twice as far from O as hq (i.e. $RR'' = 2\,(rR)$ by hypothesis), it follows, by similar triangles (i.e. Ohq and $OH'Q'$), that it is also twice as long. But hq represents a half year's installment of income. Hence $H'Q'$ represents two

APPENDIX TO CHAPTER XIII

such installments, or the annual rate of income. Therefore OK, being of the same length, also represents this annual rate of income.

In other words, the direction from O to q lies along a parallelogram of which the side OK represents the annual rate of income and the side OH' a *chord* of the discount curve OP.

Now it is evident that if, instead of a semi-annual installment, we assume greater frequency, the same statement will apply except that the point h will be nearer O. By proceeding in this

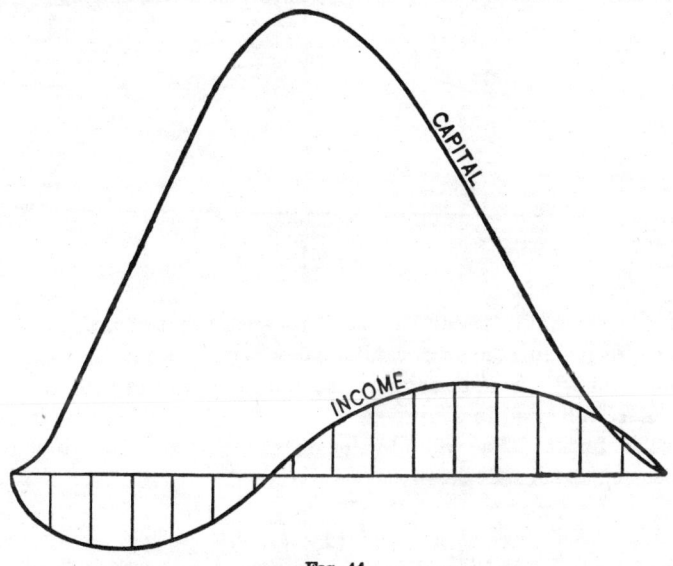

Fig. 44.

manner the chord OhH' approaches the tangent OH as its limit, and the parallelogram $OH'Q'K$ becomes at the limit the parallelogram $OHQK$ as originally described. That is, its sides are OK, the annual rate of income, and OH, the tangent to the discount curve drawn from O to a vertical line one year to the left.

That this construction and its demonstration bear a striking analogy to the construction and demonstration which apply to the composition of forces or motions is very evident. Availing ourselves of this analogy, we may say that in the case of *discontinuous* income, the point O traces the capital curve (backward) by obeying alternately two tendencies, — one, to follow the discount curve at times when no income occurs, and the other, to rise vertically whenever income occurs. In the case of *continuous* income these motions occur simultaneously instead of alternately, and the resultant is a smooth curve instead of a series of teeth.

The same principles apply when part of the income curve is below the horizontal axis, representing negative income. If

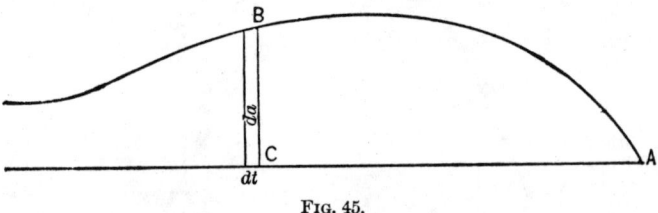

Fig. 45.

at the beginning the prospective cost just counterbalances the prospective income, the capital-value will at that instant be zero, and will from that point rise and fall again to zero at the end, as indicated in Figure 44.

The formula for capital-value in the case of a continuous income stream will be, —

$$V = \int \frac{da}{(1+i)^{t}},$$

in which da may be said to represent the infinitesimal income which flows in the infinitesimal increment of time dt. In other words, da represents an infinitesimal element of the area ABC (Fig. 45), of which element the base or breadth represents the infinitesimal time dt. For the purpose of integration we may substitute for da the expression $f(t)dt$, where $f(t)$ represents CB, or the ordinate of the income stream taken as a function of time t. If the special form of the function $f(t)$ is known, it is evidently possible to integrate the expression and obtain its value for any given limits.

APPENDIX TO CHAPTER XIII 387

§ 13 (TO CH. XIII, § 8)

Diagram showing the Accumulated "Amount" of a Given Income Stream

We reproduce in Figure 46 the diagram with which we began the study of the general case of capitalizing income. We now wish to obtain the *accumulated* value $A'''Q$, at the close of the period OA''', of the income items AB, $A'B'$, $A''B''$, and $A'''B'''$.

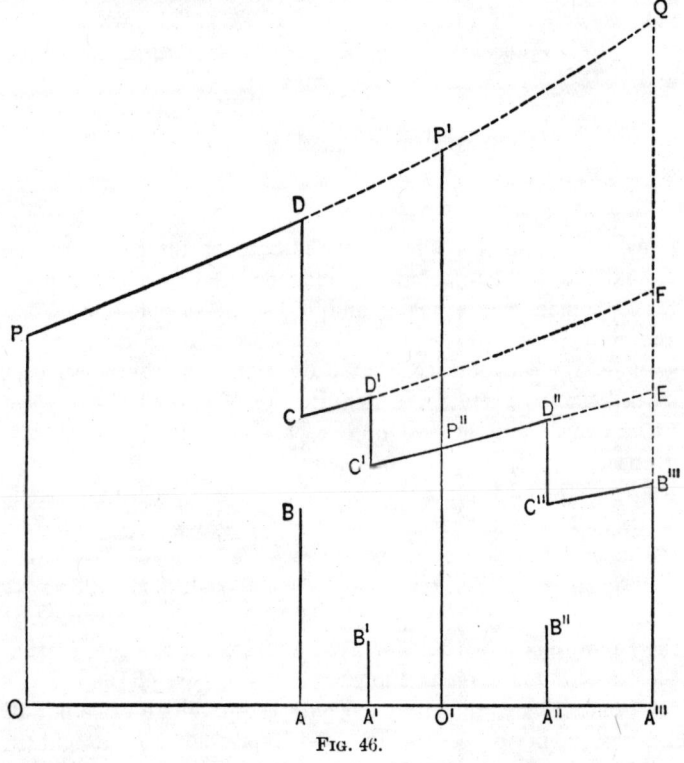

Fig. 46.

This consists of: (1) $A'''B'''$ itself; (2) $B'''E$, which is the amount of $C''D''$ (or its equal, $A''B''$), and is found by continuing the discount curve $C''D''$ to E; (3) EF, which in like manner is the amount of $C'D'$ (or its equal $A'B'$); and (4) FQ, which is the amount of CD (or its equal AB). Thus, while OP represents the price of the stream if paid for in advance, $A'''Q$ represents the price if paid for at the end. By similar reasoning it may be shown that the price at any intermediate point of the entire series is the height of any point on the one smooth curve PQ.

This result must not be confused with that which represents the capital-value of *future* income. Thus, at the point of time O', the line $O'P'$ represents the value of *all* the income items, past as well as future, AB, $A'B'$, $A''B''$, $A'''B'''$, whereas the line $O'P''$ represents the value of only the *future* items $A''B''$ and $A'''B'''$.

§ 14 (to Ch. XIII, § 10)

Effect of reckoning Semi-annually, Quarterly, and Continuously, on the Rate of Interest realized on a Stock or Store of Articles

As usual, the passage from the rate of interest reckoned annually to the rate of interest reckoned continuously, if accurately considered, is not so simple as appears on the surface and may afford to some readers no little perplexity. If we assume, for convenience, that each article in the merchant's stock remains there for a definite period, called the time of "turn-over," and the cost of purchase and all the other costs connected with the article occur at the time it *enters* the stock, while all the receipts or gross income from that article occur at the time that it *leaves* the stock, we may pass from the case of the rate of interest "reckoned annually" to that of the rate of interest "reckoned continuously" as follows: —

As a first step we assume that all of the stock is bought at the beginning of a calendar year and sold at the end, so that the time of turn-over is one year. If the cost of the stock is represented by c, including not only the purchase price but all other elements of cost, this must represent the discounted value of the receipts at the end of the year, which are therefore $c(1+i)$. The net income for the year is, therefore, $c(1+i) - c$, or ci. This bears a ratio to the total cost value reckoned at the beginning of the year, namely c, of $\frac{ci}{c}$, equal to the rate of interest, i.

For the second step we consider the stock as half purchased

on January 1 and half on July 1, six months later, and that, as before, each element of the stock remains one year before sale. The cost on January 1 is $\frac{c}{2}$, and on July 1 is also $\frac{c}{2}$. If we take inventory on July 1, the stock just purchased represents a value $\frac{c}{2}$, while that purchased six months before, and which is to be disposed of in six months more, may be taken as having a somewhat greater value, namely, $\frac{c}{2}\sqrt{1+i}$, the latter being the cost value plus interest, or, what amounts to the same thing, the expected selling value less interest. The total stock is therefore worth on July 1, —

$$\frac{c}{2} + \frac{c}{2}\sqrt{1+i}.$$

The sales or receipts from the stock will evidently be every six months $\frac{c}{2}(1+i)$, this being the accumulated value for one year of the amount purchased, $\frac{c}{2}$. For the entire year the receipts will thus be just double, or $c(1+i)$. If from this we deduct the per annum cost, c, we obtain, as before, the net income, ci. The ratio of this net income to the capital-value taken on January 1 or July 1, of any year, will therefore be, —

$$\frac{ci}{\frac{c}{2} + \frac{c}{2}\sqrt{1+i}}.$$

This expression, which is evidently the same as $\frac{2i}{1+\sqrt{1+i}}$, seems no longer to be equal to the rate of interest; but the discrepancy is due to the fact that the merchant's income accrues *semi-annually*, whereas i is reckoned *annually*. If we substitute for i its value in terms of i', the rate of interest reckoned semi-annually (namely, $i' + \frac{i'^2}{4}$, as shown in the Appendix to Chap. XII, § 2), we shall find, on simplifying, that the above expression reduces to i'. In other words, in the artificially simple case in which the merchant is supposed to accomplish all his buying and selling in two equal amounts and at semi-annual intervals, the ratio of his annual income to his capital, *reckoned at these times*, is i'. In the same manner it may be shown that if his buying and selling take place at quarterly intervals, the ratio of his income to his capital *reckoned at these times* will be i'', *i.e.* the rate of interest per annum reckoned quarterly; and so on indefinitely until we reach the limiting case, approximately true in practice, in which the merchant buys and sells daily, when we find that the annual net income, divided by the value of the capital at any instant, is equal to the rate of interest *reckoned continuously*. It will be observed that to make this proposition hold good it is necessary that the valuation of the merchant's capital shall be, not its wholesale price nor its retail price, but something intermediate, which shall take account of the fact that the stock cannot all be sold immediately, and that, on the other hand, it will not be necessary to wait a year before it is all sold. Similar reasoning may evidently be applied in case the time of turnover of the stock is more or less than a year.

§ 15 (to Ch. XIII, § 11)
Influence of Variability of Rate of Interest

Thus far we have treated the rate of interest in successive years as invariable. As a matter of fact, the rate of interest is constantly fluctuating. We shall suppose at first that these fluctuations are foreknown, and for convenience we shall confine ourselves to a year as the standard interval of time. Let us assume that the rate of interest for the first year is i_1, for the second year, i_2, for the third year, i_3, and so on indefinitely, all of these being supposed to be known in advance. By means of these rates of interest we can calculate the present value of any item or series of items of income. Thus, if $1000 is due in two years and the rate of interest for the first year (i_1) is 5%, while the rate for the second year (i_2) is 3%, we can obtain the present value of the $1000 by discounting it at 3% for one year, thus obtaining $\frac{1000}{1.03}$, or $970.87, as its value a

APPENDIX TO CHAPTER XIII

year previous to the due date, or one year from the present, and rediscounting this 970.87 at 5% for one year, giving $\frac{970.87}{1.05}$, or $924.30, as the present value.

In general, if V represents the item of income to be received, its value in one year will be $\frac{V}{1 + i_2}$ and its present value,

$$\frac{V}{(1 + i_1)(1 + i_2)},$$

which formula is, of course, easily extensible to three or any number of years.

If we represent the future value V in Figure 47 by the line AB, its value in one year is CF, found by the 3% discount

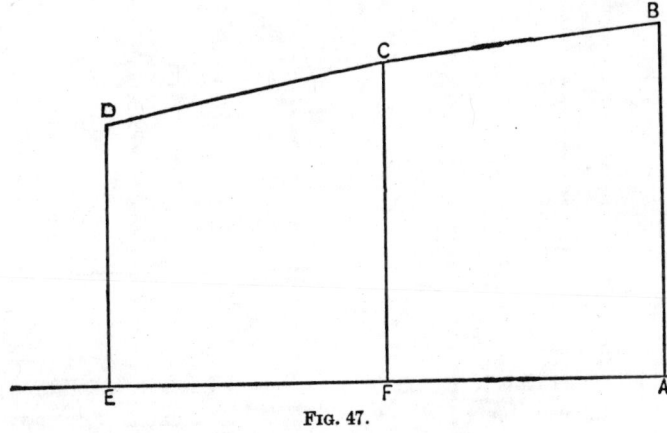

FIG. 47.

curve BC, and its present value is ED, found by the 5% discount curve DC. In other words, instead of having a uniform discount curve from B to D, we have a broken discount curve BCD, with a different percentage rate of rise for the two years considered.

In this way we may obtain the present value of any series of income items precisely as before, with the exception that the discount curves are now somewhat irregular. Thus, if the series of income items at different points of time are of the magnitude represented in Figure 48 by *AB*, *CD*, *EF*, and *GH* (read in the order of futurity), the remotest item, *AB*, is discounted by means of the discount curve *BC*, and the next to the last item is added to the capital-value at *C*, bringing the capital-value to the point *D*, from which the next discount curve *DE* is drawn, and so on until we reach the point *I*. *IJ* is thus the capital-value of the given series of income items.

In this way it is possible to review all the special cases of capitalizing income which were considered in Chapter XIII,

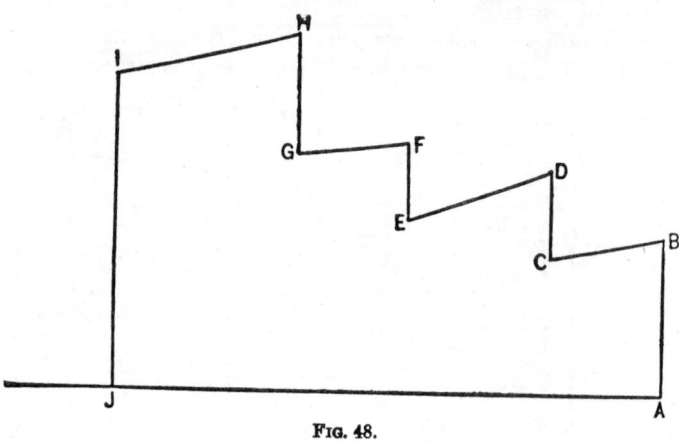

Fig. 48.

and correct them for the general case of a rate of interest which is variable but foreknown. Such a calculation, however, is of very little practical consequence, inasmuch as the variations in the rate of interest are seldom if ever foreknown.

Were it worth while to pursue the subject, it would be convenient to simplify the calculations by substituting, where possible, for the series of rates of interest i_1, i_2, i_3, etc., an average, j, such that if the given series of income items were discounted uniformly according to the rate of interest j, we should obtain exactly the same present value as when the several separate rates i_1, i_2, i_3, etc., are employed. The formula for the average rate of interest j of any particular number of individual rates, as i_1, i_2, i_3, etc., used for discounting individual items of income, a_1, a_2, a_3, would evidently be,

$$\frac{a_1}{1+j} + \frac{a_2}{(1+j)^2} + \frac{a_3}{(1+j)^3} + \cdots =$$

$$\frac{a_1}{1+i} + \frac{a_2}{(1+i_1)(1+i_2)} + \frac{a_3}{(1+i_1)(1+i_2)(1+i_3)} + \cdots$$

Various applications of such formulæ might be made, though they have little practical utility. Thus, the value of a terminable annuity of a given term is found, as before, by taking the difference in value between a perpetual annuity beginning to-day and a perpetual annuity deferred to the end of the given term. The value of the perpetual annuity beginning to-day would be found, as has just been shown, by dividing the annual income a by j_1, the average rate of interest of the individual rates from the present into the indefinite future. The value of the deferred annuity taken at the *end* of the term would be, in like manner, $\dfrac{a}{j_t}$, where j_t is the average of the individual rates from that point indefinitely forward. The present value of this deferred annuity would be found by discounting the latter value for the term of the annuity according to the rate $j_{1,t}$ where $j_{1,t}$ is the average of the individual rates of interest i_1, i_2, i_3, ... i_t for the term of the annuity.

The value of a bond would be found in a similar manner. We have just shown how to find the present value of the "interest" of the bond, and the present value of the "principal," P, due at maturity, would be evidently $\dfrac{P}{(1+j_{1,t})^t}$.

§ 16 (to Ch. XIII, § 11)
Representation of Capital and Income by Polar Coördinates

The mathematical reader may be interested in an alternative method of representing income and capital, by which polar coördinates are employed instead of rectangular. Let the radius vector in Figure 49 represent the parent capital. The time required for a complete revolution of the radius vector may be taken to represent the "purchase period." Thus, if the rate of interest is 4 %, the purchase period is twenty-five years. During one year the radius vector will move through an angle $\frac{1}{25}$ of a

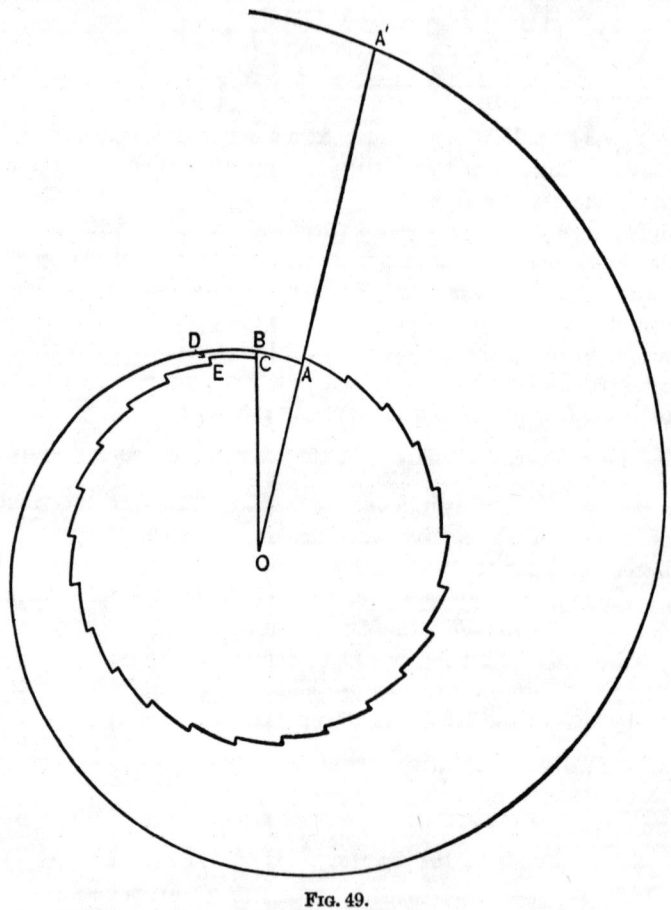

Fig. 49.

complete revolution, and the length of the radius vector will increase from OA to OB by an amount, BC, $\frac{1}{25}$ of the original OA, interest being 4 % reckoned annually. In case the interest BC is not reinvested, but detached from the principal, next

APPENDIX TO CHAPTER XIII 395

year will bring the radius vector to the position OD, at which time the same interest, DE, may be detached, and so on indefinitely, the result being a toothed wheel. Each tooth being $\frac{1}{25}$ of the radius OA, the sum of the twenty-five teeth will be exactly equal to the radius. In case the interest is reckoned semi-annually, the teeth will be fifty in number instead of twenty-five, but each will be half as large; and so on until, for "continuous" reckoning, we have an infinite number of teeth each of infinitesimal size; but the sum of the whole number in the complete revolution will still be exactly equal to OA.

In case no income is received, the accumulation of capital is represented by increasing the length of the radius vector, the end of which thus traces a spiral. The radius vector revolves around the spiral once every twenty-five years, and the ratio between the "amount," OA', after a complete revolution, and the original "principal" OA, will be e, that is, 2.718, provided the rate of interest is reckoned continuously.

The same spiral represents the accumulation of capital, whatever may be the rate of interest. For a complete revolution does not represent a definite length of time, but the purchase period; and it is clear that a more rapid rate of interest is represented by a more rapid turning of the radius vector. Thus, if the rate is not 4%, but 8%, the radius vector swings around through the same spiral once in twelve and a half years instead of once in twenty-five years. Again, if the rate is 2%, the revolution is fifty years. The spiral is what is known as the "equiangular spiral," and has the property that the tangent at any point is inclined at a constant angle to the radius vector. The angle is in this case such that its tangent is 2π. This angle is 80° 57'. The equation of this spiral is $\dfrac{\rho}{\rho_0} = e^{\frac{\theta}{2\pi}}$, in which ρ represents the radius vector, θ the angle of revolution, and ρ_0 the initial radius vector; e and π are, of course, the magnitudes ordinarily represented by these letters, namely, the base of the Napierian system of logarithms and the ratio of the circumference of a circle to its diameter.

APPENDIX TO CHAPTER XIV

§ 1 (to Ch. XIV, § 5)

When the Interest Rate varies, there are Two Rival Concepts of Standard Income.

When the rate of interest *varies* during successive years, the standard of the comparison of income and capital requires restatement. We found, when the rate of interest was assumed *constant*, that the standard income corresponding to a given capital was a perpetual and uniform flow, of which flow that capital was at any time the present value. It did not matter whether standard income was conceived as income which was constant and perpetual, or as income which would maintain its capital-value at a constant level; for under the condition of a constant rate of interest, a constant income will necessarily maintain a constant capital-value. But when we introduce the possibility of a change in the rate of interest, these two concepts of standard income are no longer equivalent; under such conditions only an inconstant income will maintain a constant capital-value. Thus, if the rate of interest for the first year is 10%, for the second, 5%, and for the third, 6%, etc., the income stream which will maintain the capital unimpaired will be, in successive years, proportional to the numbers 10, 5, 6, etc. A person possessed of $100 of capital can evidently earn with it $10 the first year and still have his $100 unimpaired, with which, in turn, he can earn $5 the second year and maintain the principal of $100; and again $6 in the third year, and so on, receiving each year an income proportional to the rate of interest. Relatively to this income stream considered as a standard of reference, the propositions stated in Chapter XIII will remain true, namely, that if the real income in any year exceeds the standard for that year, the capital will be impaired by the excess; and if the income falls short of the standard in any year, the capital will accumulate by the amount of the deficiency.

But this concept of standard income is not the only legitimate one. We may, if we choose, employ the other definition of standard income, as a perpetual and uniform flow. In this that the fall or other change in the rate of interest can never be foreseen with precision, and thus a perfectly uniform flow of income secured, whereas it is always possible, in the case of safe investments, to calculate what is necessary to maintain the value of the capital at a uniform level.

§ 2 (to Ch. XIV, § 12)
Effect of Foreknown Tax on Increase of Capital

Let us suppose that the three brothers invest in their respective annuities without realizing that a tax is to be imposed. The first brother has bought with his $10,000 a perpetual annuity of $500 a year; the second, a perpetual annuity of $1000 deferred 15 years; and the third, an annuity of $2000 for six years only. After these investments have been made, let us suppose that the tax of 10% on income is announced. If "income" is interpreted properly, *i.e.* as simply the annuities, the value of each of the three properties will immediately shrink by $1000, so that any of the three brothers could sell his annuity, subject to the tax, for $9000. But if the "income tax" is interpreted as a tax on "earnings," *i.e.* on income *and increase of capital*, the announcement of such a tax will not only reduce the values of the three properties very unequally, as has been shown, but will have the further effect of altering the very annual increase in the value of the capital which is subject to taxation. To show the effect of this "repercussion," let c represent the value of the capital of the second brother (who saves) at the end of any year during which no (true) income is received. Thus c is $18,000 at the end of the fifteenth year when the annuity of $1000 a year is purchased; for the capitalization of the perpetuity of $1000 which begins at that time is $20,000, from which $2000 is deducted as the capitalized tax. Let i represent the rate of interest (as 5%) and t the tax rate (as 10%). We wish first to find x, the capital-value *one year earlier* than c. It is clear that x is the discounted value of c $\left(i.e.\ \dfrac{c}{1+i}\right)$ *less* the discounted value of the tax, which we will suppose is due at the end of the year. The tax is laid on the increase of capital-value in the year, *i.e.* on case, it is the capital-value of such an income stream which will vary from time to time. As has been seen, the capital-value of such an income stream is found by dividing the rate of income a by the average of the individual rates of interest, such as, in the above example, 10%, 5%, 6%, etc., ad inf., the average being obtained by the formula given in Appendix to Chap. XII, § 5. If such average rate of interest be called j_1, the capital-value will be $\frac{a}{j_1}$. Suppose, for instance, that the person has a uniform perpetual income of $5 per annum. If the rate of interest to-day, j_1, is 5%, the capital-value to-day will be $100. If next year, j_2 (the average of the future rates in individual years, beginning at that time) is 4.9%, the capital-value will be $102. If, two years from date, j_3 be 5.1%, the capital-value will sink to $98. Adopting such an income stream as a standard, the propositions as to impairment or increase will still be true, provided such impairment or increase is measured with reference to the *variable* capital-value just shown. Thus, if at the end of the first year more income than $5 is received, the capital-value will be impaired by the difference, this impairment to be reckoned with respect, not to $100, but to $102, which would be the value had the income remained standard.

Thus, the effect of a difference between real and standard income may be stated in the same terms, whichever of the two definitions of standard income is adopted. In the one case the standard is with reference to constant capital and variable income; in the other, to variable capital and constant income. In practical life, the former standard is usually employed although for certain purposes the latter would be more suitable We all know of cases of investors who, twenty years ago, i1 vested at a high rate of interest, and who have taken pai1 merely to maintain the value of their capital unimpaire although they were well aware that the rate of interest w constantly sinking. In consequence, these persons are n forced, when reinvesting, to suffer a large decrease in inco1 which could have been avoided had they kept in view the m tenance, not of their capital, but of their income, and laid a each year a certain sum in order to offset the fall in the ra interest. The reason such a procedure is not commo

$c-x$. As the rate is t, the tax is $(c-x)t$. The discounted value of this tax is $\frac{(c-x)t}{1+i}$. This deducted from the discounted value, $\frac{c}{1+i}$, of next year's capital-value is this year's capital-value, x; i.e., —
$$x = \frac{c}{1+i} - \frac{(c-x)t}{1+i}.$$
Solving for x, we have, $x = \frac{c(1-t)}{1-t+i}$.

The tax itself is $t(c-x)$, which, if we substitute for x its value just found, reduces to $\frac{cit}{1-t+i}$.

If we substitute for i and t their assumed values, .05 and .10, we have $x = c \times .947$
and $\text{tax} = c \times .0053$.

Substituting for c its value at the end of the fifteenth year, namely, $18,000, we find that x, the value one year earlier, will be $18,000 \times .957$, or $17,046, and that the value one year previous will be the latter sum multiplied likewise by .947, or $16,142.56, and so on until the present is reached, when the value will be $7,952.15. The table below will show, therefore, the total effect of a 10% tax on the increase of value,

	Capital-Value	Increase of Capital-Value	10% Tax Thereon
Beginning	$ 7,952.15	....	....
End of 1 year	8,397.20	$445.05	$44.51
End of 2 years	8,867.27	470.07	47.01
End of 3 years	9,363.54	496.27	49.63
End of 4 years	9,887.58	524.04	52.40
End of 5 years	10,440.95	553.37	55.34
End of 6 years	11,025.29	584.34	58.43
End of 7 years	11,642.33	617.04	61.70
End of 8 years	12,293.91	651.58	65.16
End of 9 years	12,982.06	688.15	68.82
End of 10 years	13,708.62	726.56	72.66
End of 11 years	14,475.84	767.22	76.72
End of 12 years	15,286.00	810.16	81.02
End of 13 years	16,142.56	856.56	85.66
End of 14 years	17,046.00	903.44	90.34
End of 15 years	18,000.00	954.00	95.40

including the "repercussion" of the tax on the capital-values themselves.

The taxes in the table evidently differ somewhat from the taxes given in the text, which do not include the effect of "repercussion." The present value, therefore, of this tax on the increase of capital should be altered from $714 to $661.81. A similar correction should be made for the case of the spendthrift. Our main object, however, is not to study the effects of different methods of levying taxes, but merely to show how untenable is the theory which includes savings under income, and excludes that part of true income or services which brings about a depreciation of capital.

§ 3 (to Ch. XIV, § 13)

Unrestricted Application of a True Income Tax Impracticable

Theoretically, an income tax should tax every element of income, large or small, positive or negative. That is, all positive items should have a tax and all negative items a bounty. This system would be ideal in theory but difficult to carry out in practice.

No attempt is made in this book to contrive a practical system of taxation which would avoid all the difficulties which have been pointed out as belonging to systems now in use. It is undoubtedly true that it would be impracticable to assess taxes on each article on the basis of the actual items of income it yields; for most of such items are simply the positive sides of "interactions" and are offset as outgoes in the accounts of some other article of capital. To carry out such a system in detail would require that we levy taxes on the proceeds of every sale and remit them on every investment. It would be difficult to avoid injustice, evasion, and fraud if the attempt were made to assess taxes on such income and remit, as would be required logically, taxes on the corresponding outgo. The taxpayer would contrive to exaggerate his outgo and understate his income. Consequently, the system is not wholly unjust which exempts from taxation that part of income which stands for impairment of capital, and assesses taxes on that part which swells capital, or savings. The system would be entirely just if the impairment of one capital were always offset by the equal increase of some other capital, *i.e.* if the taxpayer's total capital-value were kept at the same level. In general, large receipts are usually reinvested and should therefore not be subject to the income tax at all. If we could assume such reinvestment to be the invariable rule, we could approve of the system by which, in England, a terminable annuity is not taxed as income at its full value, but is taxed only on that part of it which constitutes "interest." The other part, which constitutes impairment of principal, is not taxed. The system, of course, fails of justice in cases where this impairment of principal is never restored in some other form of investment but ultimately represents, like the other part of the annuity, through personal expenditure, final enjoyable income.

To illustrate the English exemption of impairment of capital, if $1000 is paid for a five-year annuity on a basis of 4% interest (reckoned semi-annually), it will purchase an annuity of $111.33 at the end of each six months, and the following will be the schedule showing the capital-value at each interval, the interest accruing upon it, the payment to the beneficiary, and the impairment of capital resulting.[1]

	Capital at Beginning	Interest Accrued at End	Total Payments at End	Impairment of Capital	Capital Left at End
1st half year	$1000.00	$20.00	$111.33	$91.33	$908.67
2d half year	908.67	18.17	111.33	93.15	815.52
3d half year	815.52	16.31	111.33	95.02	720.50
4th half year	720.50	14.41	111.33	96.92	623.59
5th half year	623.59	12.47	111.33	98.86	524.73
6th half year	524.73	10.50	111.33	100.83	423.90
7th half year	423.90	8.48	111.33	102.85	321.05
8th half year	321.05	6.42	111.33	104.91	216.15
9th half year	216.15	4.32	111.33	107.00	109.14
10th half year	109.14	2.18	111.33	109.14	000.00
			$1000.00		

If at the start he has a capital of $1000, at the end of the

[1] From *Institute of Actuaries' Text-book*, Part I, "Interest," by Ralph Todhunter, p. 57. London (Layton), 1901.

first half year, there is left $908.67, which has impaired his capital by $91.33. This being reinvested and yielding interest, would make a total combined fund of $1000 as before. At the end of the second half year, in like manner, the original security is worth $815.52, but to this must be added the capital invested last year, $91.33, and also the investment this year, $93.15, making a total again of $1000; and so on for each year.

If, then, as in England, the tax is paid on the interest annually (second column), no injustice is done, *providing the items in the fourth column are actually reinvested each year*, and that the interest on such reinvestment in some other form is used as income. In other words, each reinvestment is not accumulated at compound interest, but made a separate fund yielding perpetual interest which is converted into enjoyable income as fast as it is received. In this case the man will be receiving, from the given security and the others created out of his reinvestments, a uniform net income of $20 a year, and will maintain his capital at $1000. Consequently the exemption of "impairment of capital" works no ultimate injustice, since ultimately there is no such impairment.

But as, practically, we can never know to what extent the "impairments" are actually reinvested, the justification of taxing the sums in the first column instead of those in the third is entirely on grounds of expediency. Theoretically, the actual income from this particular form of capital as represented in the third column should be taxed, and afterward whatever is reinvested in some other form should earn remission of taxes. This method, while impracticable in such detailed application, might with advantage be applied to the taxation of an individual's income as a whole. After all the individual components are combined—all the income elements, large or small, and all the outgo elements, including reinvestments—there will be a resultant net income for the individual which, and which alone, should be taxed. A system which would accomplish this would tax, to this individual, any *net* impairment of his capital, for such impairment would mean large income; but, on the other hand, if he were not depleting but laying up capital, it would exempt the increase, for such increase would not be part of his income. Such a system would secure justice in the taxation of income. It is practically what has usually been called the system of taxing "consumption."

APPENDIX TO CHAPTER XVI

§ 1 (TO CH. XVI, § 6)

Mathematical Coefficients of Probability, Caution, and Risk

Let us call the riskless value V, the mathematical value V', the commercial value V'', the coefficient of probability P, the coefficient of caution C, and the entire coefficient of risk R. We have, —

$$P = \frac{V'}{V}, \qquad C = \frac{V''}{V'}, \qquad R = \frac{V''}{V}.$$

Whence it follows that $R = PC$.

That is, the total effect of risk on value is twofold: first, through mere *probability*, which gives mathematical value; and secondly, through *caution*, which gives commercial value. Practically, it is usually impossible to separate P and C. The object of this analysis is not so much to introduce the caution factor explicitly, as to make the general distinction between R and P, and to point out that the actual market value of securities is not their actuarial or simple "mathematical" value; that, in other words, R is not the same thing as P.

§ 2 (TO CH. XVI, § 7)

Formula for Mathematical Value of Risky Bond

Let us denote by p_1 the probability of receiving the first installment, a_1, of income due in one year, and by p_2 the probability of receiving the second installment of income, a_2, *provided the first year's is received*, and again by p_3 the probability of receiving a_3 in three years, *provided the previous two have been received*, and so on for $p_4 \ldots p_n$, where n is the number of years to the last payment. The chance of receiving the first payment is p_1; hence the "mathematical value" of the first payment, when due, is $a_1 p_1$, the present value of which is $\frac{a_1 p_1}{1+i}$. But the chance of receiving the second payment is evidently not p_2, but $p_1 p_2$; for one of the first principles of the theory of probabilities is that the chance of two successive events is the product of their successive probabilities. Thus, if the chance of heads appearing in coin tossing is $\tfrac{1}{2}$, the chance of two successive heads is $\tfrac{1}{2} \times \tfrac{1}{2}$, or $\tfrac{1}{4}$, and the chance of three successive heads is, in like manner, $\tfrac{1}{2} \times \tfrac{1}{2} \times \tfrac{1}{2}$, or $\tfrac{1}{8}$, etc. Hence the "mathematical value" of the second installment, a_2, when due is $a_2 p_1 p_2$, of which the present value is $\dfrac{a_2 p_1 p_2}{(1+i)^2}$. In like manner, the mathematical present value of the third installment is $\dfrac{a_3 p_1 p_2 p_3}{(1+i)^3}$, and so on. The sum of the expressions for present value thus obtained is the total present mathematical value of the property. If we denote this mathematical value by V_m, we have, —

$$V_m = \frac{a_1 p_1}{1+i} + \frac{a_2 p_1 p_2}{(1+i)^2} + \frac{a_3 p_1 p_2 p_3}{(1+i)^3} + \cdots + \frac{a_n p_1 p_2 p_3 \cdots p_n}{(1+i)^n}.$$

If we suppose that all the probabilities are equal, we may denote all the p's simply by p, and simplify by substituting p^2 for $p_1 p_2$, and p^3 for $p_1 p_2 p_3$, etc.

Since the p's represent the probability of receiving the installments, it is clear that the chance or risk of not receiving them is the difference between this and unity. This risk of default we shall denote by the letter q. Thus, $q_1 = 1 - p_1$, etc., and also $p_1 = 1 - q_1$, etc. If all the q's are equal, we shall denote them by q, and the present value of the property may then evidently be written, —

$$V_m = \frac{a_1(1-q)}{1+i} + \frac{a_2(1-q)^2}{(1+i)^2} + \frac{a_3(1-q)^3}{(1+i)^3} + \cdots + \frac{a_n(1-q)^n}{(1+i)^n}.$$

In case the risk of default q is very small, it is evident that the fraction $\dfrac{1-q}{1+i}$ is approximately equal to $\dfrac{1}{1+i+q}$. This may be seen by dividing the numerator and denominator of the first fraction by $1-q$, which will give for the new numerator unity, and for the denominator $1 + i + q + \dfrac{q^2 + iq}{1-q}$. In this expression the fractional term becomes negligible when q is small, because the denominator, $1-q$, is approximately unity, while the numerator, $q^2 + iq$, is made up of two terms, each of which is the product of two very small quantities. Thus, if q is $\frac{1}{100}$ and i is $\frac{4}{100}$, the value of the fractional term becomes approximately .0005, which is a negligible quantity (compared with $1 + i + q = 1 + .04 + .01$). Hence when q is small, the formula for mathematical value becomes approximately, —

$$V_m = \frac{a}{1+i+q} + \frac{a_2}{(1+i+q)^2} + \frac{a_3}{(1+i+q)^3} + \cdots + \frac{a_n}{(1+i+q)^n}.$$

In other words, when the risk of default is small, its effect is substantially the same as that which follows from a rise in the rate of interest. If the rate of interest when risk is absent is 4%, a risk of 1% will therefore merely increase the "basis" on which the loan can be contracted to about 5%. Thus, if we recur to the so-called 5% ten-year bond, and suppose that the probability of each successive payment is $\frac{99}{100}$, and the risk of default, q, is $\frac{1}{100}$, then the mathematical present value of the bond, when interest is 4%, is approximately, —

$$V_m = \frac{a_1}{1+i+q} + \frac{a_2}{(1+i+q)^2} + \frac{a_3}{(1+i+q)^3} +, \text{etc.},$$
$$= \frac{5}{1.05} + \frac{5}{(1.05)^2} + \frac{5}{(1.05)^3} +, \text{etc.}$$

In other words, the present value is approximately the same as the present value of a 5% bond on a 5% basis, which is of course par, or 100.

But if the risk is great, the approximate formula given will no longer apply. Thus, if the chance of default is $\frac{9}{10}$, or, in other words, if the chance of payment is only $\frac{1}{10}$, the formula for the mathematical value of the property becomes, —

$$V_m = \frac{a_1(\frac{1}{10})}{1+i} + \frac{a_2(\frac{1}{10})^2}{(1+i)^2} + \frac{a_3(\frac{1}{10})^3}{(1+i)^3} +, \text{etc.}$$

In this case it is evident that all terms after the first are negligible compared with the first (unless the successive items a_2, a_3, etc., increase with sufficient rapidity to offset the decreasing fractions $\frac{1}{100}$, $\frac{1}{1000}$, etc.). In the case of a 5% ten-year $100 bond, in which the risk of default is at any moment $\frac{9}{10}$, the approximate value of the bond, obtained by omitting all terms after the first, would be $\frac{5(\frac{1}{10})}{1.04}$, or approximately 50 cents! This "mathematical value" might be still further reduced by a coefficient of caution. In other words, the bond is worthless. In case of such high risk we cannot, therefore, apply the simple rule of adding to the rate of interest the rate of risk to obtain the "mathematical value"; and the "commercial value" would, of course, be even less than the mathematical value. In other words, it is practically impossible to compensate for a risky investment by increasing the rate of interest as though it were an insurance premium. In actual practice such a "bond" would be absolutely worthless; for, while the above calculations are correct on the basis of a chance of payment of one in ten, practically this chance of payment would be zero. The high risk not only makes the terms of the loan onerous, but these onerous terms make the uncertainty of repayment greater, and so on in a vicious circle. A lender who fancies he can offset a risk as high as $\frac{9}{10}$ by lending only 50 cents instead of $100 for a returnable principal of $100 will find that he has not offset that risk, but merely increased it.

In the previous calculations, we assumed that a default in one payment carried with it a default in all subsequent payments. We may, however, easily extend our formula to the general case by designating the chances of payment in successive years, whether interdependent or not, by p_1 for the first year, p_2 for the second (instead of by $p_1 p_2$ as before), p_3 for the third, etc., and changing the first equation on page 404 accordingly.

§ 3 (to Ch. XVI, § 10)

Variability about a Mean, as measured by the "Standard Deviation"

For a more minute analysis of the bearing of chance it is preferable to measure the variability with reference to the *mean*. Thus, in the case mentioned, where the dividends are successively 5%, 5%, 6%, 5%, 5%, 4%, 5%, 7%, 5%, 3%, 4%, 5%, instead of measuring the variability of dividends with reference to 5%, we should measure it with reference to the *mean* rate, which is 4.9%. The deviations from this mean during the twelve successive years were therefore: $+0.1$, $+0.1$, $+1.1$, $+0.1$, $+0.1$, -0.9, $+0.1$, $+2.1$, $+0.1$, -1.9, -0.9, $+0.1$.

APPENDIX TO CHAPTER XVI

A simple measure of the extent of variability displayed by such a series of deviations from the mean is what is called the "standard deviation." This is a sort of average of the deviations—not the ordinary arithmetical mean, but the mean found by taking the arithmetical mean of the *squares* of the deviations and extracting the square root. The standard deviation which represents the above twelve individual deviations is thus, —

$$\sqrt{\frac{(.1)^2+(.1)^2+(1.1)^2+(.1)^2+(.1)^2+(-.9)^2+(.1)^2+(2.1)^2+(.1)^2+(-1.9)^2+(-.9)^2+(.1)^2}{12}}$$

which is .95.

This "standard deviation" is used instead of other averages for several reasons. The arithmetical mean of the deviations about the mean is quite unavailable, because, unless it be reckoned by disregarding all minus signs (in which case the result is an illogical makeshift), it is zero; the standard deviation is very readily calculated, not by performing the operations indicated above, but by recourse to a theorem that the mean of the squares of the deviations about the mean is equal to the mean of the squares of the deviations about *any other* magnitude less the square of the difference between the mean and this other magnitude. The proof of this theorem is simple, and may be found in the books on probability. Applying it to the illustrated case, we first take the deviations, not about the mean, but about some other magnitude, say 5%. These deviations are 0, 0, 1, 0, 0, −1, 0, 2, 0, −2, −1, 0. The squares of these are 0, 0, 1, 0, 0, 1, 0, 4, 0, 4, 1, 0, of which the arithmetical mean is $\frac{11}{12}$, or .902. This is the mean of the squares of the deviations *about the magnitude* 5. From this we are to deduct the square of the difference between the mean 4.9 and the other magnitude 5, about which the deviations were measured. The difference is .1, its square is .01. Deducting this from .902 we have .892 as the mean of the squares of the deviations *about the mean*. The square root of this is .95, which is therefore the standard deviation sought. Calculated by this method the standard deviation may usually be obtained in less than one tenth the time required by the direct method.

The "standard deviation" plays an important rôle in the treatment of all statistics involving variation about a mean. One of its simplest uses is to change any given deviation into a deviation relative to the standard deviation (or to a fixed portion of it). This is usually done by dividing the absolute deviation by the standard deviation. Thus, in the above example, where the standard deviation is .95 %, an absolute deviation of, say, 2 % mean is a relative deviation of 2 ÷ .95 or about 2.1.

Such a reduction from absolute to relative deviation brings the different probability distributions or curves into a common comparison, so that probability tables may be constructed applicable to all. In one case the deviations may mean inches of rainfall, in another, pounds of barometric pressure, in another, the annual percentage of dividends, as in the case above. These are incommeasurable. But if each be compared with the standard deviation which applies to that particular case, and which would therefore be measured in inches, pounds, or annual percentages, respectively, we obtain three ratios which are simply pure numbers indicating the extent of the deviation compared with the standard deviation.

If we now consult a probability table we may find at once what is the probability of any given relative deviation. For the chance that dividends will, in the case supposed, deviate in any given future year by 2 % from the mean rate of 4.9 % is, from the tables, 1 in 20; for the deviation, measured relatively, is, we saw, the number 2.1 and the probability corresponding to this in the tables [1] is $\frac{19}{20}$. This expresses the chance that the deviation will keep inside the limits of 2 %; *i.e.* that the dividends will be between 2.9 % and 6.9 %.

The wider the range of deviation considered, the less the chance that the actual dividends in any year will fall outside that range. Moreover, the chance decreases *far faster* than the range increases. This relation, which follows from the theory of probability, has very important consequences in

[1] Thus on p. 55 of Davenport's "Statistical Methods," New York, Wiley, 1899, we find for a relative deviation 2.1, the number .4822 as the chance of the deviation in *one* direction. Hence the chance of the deviation in *either* direction is double this or .9644, about $\frac{19}{20}$.

the theory of distribution. From it follows as a corollary that the richer an individual, the less risk in *taking* risks. Being possessed of capital, he has a wider range within which he can safely afford to operate, and therefore he has a far greater probability of keeping within these limits of safety than his less fortunate competitors. Professor Norton has also emphasized the fact that the advantage of the capitalist is further enhanced by the tendency toward monopoly. "The result is a most interesting circle, constant combination at the top in order to force down the commercial price of the risk, and monopoly of the upper field, which pays tremendous profits, resulting in still greater increase in the financial power of the risk takers. To this there is no end, save in the divorce, through heredity, of ability and financial power." [1]

An important application of these methods is to the calculation of the chance that earnings should fall below the amount required to pay interest on bonds. This chance is found from the probability table. It is the probability corresponding to that relative deviation obtained by dividing the difference between the *mean* expected earnings and the interest by two thirds of the standard deviation. In this and other ways business men could, as Professor Norton has shown, make better use of their past experience than they do. Merely to glance over past earnings and receive an impression is not a very scientific mode of utilizing the facts which those earnings display. To average them is not of much more value. While it is important to know the mean, it is also important to know the dispersion about the mean. This dispersion is shown by the standard deviation. The best procedure would therefore seem to be to calculate first the mean of past experience as to earnings; secondly, the standard deviation from that mean; thirdly, the chances of fluctuations thus displayed (*e.g.* the chance of earnings falling below the interest-paying line); and, fourthly, to correct the results thus obtained by taking into account the degree in which it is believed that the future will not follow in the footsteps of the past. Only the last of these four

[1] From a letter to the author. Cf. also Professor Norton's "Theory of Loan Credit," *Publications of the American Economic Association*, 1904, p. 54.

operations need be done by rule of thumb. But at present all but the first and often even that are left to the merest impression.

There was a time when business men did not use bond tables, when they did not calculate cost sheets, and even when life insurance was contracted for in scornful disregard of any mortality tables. Just as these slipshod methods have been displaced by the work of expert accountants and actuaries, so should the mere guessing about future income conditions be replaced by making use of the modern statistical applications of probability.[1]

§ 4 (TO CH. XVI, § 20)

Method of computing a Pure Level Life Insurance Premium

The chief peculiarity of life insurance is that each year's premiums, in properly organized insurance companies, are calculated not on the basis of the chance of death in that year, as in the case of fire insurance, but are computed as "level premiums," which exceed this chance in the early years of the policy, and fall short of it in later years. The wisdom of such an arrangement is justified by the incentive which is produced for all "risks" to remain insured, whereas when the "natural" premium only is charged, increasing with age, there is a tendency for the better risks to withdraw, making thereby a "selection" adverse to the companies. A consequence of a "level" premium being charged is that the policy acquires an increasing mathematical value with time, so that the policy holder, after a few years, sometimes possesses a very valuable property, which he can, if he chooses, sell or use as collateral security for loans, etc. The value of such a policy, computed on the mathematical basis, is of

---

[1] Cf. "The Put and Call," by L. R. Higgins, London, 1902, pp. 65, 66. For some suggestions along this line, see Edgeworth, "Mathematical Theory of Banking," *Jour. Roy. Statis. Soc.*, March, 1888; for a statement of the modern statistical method, see Karl Pearson, *Grammar of Science*, and his journal "Biometrica"; for an application of this method to financial and industrial problems, see J. P. Norton, *Statistical Studies in the New York Money Market*, New Haven (Tuttle, Morehouse & Taylor), 1903.

APPENDIX TO CHAPTER XVI 411

course the present value of the chance of receiving the insurance, less the present value of the chance of paying the premiums. Thus, for a man aged 30, who was insured 10 years before, the chance of his death at the age of 35 will be about $\frac{732}{84720}$, or .86%, since of 84,720 living at age 30, about 732 die in their 36th year. Hence the present value of the chance of receiving his insurance of $1000 in that particular year is $\frac{1000\ (.0086)}{(1.04)^5}$, or $7.07, assuming the rate of interest to be 4%. In like manner we may determine the present value of the similar chance for every other year of possible life, and the sum total of these present values will be the total present value of the chance of receiving the insurance, $287.66. From this must be deducted the present value of the chance that he will pay premiums. Thus, the chance of his paying the premium in the above-named year, when he is 35 years of age, will be the chance that he will be living at that time, which is .958. This multiplied by his premium and discounted gives the present value of this possible premium payment; this added to the like sums for every other year will give the total present value of his obligation to pay premiums, $222.86; this, in turn, subtracted from the present value of the prospective insurance just obtained, namely $287.66, will give the present mathematical value of his property, $64.80, called the value of his insurance, or the "reserve" on his policy.

The true "commercial value," or the value which he is willing to pay, will be somewhat higher. For, in this case, the coefficient of caution operates to increase, not to diminish, the value of the property, as insurance tends, not to make a risk, but to reduce it.

The calculation of mathematical values of life insurance has been very perfectly worked out. The reader who is interested will find the most complete explanations in the *Institute of Actuaries' Text-book*, 2 vols., London (Layton), 1901.

INDEX

A

Accounting, philosophical basis of, 129, 140. *See* Capital accounts *and* Income accounts.
Accumulation of interest: not income, but increase of capital, 134-135, 224; results of, 224-226.
Adornment, services of, 165.
Agio sense of rate of interest, 195, 247, 334. *See* Premium concept.
Agriculture amenable to prediction, 291.
Amortization, definition of, 110, 332. *See* Depreciation fund.
Amount of a sum, definition of, 203, 329.
Amusement, services of, 165.
Annuity, regarded as income, 111; concept of interest based on perpetual, 191-194, on terminable, 194-195; capital-value of perpetual, 205-208; "deferred," 207; examples of perpetual, 208-209; capital-value of terminable, 209-210; examples of terminable, 210-211; the perpetual, taken as the standard income, 236-237; sinking fund based on difference between income and ideal terminable, 243-244; depreciation fund based on difference between actual income and ideal perpetual, 243-244; mathematical formula for present value of perpetual, 369; formulæ and diagrams of capital-value of, payable annually, semi-annually, etc., 369-371; formulæ for capital-value of terminable, 374-378; taxation of terminable, in England, 401.
Appraisal of labor, 172.

Appraisal of wealth, methods used in, 11-12, 34-36; based on future worth, 204-205.
Appraised price, 13; a source of inaccuracy in measurement of wealth, 16-17; discrepancies between, and actual selling price (of shares in stock company), 70-72.
Apprenticeship considered as an investment, 169-170.
Area method of representing income, 207-208, 371-374.
Assets, definition of, 67-68, 329; discrepancies in valuation of, 71-72; effect of increase or decrease in value of, 73-74; fraudulent methods of swelling, 74; relation of stability of, to capital-balance necessary for safety of a business, 81; cash, quick, and slow, 82; true value of liabilities derived from, 84-85, 139; items of, to be included in capital and income accounts, 139-140; methods employed for obtaining valuation of bank (discount paper, short-time loans), 194-195, 198-199, 204; effect of chance element on value of, 287-288; figures of, of life insurance companies, 295.
Assignment, settlement of bankruptcy by, 86.
Austria, taxation of forest lands in, 254.

B

Balances, method of: in summing capital or income accounts, 90-91, 142-143, 183, 335; taxation by, 97-98; contrasted with method of couples in income summation, 157-158.
Balance sheet, definition of, 329.

414 INDEX

Balance sheets, to show accumulation of surplus, 69; effect on, of increase or decrease in value of assets, 73–75; interdependence of, of different firms or companies, 87–92; to show methods of balances and couples, 91; to show distinction between accounting of real and of fictitious persons, 93–94; prospects of businesses shown by, 264.
Bank deposit rights, wealth underlying, 27.
Bank notes, wealth underlying, 27; nature of property right in, 32, 280; legal regulations governing, to avoid risk, 289.
Bank reserves, risk-meeting function of, 290.
Bankruptcies, communication of, 87–88.
Bankruptcy, state of, 82; laws relating to, 83; bondholders' and stockholders' position in case of, 83–86; settlement of, 86; relation of general crisis to individual, 297.
Banks, national: liability of stockholders in, 83; investments of, in government bonds, 280–281.
Basis of a security, definition of, 329.
Bemis, Edward W., cited, 39.
Bequests not counted as income, 109.
Bernoulli's Theorem, 267, 275.
Bills of exchange, 204–205.
Böhm-Bawerk, quoted on attempts to define "capital," 53–54; concept of capital of, 56; cited, 60 n.[3]; statement that interest is not an element in cost of production, 173–174; cited in connection with productivity theory, 187; concept of interest of, 195, 247; on interactions as preparatory to enjoyable services, 318.
Bondholders, nature of rights of, 31–32, 85; distinction between stockholders and, 85, 288–289; position of, in reorganization after bankruptcy, 85–86; relation of, to risks of enterprises, 289.
Bonds, wealth underlying property in, 25, 26; nature of rights of holder, 31–32, 85; capital-value of, 211–217, 382; realized vs. earned income of, 231–236; application of depreciation fund to, 242–243; as investments, 277–281; formulæ for computing value of, 378–382; formula for mathematical value of risky, 403–406.
Bond value books, 213–215.
Bougand, quoted, 168 n.
Branford, Victor, cited, 63 n.
Building and loan association, income accounts of, 127–128.
Bullock, C. J., definition of income by, 349–350.

C

Call, option known as a, 298.
Campbell, A. C., cited on moral effects of insurance, 295 n.
Canard, human beings counted as wealth by, 5 n.[2].
Cannan, Edwin, definition of wealth by, 3; cited on definition of capital, 56, n.[1]; cited in connection with wage fund theory, 59; use of term "capital" by, 60 and n.[7]; on concept of income, 102 n.[3]; savings regarded as income by, 108; concept of income of, 116; on distinction between rent and interest, 186 n.[2]; confusion of earned with realized income by, 247–248.
Capital, concept of, as stock of wealth at an instant of time, 51–52, 324; varying views of, 53–57; relation of labor to, 55; viewed as productive, 56; fancied distinction between land and, 56 n.[1]; errors resulting from narrow interpretations of, 57–58; relation of author's definition to established usage, 60–61; dictionary definitions of, 61–62; business men's view of, 63–65; two senses of, called capital-goods and capital-value, 66–67; relation of surplus or undivided profits to, 68–70; original and net, 69, 330; bookkeeper's vs. market's estimate of, 70–72; four separate meanings of term applied to person or firm, 72; classification of, 72; nominal and paid-up, 72, 330; payment

INDEX

of dividends out of, 75, 256; of "real" person and of "fictitious" person, 92-93; relation of credit to, 96; fallacious statistics of, 98; confusion of income and, 105-112, 114-115, 351; fallacy of adding to income savings of, 108, 134-135, 247-255, 349, 353; income need not leave unimpaired, 110-111; outgo is not, 124; analogous to and correlative with income, 184; physical productivity and value productivity of, 185, 186; physical return and value return of, 185, 186; mistake of distinguishing between land and, 186-187; fundamental principle of value of (value of future income), 188; increase of, equals excess of earnings over income, 237-238; relation between amount of, and risk involved, 277, 408-409; reserves of, held to avoid risk, 290; representation of income and, by polar coördinates, 393-395; effect of foreknown tax on increase of, 398-400; taxation of impairment of, 400-403.
Capital accounts, definition of, 67, 89; methods of balances and couples in summing up, 90-92; relation between income accounts and, 139, 256-264.
Capital balance, 81, 329.
Capital cost, 124-125.
Capital curves, 303-322, 369-378.
Capital-goods, meaning of term, 67, 329; classification of, 72.
Capital instruments, 66-67, 72, 329; regulation of income by combining, 127-129, 245-246.
Capitalization, definition of, 64, 330; rate of, 194; employment of rate of, as alternative to rate of interest, 199; table showing equivalent rates of interest, discount, and, 200; of income by means of rate of interest,202; dimensions of rates of discount, interest, and, 367-368.
Capitalize, use of term, 64, 330.
Capital property, 67, 72, 330.
Capital-value, 67, 72, 327, 330; determination of, from rate of interest, 202; of perpetual annuity, 205-208, 369; of terminable annuity, 209-210, 374-378; risk element in determining, 210; of a bond, 211-217, 382; of any income stream, 217-221, 387-388; of alternative income streams, 221-222; of group of articles, 223; is the discounted value of expected income, 223-224, 304-305; less than total expected income, 227-228; effect of change of interest rate on, 229, 271-273, 390-393; enumeration of causes affecting, 284-285; as mean between past cost and future income, 305-309; formula for, of sum due in one year, and of sum due at any time, 368.
Capital-wealth. See Capital goods.
Carver, cited, 117 n.².
Cash, income and outgo accounts of, 131-132, 135-136; account book of lawyer, 136-137; as an income meter, 137-138.
Caution, coefficient of: 276-277, 330; applied to insurance, 292; mathematical presentation of, 403.
Census (U. S., 1905), cited concerning railway valuation, 36 n.
Certificates, of property, 23; necessity of separating from wealth, property, services, and utility, 38; stock, 68-70; receiver's, 86.
Chance, element of, in property rights, 22, 330; involving risk of insolvency, 81; nature of, 265-269; always an estimate, 266; an affair of ignorance, 268; measurement of, 269-271; mathematical value of a, 275; in valuing stock, 280-283; effect of, on discount curve, 286-287; effect of, on bookkeeping, 287-288; effect of, on capital curves, 320-322.
Chen, Chin tao, cited on utility, 47.
Clark, J. B., cited on utility, 47; concept of capital of, 55, 56, 60; term "capital-goods" suggested by, 67; use of economic terms by, 67; "Niagara Falls" simile of, applied to income, 129; distinction between work and

INDEX

labor drawn by, 175 n.; concept of interest of, 247.
Clothing, services of, 165.
Coefficients of caution, probability, and risk. *See* Caution, *etc.*
Combination of capital instruments to standardize income, 127–129, 245–246.
Commodities, definition of, 5, 323, 331; classification of, 7; error of reckoning as income, 105–106.
Complete rights to property, 36–37, 95–96, 324–325, 335.
Composition, settlement of bankruptcy by, 86.
Computation tables, 243 n., 283–284, 408–411.
Consumption, 145, 152, 164, 165, 336, 350.
Contingent liability, 83.
Control, value of, as applied to railway ownership, 35–36.
Copyright, wealth underlying, 27, 29.
Cost, included in term "outgo," 120; influence of past, on present value, 188–190.
Cost of production, 151, 173–174, 184.
Cotgrave, definition of capital by, 62.
Couple, definition of, 331.
Couples, method of: in capital summation, 90–91, 183–184, 335; applied to accounting of railway company, 94; taxation by, 97–98; income summation by, 143–152, 183–184, 335; natural income discovered by, 150–151; contrasted with method of balances in income summation, 157–158.
Courcelle-Seneuil, use of term "capital" by, 60.
Credit, nature of property right represented by, 32–33; mistaken view of, 39; relation of, to capital, 96–97; in the sense of an item of a transaction, 158–159, 336.
"Credited," income said to be, 122, 132, 325.
Creditors, regarded as risk-takers, 83–84; bondholders contrasted with stockholders as, 85.
Crises, causes of, 296–297.

Currency inflation, mistaken idea the basis of, 38–39.
Custom (tailor's), wealth represented by, 29.

D

Daniels, use of term "capital" by, 60 n.[7].
Dargun, human beings counted as wealth by, 5 n.[2].
Davenant, on human beings as wealth, 5 n.[2].
Davenport, "Statistical Methods" by, 408 n.
Debit, an item of a transaction, 122, 132, 158–159, 336.
Debt, imprisonment for, 83; repudiation of, 84; payments on (interest or principal) are outgo, 134.
Definition, tests of a, 116.
De Foville, use of term "capital" by, 60.
Depletion of capital, not to be deducted from income, 110, 134; taxation and, 400–403.
Depreciation not outgo, 234.
Depreciation fund, regulation of income by, 125–126, 239–243; geometrical figures representing, 240, 241.
Depreciations, item of, in income and capital accounts, 257–263.
Desirability, concept of, 41, 326; discussion of term, and term "utility," 42–43. *See* Utility.
Dimension, definition of, 331.
Dimensions: wealth, price, and value, 3–15, 341–344; of income-capital ratios, 186, 357; of rates of interest, discount, and capitalization, 367–368.
Discommodities, class of articles termed, 120.
Discount, rate of, 199, 200, 327, 332; table showing equivalent rates of interest, capitalization, and, 200; total, on a sum, 209–210, 331; mathematical relations between rates of interest and, 364–366; between rates of, for different time reckonings, 366–367; dimensions of rates of interest, capitalization, and, 367–368.

INDEX 417

Discount curve (Exponential curve), 203–204, 223–224, 331–332; applications of, 206–208, 272, 284–287, 303–309, 317–322, 360–361, 378, 380–381, 391–394.
Discount paper, banks', 204.
Disservices, definition of, 20, 119–120, 325, 332; enumeration of, 120; measurement of, 120–121; examples of, 123; "necessary evils," 123; one phase of, and services termed "interactions," 144; transformations of wealth from one point of view are, 146.
Distribution curve of incomes, 142.
Distribution ledgers, 142, 143.
Disutility, criticism of term, 42.
Dividends, effect of payment of, on capital account, 75; payment of, out of capital, 75, 256; variability of, 281–282, 406–407.
"Doses" of capital, 185.
Double counting, fallacy of, in concept of income, 107–108, 113–115, 116, 347, 350; economists' attempts to avoid, 109–112.
Double entry bookkeeping, 144, 159, 325–326.
Double taxation, 39, 97–98, 250–253, 255.
Du Cange, Dufresne, definition of capital by, 62.

E

"Earning power" of stock, 71.
Earnings (Earned income), definition of, 234, 333; distinction between realized income and, 234–236, 247–253, 327–328, 353; excess of, over income, equals increase of capital, 237–238, 328.
Edgeworth, F. Y., definition of income by, 102 n.[1]; cited, 410 n.
Elements of income or outgo, 121.
Emery, H. C., cited on speculations, 300.
Endorsement, influence of, in reducing risk, 289.
Engel, human beings counted as wealth by, 5 n.[2], 17.
England, bankruptcy laws in, 83; income taxation in, 253, 401.
Enjoyable income, 105, 112–113, 118, 325–326.

Enjoyable objective services ("Consumption"), enumeration of, 165.
Exchange of wealth, 10, 11, 22, 149, 332; analysis of an, 158–159.
Expense, definition of, 119–120, 332.
Exponential curve. *See* Discount curve.

F

Factor's agreement, property right represented by, 28.
Fee simple, rights in, 23; wealth underlying, 26; definition of, 37; an asset having no counterpart liability constitutes a, 95.
Fetter, F. A., cited on utility, 47; definition of capital by, 55; cited on confusion between quantity and value of wealth, 56 n.[1]; use of term "capital" by, 60 n.[7]; use of economic terms by, 67; concept of income of, 117, 165, 350–351; on distinction between rent and capital, 186 n.[1].
Fictitious person, definition of, 335; accounting of, distinguished from that of real person, 92, 138–139, 153, 160–161.
Finished products, classification of, 7.
Flow, definition of a, 332.
Flow of wealth, income conceived as a, 51–52, 101; duration of, 52; rate of, 52, 332.
Flux, use of term "capital" by, 60; concept of income of, 117.
Forecasts, of income from capital, 283–284; by trade journals, 291; speculators experts in, 295; crises caused by a general error in, 296–297.
Foreclosure, settlement of bankruptcy by, 86.
Forests, appraisal of present value of, based on future worth, 205; taxation of, 254.
France, limited liability in, 83; taxation of forest lands in, 254; government bonds in, 281.
Franchise rights, wealth underlying, 26, 29.
Franklin fund, accumulation of interest shown by, 225.
Fund, definition of a, 332.
Fund of wealth, capital conceived as a, 51–52.

Future, value of any capital-good dependent on the, 188–199, 204–205, 223–224; estimates of, based on the past, 283–284, 291, 295, 296–297.
Futures, trading in, 298–300.

G

Gambling, uneven value of the chances in, 275; distinction between speculation and, 295.
Gaskill, Alfred, quoted on taxation of forest lands, 254.
General property tax, 253.
George, Henry, proposition of, to nationalize land, 30–31.
Germany, appraisal of forests in, 205; taxation of forest lands in, 254.
Gibbs, J. W., quoted, 65 n.^{2}.
Gide, use of economic terms by, 43.
Giffen, use of term "capital" by, 60.
Gold certificates, nature of property right in, 32.
Goods: wealth, property, and services treated under term, 41, 327; not income, 351.
Good will, wealth underlying rights of, 27, 28–29.
Government bonds, 31–32, 280–281.
Government property, wealth underlying, 27.
Government reports, reduction of risk by, 291.
Government's taxing power, nature of, 30.
"Graveyard insurance," 294.
Gross income, definition of, 121, 333.
Guaranties, method of, to avoid risk, 288–289.
Guth, Franz, on income, 356.
Guyot, use of term "capital" by, 60.

H

Hadley, A. T., "capital" according to, 60 n.^{7}; concept of income of, 117; on commutation of risks, 289, 299.
Health as wealth, 176.
Hedging, shifting risks by, 299–300.
Hermann, F. B. W. v., concept of capital of, 54, 56; perishable goods regarded as non-capital by, 63; on income, 352–353.

Hicks, use of term "capital" by, 61.
Higgins, L. R., cited, 410.
Hire, rights of, wealth underlying, 26.
Holland, T. E., cited concerning definition of "rights," 21.
Housing and warming, services of, 165.
Human beings, considered as a form of wealth, 5, 17; classification of, in scheme of wealth, 7.
Human body, transformation of services through, 167–168; effect of condition of, on subjective and objective income, 175–176.

I

Ignorance, element of, in chance, 268; reduction of risk by decrease of, 291.
Immaterial wealth, items included under, 4; disadvantage of theory of, 39.
Impairment of capital, 110, 134, 328; taxation of, 400–403.
Imprisonment for debt, 83.
Income, concept of, as flow of services during period of time, 51–52, 101, 116–118, 324; savings not to be included in, 108, 134–135, 247–255, 349, 353; varying concepts of, 101–115, 345–356; conceived as money-income, 103–104, 115, 117–118, 333; obtained in kind, 104; real, 104–106, 112–113; enjoyable, 105, 112–113, 333; services only to be regarded as, 106–107, 112, 116–118; fallacy of double counting in concept of, 107–108, 113–115, 116, 347, 350; not "regular," 109; standard, 110, 234, 236–237, 328, 333, 396–398 (*see* Standard income); need not leave capital unimpaired, 110, 328; needless distinctions between social and individual, 113–115; confusion of capital and, 114–115, 351; primary or natural, 115, 150, 333; social, 116, 141, 333, 348; net, 118, 121, 130–131, 333 (*see* Net income); use of term, in two senses (services and value), 121; element of, 121; gross, 121, 333; viewed from one point

INDEX

is outcome or yield, 122 n.; effect of depreciation fund on, 125–126, 238–243; other methods of steadying, 127–129, 243–247, 259–263, 293–294; methods of reckoning real person's (lawyer's) and fictitious person's (railway corporation's), 130–139 (*see* Income accounts); total social, 141; distribution of, 142–143; objective, 165; objective and subjective final stage of, 165–169; psychic (subjective), 167–169, 177, 333; capital analogous to and correlative with, 184; value of capital derived from future, 188; purchasing power over, 191; payable annually and semi-annually, 192; line method of representing, 206–207, 371–372; area method of representing, 207–208, 371–374; determining capital-value of, 217–221; case of capital-value less than total expected, 227–228; realized *vs*. earned, 231–236, 238, 247–255, 327–328, 353; perpetual annuity taken as the standard, 236–237; regulation of, by repair fund, 259–263; risk as applied to immediate, 275–276; forecasts of, 283–284; effect of changes in, on capital-value, 284–285; insurance a means of steadying, 293–294; increase of value is not, 351; diagrams for continuous and discontinuous, 371–374; representation of capital and, by polar coördinates, 393–395; two rival concepts of standard, when interest rate varies, 396–398.

Income accounts, services and disservices which enter into, 119–121; for house and lot, 122–126; of building and loan association, 127–128; of lawyer (real person), 131–134, 135–136, 163, 174–175; of railway corporation (fictitious person), 138–139; relation between capital accounts and, 139, 256–264, 325; items of assets and liabilities to be included in, 139–140, 325; of society as a total, 141–142; of United States, 142–143; entrance of interactions into, 143–145, 325; of logging camp and sawmill, to illustrate application of method of couples, 152–154; of dry goods company, to illustrate double entry bookkeeping, 159–162; of factory company, to show relation between capital accounts and, 258–262; summarized definition of, 333.

Income and outgo accounts, 122–140. *See* Income accounts.

Income bonds, 85.

Income meter, "cash" in income accounts termed an, 137–138.

Income-services, 121.

Income summation, by method of balances, 90–91, 142–143, 183, 335; by method of couples, 143–152, 183–184, 335; method of couples contrasted with method of balances in, 157–158.

Income tax, 250–253, 398–400; effect on capital of misconceived, 253–254; unrestricted application of, impracticable, 400–403.

Income-value, 121, 327, 333; rate of interest a link between capital-value and, 202, 327–328.

Individual income, distinctions between social and, 113–115.

Insolvency, 81; true and pseudo, 82.

Installment, payment by, as a means of regulating income, 127, 244–245.

Instrument of wealth, 5, 19, 333.

Insurance, origins of, 275–276; avoidance and shifting of risks by, 288, 291–294; a means of steadying income, 293–294; various forms of, 294.

Insurance companies, identity of creditors and stockholders in mutual, 85; terminable annuities used by, 210; bonds offered by, 217; forecast of interest rate by, 274.

Interactions between two instruments or groups of instruments, 144, 325, 334; formerly styled "productive services," 145; three classes of (transformation, transportation, and transfer), 145–152; natural services of

420   INDEX

capital consist of, 152–156; shown by diagrams to be preparatory to enjoyable services, 317–320.
Interest, is capital and not income, 134–135, 224; not an item in cost of production, 173–174; spurious distinction between rent and, 186–187; crude theories of, 187–188; nominal principal and, in case of bond, 211–212, 215, 217; accumulation of, 224–226; definition of nominal and total, 334.
Interest, rate of: defined, 191, 334; various meanings of, according to frequency of payment, 192–194, 334; payable annually and semi-annually,192; premium and price concepts of, 194–196, 246; interchangeability of premium and price concepts of, 196–199; table showing equivalent rates of discount, capitalization, and, 200; a link between capital-value and income-value, 202, 327; table of, realized per annum on three, four, and five per cent bonds, 214–215; effect on capital-value of change in, 229, 271–273, 390–393; value-return may be greater or less than, 229–234; risk as applied to, 271–274; forecast of, by insurance companies, 274; riskless, mathematical, and commercial, 279–280; on government bonds, 280–281; mathematical relations between annual, semi-annual, and quarterly rates conceived in price sense, 357–358, in premium sense, 358–362; mathematical relation between, and rate of discount, 364–366; dimensions of, and rates of discount and capitalization, 367–368; variation of, produces two rival concepts of standard income, 396–398.
Interstate Commerce Commission, Report of, cited, 39.
Inventory, distinction between quantity, price, and value of wealth shown in an, 14.
Investments, classification of, as safe and unsafe, 277; relation between amount of capital and risk of, 277, 408–409.
Irredeemable paper money, wealth underlying, 27; nature of, 30.
Item of wealth, 5, 337.

J

James, William, quoted, 168 n.
Jevons, W. S., use of phrase "final utility" by, 46; concept of capital of, 54, 57; use of term "discommodities" by, 120; cited on rent entering into cost of production, 173.
Joint stock companies, capital accounts of, 68–70; limited liability in, 82–83; shares in, as example of perpetual annuities, 209.
Joint stock rights, wealth underlying, 26.
Juglar, cited on crises, 296.

K

Kind, income obtained in, 104.
Kleinwächter, concept of capital of, 54; raw materials regarded as non-capital by, 63; on income, 102, 351–355.
Knies, on capital, 54, 57, 60.
Knowledge, reduction of risk by method of increasing, 288, 291; utility of speculation based on, 298.
Komorzynski, on capital, 65 n.².

L

Labor, economists' views of relation between capital and, 55; defined as outgo in form of human exertion, 120, 334; as form of disservice, 145; appraisal of, 172; in a sense the only true cost of production, 175; distinction drawn between work and, 175 n.
Labor power, 316–317.
Lafrentz, L. W., use of term "capital" by, 63.
Land, regarded as one class of wealth, 5, 334; classification of, 7; nationalization of, 30–31, 254; fancied distinction between capital and, 56 n¹.; view of, as non-

INDEX   421

capital by classical economists, 63; mistake of distinguishing between capital and, 186–187; an example of capital yielding an approximately perpetual annuity, 209; determination of uses of, 221; benefits of speculation in, 222; taxation of, 254.
Land improvements, 5, 7, 334.
Landry, time element in concept of capital of, 57.
Lawyer, income and outgo accounts of, 131–137, 162–164, 174–175.
Lease, wealth underlying rights of, 26, 34–35.
Liabilities, definition of, 67, 325, 334; relation of capital-balance to, looking to safety of a business, 81; true value of, derived from assets, 84–85, 139; consideration of, in income and outgo accounts, 134–135, 139–140, 162–164.
Liability, limited and contingent, 82–83.
Life insurance, steadying of income by, 294, 295; method of computing pure level premium, 410–411.
Limited liability, in case of joint stock company, 82–83.
Line method of representing income, 206–207, 371–372.
Liquidation, resulting from bankruptcy, 86; a crisis defined as a time of general and forced, 296.
Loans, short-time: interest in case of, 194–195, 198–199; rate of discount employed for, 199, 204.
Logging camp accounts, 152–157, 318.
Lowell Institute, possibilities of accumulation shown by, 225.

M

MacCulloch, on human beings as wealth, 5 n.[2]; concept of capital of, 55; quoted on wage fund theory, 59.
Machines, offsetting of depreciation in, 241–242.
MacLeod, H. D., definition of wealth by, 4; concept of capital of, 55; includes credit under capital, 96.
Marginal utility (desirability), definition of, 46, 331; mathematical expression for, 344–345.

Marshall, Alfred, use of economic terms by, 43, 46, 61; treatment of capital by, 54; on distinction between capital and non-capital, 57; on concept of income, 114, 117, 347–348; on avoidance of double counting in concept of income, 114; on transformation of wealth, 145.
Marx, distinction between capital and non-capital according to, 55; on relation between capital and labor, 55; denies that capital is productive, 56.
Measurement of psychic income, 177.
Measurement of services and disservices, 19–20, 120–121.
Measurement of wealth, by quantity, 8–9; by price, 9–11; by value, 13–14; inaccuracies in, 15–17; expressed mathematically, 341–344.
Methods of avoiding risk. See Risk.
Methods of balances and couples. See Balances and Couples.
Methods of standardizing income, 125–129, 243–247, 259–263, 293–294.
Meyer, R., on income, 355–356.
Mill, J. S., distinction between capital and non-capital by, 54; capital itself regarded as a product by, 55; quoted on wage fund theory, 59.
Miner's inch, 193, 208–209.
Mines, terminable income exemplified by, 209, 210.
Mixter, editor of Rae's *Sociological Theory of Capital*, 65 n.[1].
Money, uniformity of measurement by means of, 15; irredeemable paper, 27, 30; distinction between three elements (wealth, property, certificates) to which term is applied, 38.
Money-income, concept of, 103–104, 115, 117–118.
Money price, 335.
Money value, 337.
Money-wages not real wages, 104.
Monopoly, effect of tendency toward, on risk element, 409.
Monopoly franchise, wealth underlying rights of, 25, 27, 29.

Mortgage, use of, to maintain regularity of income, 127, 244–245; reduction of risk by, 289.
Murray, J. A. H., dictionary definition of income, 62–63, 345–346.
Mutual insurance companies, creditors and stockholders identical in, 85.

N

National banks, liability of stockholders in, 83; government bonds bought by, 280–281.
Natural income, 118, 150; ascertaining, by method of couples, 150–151.
Nau, Carl H., cited, 39.
Net capital, 69, 330.
Net income, 118, 121, 130–131, 333; example of, in case of lawyer, 136–137, 163, 174–175; lacking in case of fictitious persons, 138–139; of society, 141–143; determining by method of balances and method of couples, 157–158; of merchant's stock, 223.
Net outgo, definition of, 121, 335.
Net product, social income conceived as society's, 113–115.
Nicholson, J. S., human beings counted as wealth by, 5 n.^{2}; use of term "capital" by, 61; on credit as "revenue capital," 96.
Norton, J. P., on relation between amount of capital and risk involved, 277, 409; on use of probability computations, 283 n.^{1}, 410 n.
Notes, wealth underlying, 26, 28.
Nourishment, services of, 165.

O

Objective cost of production nonexistent, 173.
Objective income, 165–169; points of divergence of, from subjective income, 169–176.
Ofner, human beings counted as wealth by, 5 n.^{2}.
Ophelimity, 42.
Options, stock exchange (puts and calls), 298–299.

Out-come, income viewed from one point becomes, 112 n.
Outgo, definition of, 119, 326, 335; element of, 121; net, 121, 335; use of, in two senses (disservices and value), 121; viewed from one point is *ingo*, 123 n.; not capital, 124; offsetting of, by depreciation fund, 125–126; method of couples applied to, 151–152; depreciation is not, 234.
Overvaluation of capital, 79–80.
Owner-method of taxation, 97–98.
Ownership, meaning of, 18; partial and total, 34–36, 95–96, 324–325, 335; change in forms of, in reorganization after bankruptcy, 86; credit a form of divided, 96–97; proper determination of, in taxation of property, 97–98; change of, 149–152, *and see* Exchange *and* Transfer.

P

Palgrave, definition of capital by, 62.
Panama Canal, example of dependency of capital-value on future services, 188–189.
Panics, causes of, 296–297.
Pareto, human beings counted as wealth by, 5 n.^{2}; introduction of term "ophelimity" by, 42; cited on utility, 47; use of term "capital" by, 60; distribution curve of incomes of, 142.
Partial rights to property, 34–37, 95–96, 335.
Partnership, wealth underlying rights in, 26; liability of members of a, 83; income considered in respect to, 130.
Patent rights, wealth underlying, 27.
Payment by installment a means of regulating income, 127, 244–245.
Pearson, Karl, cited, 410 n.
Pension, the diminishing capital-value of a, 238–239.
Person, fictitious and real, defined, 335. *See* Fictitious *and* Real persons.
Petty, on human beings as wealth, 5 n.^{2}, 17.
Physical productivity of capital, 185, 186.

Physical return of capital, 185, 186.
Piecework, terms used in measurement of, 19-20.
Pierson, N. G., definition of income adopted by, 102 n.¹, 346.
Pigou, cited on utility, 47.
Pitt, on sinking fund, 243.
Pocket cash, risk-meeting function of, 290.
Polar coördinates, representation of capital and income by, 393-395.
Practice (physician's), wealth represented by, 29.
Prediction. *See* Forecast.
Preferred stock, 85; share of, to illustrate riskless value, 280.
Premium concept of interest, 194-196, 247, 334; interchangeability of, with price concept, 196-199, 362-366; represented mathematically and by diagram, 358-361.
Price, Richard, financial theories of, 243.
Price, definition of, 11, 335; various usages of term (money, market, and appraised or reasonable), 13-14; distinction between quantity, value, and, 14-15; relation of, to past costs and future expectations, 189-190; rate of interest called, of money or capital, 101; money, defined, 335; dimensions of wealth, value, and, 341-344.
Price concept of interest, 191-194, 196, 247, 334; interchangeability of, with premium concept, 196-199, 362-366; mathematical relations between rates reckoned annually, semi-annually, etc., according to, 357-358.
Primary (natural) income, 115.
Principal, nominal, in case of bonds, 211-212, 215, 217, 335.
Probability, a matter of human estimate, not merely mathematics, 270-271; coefficient of, 276-277, 331, 335, 403; application of principles of, to valuation of capital, 277-279, 403-406; theory of, applied to insurance, 295.
Probability computations, 283-284, 408-410.

Production, problem of, in concept of capital, 55-56, 145-148; cost of, 151, 173-174, 184.
Productive processes, 145-148, 335.
Productive services, 145.
Productivity, physical and value, 185-188, 335.
Productivity theory, 187-188.
Profits, undivided, 68.
Promises of refraining, wealth underlying, 27, 28.
Property, definition of, 18, 325, 335; rights in, 20-22; wealth and, correlative terms and coextensive, 22-23, 95-96; types of chief forms of, 26-27; partial and total rights to, 34-37, 95-96, 335; necessity of separating from wealth, certificates of property, services, and utility, 38; confusion of ideas regarding, 38-40; regulation of income by sale of, 127, 244-245.
Property rights, definition of, 18, 22, 324, 335; table illustrating existence of wealth behind, 26-27; overlying of, by one another, 31-32; classification of, 36-37; method of determining income from collection of, 130. *See* Ownership.
Pseudo-insolvency, 82.
Psychic income, 167-169, 333; measurement of, 177.
Purchase, definition of, 11, 335.
Purchasing power, use of phrase, 191.
Put, option known as a, 299.

Q

Quantity, measurement of wealth in units of, 8-9; distinction between price, value, and, 14-15; conceived as a fund (capital) or a flow (income), 51-52; measurement of services by, 120-121; ratio of, of services to quantity of capital yielding those services (physical productivity), 185; dimensions of price, value, and, 341-344.
Quarries, terminable income exemplified by, 209, 210.

R

Rae, John, use of economic terms by, 5, 65.
Railway bonds, source of income from, 130.
Railway capital, fallacious statistics of, 98.
Railway control, value of, 35-36.
Railways, disservices of, 120; income accounts of, 138-139; real sum total of income of, 151; leases of, as examples of perpetual annuities, 208; forecasting the value of property in, 284.
Rate of capitalization, 194, 330. See Capitalization.
Rate of discount, 199, 200, 327-328, 332. See Discount.
Rate of flow, 52, 332. See Flow.
Rate of interest. See Interest, rate of.
Rate of value-return, 229-238.
Ratios, income-capital, 185-186, 357.
Raw materials, classification of, 7.
Ray Act relating to bankruptcy, 83.
Real estate, regarded as one class of wealth, 5; classification of, 7; inaccuracy in appraisement of, 16-17; speculation in, 221-222, 254. See Land and Land improvements.
Real income, concept of, 104-106, 112-113.
Realized income vs. earned, 231-236, 238, 247-255, 327-328, 353.
Real persons, accounting of, distinguished from that of fictitious persons, 92-93, 138-139, 162-164, 174-175.
Real wages, money-wages not, 104.
Recapitalization of stock companies, 70.
Receiver, office of, in reorganization after bankruptcy, 86.
Rent, as example of transfer of wealth, 150-151; and cost of production, 173-174; spurious distinction between interest and, 186-187.
Reorganization resulting from bankruptcy, 86.
Repair fund, regulation of income by, 259-263.

Repairs, item of, in income and capital accounts, 257-263.
Report on Direct Taxation cited, 114.
Repudiation of debts, 84.
Reserves of capital held to avoid risk, 290.
Resources. See Assets.
Return. See Value return.
Ricardo, on relation between capital and labor, 55; theory of rent of, 187.
Rider, W., definition of capital by, 62.
Right, definition of a, 20.
Right to subscribe, 78.
Rights in common, wealth underlying, 27.
Risk, element of, in determining capital-value, 205, 210; as applied to rate of interest, 271-274; as applied to immediate income, 275-276; coefficient of, 277, 336; relation between amount of capital and, 277, 408-409; five methods of avoiding, 288; avoidance of, by method of guaranties, 288-289, of safeguards, 289-291; safety devices for meeting, 290; reduction of, by increasing knowledge, 291; avoidance and shifting of, by insurance, 291-294; shifting of, to speculators, 295-298; shifting by hedging, 299-300; effect of element of, on capital curves, 320-322; mathematical coefficient of, 403. See Chance.
Risk of insolvency, 81.
Roosevelt, Theodore, 170.
Roscher, W., human beings counted as wealth by, 5 n.[2]; treatment of capital by, 54; definition of income by, 346-347.
Runs on banks, 296, 297.

S

Safeguards, method of, to avoid risk, 288, 289-291.
Safety devices, risk-meeting function of, 290.
Sale, definition of, 11, 336.
Satisfaction, concept of, 41, 324; distinction between utility and, 43-44, 53.

INDEX

Savings, to be counted as capital, not income, 108, 134–135, 247–253, 254–255, 328, 349, 353.

Sawmill, income account for, 152–155, 157, 318–320.

Say, J. B., human beings counted as wealth by, 5 n.[2]; use of term "capital" by, 60.

Schäffle, A. E. F., treatment of capital by, 54.

Schmoller, Gustav, on income, 352–353.

Seager, H. R., definition of income by, 349.

Seligman, cited on utility, 47; use of term "capital" by, 60 n.[7].

"Selling short," 298–300.

Senior, N. W., quoted on definition of capital, 53; capital itself regarded as a product by, 55; on capital as a producer of wealth, 56.

Services, definition of, 19, 324, 336; measurement of, 19–20, 120–121; complete and partial rights to, 36–37; to be separated from wealth, property, certificates of property, and utility, 38; income conceived as flow of, 51–52, 101, 116–118, 324; commodities wrongly combined with, in concept of income, 105–106; necessity of avoiding confusion of anything else with, in income-concept, 106–107; infinite variety of, 119; one phase of, and disservices termed "interactions," 144; transformations of wealth as, 146; method of couples applied to, 152–156; enjoyable objective ("consumption"), 164, 165, 336; stage of final objective, 165; subjective, 166; classification of, 178–179.

Short-time loans, 194–195, 198–199, 204.

Simmonds, P. L., definition of capital by, 62.

Single taxation, 253–254.

Sinking fund, 243–244, 333.

Smart, William, use of term "capital" by, 60 n.[7]; definition of income by, 348–349.

Smith, Adam, on capital, 53, 54, 56, 58, 61; on rent and income, 150.

Social income, the concept of, as "net product" of society, 113–115; author's concept of, 114, 118, 141, 333; distinction between individual income and, 115–116.

Space-units for measuring wealth, 8–9.

Speculation, in real estate, 222, 230; benefits and evils of, 295–298.

Speculators, use of land deferred by, 222; position of, considered, 230; risk-meeting function of, 288, 290, 295; in futures, 298–300.

Sprague, C. E., cited on meaning of term "capital," 63 n.

Standard deviation, measurement of extent of variability by, 406–410.

Standard income, 110, 234, 333; vs. realized, 234–236, 247–253, 327–328, 353.

Stock, economic use of term, 51, 336; chance element in valuing (in commercial sense), 280–283.

Stock companies, capital accounts of, 68–70; two valuations in, 70–72.

Stockholders, liability of, in joint stock companies and in national banks, 82–83; preferred, 85; bondholders and, contrasted, 85, 288–289; position of, in case of bankruptcy, 85–86; risk-taking function of, 288–289.

Stock jobbing, 74–77.

Stock of wealth, concept of capital as a, 51–52, 323–324.

Stocks, contrasted with bonds, 85, 288–289; effect of chance on, 276–277.

Stock-watering, 79–80.

Stream of wealth, concept of income as a, 51–52, 323–324.

Subjective income, definition of, 168, 326; points of divergence of, from objective income, 169–176. See Psychic income.

Surplus, 68, 256–257.

T

Taussig, F. W., 318; definition of income by, 349.

Taxation: double, 39, 253, 255; methods of avoiding double,

97-98; owner-method and wealth-method of, 97-98; of income, 250-254, 398-403; theory of advocates of single, 254; of land, 254.
Taxing power, wealth underlying, 27; nature of government's, 30-31.
Tenant, rights of, 34-35.
Time, element of: in concept of capital, 51-52, 56-57; in considering interest, 196.
Todhunter, Ralph, cited, 401.
Total discount on a sum, 209-210, 374-378.
Total social wealth, diagrammatic summation of, 316-317.
Total utility (Total desirability), 44, 47, 331.
Trade journals, risk element diminished by, 291.
Transaction, definition of, 159, 336.
Transfer of wealth, 10-11, 149-152, 158-159, 325, 336.
Transformation of services through the human body, 167-168.
Transformations of wealth, definition of, 145, 325, 336; services or disservices according to point of view, 146; examples of, 147-148.
Transportation of wealth, 148-149, 325, 336.
Trust, property held in, 31.
Turgot, use of term "capital" by, 60.
Tuttle, definition of wealth by, 4; distinction between capital and non-capital according to, 55; use of economic terms by, 60, 67.

U

Undesirability, definition of, 42, 336.
Undesirable event, 123.
Undivided profits, 68, 256-257.
Usance of wealth, 117, 348.
Use of desirable events, "utility" to be distinguished from, 19, 43.
Usufructs, wealth underlying rights in, 26.
Utility, concept of, 19, 41, 42-43; to be separated from wealth, property, certificate of property, and services, 38; error of belief that wealth constitutes, 39-40; distinction between satisfaction and, 43-44, 53; total and marginal, 44, 331; consideration of marginal, 44-46; total, 47; definition of marginal, expressed mathematically, 344-345.

V

Valuation of railways, 35-36, 151, 284.
Valuations in stock companies (bookkeeper's and market's), 70-72.
Value, definition of, 13, 336-337; various uses of term, and of term "price," 13-14; distinction between quantity, price, and, 14; of control in case of railways, 35-36; measurement of services by, 120-121; derivation of, from future and not from past, 188-189; riskless, mathematical, and commercial, 276-277, 280-283; dimensions of wealth, price, and, 341-344; increase of, not income, 351; formulæ for, of bond, 378-380. *See* Capital-value.
Value productivity of capital, 185, 186, 335.
Value return of capital, 185-186, 188-191, 202, 336; rate of, 229-238; may be greater or less than rate of interest, 229-231.
Variation, of income, and its remedies, 125-129, 243-247, 259-263, 293-294; of rate of interest, 229, 271-273, 284-285, 390-393, 396-398; of dividends, 281-282, 406-407.
Venn, theory of chance of, 266.

W

Wage fund theory, 59.
Wages, money, are not real, 104.
Wagner, Adolf, on income, 125, 353-354.
Walker, Francis, 187.
Walras, human beings counted as wealth by, 5 n.^{2}; on capital, 54, 55-56, 63.
Waste, an example of overbalancing of services by disservices, 120.
Water-rights, an example of perpetual annuity, 193, 208-209.

Wealth, definition of, in general sense, 3–5, 337; "immaterial," 4, 39; classes of, distinguished, 5; definition of, in restricted sense, 5–6, 337; scheme showing classification of, 7; measurement of, 8–17 (*see* Measurement of wealth); transfer of, 10–11, 149–152 (*see* Exchange); appraisement of, 11–12, 34–36; distinction between quantity, price, and value of, 14–15; sources of error in measurement of, 15–17; meaning of ownership of, 18; services of instruments of, defined, 19; rights to services of, 20–22; and property correlative terms and coextensive, 22–23, 95, 96; cases in illustration of the correlation of, and property, 24–36; table illustrating existence of, behind property rights, 26–27; partial and total ownership of, 34–36; necessity of separating from property, certificates of property, services, and utility, 38; division of, into fund and flow, *i.e.* capital and income, 51–53; transformation of, 145–148; transportation of, 148–149; health as, 176; appraisal of, based on future worth, 204–205; risk-meeting function of stocks of, 290; diagrammatic summation of total social, 316–317; dimensions of price, value, and, 341–344.

Wealth-method of taxation, 97–98.

Wear and tear, depreciation due to, 210–211.

Weight-units for measuring wealth, 8–9.

Weiss, human beings counted as wealth by, 5 n.[2].

Whitman, Walt, 176.

Wieser, use of phrase "marginal utility" by, 46.

Wine, determination of present value of, based on future worth, 205.

Wittstein, on human beings as wealth, 5 n.[2].

Work, distinction between labor and, 175 n.[2].

Work dues, wealth underlying, 25, 26.

Y

Years' purchase, concept of, 194, 209, 362.

Yield, income viewed as, 122 n.

MUHLENBERG LIBRARY

3 1542 00081 6680

WITHDRAWN

Date Due

Demco 38-297